ANNETTE FLAVEL

SPEAK YOUR MIND

TEACHER'S EDITION
+ access to Teacher's App

3

macmillan education

Macmillan Education
4 Crinan Street
London N1 9XW
A division of Macmillan Education Limited

Companies and representatives throughout the world

Speak Your Mind Level 3 Teacher's Edition
ISBN 978-1-380-03145-7
Speak Your Mind Level 3 Teacher's Edition + access to Teacher's App
ISBN 978-1-380-03136-5

Written by Annette Flavel
Additional material by Mickey Rogers and Tony Prince

First published 2020

Teacher's Edition credits:
Designed by QBS Learning
Original cover design by therestless.co.uk
Cover adaptation by Roberto Martinez

The publishers would like to thank all the teachers that piloted and reviewed the series, and a special thanks to Tony Prince of the Norwich Institute for Language Education (NILE) for sharing his expertise in the article included in the Introduction.

The authors and publishers would like to thank the following for permission to reproduce their photographs:
Getty Images/Mikolette p. xxx; **NILE** p. xxviii; **Shutterstock**/Aaron Amat p. xxix; Macmillan Education Limited/Getty Images/iStockphoto/zentilia p. xxv, Macmillan Education Limited/iStockphoto/alexsl pp. xxvi–xxvii.

Student's Book credits:

Written by Mickey Rogers, Joanne Taylore-Knowles and Steve Taylore-Knowles

Designed by QBS Learning
Illustrated by QBS Learning pp. 13, 19, 41, 112; Judit Tondora (Astound) pp. 92, 125.
Picture research by Fernanda Rocha/Ikonia LLC

Full acknowledgements for photographs in the facsimile pages can be found in the Student's Book ISBN 978-1-380-03141-9.

Additional sources:
p. 24, "Abandoned Dogs Roam Detroit in Packs as Humans Dwindle" by Chris Christoff, August 21, 2013, Bloomberg website. p. 28, "Measuring Consumer Information" by Roger Bohn and James E. Short, 2012, *International Journal of Communication*, Vol. 6, pp. 980–1000. p. 40, "Is Nonverbal Communication a Numbers Game?" by Jeff Thompson, September 30, 2011, *Psychology Today* website referencing Mehrabian, A. (1972). *Nonverbal Communication*. New Brunswick: Aldine Transaction. p. 40, "What 'Personal Space' Looks Like around the World" by Amanda Erickson, April 24, 2017, The *Washington* Post website. p. 42, "The Number of Emails Sent per Day in 2019 (and 20+ Other Email Facts)" by Henry Tschabitscher, January 3, 2019, *Lifewire* website. p. 42, "Number of Mobile Phone Users Worldwide from 2015 to 2020" by Statista, November 2016, Statista website. p. 42, Data from Appfigures, Appfigures website, 2018. p. 42, Data from WhatsApp, WhatsApp Blog website, 2018. p. 42, "Number of Daily Active Snapchat Users from 1st Quarter 2014 to 3rd Quarter 2018" by Statista, October 2018, Statista website. p. 46, "Digital Advertising to Surpass Print and TV for the First Time, Report Says" by Hamza Shaban, February 20, 2019, *The Washington Post* website. p. 46, Internet World Stats website, May 9, 2019. p. 48, "IPCC Press Release #2018/24/PR" by Intergovernmental Panel on Climate Change, October 8, 2018, IPCC website. p. 98, "Musical Talent is Rooted in the Genes, Study of Twins Suggests" by Jillian Rose Lim, August 11, 2014, *Huffington Post*. p. 98, "Practice May NOT Make Perfect: Innate Talent is What's Required for Greatness in Areas Such as Games or Music" by Emma Innes, May 21, 2013, *Daily Mail* website. p. 98, Gladwell, Malcolm. (2008). *Outliers*: *The Story of Success*, Little, Brown and Company. p. 104, "Remembering How Reality TV Talent Shows First Got Started" by Bill Lucey, June 14, 2011, *The Morning Delivery* website. p. 116, "Cramming for Exams? Join the Crowd" by Justin Gerwick, June 4, 2014, *The Hawkeye*.

Printed and bound in Brazil
2025
25

Table of Contents

Speak Your Mind Philosophy

In the 21st century, it is no longer enough just to teach subject matter. Teachers need to help their students develop important skills that can lead to success in whatever they choose to do.

The core objective of ***Speak Your Mind*** is to help students become confident communicators. The focus is on using English to communicate in both local and global contexts. Most students may not live in an English-speaking country, but it is probable they will need to use English in the course of their academic and professional lives. Being a confident and competent communicator involves going beyond language skills. Students need to analyze ideas, work effectively in teams, and solve problems.

Job readiness consists of more than just a strong academic performance. The ability to communicate effectively in English and to use 21st-century skills is essential in order for young adults to enter successfully into or advance within the complex, global world in which they live. ***Speak Your Mind*** is designed to help students achieve their goals.

UNIT 3 Think About It

WHAT DO YOU ALREADY KNOW?

1 Think about words you know connected to thinking or skills. Write the words.
2 IN PAIRS Share and compare your ideas. Add more words to your lists.

Thinking/Skills

DISCUSS & SHARE

VIDEO

3 IN GROUPS Watch the video and answer the question.
SYM When do you think better: in the morning or in the evening?

In this unit, you will ...

- ask and answer questions about confirmation bias, discuss the importance of expert systems in your future career, and compare different creative uses for things.
- use thinking skills: analyze, evaluate, and apply.
- read about confirmation bias.
- use strategies and language to give yourself time to think, start a conversation, and ask for further suggestions.
- use design-thinking skills to design a new social media app.
- learn tips to create a presentation or give a talk.

Unit 3 Think About It 27

Speak Your Mind has a number of features that help students in their academic, professional, and everyday lives:

- Every lesson in ***Speak Your Mind*** ends with a specific communicative outcome. Students do a collaborative task in which they use target language from the lesson to communicate their ideas and express their opinions on a topic related to the subject of the lesson.
- Students learn skills that transfer from the classroom to real life. The lessons contain thinking questions that help improve their thinking skills as they learn English. The last lesson in every unit (Language and Life) develops problem-solving and teamwork skills by taking students through a step-by-step process in which they work together to solve a problem or produce a proposal in a real-life scenario.
- Young-adult students already have a great deal of knowledge about the world, and they are encouraged to transfer their real-life knowledge to the classroom. The topics in ***Speak Your Mind*** allow students to express their opinions on real-world events and issues and to learn more about those topics. Students are often asked to give opinions or to say what they already know about a topic before listening to or reading a text on the subject.
- Most young adults will have at least some previous knowledge of English. They are encouraged to share that knowledge and to build on it according to their personal needs and interests. Unit Openers help them be aware of how many words they already know in English and to share their knowledge with their classmates. *Make It Yours* boxes allow them to build their own personal vocabulary lists.
- Videos further help students connect their language learning to real life. For each unit, there is a video that focuses on the Unit Opener topic and acts as a prompt for discussion. For even-numbered units, there are documentary-style Follow A Pro videos that follow a day in the life of a person in a particular profession.

Unit Structure

***Speak Your Mind* Student's Books 1–3** consist of 12 units of 10 pages each. Every unit begins with a one-page Unit Opener designed to introduce the unit topic and to elicit vocabulary and other language that students are already familiar with. Each Unit Opener features a *Video* that can be used to prompt a discussion.

The Unit Opener is followed by four double-page lessons. Lessons 1–3 contain the core GRAMMAR, VOCABULARY, READING, SPEAKING, LISTENING, PRONUNCIATION, and WRITING sections for the unit. Lesson 4 is called Language and Life. It also includes a reading, but its purpose is to provide students with a task that will help them develop key 21st-century skills.

At the end of each unit, there is a REVIEW page with additional practice of the target grammar and vocabulary. This page also contains a section to introduce a study skill (in odd-numbered units) or a profession related to the topic of the unit (in even-numbered units).

At the end of each **Student's Book**, there are lessons connected to the study skills and the professions introduced on the *Review* pages. There is also a list of common irregular verbs, as well as further practice of the target grammar in the book.

Apart from the **Student's Book**, there is a **Workbook** available in print or digital form. The **Student's Resource Center** contains *Reading Worksheets* for extra reading practice, as well as lesson plans adapted from Macmillan's *OneStopEnglish* website. The **Teacher's Resource Center** contains printable tests for unit, mid-course, and end-of-course assessment.

For more information on each feature mentioned in this Introduction, please see the relevant sections that follow.

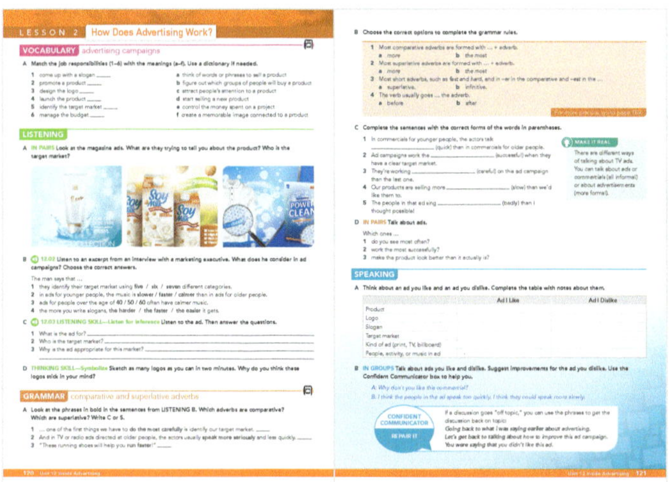

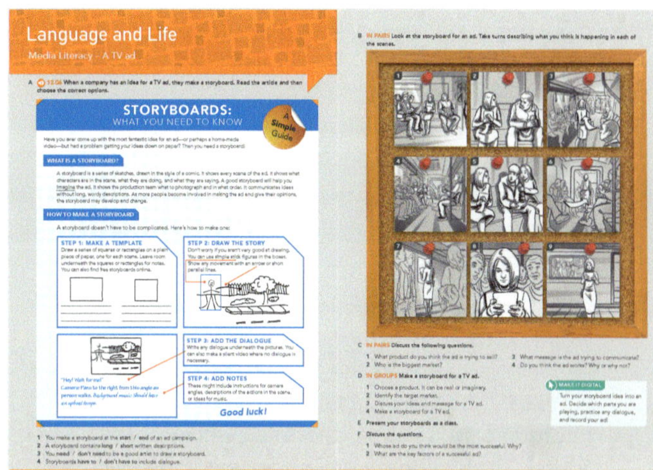

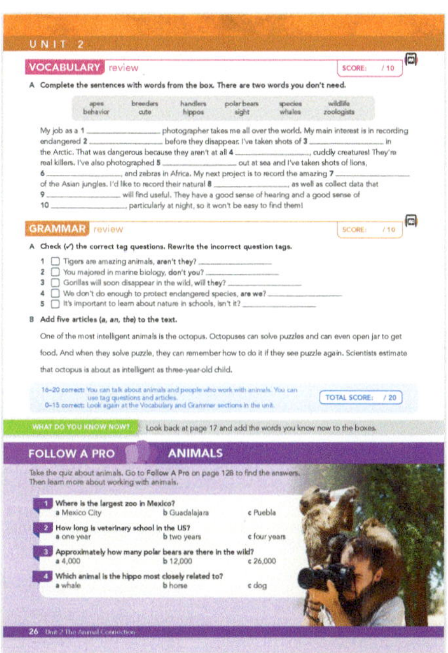

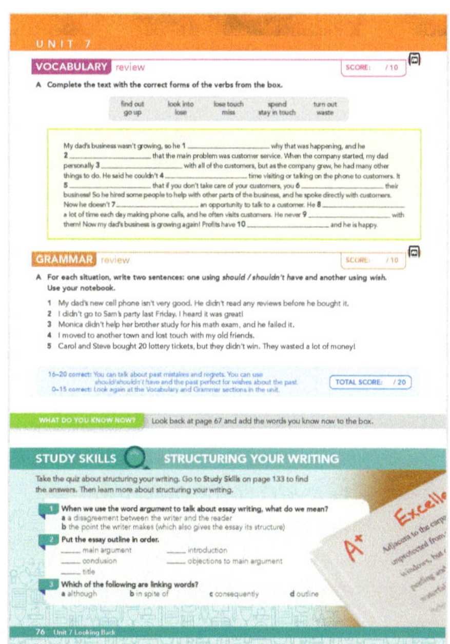

Unit Opener

Each Unit Opener introduces the general topic of the unit in a way that will stimulate the interest and curiosity of young adults. The Unit Openers give students the opportunity to think about topic-related words and phrases they already know and to discuss a question they can think about as they work through the unit. Each Unit Opener features a video to support this discussion.

The ability to use prior knowledge to support the acquisition of new knowledge is an important learning strategy. Having students think about language they already know or knowledge they already have helps them approach new material with greater confidence.

Another important concept in today's classrooms is cooperative learning. Students begin by thinking about something or doing a task individually, then work in pairs to share and build on their individual work. Finally, they work in groups to apply what they have learned individually and in pairs.

PROCEDURE: Teaching the **Unit Opener** in *Speak Your Mind*

1. **Individual work.** Have students work individually to list familiar words and phrases related to the unit topic. This helps build their confidence by highlighting the fact that they already know a lot of English. This section also gives them the chance to think about how the unit topic relates to their own lives.

2. **Peer teaching and learning.** Put students in pairs and ask them to share the words and phrases they wrote. At the beginning of the course, explain that working together and sharing what they know allows them to increase their knowledge. Note that at the end of the unit, they will be asked to come back to the Unit Opener and add new words they have learned in the unit.

3. **Video.** A short, optional video accompanies each DISCUSS & SHARE section. The purpose of these videos is to provide input that can support students in their discussion of the ***Speak Your Mind*** Question. Note that the videos are intended to provide information and context for the discussion, but the ***Speak Your Mind*** Question can easily be discussed without viewing them. Teachers are strongly encouraged to use them, as they provide fun and interesting contexts for the discussion, as well as input from both sides of the issue to help students form opinions.

4. ***Speak Your Mind* Question.** Ask students to work in groups to discuss the ***Speak Your Mind*** Question. Explain that the questions do not have specific right or wrong answers because the purpose is to make students think and allow them to express their opinions. Note that these questions are part of the critical-thinking thread in ***Speak Your Mind***. Students should think in terms of a continuum. For example, in Unit 8 A New Home?, some students may think that it's best to focus on the problems here on Earth before exploring other planets, some students may think that it's important to search for alternative homes in space, while other students may think we should solve problems on Earth as we explore space.

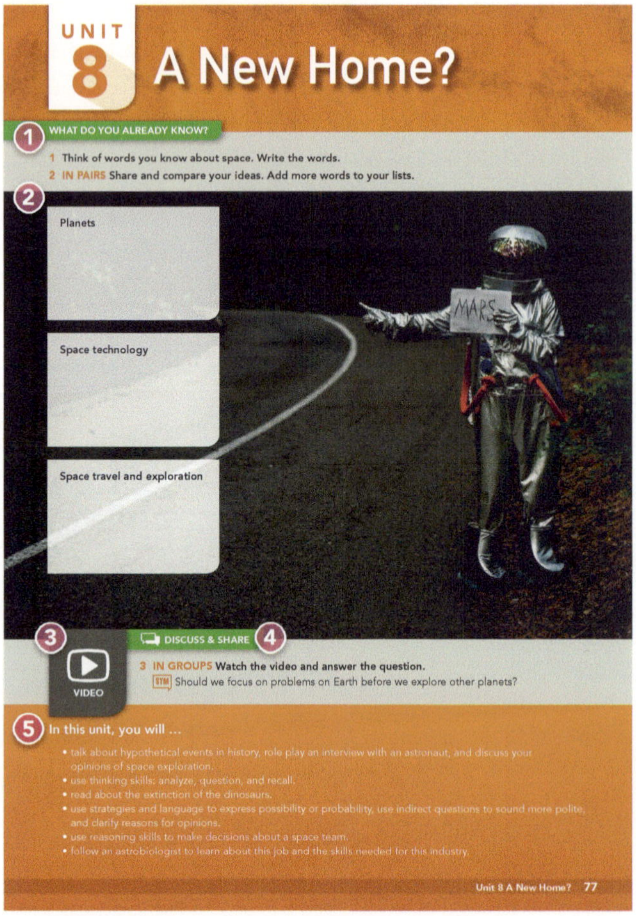

5. **Unit Summary.** At the bottom of the Unit Opener page, there is a summary of what students will learn in the unit. You may want to go over this so students know what they will learn in the unit.

Vocabulary

Vocabulary plays a very prominent role in ***Speak Your Mind***. Every unit begins with a focus on vocabulary through Unit Opener activities that elicit familiar vocabulary related to the unit topic. Students build on that knowledge through peer sharing. In Lessons 1–3, there is a VOCABULARY section to present and practice new vocabulary related to the specific lesson topic. In Lesson 4, there are opportunities for students to use vocabulary from the unit in the context of the tasks in the lesson.

In ***Speak Your Mind***, vocabulary is presented within the context of the reading or listening text in the lesson. Sometimes the vocabulary is pre-taught in order to help students understand it when they encounter it as they read or listen. Other times, the VOCABULARY section follows the READING or LISTENING section, and students are encouraged to use the context of the text to help them figure out the meaning of the words.

PROCEDURE: Teaching **Vocabulary** in *Speak Your Mind*

LESSON 3 Hope for the Future

LISTENING

A Match the environmental solutions (1–8) with the photos (a–h).

1 plant pots made from tires ____
2 recycled paper flip-flops ____
3 super trees ____
4 recycled plastic houses ____
5 fog catchers ____
6 school desks made from recycled materials ____
7 living walls ____
8 green roofs ____

B 5.04 LISTENING SKILL—Listen for details Listen to a class discussion. Under the photos a–h in A, write the name of the country where each environmental solution is taking place.

C 5.04 THINKING SKILL—Categorize Listen again and decide who should do each of the eight projects. Categorize the projects as *private companies, the government,* or *either*. Give reasons for your opinions.

I think the government would have to ... because it would be very expensive.

MAKE IT REAL
Informal ways to say strange or unusual: *weird, bizarre, wild*

VOCABULARY materials and products

A Match the descriptions with words from the box.

coconut flip-flop net pot roof rubber steel tire

1 a material with spaces made of string, rope, or metal wire: ________
2 the part of a wheel that is filled with air: ________
3 a container used to cook or to plant flowers or other plants: ________
4 the fruit of a kind of palm tree: ________
5 a strong metal made of iron and carbon: ________
6 the top of a house or other building: ________
7 a type of sandal with a V-shaped strap: ________
8 a flexible material similar to plastic that comes from a tree: ________

B IN PAIRS Think of other things that can be made from recycled materials. Discuss.

52 Unit 5 One Planet

Lexical sets. These are particularly relevant at lower levels, when students need a great deal of basic vocabulary related to topics such as food or sports. The lexical sets are often presented through visuals, and students are asked to match the words to the pictures.

When a lexical set is presented, ask students if they know or want to know any other words related to the set. This is a good way to utilize peer teaching, to make students feel that they are participating in the learning process, and to expand the target vocabulary to include words that students are interested in knowing.

Remember to have students practice saying vocabulary words that are intended for active use. It is also important for them to learn how to spell the words.

Topic-related vocabulary. Words or phrases that are related to the topic of the reading or listening are frequently presented by asking students to look at sentences from the text and match the target words to their definitions, or use them to complete sentences or a short text.

When the VOCABULARY section comes after a reading text, encourage students to go back to the text and look at the words in context to help them confirm their answers to the vocabulary activity.

When the vocabulary is presented before a LISTENING section, encourage students to listen for the words during the listening activity. Either before or after students listen, you may want to write the sentences with the vocabulary words on the board and check that they understand how each word is used.

Word formation. Students learn to use prefixes and suffixes to change the meaning or the part of speech of a word.

It is a good idea to have students make a word-formation chart in their notebooks that they can add to as they learn different prefixes and suffixes. Organize the chart into columns by parts of speech: noun, verb, adjective, and adverb. If there are equivalents to the affixes in their own language, you may want to include those in the chart to help students relate the English forms to elements in their own language.

Synonyms and antonyms. Learning synonyms and antonyms helps students expand the range and variety of their vocabulary.

There are vocabulary lessons on synonyms and antonyms in ***Speak Your Mind***, but you can teach synonyms or antonyms appropriate to the level as an extension to any vocabulary lesson. For example, if students learn *delicious*, also teach *tasty* or the slang word *yummy*. If they see *shiny* in a text, you can teach them that the opposite is *dull*.

Grammar

Grammar in ***Speak Your Mind*** is taught through an inductive approach in which students are encouraged to observe grammatical structures in context and to go through an analytical process that allows them to figure out rules of structure and function. At the beginning of the course, explain to students that they will be asked to actively participate in their own learning by using observation and thinking skills to figure out grammar rules about form and function. Point out that we tend to learn more effectively when we figure something out for ourselves rather than just being told. Each unit has two GRAMMAR sections: one in Lesson 1 and one in Lesson 2. In Lessons 3 and 4, students have opportunities to use the grammar they have just learned.

PROCEDURE: Teaching **Grammar** in *Speak Your Mind*

① **Notice the grammar in context.** Students are exposed to the new grammar structure in the context of a reading or listening text before they are asked to study and work with the grammar itself. You may want to point out one or two examples of the new structure in a reading text or explain that students will hear examples of new grammar in a listening text. It is not necessary to pre-teach the grammar in order for them to understand the text. Part of learning a new language is learning to use context to understand the meaning of new grammar or vocabulary.

② **Complete the rule.** Ask students to look at examples of the grammar from the reading or listening text. The examples are usually included in the GRAMMAR section, but sometimes students are asked to look for examples in the text. Explain that they should notice the form of the grammar and also think about the meaning, or the function, of the grammatical structure. Then ask them to do the activity that follows the examples. The activity asks them to complete grammar rules or answer questions about the grammar in order to show that they have understood it. When going over the rules, have students point out the grammar structures in the example sentences that confirm the rules.

③ **Practice.** The analysis of the grammar rules is followed by one or more written activities to practice the new structure. You may want to let students compare their answers in pairs before checking answers as a class. This will provide an opportunity for cooperative learning.

If students have had trouble with an activity, refer back to the grammar rules as you go over each answer to make sure that students understand why the answer is what it is.

④ **Oral practice.** The GRAMMAR sections often include a short pair or group communicative activity to practice the new grammar. Make sure that everyone has an opportunity to use several examples of all forms of the new grammar. For example, if they are learning questions and answers with a verb tense, make sure that students are practicing both the question forms and the answer forms.

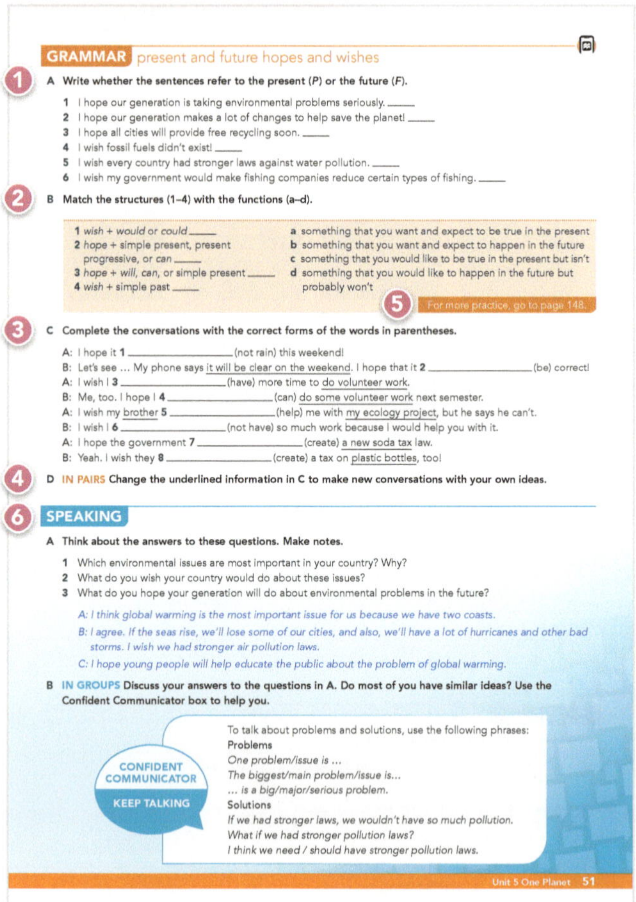
GRAMMAR present and future hopes and wishes

① A **Write whether the sentences refer to the present (*P*) or the future (*F*).**

1 I hope our generation is taking environmental problems seriously. ____
2 I hope our generation makes a lot of changes to help save the planet! ____
3 I hope all cities will provide free recycling soon. ____
4 I wish fossil fuels didn't exist! ____
5 I wish every country had stronger laws against water pollution. ____
6 I wish my government would make fishing companies reduce certain types of fishing. ____

② B **Match the structures (1–4) with the functions (a–d).**

1 *wish* + *would* or *could* ____
2 *hope* + simple present, present progressive, or *can* ____
3 *hope* + *will*, *can*, or simple present ____
4 *wish* + simple past ____

a something that you want and expect to be true in the present
b something that you want and expect to happen in the future
c something that you would like to be true in the present but isn't
d something that you would like to happen in the future but probably won't

⑤ For more practice, go to page 148.

③ C **Complete the conversations with the correct forms of the words in parentheses.**

A: I hope it **1** ________ (not rain) this weekend!
B: Let's see ... My phone says it will be clear on the weekend. I hope that it **2** ________ (be) correct!
A: I wish I **3** ________ (have) more time to do volunteer work.
B: Me, too. I hope I **4** ________ (can) do some volunteer work next semester.
A: I wish my brother **5** ________ (help) me with my ecology project, but he says he can't.
B: I wish I **6** ________ (not have) so much work because I would help you with it.
A: I hope the government **7** ________ (create) a new soda tax law.
B: Yeah. I wish they **8** ________ (create) a tax on plastic bottles, too!

④ D IN PAIRS **Change the underlined information in C to make new conversations with your own ideas.**

⑥ **SPEAKING**

A **Think about the answers to these questions. Make notes.**

1 Which environmental issues are most important in your country? Why?
2 What do you wish your country would do about these issues?
3 What do you hope your generation will do about environmental problems in the future?

A: I think global warming is the most important issue for us because we have two coasts.
B: I agree. If the seas rise, we'll lose some of our cities, and also, we'll have a lot of hurricanes and other bad storms. I wish we had stronger air pollution laws.
C: I hope young people will help educate the public about the problem of global warming.

B IN GROUPS **Discuss your answers to the questions in A. Do most of you have similar ideas? Use the Confident Communicator box to help you.**

CONFIDENT COMMUNICATOR
KEEP TALKING

To talk about problems and solutions, use the following phrases:
Problems
One problem/issue is ...
The biggest/main problem/issue is...
... is a big/major/serious problem.
Solutions
If we had stronger laws, we wouldn't have so much pollution.
What if we had stronger pollution laws?
I think we need / should have stronger pollution laws.

Unit 5 One Planet 51

⑤ **Further practice.** In the highlighted boxes, there is a reference to further practice in the *Grammar Reference* section at the back of the book. These activities could be done in class if you feel that students need more practice right away to help them understand the grammar, or they could be done as homework or as review before an exam. At the end of this section, there is a list of suggestions for further grammar practice.

⑥ **Further oral practice.** The grammar is also used in the SPEAKING section at the end of each lesson, which gives students communicative practice with the target structure. Remind them that they should use the grammar as much as possible in the speaking activities in order to become comfortable with it. You may want to elicit some examples of how they can use the grammar before they start the speaking activity.

Speak Your Mind provides a number of opportunities for further practice of the grammar:

- The *Grammar Quiz* before Unit 1 is a quick test of what students should have learned before beginning the course.
- The *Grammar Review* after Unit 12 is a review of what students should have learned in prior levels. The *Grammar Review* of Level 2 (A2) reviews language at the A1 level.
- The **Student's App** contains grammar practice. An [app icon] indicates where there is practice in the app.
- A *Grammar Reference* section at the end of the **Student's Book** gives further explanations and practice activities for the grammar points in each unit.
- Grammar practice activities in the **Workbook** reinforce the GRAMMAR sections in the lessons.

Pronunciation

In ***Speak Your Mind***, pronunciation is taught through a combination of observation and practice. There is a PRONUNCIATION section in each unit, and four main areas are emphasized: specific sounds, specific words, stress and intonation, and juncture and reduction.

Students are first asked to listen to examples and to notice a pattern or confirm a rule. It is important to allow them to listen and understand the pronunciation point before asking them to try to produce it.

The noticing activity is followed by practice of the pronunciation point, sometimes as a whole class and other times in pairs.

PROCEDURE: Teaching **Pronunciation** in *Speak Your Mind*

1

PRONUNCIATION /tʃ/ versus /ʃ/

A 11.03 **Listen to how these words are pronounced. Notice the difference between the /tʃ/ and /ʃ/ sounds.**

change   cash machine

B 11.04 **Practice saying these sentences. Then listen and check.**

1 Do you have any change?
2 I'm going to use the cash machine.

2

PRONUNCIATION *the*

A 2.04 **Listen to the sentences. What do you notice about the pronunciation of *the*?**

I have to take my dog to the vet.
My dog has to stay in the animal hospital.

B **Practice the sentence: I like to see the animals at the zoo.**

3

PRONUNCIATION word stress in verb phrases

A 5.02 **Listen to the phrases and underline the stressed word in each phrase. What type of word is stressed?**

verb + noun	verb + adjective/adverb + noun
1 reduce pollution	4 pay for plastic bags
2 provide recycling	5 require less packaging
3 create laws	6 use clean energy

B IN PAIRS **Practice reading the sentences with stress on the correct words.**

1 They should create a law that requires less packaging.
2 The city should provide recycling and support businesses that use clean energy.

4

PRONUNCIATION filler sounds and words

A 12.05 **Listen to the sentences from LISTENING B. Underline the filler sounds and words that the speakers use. Why do you think they use them?**

1 Situations that people can, um, understand and connect with.
2 I felt quite angry, hmm …
3 You might think ad companies would, you know, check the images carefully …
4 It's like, when I'm shopping, what makes me pick up certain things and buy them?

B **Think about your language. What filler sounds and words do you use?**

① **Specific sounds:** Make sure students understand the rule and can distinguish the sound. Model the sound for them, first with the sound only and then using the sound in a word. Allow them to practice the sound a number of times until they feel comfortable with it.

② **Specific words:** When students have to recognize specific words in a sentence, you may want to let them listen to the sentences more than once. If they are asked to notice a sound within a word, make sure they can all distinguish it.

③ **Stress and intonation:** You may want to read the sentences yourself before students practice them. In this way, you can exaggerate the stressed words or the intonation pattern to make sure students can recognize the pattern.

④ **Fluency sounds:** Most languages have sounds that fluent speakers use to show that they are thinking. However, in some cultures these sounds can be seen negatively, as a sign of lacking vocabulary. It is important to help students feel confident about taking their time to think in a conversation because this is a natural part of speech. If students use the same fluency sounds as native speakers, their audience will know to be patient, to give them time to search for the correct word.

Reading

Good readers unconsciously use a number of different skills when they read in their own language. When people learn a second language, they often need to become aware of those skills and learn how to use them when reading in the second language. Reading is considered a receptive skill, but that does not mean that it is a passive activity. Reading involves interacting with a text by reading it with questions in mind, comparing one's own knowledge or opinions to the information in the text, and applying skills to help one understand and interpret the text.

In the classroom, reading is usually done to develop reading skills or as a vehicle for language study. However, a text will be more effective for academic purposes if students find it interesting. In ***Speak Your Mind***, reading texts on a wide variety of topics in a number of different genres are designed to engage students' interest while providing work on key reading skills and general reading comprehension.

PROCEDURE: Teaching **Reading** in *Speak Your Mind*

① **Pre-reading.** Every READING section begins with a pre-reading activity to remind students of knowledge they already have about the topic or to raise their interest in the topic. Before students read the text, have them discuss what they know, or would like to know, about the topic, have them predict what information they think will be in the text, or have them give their opinions about the topic.

② **Reading.** The ***Speak Your Mind*** reading texts introduce vocabulary words in bold to help students focus on them. As students read, they should circle words they don't know and keep reading, then go back to unknown words and guess their meaning. Audio recordings are available for reading texts.

③ **Comprehension.** There are two types of comprehension activities that accompany reading texts: activities for general comprehension and activities to develop specific reading skills. For general comprehension activities, it is a good idea to have students read the questions before reading the text in order to help them quickly identify key information while reading. Good readers usually have an idea of what information they want to get from a text before they begin reading. You may want to ask students to underline key words and information as they read, or to make notes or write questions in the margin next to the text.

④ **Reading skill.** For READING SKILL activities, check that students understand what the skill is and why it is useful before asking them to do the activity. Each unit of the **Workbook** has an explanation of the skill presented in the **Student's Book**, as well as further practice of the skill. You may want to direct students to the explanation in the **Workbook** before having them do the activity in the **Student's Book**.

⑤ **Thinking skill.** Reading should cause us to think. In some cases, we may agree or disagree with a text. A text may raise further questions about a topic, or it may excite and motivate us to share information with others or to take some kind of action. While young adult students of a foreign language, especially at lower levels, do not have great ability with the language, they nevertheless possess adult-level thinking skills. It is more motivating for them to read texts if they know that they will be able to interact with the texts or the topics in a way that takes into account their cognitive abilities. For more on thinking skills, see *Thinking Skills* by Dr. Spencer Kagan on pages xxviii-xxxi of ***Speak Your Mind* Teacher's Edition 1**.

Further reading. For further practice of reading skills and general reading comprehension, there are *Reading Worksheets* available in the **Student's Resource Center**.

LESSON 1 Animal Intelligence

READING

① A Apart from humans, which animals do you think are intelligent?

② B 2.01 Read the blog post. Then choose *True* or *False*.

The Mirror Test

Animals are interesting, aren't they? They can be **cute**, they can be fast, and they can be strong. But are they **intelligent**?

That isn't an easy question to answer. Animals all live in different habitats and their **behavior** is right for that situation. We need a standard way to test an animal's behavior. The mirror test, developed in 1970 by Dr. Gordon Gallup Jr., gives us that.

You recognize your own reflection in a mirror, don't you? But does an animal know that it's looking at itself when it looks in a mirror, or does it think it's a different animal? If an animal passes the mirror test, there's a good chance it is intelligent. We give the animal medicine so it goes to sleep. Then, we put a colored mark on the animal's body where it can't see it in a normal way, such as on its forehead or on its ear. When the animal wakes up and sees itself in a mirror, we watch how it behaves.

Animals that pass the mirror test see the mark and touch it or try to remove it. So far, the species that have passed the test are great apes (chimpanzees, bonobos, and orangutans), elephants, dolphins, orcas, and Eurasian magpies. Some people say, though, that the test only works with animals that mainly use **sight** to explore the world, and it may not be a fair test of other animals, such as dogs, who use **smell** or sound more than sight and fail the test.

GLOSSARY
habitat (n): place where an animal naturally lives

③
1 An animal's environment changes how it acts. True / False
2 The mirror test is done while the animal is asleep. True / False
3 In the mirror test, the animal puts color on its body using the mirror. True / False
4 Animals pass the mirror test if they know they are looking at themselves. True / False

④ C READING SKILL—Understand examples Find and write examples from the text in B.
1 a good place to put a mark on an animal for the mirror test ________
2 an animal that passes the mirror test ________
3 an animal that fails the mirror test ________

⑤ D THINKING SKILL—Recall Without reading the text again, describe how the mirror test works.

VOCABULARY

A Complete the definitions (1–5) with the words in bold in READING B.
1 The sense of ________ is very important to animals that hunt with their eyes, such as cats.
2 The sense of ________ is very important to animals that use their noses a lot, such as bears.
3 An ________ person is good at understanding difficult ideas.
4 An animal's ________ is the way it acts and the things it does.
5 People often think that baby animals, such as kittens and puppies, are ________.

18 Unit 2 The Animal Connection

Listening

The importance of good listening skills cannot be over-emphasized, as listening represents 45% of adult communication. In ***Speak Your Mind***, there are listening comprehension sections in two of the four lessons in each unit. These sections are designed to help students develop key listening skills as well as general comprehension skills. The listening texts represent a variety of genres, including conversations, lectures, radio broadcasts, and podcasts, to give students exposure to as many different listening situations as possible.

Like reading, listening is a receptive skill, but it is not a passive activity. Listeners rely on their own prior knowledge of a topic, their expectations about what a speaker will say, as well as contextual clues like body language to help them predict what will be said. Listeners also employ a variety of skills while listening, such as identifying key words to help them understand the gist of a conversation as well as important details.

There are a number of things that teachers can do to help students improve their listening comprehension:

- Do not speak too slowly or enunciate too perfectly. This will make it easier for students to understand in the classroom, but much more difficult when they encounter English outside the classroom. You may want to slow down a word or a sentence occasionally, but in general you should use normal speech.
- Remind students not to worry if they do not understand every word in a listening text. Point out that we often miss words even when listening in our own language. Encourage them to identify key words to help them understand the gist of a listening text as well as important details.
- As students develop specific listening skills, remind them to use those skills when they are listening to the teacher or to their classmates. Point out that they get listening practice not only in the listening sections of their textbook, but also during speaking activities and classroom interactions.

PROCEDURE: Teaching **Listening** in *Speak Your Mind*

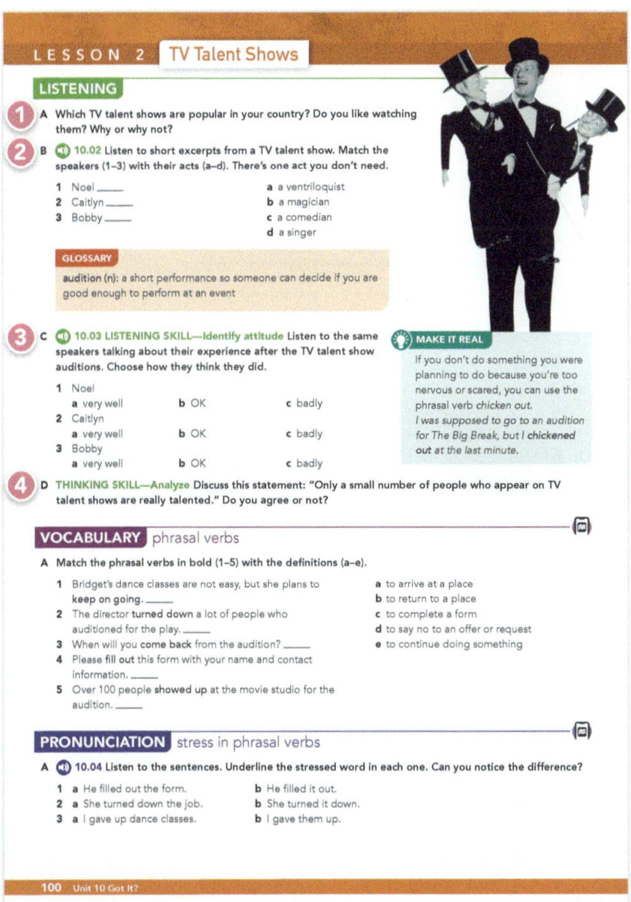
LESSON 2 TV Talent Shows

LISTENING

1 A Which TV talent shows are popular in your country? Do you like watching them? Why or why not?

2 B 10.02 Listen to short excerpts from a TV talent show. Match the speakers (1–3) with their acts (a–d). There's one act you don't need.

1 Noel ____ a a ventriloquist
2 Caitlyn ____ b a magician
3 Bobby ____ c a comedian
d a singer

GLOSSARY
audition (n): a short performance so someone can decide if you are good enough to perform at an event

3 C 10.03 LISTENING SKILL—Identify attitude Listen to the same speakers talking about their experience after the TV talent show auditions. Choose how they think they did.

1 Noel
a very well b OK c badly
2 Caitlyn
a very well b OK c badly
3 Bobby
a very well b OK c badly

MAKE IT REAL
If you don't do something you were planning to do because you're too nervous or scared, you can use the phrasal verb *chicken out.*
I was supposed to go to an audition for The Big Break, but I ***chickened out*** *at the last minute.*

4 D THINKING SKILL—Analyze Discuss this statement: "Only a small number of people who appear on TV talent shows are really talented." Do you agree or not?

VOCABULARY phrasal verbs

A Match the phrasal verbs in bold (1–5) with the definitions (a–e).

1 Bridget's dance classes are not easy, but she plans to **keep on going**. ____
2 The director **turned down** a lot of people who auditioned for the play. ____
3 When will you **come back** from the audition? ____
4 Please **fill out** this form with your name and contact information. ____
5 Over 100 people **showed up** at the movie studio for the audition. ____

a to arrive at a place
b to return to a place
c to complete a form
d to say no to an offer or request
e to continue doing something

PRONUNCIATION stress in phrasal verbs

A 10.04 Listen to the sentences. Underline the stressed word in each one. Can you notice the difference?

1 a He filled out the form. b He filled it out.
2 a She turned down the job. b She turned it down.
3 a I gave up dance classes. b I gave them up.

100 Unit 10 Got It?

(1) **Pre-listening**. Pre-listening activities help students prepare for listening by asking them to predict what speakers will say or talk about what they already know about a topic.

(2) **Listening comprehension**. Students often need a lot of support for listening comprehension. It is a good idea to allow them to read through a comprehension activity before listening in order to give them an idea of what to listen for. You may want to ask students to listen to the recording once before attempting to do the activity. After they listen, give them a few minutes to do the activity and then play the recording again for them to check their work.

(3) **Listening skill**. As with reading, every LISTENING section of ***Speak Your Mind*** includes the development of a listening skill. Check that students understand what the skill is and why it is useful. You may want to refer students to the explanation of the listening skill in the relevant unit of the **Workbook**.

(4) **Thinking skill.** In each LISTENING section of ***Speak Your Mind***, there is a thinking activity which encourages students to further analyze what they've heard and to express their opinions or to extend and apply the ideas in the listening text to their own context. For more on thinking skills, see *Thinking Skills* by Dr. Spencer Kagan on pages xxviii–xxxi of ***Speak Your Mind*** **Teacher's Edition 1**.

Speaking

Foreign-language teachers often comment that students just don't want to speak. There are a number of reasons for this. Sometimes they are afraid of making mistakes. This is especially true of young-adult and adult students who are used to thinking of themselves as competent. Other times students are just not prepared when asked to speak. It can be very difficult for them to think of what to say and how to say it if they are not able to prepare beforehand, especially at lower levels. It is important to create a classroom environment in which students feel confident and motivated to communicate in English.

It is important to provide frequent opportunities for students to speak. In ***Speak Your Mind***, there is a strong emphasis on speaking, and students are given many opportunities throughout the lessons to voice their ideas and to practice the language that they are learning:

- Unit Openers have cooperative learning opportunities and group discussion questions.
- Pre-reading and pre-listening activities often involve class discussions.
- Thinking skills sections have questions for group or class discussions.
- GRAMMAR and VOCABULARY sections frequently include group or pair speaking activities.
- Lessons 1–3 end with a SPEAKING section, which allows students to use the grammar and vocabulary of the lesson to talk about a related topic.
- Language and Life lessons (Lesson 4 in every unit) are designed as collaborative tasks that involve a variety of interactive pair, group, and class activities.

PROCEDURE: Teaching **Speaking** in *Speak Your Mind*

1. **Preparation.** SPEAKING sections are scaffolded in order to give students the support they need when they speak. They first think about the topic and make notes, fill in a form, or in some other way prepare for what they are going to say. It is important to give them enough time to do this so that they feel confident when they start speaking. You may want to add a class preparation stage before asking students to work on their own—have a class brainstorming session to help them come up with ideas, or you could elicit vocabulary and grammar structures that they may need for the speaking activity.
2. **Practice.** Once students have had a chance to prepare, they work in pairs or groups to share their ideas. Make sure that students understand what they are going to do and exactly what their roles are before you put them in their groups or pairs. You may want to model the activity with a student or ask two students to model it.
3. **Present.** Be sure to allow plenty of time for the speaking activities, as this is the communicative outcome of the lesson. The SPEAKING section frequently takes up less space on the page than other sections in the lesson, so it is easy to make the mistake of thinking that the activity is very short. In fact, it may require the most time. It is important to allow enough time for preparation and for each student to have the chance to speak.

When students are working in groups or pairs, listen for common errors, especially in the target language of the lesson. Have a short review session after the speaking activity. This generally works better than interrupting students while they are speaking. If you have a large class, you may not be able to listen to every pair or group, but you can get a good idea of things they may need more practice with by listening to as many of them as possible.

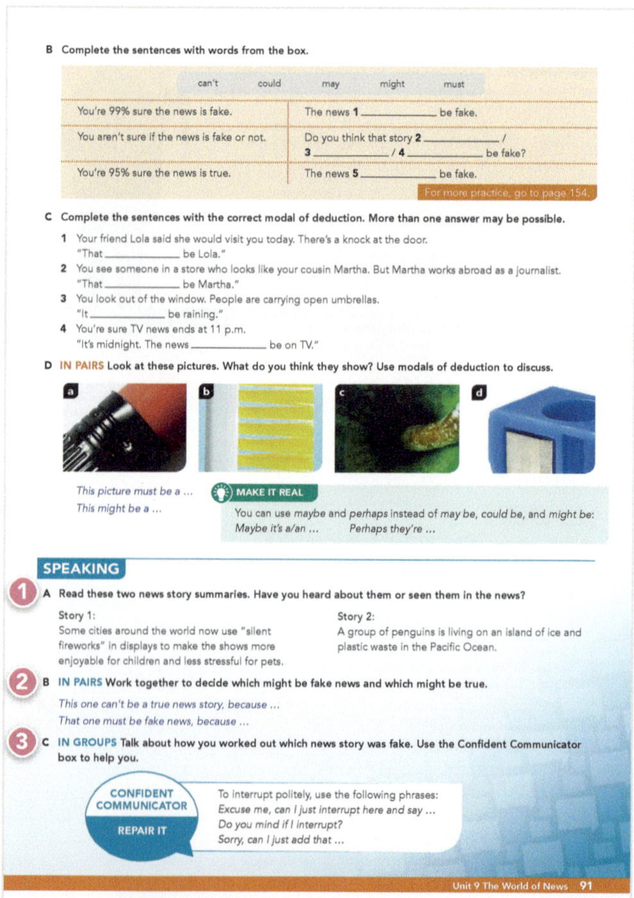
B Complete the sentences with words from the box.

can't could may might must

You're 99% sure the news is fake.	The news **1** ________ be fake.
You aren't sure if the news is fake or not.	Do you think that story **2** ________ / **3** ________ / **4** ________ be fake?
You're 95% sure the news is true.	The news **5** ________ be fake.

For more practice, go to page 154.

C Complete the sentences with the correct modal of deduction. More than one answer may be possible.

1 Your friend Lola said she would visit you today. There's a knock at the door.
"That ________ be Lola."
2 You see someone in a store who looks like your cousin Martha. But Martha works abroad as a journalist.
"That ________ be Martha."
3 You look out of the window. People are carrying open umbrellas.
"It ________ be raining."
4 You're sure TV news ends at 11 p.m.
"It's midnight. The news ________ be on TV."

D IN PAIRS Look at these pictures. What do you think they show? Use modals of deduction to discuss.

a b c d

This picture must be a ...
This might be a ...

MAKE IT REAL
You can use *maybe* and *perhaps* instead of *may be*, *could be*, and *might be*:
Maybe it's a/an ... *Perhaps they're ...*

SPEAKING

1 **A** Read these two news story summaries. Have you heard about them or seen them in the news?

Story 1:
Some cities around the world now use "silent fireworks" in displays to make the shows more enjoyable for children and less stressful for pets.

Story 2:
A group of penguins is living on an island of ice and plastic waste in the Pacific Ocean.

2 **B** IN PAIRS Work together to decide which might be fake news and which might be true.
This one can't be a true news story, because ...
That one must be fake news, because ...

3 **C** IN GROUPS Talk about how you worked out which news story was fake. Use the Confident Communicator box to help you.

CONFIDENT COMMUNICATOR
REPAIR IT
To interrupt politely, use the following phrases:
Excuse me, can I just interrupt here and say ...
Do you mind if I interrupt?
Sorry, can I just add that ...

Unit 9 The World of News 91

Confident Communicator

One of the core objectives of ***Speak Your Mind*** is that students should become confident users of English—that is, Confident Communicators. Every SPEAKING section in ***Speak Your Mind*** includes a *Confident Communicator* box that gives students tips on what to say and how to say it. Some of the tips focus on functional language, which includes words and phrases used in specific situations, such as greeting someone or asking directions. Others focus on speaking strategies, such as taking time to think or explaining what you mean. The subheadings *Start Talking*, *Keep Talking*, and *Repair It* indicate how the language in the *Confident Communicator* box functions in a conversation. For more on communicative strategies, see *Communicative Strategies* by Tony Prince on pages xxviii–xxxi of this book.

Before students get into pairs or groups to do the interactive part of the SPEAKING section, go over the language in the *Confident Communicator* box to make sure they understand how to use it. You may want to practice a few short interactions with some or all of the phrases before they start working together.

When applied to language learning, the old saying "Practice makes perfect" should probably be changed to "Practice makes perfectly adequate." Wanting students to be confident communicators does not mean that everything they say should be perfectly constructed. In our own languages, we often communicate with incomplete sentences or even just facial expressions or gestures. The goal is to give students the confidence to express their ideas in English, and the best way to do that is through a combination of frequent opportunities to speak and support with the language.

Confident Communicator feature in *Speak Your Mind*

Start Talking. With the *Start Talking* boxes, students learn phrases for initiating a conversation or topic.

CONFIDENT COMMUNICATOR
START TALKING

To introduce an anecdote or a short true story, use these phrases:
Here's something that happened to (person/company) in (date).
Listen to this. In (date), (name) made a really bad decision.

Keep Talking. With the *Keep Talking* boxes, students learn strategies and phrases to keep a conversation going even when they are not yet very proficient in the language.

CONFIDENT COMMUNICATOR
KEEP TALKING

To continue the conversation when you don't know a word, use the following phrases to communicate what you mean:
I can't think of the exact word, but It's similar to … / It's a kind of …
What's the word I'm thinking of? It means …

Repair It. With the *Repair It* boxes, students learn phrases to use when there is a problem in communication.

CONFIDENT COMMUNICATOR
REPAIR IT

When you don't understand something, use the following phrases to repair the conversation:
Sorry, what was that?
***I'm sorry—I didn't understand** what you said.*
***What do you mean by** personal achievements?*

Writing

The ability to communicate effectively in writing is more important than ever for professional success. In the past, a great deal of business communication was conducted on the phone, but now most business communication is done via email. Email is no longer considered just an informal mode of written communication. Emails, like letters in the past, can have varying degrees of informality or formality, and young adults who are about to enter a very competitive professional world will have to be able to communicate competently in writing.

Teaching students to communicate in written English is complicated by the fact that many students do not have good writing skills, even in their own language. In ***Speak Your Mind***, students are taught basic writing skills like planning before starting to write, reviewing and editing their work after they write, and how to construct different genres of written communication. Learning to write short texts in different genres gives students practice in skills such as describing a situation or event, persuading the reader to agree with a point of view, giving instructions, or presenting a proposal. While the topics they write about may not be directly related to a profession, the skills they learn can be applied later on in business communications, both in English and in their own language. There is a WRITING section in Lesson 3 of every unit in ***Speak Your Mind***.

Remember that the purpose of writing is to communicate ideas, so it is always a good idea to have students share their finished work. You could have them read their texts aloud in small groups and then have a discussion, or you could have them work with a partner and read each other's texts. They can then get together to discuss their ideas or report on each other's texts to different partners.

There is further practice in writing mechanics and editing skills in the **Workbook**. In ***Speak Your Mind***, students are given the support and the practice they need in order for them to become competent writers in English.

PROCEDURE: Teaching **Writing** in *Speak Your Mind*

① **Read the model.** A model text is provided, either in the WRITING section or in another section in the lesson. Students read the text and do an activity that asks them to notice elements of content, organization, or language commonly used in a specific genre. You may want to have students read the text and then ask some general comprehension questions before having them do the activity.

② **Organize [Pre-writing].** After students have worked with the model text, they are given a framework to provide them with cues and help them organize their ideas for their own text. You may want to start with a class brainstorming session to help generate ideas. As they work, give individual help with ideas and vocabulary as needed.

③ **Write and share.** Once students have written their texts, give them time to review and correct their work. This may be done individually or in pairs. If it is done in pairs, it is a good opportunity for cooperative learning. You may want to go over some common grammar or spelling errors before they start editing their work in order to help them spot their own errors.

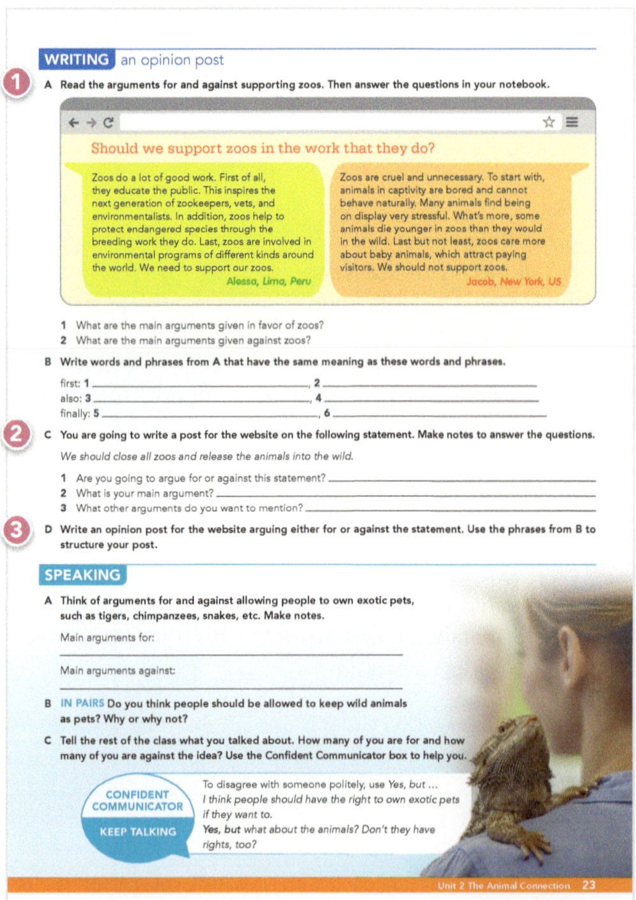

WRITING an opinion post

1 **A Read the arguments for and against supporting zoos. Then answer the questions in your notebook.**

Should we support zoos in the work that they do?

Zoos do a lot of good work. First of all, they educate the public. This inspires the next generation of zookeepers, vets, and environmentalists. In addition, zoos help to protect endangered species through the breeding work they do. Last, zoos are involved in environmental programs of different kinds around the world. We need to support our zoos.
Alessa, Lima, Peru

Zoos are cruel and unnecessary. To start with, animals in captivity are bored and cannot behave naturally. Many animals find being on display very stressful. What's more, some animals die younger in zoos than they would in the wild. Last but not least, zoos care more about baby animals, which attract paying visitors. We should not support zoos.
Jacob, New York, US

1 What are the main arguments given in favor of zoos?
2 What are the main arguments given against zoos?

B Write words and phrases from A that have the same meaning as these words and phrases.

first: **1** ______, **2** ______
also: **3** ______, **4** ______
finally: **5** ______, **6** ______

2 **C You are going to write a post for the website on the following statement. Make notes to answer the questions.**

We should close all zoos and release the animals into the wild.

1 Are you going to argue for or against this statement? ______
2 What is your main argument? ______
3 What other arguments do you want to mention? ______

3 **D Write an opinion post for the website arguing either for or against the statement. Use the phrases from B to structure your post.**

SPEAKING

A Think of arguments for and against allowing people to own exotic pets, such as tigers, chimpanzees, snakes, etc. Make notes.

Main arguments for:
______

Main arguments against:
______

B IN PAIRS **Do you think people should be allowed to keep wild animals as pets? Why or why not?**

C Tell the rest of the class what you talked about. How many of you are for and how many of you are against the idea? Use the Confident Communicator box to help you.

CONFIDENT COMMUNICATOR
KEEP TALKING

To disagree with someone politely, use *Yes, but* ...
I think people should have the right to own exotic pets if they want to.
***Yes, but** what about the animals? Don't they have rights, too?*

Unit 2 The Animal Connection 23

Language and Life

In the 21st century, the teaching of academic subjects is accompanied by the development of the types of skills that are necessary for success in academics, work, and life. These skills for success include communication, collaboration, problem-solving, creativity, self-direction, critical thinking, and media literacy.

In ***Speak Your Mind***, these skills are developed throughout each unit through collaborative activities, training in effective communication, and tasks that require critical thinking and problem-solving. The last lesson in each unit is specifically designed to focus on the development of 21st-century skills while recycling key grammar and vocabulary from the unit.

Every unit in ***Speak Your Mind*** includes a suggestion for online work outside of class. *Make It Digital* often occurs in Lesson 4 because the Language and Life tasks tend to lend themselves to further investigations or to a product that can be posted on a school website. You could have students do the research for homework and then report back to the class.

The lesson ends with questions that encourage students to reflect on the process they followed to achieve the outcome of the lesson and to think about what they might do better in a similar situation in the future. It is a good idea to discuss these questions as a class.

PROCEDURE: Teaching **Language and Life** in *Speak Your Mind*

1. **Present the life skill.** The heading is in two parts. The first part indicates the target 21st-century skill. The second part indicates the outcome of the task sequence in the lesson. Check that students understand both the skill that they will be using and the objective of the task.
2. **Read the text.** The lesson begins with a text that introduces students to the topic of the lesson. The topic is directly related to the overall unit topic. After students have read the text and done the activity, you may want to ask some further questions to check comprehension.
3. **Read the task.** Students are then given a problem or a task, and they have to work through a series of steps in order to achieve an outcome. They work individually to decide how they would solve the problem or carry out the task. Make sure they understand exactly what to do at this stage because everyone's input will be needed for the subsequent activities.
4. **Collaborate.** In the next stage, students work in pairs or in groups, to share the ideas from the previous stage. Depending on the topic and task type, you may want to organize students in different ways. Pair more confident with less confident students, or group students by academic major or interest areas.

   The pairs or groups discuss and combine their ideas and then produce a proposal or set of recommendations in the form of a concrete outcome such as a guide, a presentation, a poster, or an online post. If the final product is a written document, have students write it in the correct format in their notebooks. If it is a presentation, have them write notes on notecards for use during their presentation.
5. **Present.** Students share their proposals or recommendations. They frequently finish the task sequence by discussing their ideas as a whole class and reaching a consensus on the best ideas. Have them work in pairs or small groups so that everyone will have plenty of time to talk, as this is the communicative outcome of the lesson.
6. **Reflect.** Students are asked to reflect on the process of working together through discussion questions.

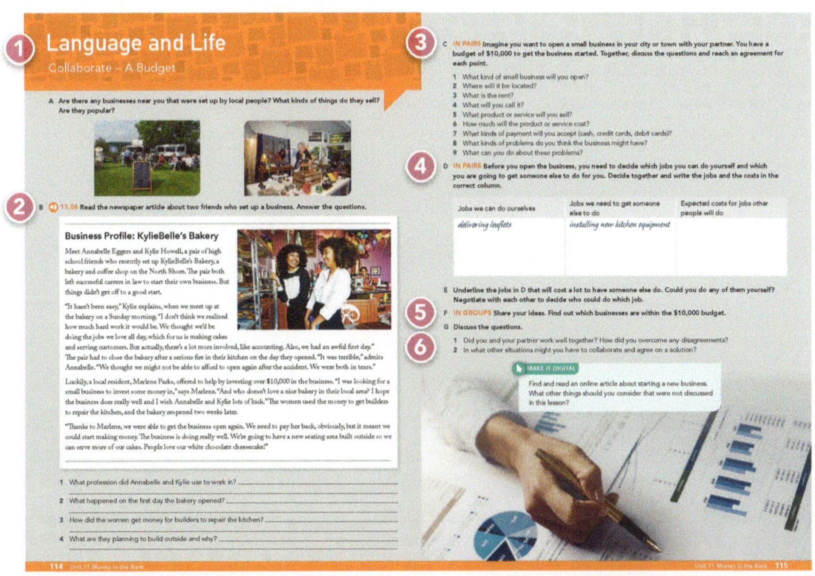

Make It ...

Personalization is an important part of building vocabulary for English language learners. The *Make It ...* features in ***Speak Your Mind*** show students where they should add the words and phrases they need to use for work or study. Students should be encouraged to build a list of words, phrases, or expressions that are meaningful to them.

PROCEDURE: Using the **Make It ...** features in *Speak Your Mind*

Make It Yours. *Make It Yours* boxes encourage students to expand their vocabulary by making a list of words that are useful for them personally or by using target vocabulary in a personalized way. Go over the information in the boxes and elicit words from the class, or ask them to do the task suggested in the box for homework.

> **MAKE IT YOURS**
>
> Some people think technology is amazing. Others are terrified. How do the different types of technology around you make you feel?

Make It Happen. The Study Skills page ends with a *Make It Happen* box that has a suggestion for an activity in which students would use the skill they have just learned. These could work well as homework assignments or even short projects.

> **MAKE IT HAPPEN**
>
> Work with a partner. Look online and choose a text at an appropriate level that you think your partner would find interesting. Ask your partner to read the text using some of the tips outlined in these lessons. Share your findings in a group.

Make It Real. GRAMMAR and VOCABULARY sections are often accompanied by a *Make It Real* box. The purpose of this feature is to provide students with examples of language that they may not be formally taught but which are commonly used by native speakers. This helps them understand more easily when they listen to a native speaker, and it can help them sound more natural when they speak English.

> **MAKE IT REAL**
>
> To *splurge* means to spend a lot of money. *Maria used her birthday money to splurge on expensive new shoes.*

Make It Digital. Every unit in ***Speak Your Mind*** includes a suggestion for online work outside of class. The *Make It Digital* box always appears in Lesson 4 because the Language and Life tasks lend themselves to further investigations or to a product that can be posted on a school website. You could have students do the research for homework and then report back to the class.

> **MAKE IT DIGITAL**
>
> Record the talent contest. Decide whose performance was the best. Who definitely has talent?

Unit Review

Every unit in ***Speak Your Mind*** includes an end-of-unit review of the target grammar and vocabulary from the unit. The activities are designed as a general review to help students and teachers identify areas of strength and weakness so that students know what to focus on when studying for their exams.

PROCEDURE: Teaching the **Unit Review** in *Speak Your Mind*

1. **Review.** The VOCABULARY and GRAMMAR *Review* sections each have one or two activities for a total of 10 items per section. The activities are written in a variety of formats that reflect the different activity types that students may encounter on an exam.

   For Unit Tests, Mid-Course Tests, and End-of-Course Tests, use the Ready to Go tests or make customized tests with the ***Speak Your Mind* Test Generator**. If possible, it is a good idea to have students do the *Review* section a couple of days before a unit exam so that they have plenty of time to study their weak areas before the exam. The *Review* may be assigned as homework or done in class as a practice test.

2. **Score.** There are 10 points per section for a combined total of 20 points for the two sections. Students should write the number of correct answers in the blank in each section and the total number of correct answers in the *Total Score* box. Point out the score interpretations under the *Total Score* box. Remind students that they will be tested on the grammar and vocabulary of the unit, and if they have a low score on the *Review*, they need to go back to the relevant sections in the unit and study the material.

   When you go over the answers to the *Review* section, make sure that students understand their errors and that they know which section of their **Student's Book** to study for each incorrect item. Remind them that they need to study all of the vocabulary items in the three VOCABULARY sections in the unit, not just the items that were included in the *Review* activities.

3. **Further review.** Every *Review* section ends with the question WHAT DO YOU KNOW NOW? Students are asked to go back to the vocabulary activity in the Unit Opener and add words that they have learned in the unit. This is useful both as a reflection activity and as a review tool. It raises students' awareness that they are increasing their vocabulary in English. Also, by looking back at the words they listed in the Unit Opener, they are reviewing vocabulary related to the unit topic.

4. **Study Skill / Follow A Pro.** Please see the following pages for explanations of the STUDY SKILLS and FOLLOW A PRO sections on the *Review* page.

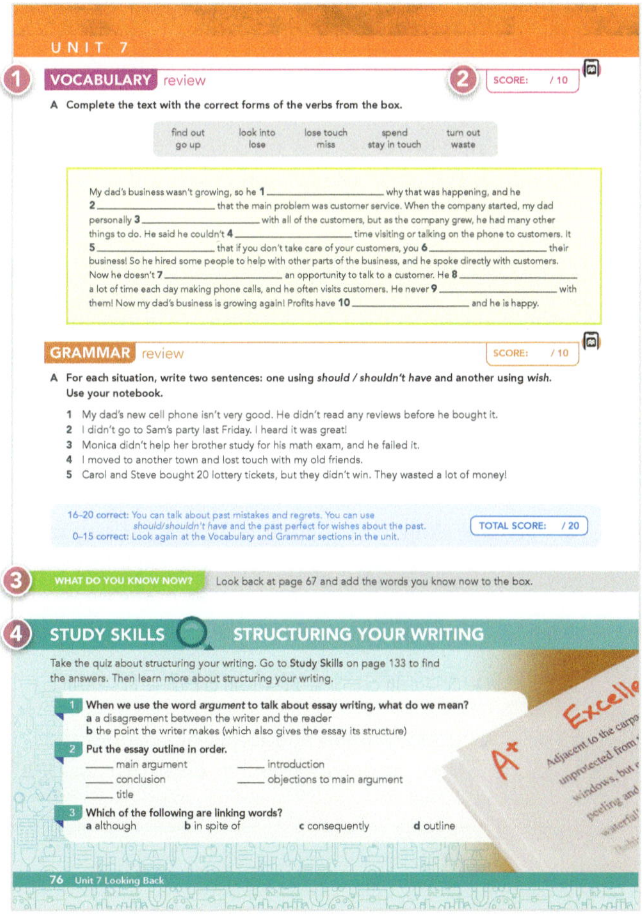
UNIT 7

① VOCABULARY review ② SCORE: / 10

A Complete the text with the correct forms of the verbs from the box.

find out, look into, lose touch, spend, turn out, go up, lose, miss, stay in touch, waste

My dad's business wasn't growing, so he 1 ______ why that was happening, and he 2 ______ that the main problem was customer service. When the company started, my dad personally 3 ______ with all of the customers, but as the company grew, he had many other things to do. He said he couldn't 4 ______ time visiting or talking on the phone to customers. It 5 ______ that if you don't take care of your customers, you 6 ______ their business! So he hired some people to help with other parts of the business, and he spoke directly with customers. Now he doesn't 7 ______ an opportunity to talk to a customer. He 8 ______ a lot of time each day making phone calls, and he often visits customers. He never 9 ______ with them! Now my dad's business is growing again! Profits have 10 ______ and he is happy.

GRAMMAR review SCORE: / 10

A For each situation, write two sentences: one using *should / shouldn't have* and another using *wish*. Use your notebook.

1 My dad's new cell phone isn't very good. He didn't read any reviews before he bought it.
2 I didn't go to Sam's party last Friday. I heard it was great!
3 Monica didn't help her brother study for his math exam, and he failed it.
4 I moved to another town and lost touch with my old friends.
5 Carol and Steve bought 20 lottery tickets, but they didn't win. They wasted a lot of money!

16–20 correct: You can talk about past mistakes and regrets. You can use *should/shouldn't have* and the past perfect for wishes about the past.
0–15 correct: Look again at the Vocabulary and Grammar sections in the unit.

TOTAL SCORE: / 20

③ WHAT DO YOU KNOW NOW? Look back at page 67 and add the words you know now to the box.

④ STUDY SKILLS STRUCTURING YOUR WRITING

Take the quiz about structuring your writing. Go to **Study Skills** on page 133 to find the answers. Then learn more about structuring your writing.

1 When we use the word *argument* to talk about essay writing, what do we mean?
a a disagreement between the writer and the reader
b the point the writer makes (which also gives the essay its structure)

2 Put the essay outline in order.
____ main argument ____ introduction
____ conclusion ____ objections to main argument
____ title

3 Which of the following are linking words?
a although b in spite of c consequently d outline

76 Unit 7 Looking Back

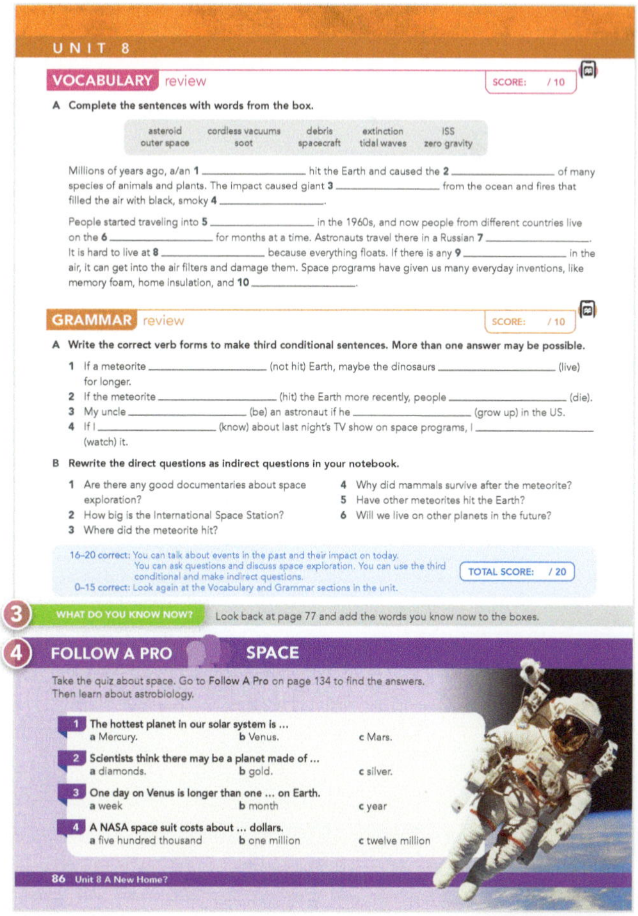
UNIT 8

VOCABULARY review SCORE: / 10

A Complete the sentences with words from the box.

asteroid, cordless vacuums, debris, extinction, ISS, outer space, soot, spacecraft, tidal waves, zero gravity

Millions of years ago, a/an 1 ______ hit the Earth and caused the 2 ______ of many species of animals and plants. The impact caused giant 3 ______ from the ocean and fires that filled the air with black, smoky 4 ______.

People started traveling into 5 ______ in the 1960s, and now people from different countries live on the 6 ______ for months at a time. Astronauts travel there in a Russian 7 ______. It is hard to live at 8 ______ because everything floats. If there is any 9 ______ in the air, it can get into the air filters and damage them. Space programs have given us many everyday inventions, like memory foam, home insulation, and 10 ______.

GRAMMAR review SCORE: / 10

A Write the correct verb forms to make third conditional sentences. More than one answer may be possible.

1 If a meteorite ______ (not hit) Earth, maybe the dinosaurs ______ (live) for longer.
2 If the meteorite ______ (hit) the Earth more recently, people ______ (die).
3 My uncle ______ (be) an astronaut if he ______ (grow up) in the US.
4 If I ______ (know) about last night's TV show on space programs, I ______ (watch) it.

B Rewrite the direct questions as indirect questions in your notebook.

1 Are there any good documentaries about space exploration?
2 How big is the International Space Station?
3 Where did the meteorite hit?
4 Why did mammals survive after the meteorite?
5 Have other meteorites hit the Earth?
6 Will we live on other planets in the future?

16–20 correct: You can talk about events in the past and their impact on today. You can ask questions and discuss space exploration. You can use the third conditional and make indirect questions.
0–15 correct: Look again at the Vocabulary and Grammar sections in the unit.

TOTAL SCORE: / 20

③ WHAT DO YOU KNOW NOW? Look back at page 77 and add the words you know now to the boxes.

④ FOLLOW A PRO SPACE

Take the quiz about space. Go to **Follow A Pro** on page 134 to find the answers. Then learn about astrobiology.

1 The hottest planet in our solar system is …
a Mercury. b Venus. c Mars.

2 Scientists think there may be a planet made of …
a diamonds. b gold. c silver.

3 One day on Venus is longer than one … on Earth.
a week b month c year

4 A NASA space suit costs about … dollars.
a five hundred thousand b one million c twelve million

86 Unit 8 A New Home?

Study Skills

In order to be successful, not only in learning English but also in academics in general, students must develop good study skills, such as how to do efficient research, how to give presentations, and how to improve their memory. In ***Speak Your Mind***, there is a study skills syllabus that is based on universal needs regardless of the subject but modified when appropriate to focus on skills specific to learning a new language.

In each level of ***Speak Your Mind***, study skills are presented and practiced in every other unit. To raise students' interest in the study skill and to give them an idea of what they already know about the skill, there is a short quiz at the end of the *Review* page in odd-numbered units.

PROCEDURE: Teaching **Study Skills** in *Speak Your Mind*

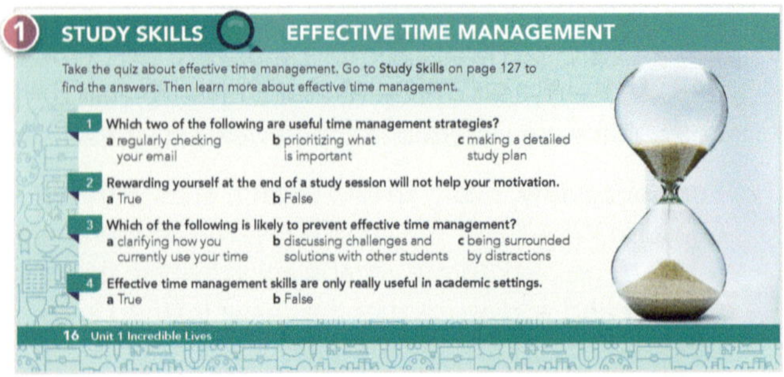

1 STUDY SKILLS — EFFECTIVE TIME MANAGEMENT

Take the quiz about effective time management. Go to **Study Skills** on page 127 to find the answers. Then learn more about effective time management.

1 **Which two of the following are useful time management strategies?**
a regularly checking your email **b** prioritizing what is important **c** making a detailed study plan

2 **Rewarding yourself at the end of a study session will not help your motivation.**
a True **b** False

3 **Which of the following is likely to prevent effective time management?**
a clarifying how you currently use your time **b** discussing challenges and solutions with other students **c** being surrounded by distractions

4 **Effective time management skills are only really useful in academic settings.**
a True **b** False

16 Unit 1 Incredible Lives

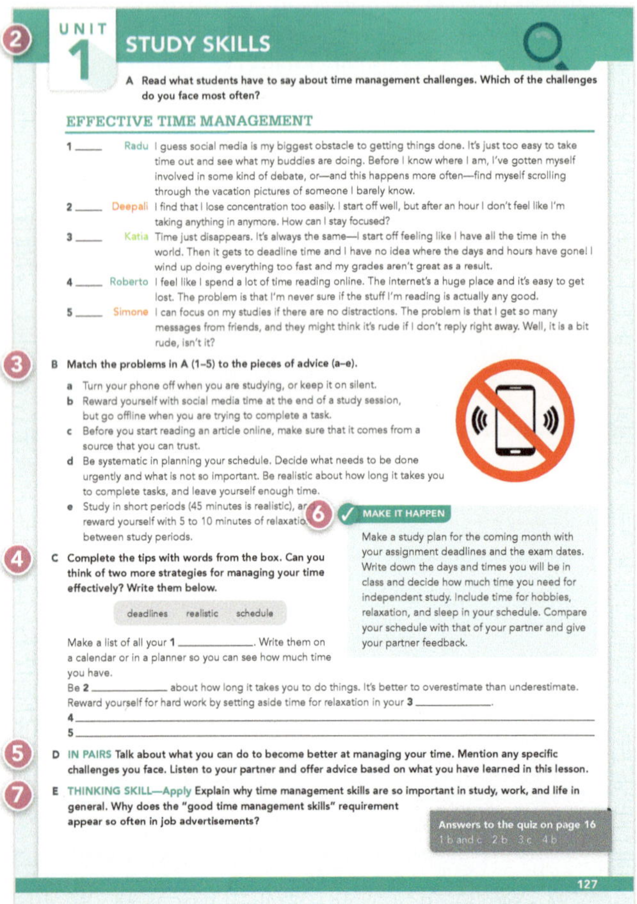

2 UNIT 1 STUDY SKILLS

A Read what students have to say about time management challenges. Which of the challenges do you face most often?

EFFECTIVE TIME MANAGEMENT

1 ____ Radu I guess social media is my biggest obstacle to getting things done. It's just too easy to take time out and see what my buddies are doing. Before I know where I am, I've gotten myself involved in some kind of debate, or—and this happens more often—find myself scrolling through the vacation pictures of someone I barely know.

2 ____ Deepali I find that I lose concentration too easily. I start off well, but after an hour I don't feel like I'm taking anything in anymore. How can I stay focused?

3 ____ Katia Time just disappears. It's always the same—I start off feeling like I have all the time in the world. Then it gets to deadline time and I have no idea where the days and hours have gone! I wind up doing everything too fast and my grades aren't great as a result.

4 ____ Roberto I feel like I spend a lot of time reading online. The internet's a huge place and it's easy to get lost. The problem is that I'm never sure if the stuff I'm reading is actually any good.

5 ____ Simone I can focus on my studies if there are no distractions. The problem is that I get so many messages from friends, and they might think it's rude if I don't reply right away. Well, it is a bit rude, isn't it?

3 **B Match the problems in A (1–5) to the pieces of advice (a–e).**

a Turn your phone off when you are studying, or keep it on silent.
b Reward yourself with social media time at the end of a study session, but go offline when you are trying to complete a task.
c Before you start reading an article online, make sure that it comes from a source that you can trust.
d Be systematic in planning your schedule. Decide what needs to be done urgently and what is not so important. Be realistic about how long it takes you to complete tasks, and leave yourself enough time.
e Study in short periods (45 minutes is realistic), and reward yourself with 5 to 10 minutes of relaxation between study periods.

6 MAKE IT HAPPEN

Make a study plan for the coming month with your assignment deadlines and the exam dates. Write down the days and times you will be in class and decide how much time you need for independent study. Include time for hobbies, relaxation, and sleep in your schedule. Compare your schedule with that of your partner and give your partner feedback.

4 **C Complete the tips with words from the box. Can you think of two more strategies for managing your time effectively? Write them below.**

deadlines realistic schedule

Make a list of all your **1** ____________. Write them on a calendar or in a planner so you can see how much time you have.
Be **2** ____________ about how long it takes you to do things. It's better to overestimate than underestimate.
Reward yourself for hard work by setting aside time for relaxation in your **3** ____________.
4 ____________
5 ____________

5 **D IN PAIRS Talk about what you can do to become better at managing your time. Mention any specific challenges you face. Listen to your partner and offer advice based on what you have learned in this lesson.**

7 **E THINKING SKILL—Apply Explain why time management skills are so important in study, work, and life in general. Why does the "good time management skills" requirement appear so often in job advertisements?**

Answers to the quiz on page 16
1 b and c 2 b 3 c 4 b

127

① **Take the quiz.** Direct students' attention to the skill in the heading and make sure they understand what the skill is. Have them take the quiz. You may want to let them do the quiz in pairs or check their answers with a partner before going to the STUDY SKILLS page at the back of the **Student's Book** to check their answers. The answers are at the bottom of the STUDY SKILLS page.

② **Present the study skill.** The quiz on the Unit Review page leads students to the Study Skills page at the back of the book. In the first activity, students are asked to apply critical-thinking skills to do a broad analysis of a text in relation to the target study skill. The topic of the text is often related to the topic of the unit. Have students read the text and then answer the question or do the task as a whole-class activity.

③ **Do the task.** The second activity goes into more detail about the study skill. After students have done the activity, go over it as a class to make sure they have understood the skill.

④ **Read the tips or rules.** The third activity is usually focused on tips and rules for carrying out the study skill effectively. Encourage students to refer back to these from time to time to help them remember the skill.

⑤ **Apply the skill.** In the fourth activity, students apply what they have learned and use the study skill to do an academic task or discuss how they can use the skill in their own studies. This is the productive outcome of the lesson, so be sure to allow enough time for the activity.

⑥ **Transfer the skill.** The *Make It Happen* box suggests a task that allows students to apply the skill they have just learned. These could work well as homework assignments or even short projects.

⑦ **Reflect.** The last activity develops a thinking skill. Students are asked to discuss how the study skill can be applied in real-life academic or professional situations. These often work well as class discussions.

Follow A Pro

Speak Your Mind has a strong emphasis on professional readiness, and in every other unit, a job is highlighted in a section called Follow A Pro. As with the Study Skills section, there is a short quiz at the end of the *Review* page in even-numbered units to generate interest in and highlight previous knowledge of a particular job or professional field.

PROCEDURE: Teaching **Follow A Pro** in *Speak Your Mind*

① **Take the quiz.** Ask students to take the quiz about a specific job or a general professional area, and then go to the corresponding page at the back of the **Student's Book** to check their answers. Answers are at the bottom of the page.

② **Read about a professional.** Ask students to read the text about a person who does a particular job or about a job in general. The topic of the text is related to an aspect of the topic of the unit. When students have finished reading, have them answer the comprehension questions individually. Check the answers as a class.

③ **Discuss the job.** Have students discuss different aspects of the job in the text and whether they would be good at or enjoy doing that job themselves. If you have a large class, you may prefer to do the discussion in small groups so that all students will have an opportunity to talk.

④ **Watch the video.** A video follows a professional in a job that is related to or in the same general field as the job in the text. There is an option to view the video script, if desired. Have students answer comprehension questions about the video. For this activity, students work in small groups. It is a good idea to have students read the questions before they watch the video so that they can more easily pick out the information that they need to remember. You may want to play the video once without the video script and ask students to answer the questions as well as they can, and then play it again with the video script in view to reinforce their comprehension. They can then go back and complete or revise their answers to the questions.

⑤ **Talk about the industry or field.** The final set of discussion questions asks students to think about the job and industry in general. Have students work in pairs or small groups to explain what they know about the job and the skills it requires. Because these questions do not refer specifically to the video, the discussion can be done even if the video is not used.

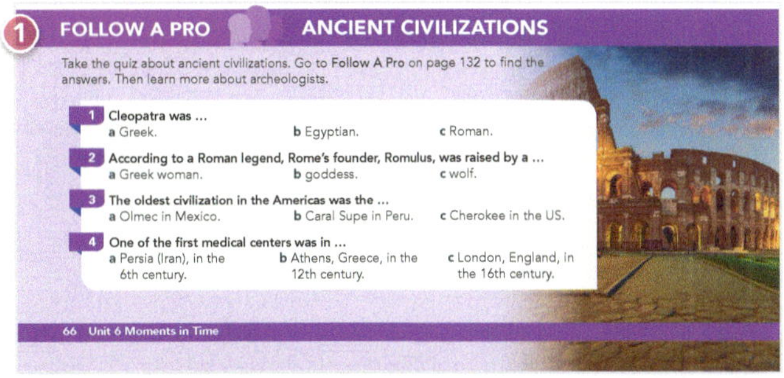
① FOLLOW A PRO — ANCIENT CIVILIZATIONS

Take the quiz about ancient civilizations. Go to **Follow A Pro** on page 132 to find the answers. Then learn more about archeologists.

1. **Cleopatra was ...**
   a Greek. b Egyptian. c Roman.
2. **According to a Roman legend, Rome's founder, Romulus, was raised by a ...**
   a Greek woman. b goddess. c wolf.
3. **The oldest civilization in the Americas was the ...**
   a Olmec in Mexico. b Caral Supe in Peru. c Cherokee in the US.
4. **One of the first medical centers was in ...**
   a Persia (Iran), in the 6th century. b Athens, Greece, in the 12th century. c London, England, in the 16th century.

66 Unit 6 Moments in Time

② UNIT 6 FOLLOW A PRO

A Read about an archeologist. Answer the questions below in your notebook.

AN ARCHEOLOGIST

Many people think archeologists work outside, discovering the secrets of ancient civilizations in the mountains of Peru or the deserts of Egypt. Well, that's true, but is archeology really just about that? Archeology is a part of the larger field of anthropology, which is the study of human culture. Archeologists study structures and objects from ancient civilizations to try to understand what the ancient cultures were like and how ancient people lived. To be an archeologist, you will need a master's degree or a PhD. Your studies will include a large amount of research and probably some fieldwork. The chance of making a great discovery is what most archeologists dream of. However, even when it happens, archeologists have to carefully analyze their findings, to prove their importance. If you want to find out more about archeology before you spend a lot of time and money getting advanced degrees, research what an archeologist does online. You need to understand that archeologists do not all work in exciting places. Most of us work at places like historic sites, national parks, museums, or universities. We also often do not have regular working hours. We might work seven days a week for several weeks if there is an important project. We also have to work in all kinds of weather at all times of day. Archeology is an interesting job, and sometimes it's exciting, but you have to study a lot to become an archeologist, and you have to work very hard when you get a job!

1 What field is archeology a part of?
2 What do archeologists study? Why?
3 What do archeologists most want to achieve?
4 What is a good way to find out more about archeology before you decide to study it?
5 Where do archeologists work?

③ **B Discuss the questions as a class.**

1 In what ways is archeology a hard job?
2 Is archeology an important field in your country?

VIDEO — WATCH THE VIDEO AND FOLLOW A MECHANICAL ENGINEER.

④ **C IN GROUPS Answer the questions.**

1 What does the person do? ______
2 What skills does the person need for the job? ______
3 Where does the person often work? ______
4 What kind of special equipment does the person use? ______
5 Does the person work alone or in a team? ______
6 Is the person happy with the job? Why? ______

⑤ **D IN GROUPS Check your answers to the quiz on page 66 and discuss the questions.**

1 What old or ancient civilizations were in your country? Have you ever visited any of their sites? If so, which ones?
2 What other archeological or historical sites in the world would you like to visit?

Answers to the quiz on page 66
1a 2c 3b 4a

132

Unit Opener Videos

The Discuss & Share section of the Unit Opener features an optional ***Speak Your Mind*** video. The video provides information and context for the discussion of the question. In each video, two vloggers answer the ***Speak Your Mind*** SYM **question**. One vlogger expresses one point of view, while the other one answers with the opposite point of view. The video ends with the vloggers posing the question to the students. The two opposing answers provide a model for the students' own responses. In most cases, the students' opinions will fall somewhere between the two opposing points of view. You should encourage students to state their opinion and explain where they are on the continuum of the two opposite points of view.

PROCEDURE: Using the **Unit Opener Videos** in *Speak Your Mind*

1. ***Speak Your Mind*** **question.** Make sure students understand the two points of view. You may want to draw a line with the opposing views at either end to show the continuum.

   natural causes ———— caused by people

2. **Before viewing.** The teacher's page provides a question or questions to ask students before they watch the video. Use the question(s) to focus the students' attention on the differing points of view.
3. **Mark the continuum.** After viewing the video, have students mark where they are on the continuum by placing an X on the line between the points of view. Alternatively, ask students to form a line in the classroom, placing themselves between the two ends of the line, according to their opinion.
4. **Discuss & Share**. Ask students to explain why they have placed themselves at their selected point on the continuum. Encourage them to use the words they wrote in the What Do You Already Know? word list.

Follow A Pro Videos

The Follow A Pro videos follow professionals through their daily work lives. The job in the video is in the same industry or field as the job on the Follow A Pro page. Students should be able to recycle some of the vocabulary from the text and discussion in activities **A** and **B** as they answer the questions about the video in **C**. There are many ways to maximize learning when using videos. These suggestions support vocabulary acquisition and listening comprehension.

PROCEDURE: Using the **Follow A Pro Videos** in *Speak Your Mind*

1. **Look for images.** Tell students they are going to watch the video with the sound off. Give them the list of words to look for, provided on the **Teacher's Edition** page. If they see any of the things on the list, they should circle the words. For further challenge, ask students to predict what the professional will say about his or her life based on the images in the video.
2. **Listen for words.** Play the video with the sound on. Provide the list of words or phrases from the Teacher's Edition page. Ask students to circle any words or phrases they hear. Have students answer the questions in activity **C**. A challenge question is provided on the **Teacher's Edition** page to check students' comprehension of the video.
3. **Watch again.** Play the video again with or without the video script visible. Students can check or correct their answers to the questions in activity **C** and the challenge question.

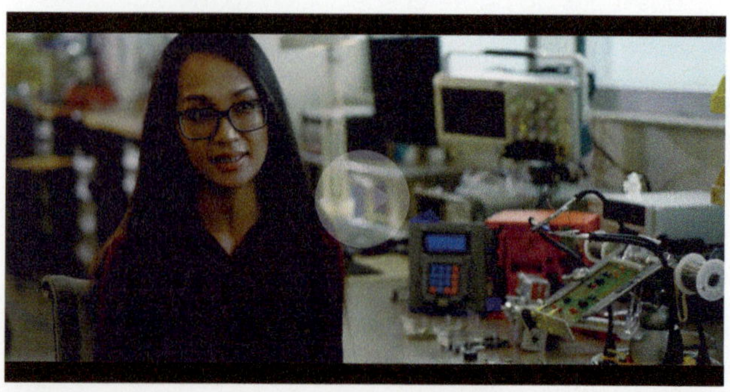

Grammar Quiz

Before students begin their course, have them take the *Grammar Quiz* on page 6. This quiz is a quick review of language from the Starter level of ***Speak Your Mind***. For a longer review, go to the *Grammar Review* on page 140.

Grammar Review

At the back of the ***Speak Your Mind*** **Student's Book**, there is a *Grammar Review* section. The section starts with a page containing a list of common irregular verbs.

The *Grammar Review* pages review language that was taught in the previous level of ***Speak Your Mind***. You can use the *Grammar Review* when students begin their level to test what they have retained from previous classes.

Grammar Reference

Following the *Grammar Review* are the *Grammar Reference* pages. They provide an expanded explanation of the function of the grammar points. The form of the grammar is shown in a table. Practice activities follow the explanation. Note that the *Reference* section is in the **Student's Book** only, but the *Answer Key* for the practice activities in this section is at the back of this **Teacher's Edition**. Grammar points are labeled clearly with a heading.

The *Grammar Reference* pages can be used in several ways:

- **Further practice.** When a new grammar point is introduced in a unit, you may want to refer students to the relevant section in the *Grammar Reference* and go over the explanations of form and function with them, pointing out the examples in the table(s). You could do this before or after doing the grammar presentation in the unit.
- **Homework.** You may want to do the grammar practice activity in the unit in class and assign the activities in the *Grammar Reference* section for homework, along with or instead of the activities in the **Workbook**.
- **Review.** The *Grammar Reference* activities can be used for review before an exam.

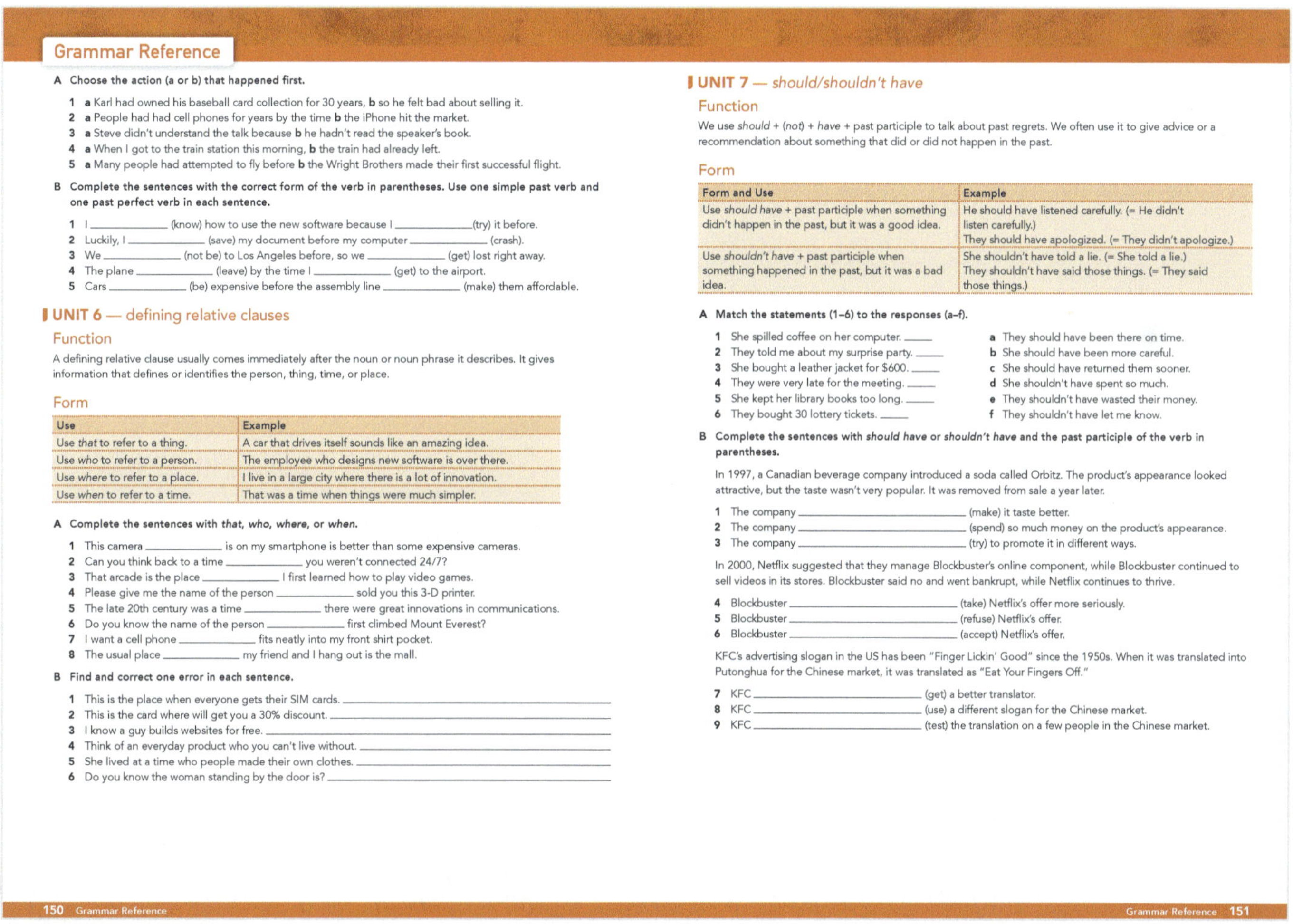

Grammar Reference

A Choose the action (a or b) that happened first.

1 **a** Karl had owned his baseball card collection for 30 years, **b** so he felt bad about selling it.
2 **a** People had had cell phones for years by the time **b** the iPhone hit the market.
3 **a** Steve didn't understand the talk because **b** he hadn't read the speaker's book.
4 **a** When I got to the train station this morning, **b** the train had already left.
5 **a** Many people had attempted to fly before **b** the Wright Brothers made their first successful flight.

B Complete the sentences with the correct form of the verb in parentheses. Use one simple past verb and one past perfect verb in each sentence.

1 I __________ (know) how to use the new software because I __________(try) it before.
2 Luckily, I __________ (save) my document before my computer __________ (crash).
3 We __________ (not be) to Los Angeles before, so we __________ (get) lost right away.
4 The plane __________ (leave) by the time I __________ (get) to the airport.
5 Cars __________ (be) expensive before the assembly line __________ (make) them affordable.

UNIT 6 — defining relative clauses

Function

A defining relative clause usually comes immediately after the noun or noun phrase it describes. It gives information that defines or identifies the person, thing, time, or place.

Form

Use	Example
Use *that* to refer to a thing.	A car that drives itself sounds like an amazing idea.
Use *who* to refer to a person.	The employee who designs new software is over there.
Use *where* to refer to a place.	I live in a large city where there is a lot of innovation.
Use *when* to refer to a time.	That was a time when things were much simpler.

A Complete the sentences with *that, who, where,* or *when.*

1 This camera __________ is on my smartphone is better than some expensive cameras.
2 Can you think back to a time __________ you weren't connected 24/7?
3 That arcade is the place __________ I first learned how to play video games.
4 Please give me the name of the person __________ sold you this 3-D printer.
5 The late 20th century was a time __________ there were great innovations in communications.
6 Do you know the name of the person __________ first climbed Mount Everest?
7 I want a cell phone __________ fits neatly into my front shirt pocket.
8 The usual place __________ my friend and I hang out is the mall.

B Find and correct one error in each sentence.

1 This is the place when everyone gets their SIM cards. __________
2 This is the card where will get you a 30% discount. __________
3 I know a guy builds websites for free. __________
4 Think of an everyday product who you can't live without. __________
5 She lived at a time who people made their own clothes. __________
6 Do you know the woman standing by the door is? __________

150 Grammar Reference

UNIT 7 — *should/shouldn't have*

Function

We use *should* + (*not*) + *have* + past participle to talk about past regrets. We often use it to give advice or a recommendation about something that did or did not happen in the past.

Form

Form and Use	Example
Use *should have* + past participle when something didn't happen in the past, but it was a good idea.	He should have listened carefully. (= He didn't listen carefully.) They should have apologized. (= They didn't apologize.)
Use *shouldn't have* + past participle when something happened in the past, but it was a bad idea.	She shouldn't have told a lie. (= She told a lie.) They shouldn't have said those things. (= They said those things.)

A Match the statements (1–6) to the responses (a–f).

1 She spilled coffee on her computer. ____
2 They told me about my surprise party. ____
3 She bought a leather jacket for $600. ____
4 They were very late for the meeting. ____
5 She kept her library books too long. ____
6 They bought 30 lottery tickets. ____

a They should have been there on time.
b She should have been more careful.
c She should have returned them sooner.
d She shouldn't have spent so much.
e They shouldn't have wasted their money.
f They shouldn't have let me know.

B Complete the sentences with *should have* or *shouldn't have* and the past participle of the verb in parentheses.

In 1997, a Canadian beverage company introduced a soda called Orbitz. The product's appearance looked attractive, but the taste wasn't very popular. It was removed from sale a year later.

1 The company __________ (make) it taste better.
2 The company __________ (spend) so much money on the product's appearance.
3 The company __________ (try) to promote it in different ways.

In 2000, Netflix suggested that they manage Blockbuster's online component, while Blockbuster continued to sell videos in its stores. Blockbuster said no and went bankrupt, while Netflix continues to thrive.

4 Blockbuster __________ (take) Netflix's offer more seriously.
5 Blockbuster __________ (refuse) Netflix's offer.
6 Blockbuster __________ (accept) Netflix's offer.

KFC's advertising slogan in the US has been "Finger Lickin' Good" since the 1950s. When it was translated into Putonghua for the Chinese market, it was translated as "Eat Your Fingers Off."

7 KFC __________ (get) a better translator.
8 KFC __________ (use) a different slogan for the Chinese market.
9 KFC __________ (test) the translation on a few people in the Chinese market.

Grammar Reference 151

The following features are accessible via the ***Speak Your Mind*** Resource Centers.

Student's Resource Center

- **Reading Worksheets**
- **Student's Book** and **Workbook** audio files
- **Student's Book** videos
- **Word Lists**

Teacher's Resource Center

- **Reading Worksheets**
- ***OneStopEnglish*** **Worksheets**
- **Student's Book** and **Workbook** audio files
- **Student's Book** videos
- **Printable Ready-to-Go Tests**
- **CEFR Correlations**
- **Word Lists**

Reading Worksheets

Each unit of ***Speak Your Mind*** has three extensive **Reading Worksheets**, for a total of 36. The topics of the worksheets extend the themes and vocabulary sets of the units in the areas of General English, Business, Science, and Services. They are designed to appeal to students who are studying academic subjects and young adults who are already working in their careers.

The **Reading Worksheets** have a text with a VOCABULARY activity and COMPREHENSION questions. A THINKING question at the end of the worksheet can be used as a departure for discussion in the classroom or a writing assignment for homework.

OneStopEnglish Worksheets

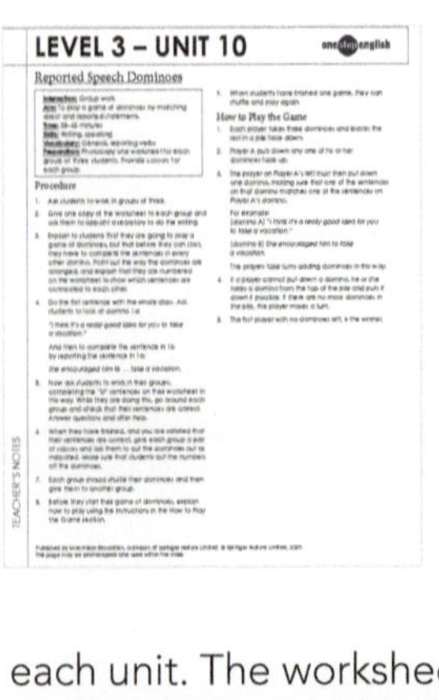

The ***OneStopEnglish*** **Worksheets** give students further speaking practice in a fun and engaging way. Speak Your Mind has chosen select worksheets from the OneStopEnglish website, the world's number one teacher resource site for English Language teachers. The ***OneStopEnglish*** **Worksheets** have been adapted for the course, with one worksheet for each unit. The worksheets consist of one page of teacher's notes, which includes the aim, procedure, and estimated activity time, and one page with the student's activity.

Printable Ready-to-Go Tests

All the tests for ***Speak Your Mind*** can be found in the **Teacher's Resource Center**. This includes a Placement Test, Unit Tests, a Mid-Course Test, and an End-of-Course Test. All tests are available as ready-to-print PDFs. Tests can be customized using the **Test Generator** (see the **How to Use the Digital Components** section, page xxvii).

- The Placement Test places students in a ***Speak Your Mind*** level.
- The Unit Tests include vocabulary, grammar, listening, reading, writing, and speaking items for each unit.
- The Mid-Course Test include vocabulary, grammar, listening, reading, writing, and speaking items for units 1–6.
- The End-of-Course Test includes vocabulary, grammar, listening, reading, writing, and speaking items for units 7–12.

CEFR Correlations

The Common European Framework of Reference for Languages (CEFR) is an international standard that aims to provide a transparent, coherent, and comprehensive means of describing language ability. It describes what language learners can do in different skills across six broad levels, from A1 to C2, and consists of a set of scales containing descriptors indicating what a learner can do in that context. The **CEFR Correlations** document is a map is organized unit by unit, which allows you to browse the course learning outcomes chronologically. These are mapped to the relevant CEFR descriptors, levels, and scales.

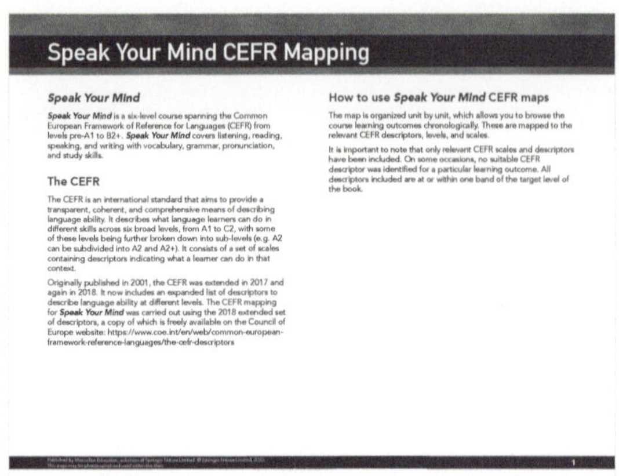

Word Lists

The **Word Lists** are a list of the main vocabulary that appears in ***Speak Your Mind***. These include words that appear in the **Student's Book** and **Student's App** VOCABULARY sections, as well as the glossaries of the **Student's Book** READING sections. The word lists include the word, part of speech, IPA pronunciation, definition, and frequency, as well as an example sentence using the word.

How to Use the Teacher's Edition

The up-to-date, innovative approach to the ***Speak Your Mind*** **Teacher's Edition** takes into account that teachers have very busy lives and want the class-planning process to be as streamlined as possible. The introductory pages of the **Teacher's Edition** are designed to provide general explanations and instructions that are needed to teach each section of the unit and use the special features.

The introductory pages also include information on how to use the special features, the **Workbook**, the *Videos*, and the digital material included in the ***Speak Your Mind*** series. The *Answer Keys* for the **Workbook** activities and the **Student's Book** *Grammar Reference* activities are at the back of this book, as are the *Audio Scripts* for the listening activities in the **Student's Book** and **Workbook**.

The core pages of the **Teacher's Edition** include:

① ***GO TO***. Teachers can read the introductory information once for guidelines on how to teach these sections throughout the book. *GO TO* pointers help teachers find the procedure pages they need quickly.

② **Answer Key.** The core pages have the detailed information a teacher needs to teach specific activities. The **Teacher's Edition** has reduced **Student's Book** pages with answers in place or in the margin next to the Student's Book pages.

③ **Specific notes.** Notes below the **Student's Book** reduced page include relevant background information for texts, tips for dealing with specific language issues, common errors to watch out for, cultural information, classroom management ideas, and suggestions for extra or alternative activities.

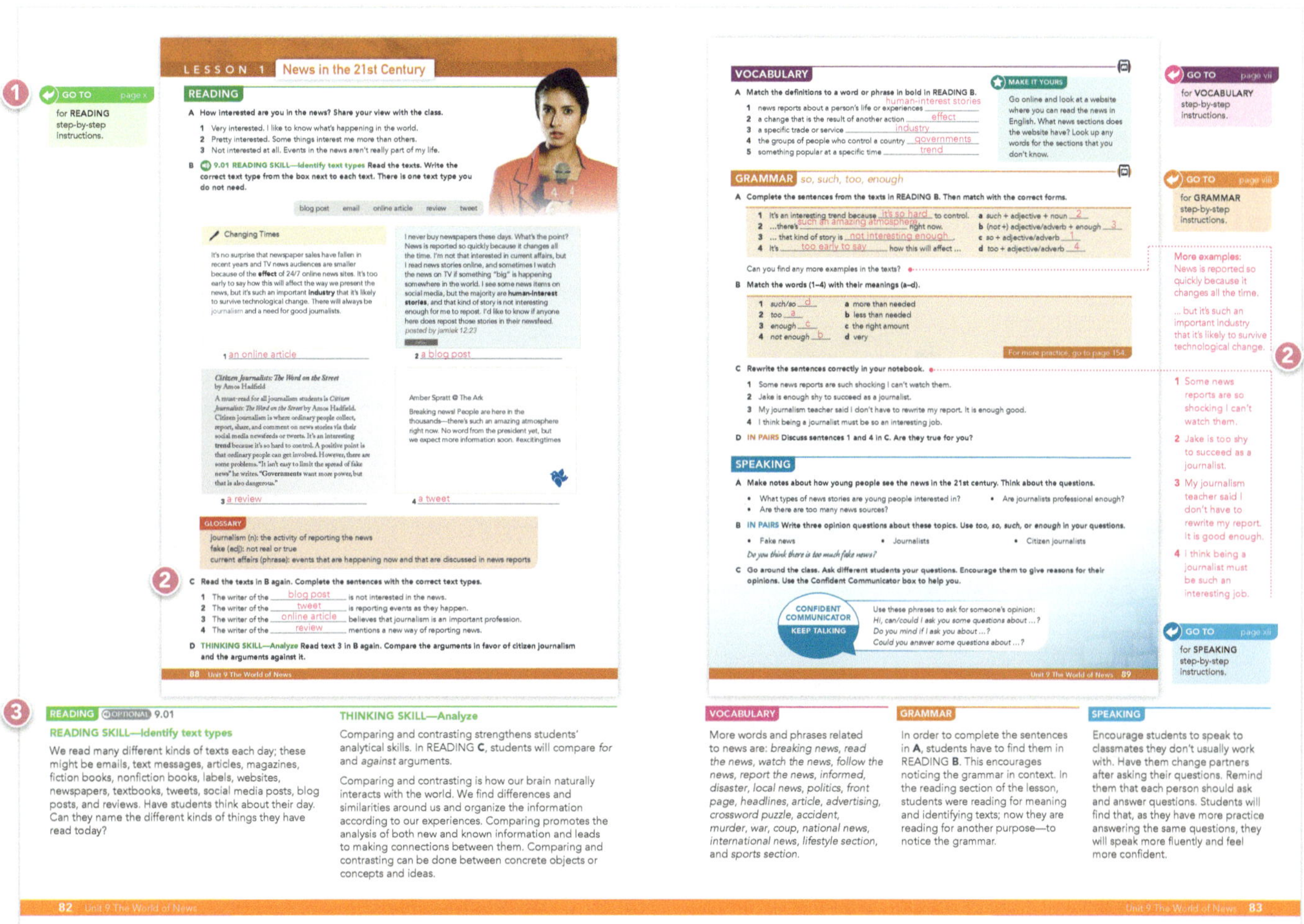

The ***Speak Your Mind* Workbook** is designed to give students further practice in grammar and vocabulary, as well as the listening, reading, and writing skills taught in the **Student's Book**. The **Workbook** is available in both print and digital form. The **Digital Workbook** can be accessed through the **Student's App**. At the end of the **Workbook**, there are five pages of activities designed to familiarize students with the most common exam formats (Cambridge suite, TOEFL, and IELTS).

The **Workbook** activities can be used in several ways:

- As homework or further classroom practice after teaching a section in the **Student's Book**.
- As a review of a whole lesson after finishing the lesson.
- As a review session before a unit exam.

① **Reading and listening skills expansion.** Skills boxes give explanations of the reading and listening skills taught in the **Student's Book**. You may want to refer students to the explanation in the **Workbook** before asking them to do the skill activity in the **Student's Book**. Following each skill box, there is an activity to practice the skill.

② **Vocabulary practice.** There is additional practice of the target vocabulary of the lesson.

③ **Grammar practice.** The grammar of the lesson is practiced in a variety of ways.

④ **Writing skills.** In the WRITING section, there is practice in the mechanics of writing.

⑤ **Progress check.** Students check the areas they feel competent in. If they feel that they need to review a particular point, they are directed to the relevant section in the **Student's Book**.

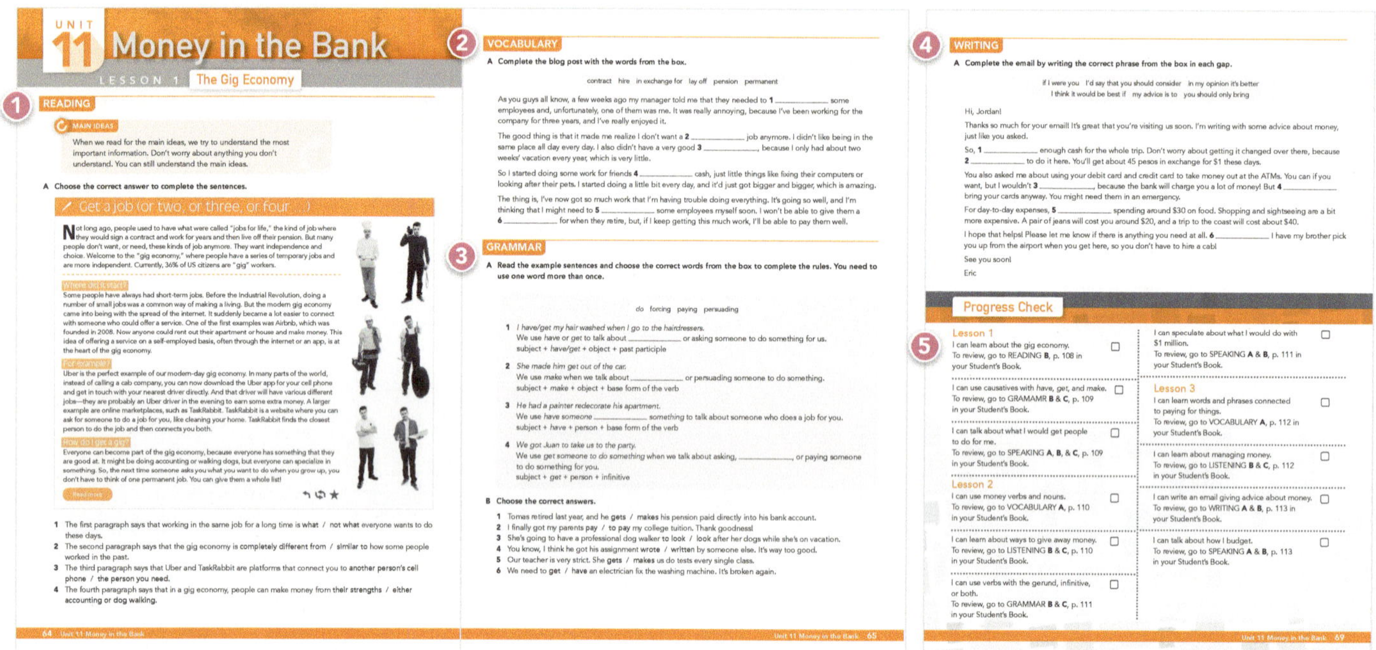

Teacher's App

The ***Speak Your Mind*** **Teacher's Edition** comes with an innovative **Teacher's App**, which gives access to the **Classroom Presentation Kit**, **Homework Manager**, **Progress Tracker**, **Test Generator**, and **Teacher's Resource Center**.

Classroom Presentation Kit

The **Classroom Presentation Kit** is a page-faithful view of the **Student's Book** and **Workbook**. It is designed to be displayed on an interactive whiteboard (IWB) or using a projector. It is user-friendly for teachers and students, with activities clearly visible for the whole class.

The **Classroom Presentation Kit** allows teachers to play the audio tracks, show the course videos, and present the interactive versions of the book activities from the page. Teachers can zoom in on each activity with one click, then move smoothly through the activities or zoom out to see the whole page. Answer reveal enables teachers to elicit students' responses and check answers one by one or all together.

Embedded tools make it possible to highlight and annotate texts to prompt noticing or self-correction. Teachers also have the option to show scripts when listening to audio or watching video for easy clarification. There is also the option to create a whiteboard area for additional notes.

Homework Manager

Using the practice activities available in the **Student's App**, teachers can assign homework by selecting and publishing content directly to their students' devices. Students will then be alerted by a push notification telling them they have activities to complete. This enables teachers to personalize the amount and kind of practice students have each week and to track their progress using the **Progress Tracker**.

Progress Tracker

The **Progress Tracker** gives teachers an overview of students' progress, allowing teachers to monitor scores and see at a glance that students are performing well or that they may need additional support. Student data is presented in a way that is clear and easy to understand.

Test Generator

Ready-to-Go print tests are available in the **Teacher's Resource Center** for teachers who want to give a test on every skill. If you prefer to customize tests for your students, you can do so through the **Test Generator** in the **Teacher's App**. The **Test Generator** allows you to create tests by selecting only the activities you want from a menu. You can save and print out the tests from the **Test Generator**. You may also use a randomized function to create different tests for the same unit.

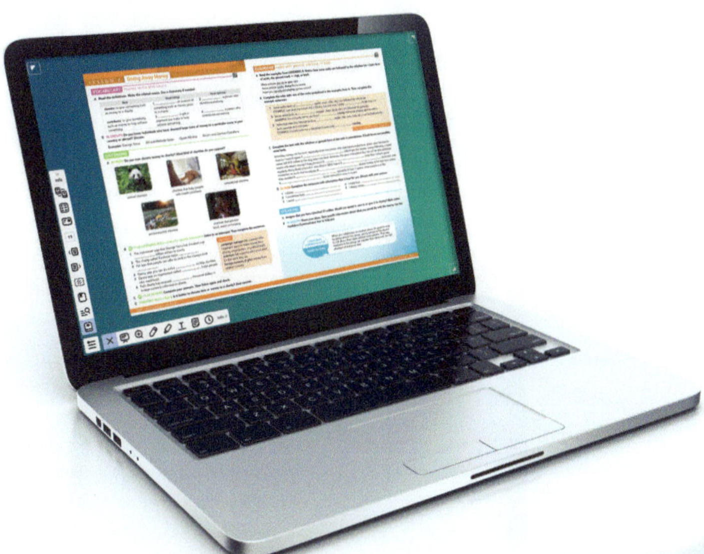

Student's App

Each **Student's Book** includes a code for the **Student's App**, which gives access to new **On-the-Go Practice** activities, **Progress Tracker**, **eBook**, **Digital Workbook**, and the **Student's Resource Center**.

On-the-Go Practice

Through the **Student's App**, students will have access to new grammar, vocabulary, and pronunciation activities that have been mapped to the course scope and sequence. These bite-sized activities have been specifically designed for use on smartphones. They include game-like elements to encourage repetition and deeper retention of key language. Questions are shown in random order to increase interest and ensure a thorough understanding of each language point. Students are able to complete activities in a standard practice mode or in a more difficult challenge mode, where they can earn medals based on their performance.

Each **Student's App** unit also contains a new speaking activity that recycles the Unit Opener video, providing an opportunity to review the Unit Opener topic and the language encountered throughout the unit. These activities have been designed to increase students' confidence as they see how their language competence has developed over the course of each unit, while reinforcing what they have learned.

Progress Tracker

The **Student's App** gives a clear overview of students' progress, clearly highlighting areas of strength and areas for improvement. Students have the opportunity to review their weakest activities and repeat them to improve their scores.

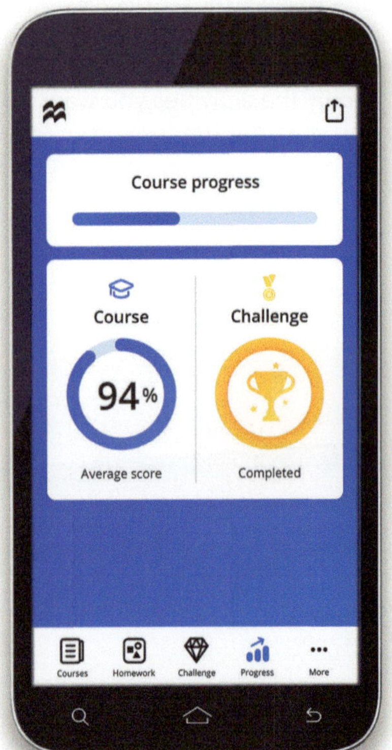

eBook

The **eBook** is a digital version of the **Student's Book** with embedded audio and video files, so students can access the book and its media on their desktop, in their classroom, or at home.

Digital Workbook

The **Digital Workbook** is a new, digital version of the students' **Workbook** designed to be accessible on students' devices. The **Digital Workbook** contains digital versions of the **Workbook** activities designed to work across mobile, tablet, and desktop to provide a rich interactive experience. The **Workbook** audio and video files can be accessed from the page so students have everything they need in one place. Built-in answer keys give instant feedback, while students' scores feed to the **Progress Tracker** for easy monitoring.

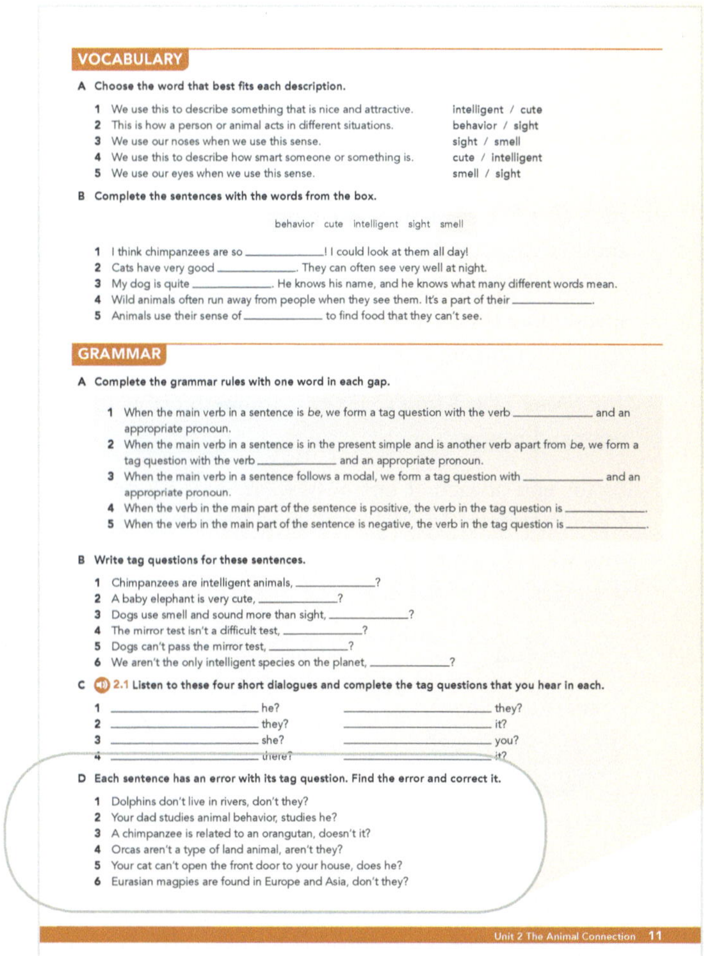

VOCABULARY

A Choose the word that best fits each description.

1 We use this to describe something that is nice and attractive. intelligent / cute
2 This is how a person or animal acts in different situations. behavior / sight
3 We use our noses when we use this sense. sight / smell
4 We use this to describe how smart someone or something is. cute / intelligent
5 We use our eyes when we use this sense. smell / sight

B Complete the sentences with the words from the box.

behavior cute intelligent sight smell

1 I think chimpanzees are so ___________! I could look at them all day!
2 Cats have very good ___________. They can often see very well at night.
3 My dog is quite ___________. He knows his name, and he knows what many different words mean.
4 Wild animals often run away from people when they see them. It's a part of their ___________.
5 Animals use their sense of ___________ to find food that they can't see.

GRAMMAR

A Complete the grammar rules with one word in each gap.

1 When the main verb in a sentence is *be*, we form a tag question with the verb ___________ and an appropriate pronoun.
2 When the main verb in a sentence is in the present simple and is another verb apart from *be*, we form a tag question with the verb ___________ and an appropriate pronoun.
3 When the main verb in a sentence follows a modal, we form a tag question with ___________ and an appropriate pronoun.
4 When the verb in the main part of the sentence is positive, the verb in the tag question is ___________.
5 When the verb in the main part of the sentence is negative, the verb in the tag question is ___________.

B Write tag questions for these sentences.

1 Chimpanzees are intelligent animals, ___________?
2 A baby elephant is very cute, ___________?
3 Dogs use smell and sound more than sight, ___________?
4 The mirror test isn't a difficult test, ___________?
5 Dogs can't pass the mirror test, ___________?
6 We aren't the only intelligent species on the planet, ___________?

C 2.1 Listen to these four short dialogues and complete the tag questions that you hear in each.

1 ___________ he? ___________ they?
2 ___________ they? ___________ it?
3 ___________ she? ___________ you?
4 ___________ there? ___________ it?

D Each sentence has an error with its tag question. Find the error and correct it.

1 Dolphins don't live in rivers, don't they?
2 Your dad studies animal behavior, studies he?
3 A chimpanzee is related to an orangutan, doesn't it?
4 Orcas aren't a type of land animal, aren't they?
5 Your cat can't open the front door to your house, does he?
6 Eurasian magpies are found in Europe and Asia, don't they?

Unit 2 The Animal Connection 11

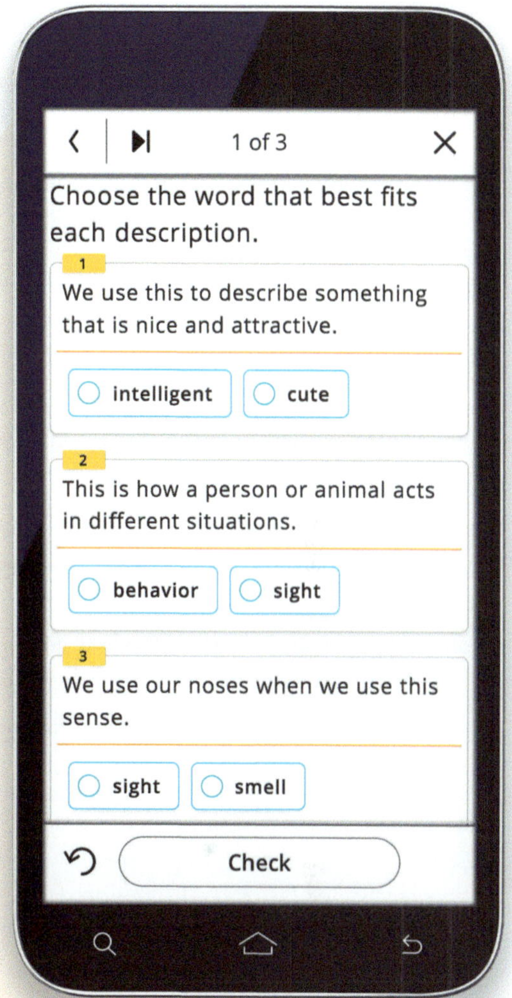

Communicative Strategies

Tony Prince
Academic Director – NILE : Norwich Institute for Language Education

NILE
PART OF THE **INTO** GROUP

What Are Communicative Strategies?

Everyone has experienced a problem communicating at some time. Even if you are speaking your first language or a language you are very confident in speaking, you might struggle to explain the idea you want to communicate. You might find it hard to talk about technical topics or to engage in "small talk." There are times and places, topics, and people that can make communication difficult.

When we encounter these problems in our first language, we often unconsciously use strategies to overcome them. These strategies include:

- using gestures and body language
- indicating the shape or size of something we are trying to describe
- frowning, grimacing, or smiling to show how we feel about what we are trying to explain
- using alternative words or phrases when we cannot remember the word we want:

> ***A:*** *So what do you think?*
> ***B:*** *Well, it seems there might be an issue with the … solution? No, the suggestion. I mean the … proposal, that's it! There might be an issue with the proposal.*

- describing the thing with identifying details in place of the word:

> ***A:*** *Can I help?*
> ***B:*** *Sure. Can you pass me the thingamabob?*
> ***A:*** *Sorry?*
> ***B:*** *The metal thing, two teeth, closes around a bolt.*
> ***A:*** *The wrench?*
> ***B:*** *The wrench! Thank you.*

- giving the listener the chance to provide the word we can't find:

> ***A:*** *We'll meet at the … you know, the place with the books.*
> ***B:*** *The bookshop?*
> ***A:*** *No, the place where you borrow them.*
> ***B:*** *Oh, you mean the library?.*
> ***A:*** *Exactly!*

Three Parts of Communication

An explanation of the importance of body language from Unit 4 page 40

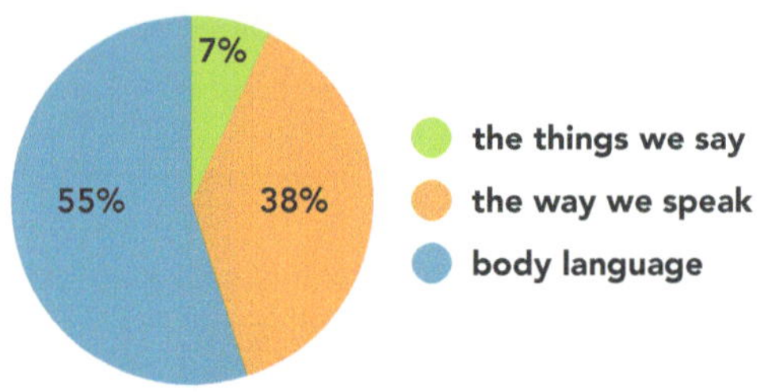

In learning to use language, we learn strategies for situations where we do not know the word we need or we have forgotten it. It is a natural part of speaking. No one expects others to be clear and fluent communicators all the time.

But when we learn another language, we often forget these strategies. We seem to assume that our communication in another language has to be clear and fluent all the time. The result is that we often say less than we would like to or we spend more time thinking before we speak. This is because we want to be fluent before we even say a single word.

The ***Speak Your Mind*** series puts communicative strategies front and center.

At the end of each of Lessons 1–3, there is a *Confident Communicator* box, which aims to provide students (and you) with strategies that will help with communication. These strategies are divided into three categories:

CONFIDENT COMMUNICATOR
START TALKING

Start Talking: This is intended to provide students with phrases, prompts, and strategies for starting the conversation.

CONFIDENT COMMUNICATOR
KEEP TALKING

Keep Talking: This helps students maintain the conversation and keep the communication going.

CONFIDENT COMMUNICATOR
REPAIR IT

Repair It: This offers students ways of overcoming problems in communication, through strategies, phrases, and prompts.

What Advantages do Communicative Strategies Offer the Teacher and the Student?

Changing Mindsets

For the student, one of the principal benefits of the explicit inclusion of communicative strategies in the ***Speak Your Mind*** series is that students realize that problems in speaking are a normal part of communication and not an indication of their lack of ability. This change in mindset is an important aspect of language acquisition. If students can see that it is common to experience communication difficulties and that strategies are employed by everyone, then they are more likely to start speaking, to keep talking, and to try to overcome their difficulties in understanding or being understood.

Seeing the communicative strategies throughout the **Student's Book** is an important aspect of changing the students' mindset. In sociology, there is an expression that "you cannot be what you cannot see," meaning that you have to be able to see examples of people doing things (e.g. women as managers, men as caregivers) in order to believe that you can do it—that it is normal. In the same way, students need to see the strategies and to be asked to use them repeatedly in order to begin to believe that they are normal.

CONFIDENT COMMUNICATOR START TALKING

CONFIDENT COMMUNICATOR KEEP TALKING

CONFIDENT COMMUNICATOR REPAIR IT

Communicative strategies can also help to change the mindset of teachers and managers. Often, there is a lot of attention on results—on students getting the right answers. Here, the focus is on accuracy, on precision, and on being correct. But the focus on communicative strategies shifts the focus away from correctness toward competence. Now, it is not as important to pay attention to the accuracy of what is said, but instead to understand how effectively the communicative task is achieved. This does not mean that mistakes are ignored or that there is no feedback or correction. It means simply that if there is feedback or correction, it is offered in service of the communication.

A: *What do you in the summer?*
B: *No … nothing.*
A: *Really nothing? Nothing, nothing?*
B: *I go to Santa Monica.*
A: *Where is this?*
B: *In the US, in California.*
A: *Oh. Tell me more. Is nice?*
B: *Is very nice.*
A: *What to do there?*
B: *Sorry. I don't understand.*
A: *I go there. What to do. For me?*
B: *Ahh, OK. There is beach. There is parks. There is shops. There is activity.*
A: *Tell me more the activities.*

Clearly, there are a number of grammatical errors in this conversation. And if the students were taking an exam focused on grammatical accuracy or range, they would likely receive a very low score. But they have each used a number of communicative strategies. They're interested in communicating with each other and are using the language they know to communicate. Teachers should encourage communication as much as possible, and the communicative strategies in ***Speak Your Mind*** allow you to do this.

Forming Habits

It is only when language becomes automatic that we begin to use it effectively. For something to become automatic, we have to make it into a habit. This goes for all kinds of things in our lives, from brushing our teeth, to eating healthily, to resisting distracting cat videos online. The good news is that we can develop habits relatively easily; the bad news is that it takes time and that it requires a systematic approach. For a new practice to become a habit, it can take anywhere between 15 and 254 days, with the average being 66 days. Clearly, that is a lot of time. But the secret to putting practice into action is to make it as simple as possible. Want to brush your teeth every day? It may make sense to put the toothbrush in the shower rather than by the sink. Want to practice communicative strategies? Put them into every lesson. This is another reason why the presence of communicative strategies in every lesson of the **Student's Book** is so important. Students see them all the time and using them becomes habitual.

Encouraging Communication

One of the major difficulties with the communicative way has always been that there are some students (if not many) who focus on completing a task instead of using the task as an opportunity to communicate. Most (if not all) teachers have experienced the frustration of taking the time to set up the task, giving clear instructions, ensuring everyone understands, only to find that no sooner has the class started then one or two groups have put up their hands to say that they have finished.

One of the benefits of having communicative strategies in the **Student's Book** is that it gives the teacher a series of phrases, prompts, and techniques that they can use to motivate students to keep talking. Also, the students can refer to those same phrases and prompts. The explicitness of this strategy within the **Student's Book** will hopefully make it clear to students that maintaining communication is a more important aspect of the task than completing it.

Then there are students who believe that they do not have an aptitude for language because they are not able to speak fluently. Others may think that they have nothing to say. In each case, the students' problem is that they believe that they lack language. This belief and how it demotivates students is a bigger problem than actually lacking language.

Communicative strategies not only provide students with a different attitude about their problems (suggesting that all communication involves difficulty) but also provide them with a series of practical solutions to use. In the beginning, these phrases and prompts may feel a little artificial. But repeated use builds the automaticity that leads to fluency. Then fluency builds confidence, which motivates students to communicate.

One way of looking at motivation is to see it as:

Belief in Success × Value of the Goal = Motivation

We have to believe that we can succeed before we can find something motivating. If we believe in our success, this multiplies the value of the goal, which creates motivation. Many teachers seek to motivate their students by making the lessons more interesting or the topics more relevant. All of this is a worthwhile effort toward a valuable goal. However, by increasing the students' belief in their success, their motivation will automatically increase as a result.

Communicative strategies work at a very practical level to increase belief in success. But their explicit presence in the **Student's Book** also works on a psychological level to change students' attitudes about communication and make communicative success more attainable.

What Approaches Can You Take to Use Communicative Strategies?

The Learning Journey

In some ways, the communicative strategies in ***Speak Your Mind*** represent the learning journey.

In the beginning, our main task is to get the students to start talking. As teachers, we may do this by exposing students to vocabulary that is relevant to the topic, useful for the task, or simply high frequency enough that the students will need it more generally. We may explain appropriate grammatical structures and provide exercises that will help students in both controlled and free practice.

You will see from even a brief glance at the **Student's Book** that all of this is included within the lessons. However, all teachers know that despite providing the relevant vocabulary and the appropriate grammar, and even after clear explanation and extensive, controlled practice, many students struggle when they start to talk. If we cannot get the students to start talking, any effort we make to keep them talking or to repair their communication is pointless.

The learning journey begins with an examination of the strategies related to getting students to start talking. It is also necessary to discuss the underlying issues that are blocking these students from communicating:

- Is it their attitude about communication in general?
- Do they see communication as requiring an extensive knowledge of vocabulary and understanding of grammar?
- Do they feel that what they say has to be correct?
- Do they want to spend a great deal of time thinking before they speak?

For this reason, it may be useful to look at communication and communicative strategies in general. Unit 4, "Beyond Words," may prove to be very useful, as it provides texts that discuss what it means to be a good communicator and how all kinds of people find it difficult to keep talking.

UNIT 4 Beyond Words

WHAT DO YOU ALREADY KNOW?

1 Think about words you know about communication. Write the words.
2 IN PAIRS Share and compare your ideas. Add more words to your lists.

Personal communication

Digital communication

VIDEO

DISCUSS & SHARE

3 IN GROUPS Watch the video and answer the question.
STM Would you rather call someone or text them?

In this unit, you will ...

- present a subject you know, ask questions and assess someone's body language, and decide on the best means of communication for different situations.
- use thinking skills: evaluate, apply, and predict.
- read about how to be a good communicator.
- learn strategies to use eye contact, use language to ask for more information, and to make your meaning clearer.
- use reasoning skills to discuss the pros and cons of a company proposal.
- follow a PR professional to learn about this job and the skills needed for this industry.

Unit 4 Beyond Words 37

It may be necessary to emphasize to students the importance of making mistakes. If there are no errors in the class, if there are no difficulties in communication, then there is no opportunity for them to practice repairing communication. If they do not practice repairing communication, then it cannot become automatic, meaning that when they communicate outside the class, it will be much more difficult. Getting students to start talking before they are completely ready is an important part of providing them with the opportunity to practice repairing their communication. If students are really fully prepared to speak, then activities in repairing communication can become rather artificial. So, pushing students to begin before they are fully ready may be a key aspect of allowing practice in repairing.

An alternative tactic is to push students out of their comfort zone in terms of the detail and depth with which they discuss a topic. This requires them to keep talking long after they may feel comfortable doing so. We often have things that we are familiar with saying on certain topics, opinions that we commonly express, examples that we may give, and evidence that we may refer to. But once these resources have all been used, what happens? We struggle. It is in this struggle that we start to fight to find the words we need. It is in this struggle to keep talking that we really start to reach for the communicative strategies.

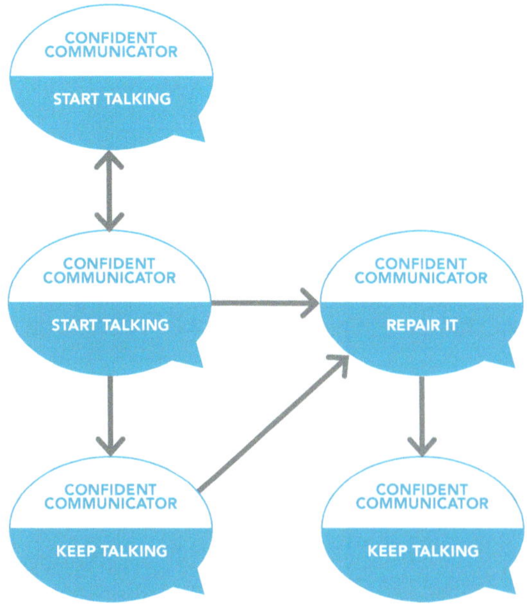

This is why it is important not to present the learning journey as a linear progression.

Each element of the learning journey should be presented as a station that we might move to before we move to another, with the possibility that we might return again and move back and forth between stations.

This may seem somewhat complex, but this is an accurate representation of real-life communication and the use of communicative strategies. How often have you been involved in a conversation that seemed to take a very long time to get going, but then, once you hit on a particular topic, you were not able to stop? Equally, have you spoken to a person who could not seem to understand what you were saying until you found the right metaphor or right set of words? Then suddenly, the conversation takes off.

Communicative strategies offer a series of phrases, prompts, and techniques that we can use to help students and that students can use to become more communicative. We can use these strategies to help students accomplish the tasks, or we can take these basic blocks and connect them into more complex sequences that push students to communicate in extended sequences, making real use of the strategies.

Overall though, the strategies offer an approach to communication that reflects real-life communication. Both teachers and students will be encouraged to be more realistic about how communication takes place and how accurate students can or need to be. This realistic view of communication will improve the students' belief in their success, and they will be much more motivated and relaxed about speaking English.

Student's Book Scope and Sequence

	Outcomes	Vocabulary	Grammar	Speaking
Unit 1 Incredible Lives pp. 7–15	• Discuss possible devices that could help disabled people • Ask and answer questions about your achievements • Describe survival situations	• Technology and disability • Noun suffixes • Character adjectives	• Stative and dynamic verbs • Expressing ability Grammar Reference pp 142–143	• Describe a device to help disabled people • Talk about personal achievements • Talk about survival situation
	Language and Life—Decision Making: Manage a Survival Situation			
Unit 2 The Animal Connection pp. 17–25	• Talk about which are the most intelligent animals • Discuss possible jobs with animals • Make arguments for and against people owning exotic pets	• Animal intelligence • Careers with animals • Animals	• Tag questions • Articles Grammar Reference pp 143–144	• Discuss which animals are most intelligent • Talk about working with animals • Argue for and against keeping wild animals
	Language and Life—Problem Solving: Find Solutions to Help Stray Animals			
Unit 3 Think About It pp. 27–35	• Ask and answer questions about confirmation bias • Discuss the importance of expert systems in your future career • Compare different creative uses for things	• Confirmation bias • Word formation • Phrasal verbs	• Future time clauses (*after*, *as soon as*, *before*, *until*, *when*) • Present perfect progressive Grammar Reference pp 145–146	• Discuss confirmation bias • Talk about expert systems • Compare different objects
	Language and Life—Design Thinking: Design an App			
Unit 4 Beyond Words pp. 37–45	• Present a subject you know • Ask questions and assess someone's body language • Decide on the best means of communication for different situations	• Communication • Ways to communicate • Emojis	• Infinitives with *to* • Separable and non-separable phrasal verbs Grammar Reference pp 146–147	• Give a presentation • Make statements about yourself • Discuss ways to communicate
	Language and Life—Reason Effectively: Discuss Ideas to Improve Communication Problems			
Unit 5 One Planet pp. 47–55	• Discuss global warming problems • Talk about solutions • Brainstorm products	• Climate change • Taking action • Materials and products	• Review of conditionals • Present and future hopes and wishes Grammar Reference pp 148–149	• Discuss global warming • Discuss environmental solutions • Discuss if measures are practical
	Language and Life—Global Competence: Explain and Discuss Ideas about Environmental Issues			
Unit 6 Moments in Time pp. 57–65	• Compare different generational use of technology • Share your opinions about inventions • Brainstorm quiz questions about people in history	• Change • *–ed* and *–ing* adjectives • Adjective suffixes	• Past perfect • Defining relative clauses Grammar Reference pp 149–150	• Compare lists • Discuss an opinion poll • Create a quiz
	Language and Life—Decision Making: Choose a New UNESCO Site			

Confident Communicator	Pronunciation	Listening/Reading	Thinking Skills	Writing
Start Talking • Start a discussion *Repair It* • Express lack of understanding *Keep Talking* • Justify choices	• Word stress with *–ity*	Read an article about technology and disability • Skill—Predict information Listen to part of a lecture about amazing abilities • Skill—Recognize signposts Listen to a podcast about Juliane Koepcke • Skill—Listen for specific information	• Apply • Evaluate • Analyze	Write a blog post about a survival situation
Unit Review p. 16 **Study Skills**—Effective Time Management				
Keep Talking • Invite agreement *Start Talking* • Hypotheticals *Keep Talking* • Disagree politely	• *The*	Read a blog post about animal intelligence • Skill—Understand examples Listen to a careers talk • Skill—Use key information to predict content Listen to a zoo's presentation • Skill—Listen for key words	• Recall • Analyze • Evaluate	Write an opinion post
Unit Review p. 26 **Follow A Pro**—A Wildlife Photographer ▶ Marine Biologist				
Keep Talking • Give yourself time to think *Start Talking* • Start talking *Keep Talking* • Further suggestions	• say, says, said	Read an article about confirmation bias • Skill—Identify the topic Listen to a radio call-in show about AI • Skill—Listen for attitude Listen to a talk about being creative • Skill—Listen for main ideas	• Analyze • Evaluate • Apply	Write an informal email about being productive
Unit Review p. 36 **Study Skills**—Making a Presentation or Giving a Talk				
Keep Talking • Speak to a group *Keep Talking* • Provide more information *Keep Talking* • Make meaning clearer	• Electronic communication	Read an article about communication • Skill—Read for gist Listen to a podcast • Skill—Listen for specific information Listen to a lecture about communication technology • Skill—Listen for the order of events	• Evaluate • Apply • Predict	Write an informal text message as a formal email
Unit Review p. 46 **Follow A Pro**—A PR Professional ▶ Translator/Interpreter				
Start Talking • Speak for a group *Keep Talking* • Talk about problems and solutions *Keep Talking* • Comment on ideas	• Word stress in verb phrases	Read an online article about climate change • Skill— Identify explanations, definitions, and examples Listen to a radio show about environmental problems • Skill—Listen for main ideas Listen to a class discussion about environmental solutions • Skill—Listen for details	• Summarize • Analyze • Categorize	Write an essay about environmental projects
Unit Review p. 56 **Study Skills**—Improving Reading Speed				
Keep Talking • Circumlocution *Keep Talking* • Interrupting politely *Keep Talking* • Express interest and surprise	• Stress in multisyllable adjectives	Read an article about technological changes • Skill—Scan Listen to some interviews about inventions • Skill—Listen for supporting details Listen to a podcast about a famous person • Skill—Listen for numerical information	• Predict • Evaluate • Question	Write a short biographical essay
Unit Review p. 66 **Follow A Pro**—An Archeologist ▶ Mechanical Engineer				

	Outcomes	Vocabulary	Grammar	Speaking
Unit 7 Looking Back pp. 67–75	• Talk about things that a business should have done differently • Discuss things you should not have bought • Recall events you regret	• Phrasal verbs • *spend, lose, waste* • Collocations	• *Should/shouldn't have* • Past perfect for wishes about the past Grammar Reference pp 151–152	• Talk about what people should have done differently • Talk about things you regret buying • Tell an anecdote
	Language and Life—Interpersonal Communication: Plan and Give a Presentation about a Product			
Unit 8 A New Home? pp. 77–85	• Talk about hypothetical events in history • Role play an interview with an astronaut • Discuss your opinions of space exploration	• Extinction of the dinosaurs • Space • Space program inventions	• Third conditional • Indirect questions Grammar Reference pp 152–153	• Speculate about alternative histories • Role-play an interview • Discuss space exploration
	Language and Life—Reason Effectively: Select a Space Team			
Unit 9 The World of News pp. 87–95	• Give your opinions on fake news, journalists and citizen journalists • Compare real and fake news stories • Role-play a job interview for a news career	• News • News stories • News careers	• *So, such, too, enough* • Modals of deduction Grammar Reference pp 154–155	• Discuss news now • Discuss how you knew a news story was true or fake • Role-play a job interview
	Language and Life—Problem Solving: Discuss Ideas to Improve Newspaper Sales			
Unit 10 Got It? pp. 97–105	• Talk about your talents and abilities • Ask and answer questions for a talent show audition • Share advice on how to succeed in the music industry	• Talents and abilities • Phrasal verbs • Idioms and sayings connected to success	• Reported speech: statements • Reported speech: questions Grammar Reference pp 155–156	• Talk about something someone can do well • Talk about talent show contestants • Discuss the usefulness of advice
	Language and Life—Communication: Hold a Talent Contest			
Unit 11 Money in the Bank pp. 107–116	• Discuss who you would employ if you were a millionaire • Share ideas about what to do with a fortune • Compare your budget with that of a partner	• Money • Money verbs and nouns • Paying for things	• Causatives with *have, get* and *make* • Verbs with gerund, infinitive or both Grammar Reference pp 156–158	• Discuss jobs to do yourself • Talk about how to use a lot of money • Talk about monthly budgets
	Language and Life—Collaborate: Manage a Budget			
Unit 12 Inside Advertising pp. 117–126	• Discuss the advertising of energy drinks • Talk about ads that you like and dislike • Debate the effects of advertising	• From the reading Advertising • Advertising campaigns • Discourse markers	• Passive voice: other tenses • Comparative and superlative adverbs Grammar Reference pp 158–159	• Discuss whether to ban advertisements • Talk about improving ad campaigns • Debate the effects of images in advertising
	Language and Life—Media Literacy: Make a TV Ad			

Confident Communicator	Pronunciation	Listening/Reading	Thinking Skills	Writing
Start Talking • Tell an anecdote *Keep Talking* • Give reasons *Start Talking* • Set the scene	• /s/ and /z/	Read an online article about famous mistakes • Skill—Synthesize Listen to a radio interview about regret • Skill—Listen for reasons Listen to a talk about types of regret • Skill—Listen for main ideas	• Evaluate • Analyze • Apply	Write a blog post about regrets
Unit Review p. 76 **Study Skills**—Structuring Your Writing				
Keep Talking • Express probability *Keep Talking* • Ask polite questions *Keep Talking* • Clarify reasons for opinions	• Consonant clusters with /s/	Read an article about the dinosaurs • Skill—Predict Listen to an interview about life in space • Skill—Listen for specific information Listen to a panel discussion about space • Skill—Listen for main ideas	• Analyze • Question • Recall	Write a blog post about space exploration
Unit Review p. 86 **Follow A Pro**—An Astrobiologist ▶ Astronomer				
Keep Talking • Ask for opinions *Repair It* • Interrupt politely *Keep Talking* • Interview techniques	• /ə/ versus /r/	Read texts about news • Skill—Identifying text types Listen to a lecture about fake news • Skill—Listen for information order Listen to an interview about being a foreign correspondent • Skill—Listen for opinions	• Analyze • Apply • Deduce	Write about a job
Unit Review p. 96 **Study Skills**—Making Notes				
Keep Talking • Your achievements *Keep Talking* • Talk in front of a group *Keep Talking* • Use idioms carefully	• Stress in phrasal verbs	Read a text about great artists • Skill—Recognize fact and opinion Listen to excerpts from a TV talent show • Skill—Identify attitude Listen to a radio call-in show about the music industry • Skill—Listen to take notes	• Question • Analyze • Evaluate	Write an informal email
Unit Review p. 106 **Follow A Pro**—A Talent Scout ▶ Musician				
Start Talking • Talk about imagined future situations *Start Talking* • Collaborate on creative ideas *Keep Talking* • Talk or avoid talking about money	• /tʃ/ versus /ʃ/	Read a job ad, article and business profile about the gig economy • Skill—Read for the main idea Listen to an interview about charity • Skill—Listen for specific information Listen to a radio show about managing money • Skill—Listen for the main idea	• Question • Apply • Recall	Write an email listing key points
Unit Review p. 116 **Study Skills**—Personal Development				
Keep Talking • Take turns in a discussion *Repair It* • Getting back on track *Keep Talking* • Paraphrase	• Filler sounds and words	Read an article about advertising • Skill—Identify missing sentences Listen to an ad • Skill—Listen for inference Listen to an interview about advertising • Skill—Recognize discourse markers	• Evaluate • Symbolize • Induce	Write a 'for' and 'against' essay about retouching images
Unit Review p. 126 **Follow A Pro**—A Digital Copywriter ▶ Video Editor				

GO TO page xxi
for **GRAMMAR REVIEW** step-by-step instructions.

1 's worked / has worked
2 was working
3 started
4 hasn't / has not stopped
5 was visiting
6 became

Grammar Quiz: What Do You Already Know?

A Complete the paragraph with the simple past, past progressive, or present perfect form of the verbs in parentheses.

Colombian teen Yadis Xiomara Chocó Mina has a clear goal: to help others. She **1** ___________ (work) to improve the lives of young girls since she was nine years old. She **2** ___________ (work) with a group called Plan International Colombia when she first **3** ___________ (start) to mentor young girls in her community. Since then, she **4** ___________ (not stop). A few years ago, while she **5** ___________ (visit) Spain, she **6** ___________ (become) mayor of Madrid for a day as part of International Day of the Girl. Yadis has big plans: someday she wants to be Colombia's minister of education.

B Complete the email message with the correct quantifiers from the box.

a few | a little | a lot of | any | enough | too much

New Message

Hi Anna,

I'm home preparing for Ricardo's graduation party. I've finished most of the preparations, but I could use **1** ___a little___ help. There are going to be **2** ___a lot of___ people here—I think about 45 of his friends are coming. We have 40 chairs, but it's not **3** ___enough___. Can you bring **4** ___a few___ chairs—maybe three or four? I know we have **5** ___too much___ food, so there will be leftovers for the guests to take home. So, please don't bring **6** ___any___ more food. There is nowhere to put it!

See you soon,
Bev

C Choose the correct option.

1 Can / **Would** you like to join us?
2 I'm sure Oscar **will** / may be here.
3 Will / **May** I put my jacket here?
4 **Could** / May you please take a seat?
5 Lena **might** / would be late for the wedding.
6 They probably **won't** / might not be there.

5 would not / wouldn't go
6 will not / won't feel

D Complete the sentences with the correct form of the verb in parentheses.

1 If you ___eat___ (eat) a lot of sugar, you gain weight.
2 If I ___had___ (have) more time, I would exercise more.
3 You will enjoy these brain puzzles if you ___try___ (try) them.
4 If I ___get___ (get) tired at the library, I usually take a short nap.
5 I probably ___________ (not go) to the hospital if I had a bad cold.
6 You ___________ (not feel) better if you don't take this medicine.

E Find one error in each sentence. Then rewrite the sentences correctly.

1 Maggie has belonged to a gym since 15 years.
Maggie has belonged to a gym for 15 years.
2 Rafael hasn't graduated from high school already.
Rafael hasn't graduated from high school yet.
3 A lot cans and plastic are recycled these days.
A lot of cans and plastic are recycled these days.
4 People use to buy a lot of music CDs in the 1990s.
People used to buy a lot of music CDs in the 1990s.
5 Jae is the more adventurous person in my family.
Jae is the most adventurous person in my family.
6 Students need to introduce themself in class.
Students need to introduce themselves in class.

Go to the Grammar Review on pages 140–141.

GRAMMAR QUIZ

This quiz tests students' knowledge of language presented in **Student's Book** level 2. For further review of level 2, have students do the *Grammar Review* on pages 140–141.

UNIT 1 Incredible Lives

GO TO page vi
for UNIT OPENER step-by-step instructions.

WHAT DO YOU ALREADY KNOW?

1 Think about your family: what characteristics do you share with them and which are unique to you? Write the words.

2 IN PAIRS Share and compare your ideas. If possible, add more words about yourself or your partner.

Shared characteristics

Unique characteristics

STUDENTS MAY ALREADY KNOW:

- Positive words: cheerful, creative, curious, easygoing, generous, healthy, honest, independent, intelligent, optimistic, organized, outgoing, patient, smart, successful, worried.
- Negative words: bossy, depressed, disorganized, impatient, lazy, pessimistic, rude, selfish, unhappy, unhealthy.

VIDEO

DISCUSS & SHARE

3 IN GROUPS Watch the video and answer the question.
SYM What influences a person's character: family values or life experience?

GO TO page xx
for VIDEOS IN SYM step-by-step instructions.

In this unit, you will ...

- discuss possible devices that could help the lives of others, ask and answer questions about your achievements, and describe survival situations.
- use thinking skills: apply, evaluate, and analyze.
- read about technology for an accessible world.
- use strategies to start a discussion, use language to say you do not understand to repair a conversation, and justify reasons in a discussion.
- use decision-making skills to choose items and write a survival list.
- learn skills for effective time management.

WHAT DO YOU ALREADY KNOW?

If students are struggling to understand what to do, you can ask them some questions to prompt their thinking:

- Do you think you're outgoing?
- Are you bossy or selfish?
- Do you consider yourself to be lazy?
- Are you a leader?
- Have you ever been called a workaholic?
- Are you generous?

VIDEO

Before viewing, ask:

For Andrea, what is a family value? *sharing with others*

What happened to Sean's family? *his dad had to look for another job, they had to move out of the house*

After viewing, put the continuum on the board.

family values —— life experience

Have students mark the continuum and explain their preferences.

DISCUSS & SHARE

Students should place themselves on a continuum of opinion. Ask students to consider whether family values influence character or if character is shaped by life experiences. How strongly do family values influence a person's character? What life experiences change a person's character? Students should choose one viewpoint, plot it, and then defend it with examples.

LESSON 1 Life-Changing Technology

GO TO page x for **READING** step-by-step instructions.

Suggested answer: a man with bionic legs

READING

A READING SKILL—Predict information Look at the picture. What do you think the article is going to be about?

B 1.01 Read the article. Then answer the questions.

Technology Creating an Accessible World

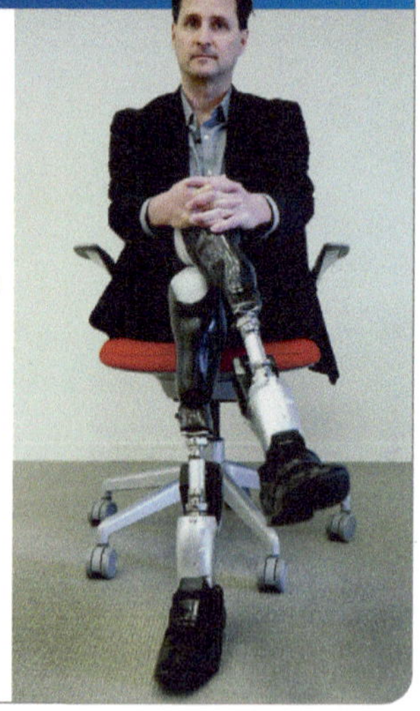

Through the use of technology, we are changing the world that is accessible to us. People such as Hugh Herr, co-director of the MIT Center for Extreme Bionics, are responsible for these changes. After losing both of his legs in a mountain climbing accident, Hugh Herr designed and developed new bionic legs. These new legs have a number of features that were previously **impossible**. The legs can be made longer or shorter. The feet can change depending on the surface of the mountain. It is even possible to attach different climbing equipment. All of these advances mean that Hugh Herr can **achieve** climbs that no one else has ever been able to do before. The MIT Center for Extreme Bionics is currently working on a digital nervous system which will connect the brain with a computer that can control artificial arms and legs.

Another area in which connections with computers are having a huge effect is communication. Facebook is currently working on a "silent speech" project: computers that can **recognize** what people are thinking so they can type messages with their brain. This system can help people who are **disabled** because of **disease** or injury. It can also help **able-bodied** people who want a faster way to type their ideas. Early tests in similar systems have used a person's thoughts to **select** letters and then write words. However, systems will get much faster. The aim of the silent speech project is for thoughts to be **turned into** text at a speed of 100 words per minute. How would you use technology to access a whole new world?

GLOSSARY

artificial (adj): made by people and used instead of something natural
accessible (adj): when a place or object can be easily used by all.

1. What technology did Hugh Herr develop? He continued to climb after losing his legs.
2. What is special about that technology? He can make his legs longer and attach equipment.
3. How else can systems that connect people to computers help us? communication problems
4. What advantages of these systems are mentioned in the text? There are systems that know what a person is thinking and help the person communicate.

C THINKING SKILL—Apply Explain how technology improves your ability to work, travel, socialize, and study.

GO TO page vii for **VOCABULARY** step-by-step instructions.

VOCABULARY

A Match the words in bold in READING B with the definitions (1–8).

1. turned into (phr v): made one thing become another
2. disabled (adj): unable to use part of your body in the way most other people can
3. impossible (adj): not possible
4. selects (v): chooses
5. recognize (v): know what you are seeing because you have seen it before
6. able-bodied (adj): able to use your body in the way most other people can
7. achieve (v): be successful, usually after hard work
8. disease (n): illness

READING OPTIONAL 1.01

READING SKILL—Predict information

Be open to all predictions and make notes on the board. Making predictions when reading is an important reading comprehension strategy. Then tell students to read through the article quickly to find out if their predictions were accurate.

The prediction activity may have raised questions about Hugh Herr that were not answered in the article. Have students research him online.

THINKING SKILL—Apply

To apply what they have learned about how technology has helped Hugh, have students think about how technology improves their ability to work (remotely), travel (by sharing reviews and experiences), socialize (by communicating where to meet and how to get there), and study (by giving us access to databases and current information).

VOCABULARY Alternative Activity

Play *Find a Word That Means …* Give a definition, synonym, or antonym of a word in READING **B**. Have students search for the word in the text. The first person to find it gets a point. The first person to reach five points wins. For example, *The opposite of shorter.* (*longer*) *A word that means connect.* (*attach*)

GRAMMAR stative and dynamic verbs

GO TO page viii for GRAMMAR step-by-step instructions.

A Complete the sentences from the text in READING A.

1 Through the use of technology, we ___are changing___ the world that is accessible to us.
2 These new legs ___have___ a number of features that were previously impossible.
3 Another area in which connections with computers ___are … having___ a huge effect is communication.
4 Computers that can recognize what people ___are thinking___ so they can type messages with their brain.

B Read the sentences in A and choose the correct options.

1 Stative verbs, e.g., *know, have,* and *like*, describe actions / **states**.
2 Dynamic verbs, e.g., *write, walk,* and *use*, describe **actions** / states.
3 **Stative** / Dynamic verbs are not usually used in progressive tenses.
4 Some verbs, e.g., *be, have,* and *think*, can be used both ways with the same / **a different** meaning.

For more practice, go to page 142.

C Check (✓) the correct sentences. Both sentences may be correct.

1 ☑ Do you know how disabled people use technology?
☐ Are you knowing anything about technology and disability?
2 ☐ I'm not understanding how the technology will help people.
☑ I don't understand what you're saying.
3 ☑ What do you think we can do to improve people's lives?
☑ What were you thinking about before this lesson began?
4 ☑ Do you have any problems that technology could solve?
☑ Are you having any problems with what I'm saying?

D IN PAIRS Ask and answer the questions.

1 What careers do you know that involve working with disabled people?
2 Which of those careers do you think would be most suitable for you?

MAKE IT REAL

Some people might use verbs such as *like* and *love* with progressive tenses, e.g., *Are you liking your new apartment? Yes, I'm loving it!* This makes the statement more intense. Remember, though, that some people don't think it's correct.

SPEAKING

GO TO page xii for SPEAKING step-by-step instructions.

A IN PAIRS Decide which of these pieces of technology you think would make the most difference in people's lives. Say why.

- a device that knows what you are thinking about and says the words aloud
- a device that knows what you are looking at and recreates the image on a computer screen

B Think of another device that would help the lives of others. Draw a simple picture or write a short explanation. Tell the class about your device. Use the Confident Communicator box to help you.

CONFIDENT COMMUNICATOR
START TALKING

To start a discussion, use *What do you think about …*
***What do you think about** a device to help people with reading?*

GRAMMAR

Stative verbs express like or dislike, thoughts, emotions, and relationships. Some common stative verbs are *agree, feel, know, need,* and *surprise*.

Some more verbs that are stative in the present and dynamic in the present progressive are those that describe the senses. For example, *It tastes like lemon* (stative). *The cook is tasting the soup* (dynamic).

CULTURE NOTE

Another device that helps disabled people is a wheelchair operated by joystick controls, the chin, or the voice. There are computers that respond to eye contact, a device that converts sign language to speech helps the deaf communicate with people who don't understand sign language, and voice-activated phones and other gadgets that help those with mobility difficulties. Now there's a phone that responds to head movements instead of finger swipes.

LESSON 2 Amazing Abilities

VOCABULARY noun suffixes

A Complete the table with words from the box and nouns formed from the words.

achieve, argue, available, develop, hard, ill, impossible, kind, possible, responsible, sad

Verb + *–ment*	Adjective + *–ness*	Adjective ending in *–able/–ible* + *–ity*
entertain–entertainment	*happy–happiness*	*able–ability*
achieve–achievement	hard–hardness	available–availability
argue–argument	ill–illness	impossible–impossibility
develop–development	kind–kindness	possible–possibility
	sad–sadness	responsible–responsibility

B IN PAIRS Ask and answer the questions.

1 What do you think your greatest achievement is?
2 What was the last argument you had? What happened?

GO TO page xi for LISTENING step-by-step instructions.

GO TO page 137 for AUDIO SCRIPT.

Suggested answer: Daniel went to Iceland and spent the week with an Icelandic tutor, who was amazed at Daniel's ability to quickly learn Icelandic vocabulary, grammar, and pronunciation. Students who are interested in his story should search online for "Daniel Tammet Icelandic" and they will find videos describing his story and Daniel himself talking about it.

LISTENING

A 1.02 You are going to listen to part of a lecture. Look at the pictures and say why you think these two people might be mentioned in the lecture. Listen and check.

Wolfgang Amadeus Mozart (1756–1791)

Daniel Tammet (1979–)

B 1.02 LISTENING SKILL—Recognize signposts Listen again and complete the sentences.

1 Over the ___last___ few lectures, we looked at …
2 To ___begin___ with, people with perfect pitch can …
3 As you ___probably___ know, Mozart could play …
4 Moving ___on___ to language learning, we all have …

C 1.02 Listen again and complete the notes with the relevant numbers.

1 People with perfect pitch: 1 in ___10,000/ten thousand___
2 Mozart played violin and keyboard, age ___5/five___
3 Mozart wrote symphony, age ___8/eight___
4 Daniel Tammet speaks ___10/ten___ languages.
5 David Tammet learned Icelandic in ___1/one___ week.

D THINKING SKILL—Evaluate Consider how Daniel Tammet was able to learn Icelandic so quickly.

VOCABULARY

Tell students to do VOCABULARY **A** in two phases. First, have them categorize the words. Then have them change the words to nouns. Tell them to observe the patterns they see emerge.

More suffixes for nouns are *–age* (*marriage*), *–ance* (*importance*), *–er* (*painter*), *–ery* (*bakery*), *–ing* (*painting*), *–ion* (*communion*), and *–ism* (*capitalism*).

LISTENING

LISTENING SKILL—Recognize signposts

Signposts in speech are phrases a speaker uses during a presentation to help the audience follow their discourse. A presentation should have a structure: a beginning, middle, and end. There should be higher-energy moments, lower-energy moments, or moments to look at a slide, a chart, and so on. A good presenter will use signposting phrases to help guide the audience through the different parts of the talk. Some signpost examples in the lecture are when the speaker introduces main points: *I want to talk about …*; *To begin with, people with perfect pitch …*; and *Moving on to language learning …*

GRAMMAR expressing ability

A **Match the sentences (1–5) with the correct explanations of the language of ability (a–c). You will use some explanations more than once.**

1 People with perfect pitch **can** hear a musical note and tell you exactly what it is. __a__
2 Mozart **could** play the violin and the keyboard at the age of five. __b__
3 And he **managed to** write his first symphony at the age of eight. __c__
4 And many of us **have succeeded in** learning one or two foreign languages. __c__
5 Some people **are able to** learn languages amazingly quickly. __a__

a a general ability in the present
b a general ability in the past
c an ability that has been achieved despite difficulty

For more practice, go to page 142.

B **Choose the correct options.**

1 Some people … speak more than one language.
a don't succeed in **b** aren't able to **c** don't manage
2 How many languages … now?
a can you speak **b** could you speak **c** did you manage to speak
3 After a lot of practice, I finally … to learn how to play the piano.
a succeeded **b** could **c** managed
4 I … ride a bike by the time I was six.
a managed **b** can **c** could
5 Even though my brother has perfect pitch, he … becoming a professional musician.
a couldn't **b** wasn't able to **c** didn't succeed in

C IN PAIRS **Tell your partner one thing you managed to do this week.**

PRONUNCIATION word stress with *–ity*

A 1.03 **Underline the stressed syllable in each word. Listen, check, and practice.**

1 able ability 2 available availability

GO TO page ix for **PRONUNCIATION** step-by-step instructions.

SPEAKING

A **Think of a time when you did something that was hard, e.g., passed an exam, learned a new skill, etc. Make notes about any details you remember.**

B IN PAIRS **Ask and answer the questions about your achievements. Use the Confident Communicator box to help you.**

1 Do you have an achievement you are proud of?
2 How did you manage to do it?
3 What did you do in the beginning? How did you feel?
4 What did you manage to do that helped you?
5 How did that help you? What were you able to do then?
6 What happened in the end?

CONFIDENT COMMUNICATOR
REPAIR IT

When you don't understand something, use the following phrases to repair the conversation:
Sorry, what was that?
I'm sorry—I didn't understand what you said.
What do you mean by personal achievements?

GRAMMAR

Check that students also know how to use expressions for ability in the negative: *can't play, couldn't hear, haven't succeeded in learning, are not able to …*

Additional Activity

Have students draw a table in their notebooks with the following titles: *Things I can't do, Things I tried but couldn't do,* and *Things I haven't succeeded in doing ever*. Then tell them to complete the table.

PRONUNCIATION

For more pronunciation practice, have students identify the stressed syllables in the nouns in VOCABULARY **A**. Have them work in pairs to practice saying the nouns with the right stress.

SPEAKING

Here are some examples of some more things that are hard to learn to do when you are very young: drive a car, start a job, learn to cook, live on your own, share an apartment or house, find your way around, sew a button, or do an oil change on your car.

LESSON 3 Three Stories of Survival

VOCABULARY character adjectives

A Find and underline the negative character adjective. Use a dictionary if necessary.

brave calm confident creative curious generous independent <u>selfish</u> reliable

MAKE IT YOURS

Do these adjectives describe you? What other words could you use to describe your character?

B Write an adjective from the box for each description.

1 Danielle never thinks about other people's feelings. selfish
2 Lauren isn't afraid of anything. She likes dangerous situations! brave
3 Kyle never seems to be nervous. He really believes in himself. confident
4 Juan Carlos will happily give you money if you need some. generous
5 Madison always wants to know more about things and asks lots of questions. curious
6 Joshua doesn't like asking for help and wants to do things himself. independent
7 Sophie never gets angry or worried. She always seems to be relaxed. calm
8 Chelsea always does what she says she will. She won't disappoint you. reliable

Suggested answers: 1 a year or a place 2 probably a number: her age 3 a number 4 a person, an object, or an action 5 a type of food 6 a period of time 7 an adjective or a profession 8 a year or a place

LISTENING

A Look at B. Before you listen, predict what kind of information you need to write.

B 1.04 LISTENING SKILL—Listen for specific information
Listen to a podcast. Then complete the notes with a number, word, or short phrase.

1 Born: Lima, Peru
2 Crash happened when she was: 17
3 Height of plane: 3.2 kms
4 Saved by: her seat
5 Food: a bag of candy
6 In rain forest for: 10 days
7 Later, became: a scientist
8 *When I Fell From the Sky* published in: 2011

Juliane Koepcke

GO TO page 137 for AUDIO SCRIPT.

People often live near sources of water, so following a stream is a good way of finding an area where people live.

C 1.04 THINKING SKILL—Analyze Listen again and explain why you think Juliane followed a stream.

GO TO page xiv for WRITING step-by-step instructions.

WRITING a blog post

A Read the blog post and choose *True* or *False*.

AN AMAZING STORY

Hi, guys! I want to share with you an amazing story of survival. Some of you might know about it already. In 2018, 12 teenagers and their football coach went into caves in Thailand. It started to rain and they couldn't get out because of the water. They were in there for nine days without any food or light. They drank water from the cave walls! Divers managed to find them after a long search, but they still had a problem. The water made it very hard to get the boys out, and most of them couldn't swim. And it was the start of the rainy season, so they didn't have a lot of time. Finally, the divers succeeded in getting all the boys out, but it wasn't easy.

I hate the idea of being stuck in a dark cave! I'd be very scared. You need to be calm and independent to survive a situation like that. I think the boys were really brave, and so were the divers who rescued them. They had to be creative to find a solution to the problem, but they did it. If you are curious, search online and read the whole story.

VOCABULARY Additional Activity

Have students count the number of syllables in the words and guess the correct pronunciation. Show them where to find the pronunciation of a word in a dictionary. Ask them which dictionary apps they use and if the apps provide the pronunciation of words.

LISTENING

When students are predicting the kinds of information they have to listen for, elicit what they think they'll listen for: *age*, *year*, *measurement*, *period of time*. Elicit examples: *26 years old*, *1947*, *350 meters*, *15 days*.

THINKING SKILL—Analyze

As teachers, we want students to activate their curious minds. Throughout ***Speak Your Mind***, you will encounter many circumstances where students are asked to take the information they have been reading about or listening to, analyze it, and apply it in a new setting or bring new information to a problem.

The writer …

1 speaks directly to the readers to create a friendly style. True / False
2 gives his or her personal reaction and then describes what happened. True / False
3 explains what problems different people faced. True / False
4 imagines himself or herself in the survival situation. True / False
5 gives his or her opinion of the people in the situation. True / False
6 tells readers to write their own blog posts. True / False

B Choose the correct spelling.

1 **a** surviveal **b** survival
2 **a** achievement **b** achievment
3 **a** possibileity **b** possibility
4 **a** amazement **b** amazment
5 **a** amazeing **b** amazing

C Make notes about a story of survival. You can use the story in LISTENING B, the story in WRITING A, or another story of survival you know about.

1 When did this happen? ______
2 Who was involved? ______
3 What happened first? ______
4 Then what happened? ______
5 What happened in the end? ______
6 What's your reaction? ______
7 What do you think of the people involved? ______

D Write a blog post about a story of survival.

SPEAKING

A Choose one of these survival situations. Make notes.

a hurricane

an earthquake

a flood

How I would feel:

______

______

What I would do:

______

______

B IN PAIRS Tell your partner about the survival situation you have chosen. Then ask and answer the questions. Use the Confident Communicator box to help you.

1 What personal qualities does it take to survive in a hard situation?
2 Do you think you have those personal qualities?

CONFIDENT COMMUNICATOR
KEEP TALKING

To justify reasons in a discussion, it helps to describe your feelings and explain your choices:
In a hurricane / an earthquake / a flood, I would feel nervous and frightened.
I'd hate to be in a hurricane / an earthquake / a flood because it would be very frightening.

WRITING

Allow students to research some stories of survival online and make notes. Give them a list of famous incidents to get their research started, such as a group of Chilean miners who were trapped underground in 2010, five Mexican fishermen who were lost at sea for more than nine months in 2005, and Aron Ralston, who was trapped in rocks in Utah in 2003.

SPEAKING

After students have made notes about each survival situation, have them write words on the board under these headings: *hurricane*, *earthquake*, and *flood*. Elicit as many vocabulary words as possible to create a good bank of words to refer to during the speaking activity:

- **hurricane:** wind, storm, power outage, evacuation, supplies, communication blocked
- **earthquake**: suddenly, buildings, shake, collapse, noise, hide, take cover, protection
- **flood:** water, river, rain, rise, plan, rescue

GO TO page xv

for **LANGUAGE AND LIFE** step-by-step instructions.

Language and Life

Decision Making – Survival Situation

A 1.05 Read the description. Then answer the questions.

Surviving in the Desert

It is 9 o'clock in the morning on a warm July day. You and your three colleagues were on a short flight to a conference in Southern California when your plane developed mechanical problems. The plane was forced off course by a few miles. Finally, the mechanical problems got worse, the pilot lost control of the plane, and you all crash-landed in the desert. You and your three colleagues find yourselves quite far from the plane. Although you keep looking, unfortunately it seems that the pilot is missing. You and your colleagues are on your own.

The nearest town, which you saw from the window when you flew over it half an hour ago, is about 30 kilometers away. That is an extremely long walk, and you know that it will be very difficult. None of you can get any signal at all on your cell phones, and without signal, none of the apps work. Daytime temperatures in this area can reach 40°C, and at night, they can fall below 0°C. It is already starting to get very warm, and you know that soon you will be in danger. One of your colleagues remembers reading an article about the desert, and he says it is better to move around during the evening, because it is less hot. He says that between late afternoon and sunset is the best time to move.

In different parts of the desert around you, you see a variety of different things, including a map, an empty lighter, and a few items of clothing. You discuss ideas with your colleagues and as you talk, you realize that you need to come up with a plan if you are going to manage to survive. Suddenly, there is a smell of smoke in the air. You look towards the plane and you see that it is beginning to catch fire. You know that this means that there is not much time to decide what to do because the fuel in the plane's tanks could explode. What do you do?

1. How would you feel in a situation like this? Students' own answers
2. What skills do you think you would need in a situation like this? **Suggested answers:** practical skills, like the ability to start a fire; teamwork; problem-solving skills
3. What are the main problems you and your group face? You need food and water, and you need to keep warm at night.

B IN GROUPS Look at the items you have recovered from the crash. Decide how important each one is to you. Number them from 1 (most important) to 8 (least important). How might you use each item? Make sure everyone in your group agrees.

OBJECTIVE

In this lesson, students learn how to make choices and prioritize actions in a survival game. This activity will have students think about the reasons behind their choices, and it will require them to defend their choices with explanations. Point out that the decision-making skills they use in the game translate to their personal and work lives. Ask them to reflect on the choices they make.

PROCESS OPTIONAL 1.05

Students read the description about a plane crash, consider how they would feel in this situation, list skills they would need, and then identify main problems they would be faced with. Groups look at items recovered from the crash, put them in order of importance for survival, and give reasons for their choices. Each group will share their choices and reasons. Students then complete a text that explains why some items are better than others and how they help. They will score their choices and discover if they "survived." Finally, students reflect on the reasons for their choices and discuss other situations where they might have to explain reasons for choices.

lighter

clothes

map of the area

chocolate bars

mirror

flashlight

radio

container of water

C Write your top four items from B. Explain to the class what they are and why you have chosen them instead of the other items. Take turns to explain an item so that each person in your group gets to speak. Leave the scores for each item until later.

Top 4 items:

1	________	Score: ____	**3**	________	Score: ____
2	________	Score: ____	**4**	________	Score: ____

D Complete each sentence with an object from B. Then calculate the scores for your choices in C.

The best survival strategy is to stay where you are. Each pilot files a flight plan before taking off, and so rescuers will follow that when the flight doesn't arrive at your destination. The worst strategy is to set off to try to reach the town. You would be unlikely to get there before becoming exhausted. Therefore, the **1** map of the area is not very useful: 0 points. The **2** radio is also unlikely to be much help, because you can only receive a signal, not send one: 0 points. The **3** clothes will be useful when the temperature drops at night: 5 points. The **4** lighter will make a spark and can be used to start a fire: 10 points. The **5** chocolate bars will provide you with some energy and are easy to digest: 10 points. The **6** flashlight is useful for signaling at night: 10 points. The **7** container of water is essential for when you get thirsty: 15 points. The **8** mirror is also extremely important. You can use it to reflect the sun to signal to any rescuers: 15 points.

E Add the scores of each of your top four items and record your total score.

Total Score	
45–65	Congratulations! You've got great survival skills. You are finally rescued when you are able to signal a plane overhead. Perhaps your adventures have given you a taste for the great outdoors!
35–45	Good job. It wasn't easy, but you succeeded in getting the attention of the rescuers. Think twice before going out into the wilderness again.
Less than 35	Uh-oh. It looks like the desert was the winner this time. You need to think clearly and stay calm if you're going to come out on top next time!

F Discuss the questions.

1 What approach did you use to decide which items to choose?
2 In what other situations might you use this approach?

MAKE IT DIGITAL

Go online and find other stories of survival. How did those people survive and what did they use?

CLASSROOM MANAGEMENT

Encourage balanced group participation in speaking activities by giving everyone a token (a chip or a piece of paper) that they put in the middle of the table each time they take a turn to speak. Once a person has used up all their tokens, they must wait for others to use their tokens before participating again.

CULTURE NOTE

How do different cultures approach decision-making? Depending on the country, a decision will be made quickly or slowly. In the United States, people value speed and efficiency, so a boss may be trusted to make a decision. In China, speed is not valued but seen as a weakness. A company culture can override country culture. A company can be hierarchical and expect decisions to be made at the top or more egalitarian and ask for input from everyone.

GO TO page xvii
for UNIT REVIEW step-by-step instructions.

UNIT 1

VOCABULARY review

SCORE: / 10

A Complete the sentences with words from the box. There are three words you don't need.

able-bodied brave calm creative curious disabled reliable selfish

1 If you are creative, you are good at making things or coming up with new ideas.
2 If you are disabled, you are unable to use part of your body.
3 If you are selfish, you don't care about other people.
4 If you are brave, you have courage and you are not afraid.
5 If you are curious, you want to know more about a subject.

B Complete the sentences with nouns.

1 Jack took a lot of days off work last year because of illness (ill).
2 I like working here because there are opportunities for professional development (develop).
3 Is there any possibility (possible) that you're wrong about this issue?
4 I had an argument (argue) with the janitor because I couldn't get into the building in my wheelchair.
5 My greatest achievement (achieve) is learning to climb again after my accident.

GRAMMAR review

SCORE: / 10

A Choose the correct words and phrases.

The *Jascon-4*, a small boat, went down in heavy seas near Nigeria on May 26, 2013. No one **1** thought / was thinking that there were any survivors. However, one man, Harrison Odjegba Okene, the ship's cook, managed **2** surviving / to survive. At a depth of 30 meters, it was totally dark and he **3** can't / couldn't see a thing. He **4** knew / was knowing that he needed to find a safe space. Time **5** ran / was running out, but luckily, he succeeded **6** to find / in finding a pocket of air in the engineer's office. It **7** can / is able be dangerous in cold water, but he was able **8** make / to make a small platform from a mattress that kept his upper body out of the water. He was there for three days. Finally, he **9** can / could hear a noise. It was the divers who **10** searched / were searching for the boat. He was rescued, but he said he would never go to sea again!

16–20 correct: You can describe people's characters and form nouns with suffixes. You can use stative and dynamic verbs and express ability.
0–15 correct: Look again at the Vocabulary and Grammar sections in the unit.

TOTAL SCORE: / 20

WHAT DO YOU KNOW NOW? Look back at page 7 and add the words you know now to the boxes.

GO TO page xviii
for STUDY SKILLS step-by-step instructions.

STUDY SKILLS EFFECTIVE TIME MANAGEMENT

Take the quiz about effective time management. Go to **Study Skills** on page 127 to find the answers. Then learn more about effective time management.

1 Which two of the following are useful time management strategies?
a regularly checking your email
b prioritizing what is important
c making a detailed study plan

2 Rewarding yourself at the end of a study session will not help your motivation.
a True
b False

3 Which of the following is likely to prevent effective time management?
a clarifying how you currently use your time
b discussing challenges and solutions with other students
c being surrounded by distractions

4 Effective time management skills are only really useful in academic settings.
a True
b False

VOCABULARY

For VOCABULARY **A**, have students cover the words in the box and see if they can figure out the answers based on context.

If students have trouble with VOCABULARY **B**, direct them to Lesson 2, VOCABULARY **A**.

GRAMMAR

Role-play an interview with one of the survivors from the unit. Have students work in pairs to choose a person to portray. Ask them to work together to prepare three interview questions and answers. Then give them time to practice the interview. Ask pairs to present their interview to the class.

FURTHER DISCUSSION

Write the following questions on the board. Then have students form groups of three and ask each other:

- Do you know of any survival stories in your community?
- Do you know anyone who uses prosthetics? What do they use?
- Have you ever been in a hurricane, earthquake, or a flood?

UNIT 2 The Animal Connection

WHAT DO YOU ALREADY KNOW?

1 Think about animals you know and their characteristics. Write the names of the animals.

2 IN PAIRS Share and compare your ideas. Add more words to your list.

Domestic animals / Characteristics

Wild animals / Characteristics

VIDEO

DISCUSS & SHARE

3 IN GROUPS Watch the video and answer the question.

SYM Are you a dog person or a cat person?

In this unit, you will ...

- talk about intelligent animals, discuss possible jobs with animals, and make arguments for and against owning exotic pets.
- use thinking skills: recall, analyze, and evaluate.
- read about animals and the mirror test for intelligence.
- use strategies and language to move on to your next point, start a conversation about hypothetical situations, and disagree politely.
- use problem-solving skills to find solutions to help stray animals.
- follow a wildlife photographer to learn about this job and the skills needed for this industry.

Unit 2 The Animal Connection 17

GO TO page vi
for UNIT OPENER step-by-step instructions.

STUDENTS MAY ALREADY KNOW:

- **Domestic animals / Characteristics:** the names of domestic and farm animals, products that we get from domestic animals, tamed, friendly.
- **Wild animals / Characteristics:** the names of wild animals, jungle, savannah, desert, hole, forest, den, claws, fur, mane, endangered.

GO TO page xx
for VIDEOS IN SYM step-by-step instructions.

WHAT DO YOU ALREADY KNOW?

If students are struggling to understand what to do, you can ask them some questions to prompt their thinking:

- What domestic animals do you like?
- Have you seen any animals in the wild?
- Do you have any pets?
- Do you consider yourself to be an animal lover?

VIDEO

Before viewing, ask:

What do dogs need? *time, attention, lots of exercise*

Why do Elena have a cat? *She works all day and cats are independent.*

After viewing, put the continuum on the board.

dogs —— cats

Have students mark the continuum and explain their preferences.

DISCUSS & SHARE

Students should place themselves on a continuum of opinion. Ask students if they prefer cats or dogs. Often, the opinion about which animal is a better pet is polarizing. Or it may be that people identify with one animal over the other. Students should choose one viewpoint and defend it with examples.

GO TO page x

for **READING** step-by-step instructions.

LESSON 1 Animal Intelligence

READING

A **Apart from humans, which animals do you think are intelligent?**

B 2.01 **Read the blog post. Then choose *True* or *False*.**

The Mirror Test

Animals are interesting, aren't they? They can be **cute**, they can be fast, and they can be strong. But are they **intelligent**?

That isn't an easy question to answer. Animals all live in different habitats and their **behavior** is right for that situation. We need a standard way to test an animal's behavior. The mirror test, developed in 1970 by Dr. Gordon Gallup Jr., gives us that.

You recognize your own reflection in a mirror, don't you? But does an animal know that it's looking at itself when it looks in a mirror, or does it think it's a different animal? If an animal passes the mirror test, there's a good chance it is intelligent. We give the animal medicine so it goes to sleep. Then, we put a colored mark on the animal's body where it can't see it in a normal way, such as on its forehead or on its ear. When the animal wakes up and sees itself in a mirror, we watch how it behaves.

Animals that pass the mirror test see the mark and touch it or try to remove it. So far, the species that have passed the test are great apes (chimpanzees, bonobos, and orangutans), elephants, dolphins, orcas, and Eurasian magpies. Some people say, though, that the test only works with animals that mainly use **sight** to explore the world, and it may not be a fair test of other animals, such as dogs, who use **smell** or sound more than sight and fail the test.

GLOSSARY

habitat (n): place where an animal naturally lives

1	An animal's environment changes how it acts.	**True** / False
2	The mirror test is done while the animal is asleep.	True / **False**
3	In the mirror test, the animal puts color on its body using the mirror.	True / **False**
4	Animals pass the mirror test if they know they are looking at themselves.	**True** / False

C **READING SKILL—Understand examples** **Find and write examples from the text in B.**

1 a good place to put a mark on an animal for the mirror test forehead/ear

2 an animal that passes the mirror test ____________

3 an animal that fails the mirror test dog

chimpanzee / bonobo / orangutan / elephant / dolphin / orca / Eurasian magpie

D **THINKING SKILL—Recall** **Without reading the text again, describe how the mirror test works.**

GO TO page vii

for **VOCABULARY** step-by-step instructions.

VOCABULARY

A **Complete the definitions (1–5) with the words in bold in READING B.**

1 The sense of sight is very important to animals that hunt with their eyes, such as cats.
2 The sense of smell is very important to animals that use their noses a lot, such as bears.
3 An intelligent person is good at understanding difficult ideas.
4 An animal's behavior is the way it acts and the things it does.
5 People often think that baby animals, such as kittens and puppies, are cute.

READING OPTIONAL 2.01

Some intelligent animals are bees, chimpanzees, cats, dogs, dolphins, elephants, goats, octopuses, parrots, and rats. Accept all answers at the beginning of the activity.

Before reading, you may want to preview the topic some more. Elicit information from students about how intelligence is measured.

THINKING SKILL—Recall

Recall is the ability to remember facts, events, and situations. To recall is to bring something to mind. Tell students that if they practice going over facts in their minds, they will improve their memory. Have students close their eyes and think about what they have learned recently.

VOCABULARY Extra Practice

For further practice of the vocabulary, ask students to write a paragraph with as many of the vocabulary words in it as possible. Ask volunteers to read their paragraphs, and have the class nominate the writing that is creative and that best illustrates the newest words.

GRAMMAR tag questions

A Read the tag questions and choose the correct options.

Animals are interesting, aren't they?
You recognize your own reflection in a mirror, don't you?

1 To form a tag question with the verb *be*, we use the verb **be** / do and an appropriate pronoun.
2 To form a tag question with other verbs, we use the verb be / **do** and an appropriate pronoun.
3 To form a tag question with a modal, **use the verb *be*** / repeat the modal.
4 When the verb in the main part of the sentence is positive, the verb in the tag is **negative** / positive.

For more practice, go to page 143.

GO TO page viii for GRAMMAR step-by-step instructions.

B Complete the tag questions.

1 You're James, ___aren't you___?
2 It's cold today, ___isn't it___?
3 Jack's a really smart dog, ___isn't he___?
4 Horses are very intelligent, ___aren't they___?
5 Dolphins can be taught tricks, ___can't they___?
6 Your mom works with animals, ___doesn't she___?

MAKE IT REAL

In informal situations, some people might use *right* at the end of a sentence instead of using a tag question, e.g., *You're a vet, right?*

SPEAKING

GO TO page xii for SPEAKING step-by-step instructions.

A Put the animals in order of intelligence from 1 (most intelligent) to 5 (least intelligent).

 ___

 ___

 ___

 ___

 ___

B IN PAIRS Tell each other what order you have put the animals in. Explain your reasons. Use the Confident Communicator box to help you.

A: Parrots can talk, can't they? I think that means they're smart.
B: Maybe, but dolphins are smarter, aren't they? They can learn lots of tricks.

CONFIDENT COMMUNICATOR
KEEP TALKING

Use the following phrases to move on to your next point for discussion.
***What about** horses? Do you think they're intelligent?*
***Let's move on to** rabbits. Are they intelligent?*
***Next, let's think about** parrots. They're intelligent, aren't they?*

GRAMMAR

The intonation of a tag question influences the meaning. Rising intonation makes a tag question a real inquiry: *You're James, aren't you?* (You're not sure if he's James.) Falling intonation in the tag indicates a confirmation: *You're James, aren't you?* (You're pretty sure he's James.)

SPEAKING

Ordering activities promote speaking by having students engage with the content. Tasks like SPEAKING **B** promote discussion because there is a purpose to speaking. Give students time to consider the order of intelligence and then some more time to think about why they put the animals in a certain order. Additionally, students will need some more time to prepare to defend their opinions.

You may want to extend the activity by having students then research other animals' intelligence and investigate other studies that have been done about animals' intelligence.

LESSON 2 Working With Animals

VOCABULARY careers with animals

Although the precise requirements of careers may vary from country to country, students should check vet, marine biologist, and zoologist. Zookeepers may also need a degree in some places.

A Check (✓) the careers you need a degree to do.

☐ dog handler

☐ vet/veterinarian

☐ zookeeper

☐ wildlife photographer

☐ breeder

☐ marine biologist

☐ horse trainer

☐ zoologist

dog handler or breeder

B IN PAIRS Decide which career(s) from A would be most appropriate for Holly.

Holly is 18 and is considering a career with animals. She loves small animals and has always had a number of pets. She has good exam results, but she would rather take a practical course than an academic course.

GO TO page xi for **LISTENING** step-by-step instructions.

GO TO page 138 for **AUDIO SCRIPT**.

GO TO page 138 for **AUDIO SCRIPT**.

LISTENING

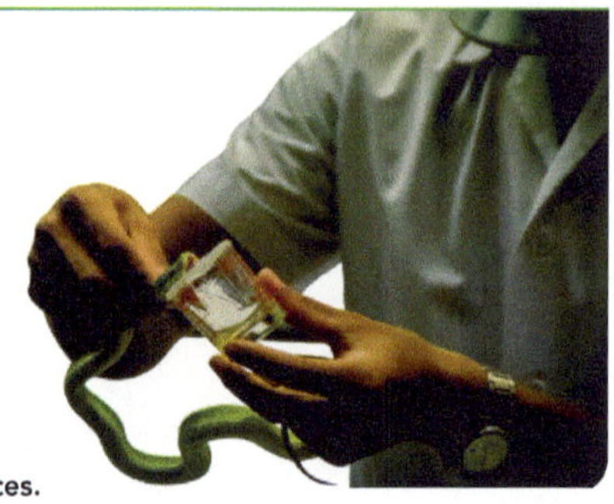

A What do you think this person is doing?

B 2.02 LISTENING SKILLS—Use key information to predict content Listen to Part 1 of a talk. Then check what topics you expect to hear in the rest of the talk.

- ☐ academic qualifications
- ☐ salary
- ☐ work experience
- ☐ personal qualities

Answers may vary. Topics covered in Part 2 are academic qualifications, work experience, and personal qualities.

C 2.03 Listen to Part 2 of the talk. Then complete the sentences.

1 A marine biologist is someone who studies animals that live __in the sea__.
2 Some marine biologists do __research__ in the summer months.
3 To be a marine biologist, you'll need a __degree__ in biology or marine biology.
4 The person who gets venom from a snake is known as a __snake milker__.
5 Venom is used to make antivenom for when a snake __bites someone__.

D THINKING SKILL—Analyze Decide what kind of person would make a good snake milker. Say whether you think you would be good at that job.

VOCABULARY

Ask students to work in pairs to check each other's pronunciation of the animal-related careers. Tell them that one person should point, in random order, to the pictures and ask *What's this job?* or *What does this person do?* The other person responds *He's a dog handler. She's a zoologist.* Then, have them change roles.

LISTENING

LISTENING SKILL—Use key information to predict content

There are two prediction tasks in the LISTENING section. First, students will predict what they think the person in the picture is doing. This activates their previous knowledge about the topic. Then, they will use key information to predict the second part of a talk after listening to the first part. Prediction is a useful skill to employ in listening tasks and will be a vital strategy for standardized certifications that have a listening component.

GRAMMAR articles

A Match the sentence beginnings (1–3) with the ends (a–c).

A marine biologist is someone who studies animals that live in the sea.
A snake milker takes venom from a snake. The venom is very useful.

1 We use the indefinite article (*a*, *an*) __c__
2 We use the definite article (*the*) __a__
3 We use no article __b__

a with singular countable nouns, with plural countable nouns when we are being specific, and when there is only one of something (*the sun, the sky, etc.*).
b with plural countable nouns and uncountable nouns when we are talking generally.
c with singular countable nouns when we are not being specific or when we mention something for the first time.

For more practice, go to page 144.

B Complete the sentences with *a*, *an*, or *the*. If no article is needed, put an X.

When **1** ____a____ director needs **2** ____an____ animal for **3** ____a____ movie, they turn to **4** ____an____ animal trainer. **5** ____The____ animal trainer then provides **6** ____a____ trained animal to do whatever **7** ____the____ director wants them to do. But what does it take to become **8** ____an____ animal trainer? Of course, you need to enjoy working with **9** ____X____ animals. More than that, though, you have to be interested in **10** ____X____ animal behavior. You should also be in shape and able to work outdoors.

C IN PAIRS Say if you think you would be a good animal trainer.

PRONUNCIATION the

A 2.04 Listen to the sentences. What do you notice about the pronunciation of *the*?

I have to take my dog to the vet.
My dog has to stay in the animal hospital.

B Practice the sentence: I like to see the animals at the zoo.

GO TO page ix for PRONUNCIATION step-by-step instructions.

Before a consonant, *the* is pronounced /ðə/. Before vowels, *the* is pronounced /ðiː/.

SPEAKING

A Read the questions and make notes.

1 If you were going to work with animals, what kind of animals would you like to work with (small, large, marine, etc.)? ____________
2 What kind of place (lab, outdoors, etc.) would you like to work in? ____________
3 How closely would you like to work with animals? ____________

B IN PAIRS Talk about your answers to the questions in A. Discuss what careers with animals each of you might enjoy. Use the Confident Communicator box to help you.

CONFIDENT COMMUNICATOR
START TALKING

To start a conversation about hypothetical situations, use the following phrases:
If I were going to work with animals, I would like to work with small animals, such as cats and dogs.
The animals I'd like to work with are marine animals.

GRAMMAR

More examples of using *the* for something that is unique are *the world* and *the universe*. We also use *the* when referring to groups of people: *the Dutch* and *the elderly*. We use *the* for decades: *She was born in the '90s*. Geographic regions also use *the*: *the Great Smoky Mountains*, *the Antarctic*, and *the Pacific Ocean*.

PRONUNCIATION

Some learners have a hard time identifying when to use *the* because naturally when we listen, we listen for meaning and don't notice it. Interestingly, *the* is the most commonly used word in English, but as it is a grammar word, it does not carry a message as nouns and verbs do.

SPEAKING

Some more examples of jobs working with animals might be *kennel worker*, *elephant sanctuary caretaker*, *dog walker*, *research scientist*, *farmer*, *police officer* (in a horse or dog unit), or *rescue worker*. Some students may already have had experience working with animals. You may want to allow them to talk about that experience.

LESSON 3 Endangered Species

VOCABULARY animals

A Name the animals. Then check (✓) the ones you think are endangered.

☐ crocodile	☐ dolphin	☐ hippo	☐ polar bear	☐ porcupine
☐ puma	☐ shark	☐ tiger	☐ turtle	☐ whale

1  hippo

2  whale

3  turtle

4  tiger

5  crocodile

6  shark

7  dolphin

8  porcupine

9  puma

10  polar bear

B IN PAIRS Compare your answers. Say why you think some of the animals are endangered.

LISTENING

A Have you visited a zoo? What was it like?

B 2.05 LISTENING SKILL—Listen for key words Look at the word cloud. Listen to a presentation and circle words and phrases you hear.

GO TO page 138 for AUDIO SCRIPT.

C 2.05 Listen again and choose the correct options.

1 The zoo tries to make ...
 a the zoo environment as natural as possible. b animals behave in different ways.

2 The zoo wants to educate people about ...
 a the work the zookeepers do with the animals. b the problems some animals face in the wild.

3 The zoo's breeding program ...
 a provides animals for other zoos. b aims to help endangered species in the wild.

D THINKING SKILL—Evaluate What arguments can you think of against zoos? Choose the most persuasive points.

Suggested answers: Animals often live in unsuitable conditions. Animals are often bored in zoos, which can lead to psychological problems. Baby animals are cute and attract visitors, which may mean that zoos breed young animals but don't take care of older animals properly. Most animals are never released into the wild. Some animals, e.g., elephants, might have shorter lives in zoos.

VOCABULARY

According to the World Wildlife Federation, some endangered, vulnerable, or critically species are rhino, tiger, dolphin, turtle, panda, whale, polar bear, shark, hippo. In Latin America: sloths, sea turtles, jaguars, howler monkeys, macaws, Amazonian manatees, and short-tailed chinchillas. Ask students if they have ever seen any of these animals. If not, encourage students to look for pictures online. Ask students if they have participated in any programs to save them from extinction.

LISTENING

LISTENING SKILL—Listen for key words

Have students preview the word cloud before listening. All of the words are nouns and adjectives. Nouns usually carry most of the meaning in a text. Students should listen for key words (nouns) when trying to understand a conversation or passage.

THINKING SKILL—Evaluate

Students are required to think of negative aspects of zoos. This takes their thinking outside the box. They are applying what they have learned to the wider topic. They must form their own opinions.

WRITING an opinion post

GO TO page xiv for WRITING step-by-step instructions.

A Read the arguments for and against supporting zoos. Then answer the questions in your notebook.

Should we support zoos in the work that they do?

Zoos do a lot of good work. First of all, they educate the public. This inspires the next generation of zookeepers, vets, and environmentalists. In addition, zoos help to protect endangered species through the breeding work they do. Last, zoos are involved in environmental programs of different kinds around the world. We need to support our zoos.

Alessa, Lima, Peru

Zoos are cruel and unnecessary. To start with, animals in captivity are bored and cannot behave naturally. Many animals find being on display very stressful. What's more, some animals die younger in zoos than they would in the wild. Last but not least, zoos care more about baby animals, which attract paying visitors. We should not support zoos.

Jacob, New York, US

1 What are the main arguments given in favor of zoos?
2 What are the main arguments given against zoos?

1 Zoos tell people about animals. They make people want to work with animals. They breed animals to help endangered species. They do other kinds of environmental work.

2 Animals in zoos have problems, such as being bored and being under stress. Some don't live as long as animals in the wild. Zoos focus too much on baby animals.

B Write words and phrases from A that have the same meaning as these words and phrases.

first: 1 First of all, 2 To start with
also: 3 In addition, 4 What's more
finally: 5 Last, 6 Last but not least

C You are going to write a post for the website on the following statement. Make notes to answer the questions.

We should close all zoos and release the animals into the wild.

1 Are you going to argue for or against this statement? ______
2 What is your main argument? ______
3 What other arguments do you want to mention? ______

D Write an opinion post for the website arguing either for or against the statement. Use the phrases from B to structure your post.

SPEAKING

A Think of arguments for and against allowing people to own exotic pets, such as tigers, chimpanzees, snakes, etc. Make notes.

Main arguments for:

______

Main arguments against:

______

B IN PAIRS Do you think people should be allowed to keep wild animals as pets? Why or why not?

C Tell the rest of the class what you talked about. How many of you are for and how many of you are against the idea? Use the Confident Communicator box to help you.

CONFIDENT COMMUNICATOR
KEEP TALKING

To disagree with someone politely, use *Yes, but …*
I think people should have the right to own exotic pets if they want to.
Yes, but what about the animals? Don't they have rights, too?

WRITING

After WRITING **D** you could do a gallery feedback session. Have students post their writings on the walls of the classroom. Give them 10–15 minutes to walk around reading each other's writing. Ask them to give feedback. Give everyone three sticky notes, and ask them to write positive comments and stick them next to the writing they admire. Comments have to be nice, and they should be descriptive of the work.

SPEAKING

Students will use the strategies from the writing exercise in a speaking scenario. They will apply the structures and functions they have used before to talk about the topic of owning exotic pets. Encourage students to look up an article about owning exotic pets online and then scroll down to the comments section. There, they will find plenty of debate for and against the right to own exotic pets.

GO TO page xv
for LANGUAGE AND LIFE step-by-step instructions.

Language and Life

Problem Solving – Strays

A 2.06 **Read the article. Then answer the questions.**

The Trouble With Strays

Puppies are cute, aren't they? And kittens are adorable. But those puppies and kittens grow up to be adult dogs and cats. Often the demands of being a pet owner just get to be too much for people and the cats and dogs end up on the street as strays. Sometimes it's the responsibility of looking after an adult animal that causes problems, and sometimes there are financial reasons. It's a growing problem. In the city of Detroit in the US, it is estimated that there are 50,000 stray dogs. The World Health Organization estimates that there are about 200 million stray dogs worldwide.

This situation causes a number of problems. First of all, the lives of stray animals are hard and stressful. Every day is a struggle to find enough to eat and a safe place to sleep. That means the animals are often in poor condition and get injured or die young. In addition to that, stray animals cause a number of problems for city residents. They can run into the road and cause traffic accidents. Stray animals can also carry diseases. They can pass these diseases on to people or to domestic pets. Last, packs of dogs can be dangerous and may attack people.

However, there may be a solution to the problem. One country that has reduced the number of stray dogs is the UK. In 2016, a new law was introduced. All dogs must be microchipped. This means that a small chip—the size of a grain of rice—is inserted under the dog's skin. It's a quick and painless procedure. Microchips contain a unique code that is connected to a national database. When the chip is scanned, it shows the owner's address. If your dog does not have a chip, you can receive a fine of up to £500. Microchipping is useful if your dog is lost or stolen, and it also encourages people to take more responsibility for their pets. According to the Dogs Trust's *Stray Dogs Survey Report*, in 2018, the number of stray animals in the UK was at its lowest level in 21 years—so this is a step in the right direction.

1 What are the causes of the stray animal problem? People throw their animals onto the streets because they can't handle the responsibility and because they can't afford to feed them.

2 What problems do stray animals cause for city residents? The animals cause traffic accidents. They carry diseases. They can be dangerous.

3 How did the UK solve this problem? The UK introduced microchipping which helped people find lost dogs and made them more responsible.

B IN GROUPS **Talk about the situation in your own city or area. Check (✓) the main problems with animals and add details and ideas of your own.**

Main animal problems in our city/area

☐ stray dogs
packs of dogs in some neighborhoods

☐ stray cats

☐ unwanted pets

☐ other problems

OBJECTIVE

Students learn how to brainstorm solutions. Sometimes we opt for the easiest solution without thinking about all of the options available. Learning how to brainstorm solutions can be empowering and may help in real-life situations. Students will also estimate costs related to the solutions. Cost is always an issue, so thinking about financial burdens related to solutions is practical.

PROCESS OPTIONAL 2.06

Students first read an article about the problem of stray dogs. They should understand the problem and demonstrate their understanding by answering questions. Then, they apply that knowledge to their own city or town. They should make detailed notes of the problems caused by stray animals in their hometowns. Next, they will read opinions about the problems of stray animals and use the opinions as models to brainstorm possible solutions to the problems in their areas. Students are required to then think about costs related to the solutions they proposed. Finally, they will present their solutions and estimated costs to the class.

C **Read and assess the opinions. Do you think they are good suggestions? Why or why not?**

Amy2001 *We need more shelters. We should take the animals off the streets.*

CityGirl *We should make sure the animals can't breed. And then release them back onto the streets.*

Ed_99 *We need to educate people more and stop the problem where it begins, in people's homes.*

A: Having more shelters is a good idea.
B: I agree, but maybe that's a short-term solution.

D **Brainstorm solutions for your city or area. Try to estimate the costs.**

Possible solutions for our city/area

Our estimated costs

E **Present your solutions to the class. Vote to choose the best ideas at a realistic cost.**

F **Discuss the questions.**

1. How did the costs of the solutions affect your choice?
2. What other factors did you consider when choosing solutions?
3. Why is it important to consider many factors when solving a problem?
4. What problems have you solved recently? How did you solve them?

MAKE IT DIGITAL

Find websites where people debate ideas. Read some of the posts and see what phrases they use for starting, for introducing further points, and for concluding.

CLASSROOM MANAGEMENT

The ideal size of a group in activity **B** is four students. Physically, it is easy to manage groups of four—they can sit comfortably around a table or in a circle in chairs. Make a couple of groups of three or five if the class doesn't divide evenly into fours.

CULTURE NOTE

India has the highest number of stray dogs in the world. The World Health Organization estimates there are 35 million stray dogs.

Holland is the country with the fewest stray dogs. After a big problem with strays, they took strict measures to fine and imprison people for abandoning or mistreating animals.

MAKE IT DIGITAL

Some stray animals have not been abandoned; they just got lost. Social media has made finding your lost dog much easier. People post in lost pet sites or in neighborhood sites when they have lost a pet or found a pet wandering around. Shelters post pets for adoption online.

GO TO page xvii
for UNIT REVIEW step-by-step instructions.

UNIT 2

VOCABULARY review

SCORE: / 10

A Complete the sentences with words from the box. There are two words you don't need.

apes	breeders	handlers	polar bears	species	wildlife
behavior	cute	hippos	sight	whales	zoologists

My job as a **1** ___wildlife___ photographer takes me all over the world. My main interest is in recording endangered **2** ___species___ before they disappear. I've taken shots of **3** ___bears___ in the Arctic. That was dangerous because they aren't at all **4** ___cute___, cuddly creatures! They're real killers. I've also photographed **5** ___whales___ out at sea and I've taken shots of lions, **6** ___hippos___, and zebras in Africa. My next project is to record the amazing **7** ___polar bears___ of the Asian jungles. I'd like to record their natural **8** ___behavior___, as well as collect data that **9** ___zoologists___ will find useful. They have a good sense of hearing and a good sense of **10** ___sight___, particularly at night, so it won't be easy to find them!

GRAMMAR review

SCORE: / 10

A Check (✓) the correct tag questions. Rewrite the incorrect question tags.

1 ☑ Tigers are amazing animals, aren't they? ______
2 ☐ You majored in marine biology, don't you? ___didn't you___
3 ☐ Gorillas will soon disappear in the wild, will they? ___won't they___
4 ☐ We don't do enough to protect endangered species, are we? ___do we___
5 ☑ It's important to learn about nature in schools, isn't it? ______

One of the most intelligent animals is the octopus. Octopuses can solve puzzles and can even open **a** jar to get food. And when they solve **a** puzzle, they can remember how to do it if they see **the** puzzle again. Scientists estimate that **an/the** octopus is about as intelligent as **a** three-year-old child.

B Add five articles (*a*, *an*, *the*) to the text.

One of the most intelligent animals is the octopus. Octopuses can solve puzzles and can even open jar to get food. And when they solve puzzle, they can remember how to do it if they see puzzle again. Scientists estimate that octopus is about as intelligent as three-year-old child.

16–20 correct: You can talk about animals and people who work with animals. You can use tag questions and articles.
0–15 correct: Look again at the Vocabulary and Grammar sections in the unit.

TOTAL SCORE: / 20

WHAT DO YOU KNOW NOW? Look back at page 17 and add the words you know now to the boxes.

GO TO page xix
for FOLLOW A PRO step-by-step instructions.

FOLLOW A PRO ANIMALS

Take the quiz about animals. Go to Follow A Pro on page 128 to find the answers. Then learn more about working with animals.

1 Where is the largest zoo in Mexico?
a Mexico City **b** Guadalajara **c** Puebla

2 How long is veterinary school in the US?
a one year **b** two years **c** four years

3 Approximately how many polar bears are there in the wild?
a 4,000 **b** 12,000 **c** 26,000

4 Which animal is the hippo most closely related to?
a whale **b** horse **c** dog

CLASSROOM MANAGEMENT

Give students a five-minute time limit to finish VOCABULARY **A**. Then allow students a few minutes to review tag questions on page 19 and articles on page 21 before they do the grammar exercises.

For further practice have students work in pairs. Tell them to look over the unit and then think of five questions to ask their partner about the vocabulary in the units and five questions about the grammar in the unit. Then have them ask each other about the content of the unit.

FURTHER DISCUSSION

Write the following questions on the board. Then have students form groups of three and ask each other:

- How do you think animals demonstrate their intelligence?
- If you have pets, are they smart?
- What would be the best and worst things about working with animals?
- What can we tell our children about extinct animals?

UNIT 3 Think About It

WHAT DO YOU ALREADY KNOW?

1 Think about words you know connected to thinking or skills. Write the words.

2 IN PAIRS Share and compare your ideas. Add more words to your lists.

Thinking/Skills

DISCUSS & SHARE

VIDEO

3 IN GROUPS Watch the video and answer the question.

SYM When do you think better: in the morning or in the evening?

In this unit, you will ...

- ask and answer questions about confirmation bias, discuss the importance of expert systems in your future career, and compare different creative uses for things.
- use thinking skills: analyze, evaluate, and apply.
- read about confirmation bias.
- use strategies and language to give yourself time to think, start a conversation, and ask for further suggestions.
- use design-thinking skills to design a new social media app.
- learn tips to create a presentation or give a talk.

GO TO page vi

for **UNIT OPENER** step-by-step instructions.

STUDENTS MAY ALREADY KNOW:

- **Thinking/ Skills:** listen, read, write, understand, comprehend, interpret, evaluate, analyze, study, remember, wonder, know, create, make, imagine, guess, reflect, meditate, brain, competent, do, act, abilities, mastery, knowledge, talk, discuss, learn, express, compare, problem solving.

GO TO page xx

for **VIDEOS IN SYM** step-by-step instructions.

WHAT DO YOU ALREADY KNOW?

If students are struggling to understand what to do, you can ask them some questions to prompt their thinking:

- What is thinking?
- What does it mean to you?
- Why do you think?
- What is the outcome of thinking?
- What are thinking skills?
- When do you use thinking skills?

VIDEO

Before viewing, ask:

What did Sean do in the morning? *went running, had a big breakfast, and study math and chemistry*
At what time does Andrea start her history essay? *at 10:30 p.m.*

After viewing, put the continuum on the board.

morning —— evening

Have students mark the continuum and explain their preferences.

DISCUSS & SHARE

Students should place themselves on a continuum of opinion. When do they do their best thinking: in the morning or in the evening? When do they have more energy? Do they have any preferences for when to study? Does anyone consider themselves an early bird or a night owl? Students should choose one viewpoint and defend it with examples.

GO TO page x
for **READING** step-by-step instructions.

LESSON 1 **How We Think**

READING

A **Do you think the world is generally getting better or getting worse? Why do you think that?**

B **3.01 READING SKILL—Identify the topic** **Read the article. Then choose the best definition.**

a confirmation bias (*n*): the mistake we make when we don't think carefully enough about a subject and think that our first idea is correct

b confirmation bias (*n*): the thinking habit that means we accept evidence that supports the opinion we already have and don't accept other evidence

CONFIRMATION BIAS

Scientists believe that the average person receives about 34 gigabytes of information and sees or hears 100,500 words every day. That's a lot of information, and no one can possibly **concentrate on** all of it. We choose what we **pay attention to** and what we think is important. That creates a problem: confirmation bias. We like to be right, and so we listen to **evidence** that supports what we already believe and we **ignore** evidence that goes against what we believe. For example, if you believe that the world is generally getting worse, you will see only evidence to support your opinion when you hear the news. You will pay attention to stories about rising crime and environmental problems. And you will ignore evidence that suggests people around the world are getting richer, becoming healthier, and living longer.

Confirmation bias means we see what we want to see. It can create problems. For instance, a business may try a new strategy. The managers will notice positive results, such as increased sales, before they notice negative ones, such as increased costs. That could be expensive for the business. Social media and other websites can make confirmation bias worse. Groups of online friends often agree with each other. They easily share information and news stories that support their opinions. They **rarely** hear the other side of the argument and miss **relevant** information. Some people are worried that this kind of "social media bubble" is bad for society.

Is there anything you can do to question your own confirmation bias? You can **make an effort** to listen to people with different views. You can visit websites that present a different opinion from yours. As soon as you do that, you will learn something about how other people think.

1 The fact that with so much information, we select what to focus on.

2 The managers might not notice negative results of a new strategy.

3 Because we communicate online with people who think the same way and it's easy to share evidence that supports our views.

C **Write short answers to the questions.**

1 What is the cause of confirmation bias? ______
2 Why might confirmation bias cause problems for a business? ______
3 Why can social media make confirmation bias worse? ______
4 What can you do to prevent confirmation bias? You can try to hear different points of view.

Suggested answer:
A person might try to make a change in their life (e.g., lose weight, get in shape) and only pay attention to evidence that shows it is working and ignore negative evidence. A person might want to learn a new skill and only focus on what they enjoy and what they can already do and not focus on the things they really need to practice.

D **THINKING SKILL—Analyze** **Explain other ways in which confirmation bias could be a problem.**

VOCABULARY

A **Complete the sentences with the words and phrases in bold in READING B.**

1 If you pay attention to the lecturer, you will understand the topic better.
2 People rarely listen carefully to other people's opinions—in fact, they almost never do!
3 Please don't ignore me! Listen to what I'm saying.
4 What evidence do you have that supports your opinion?
5 I know learning to play an instrument is hard, but if you make an effort, you'll improve.
6 I like to collect all the relevant information before I make an important decision.
7 I can't concentrate on my work with all this noise!

GO TO page vii
for **VOCABULARY** step-by-step instructions.

READING OPTIONAL 3.01

Ask the pessimists, those who think the world is getting worse, to stand up and give their examples. Then ask the optimists to stand up and give their examples of how they think the world is getting better. Don't agree, disagree, or give them any feedback—just encourage them to speak.

THINKING SKILL—Analyze

One example of how confirmation bias could be a problem is when dealing with a medical condition or health in general. If you only listen to information that matches your preconceived notions and are not open to research or evidence that contradicts that, it might be dangerous.

VOCABULARY

A strategy for learning new vocabulary is for students to write the word in a sentence of their own creation. This will help them remember the words and how to use them. Writing words in their own sentences will also help students practice collocating words and putting words together naturally.

GRAMMAR future time clauses (*after, as soon as, before, until, when*)

A Choose the correct option.

1 You will see only evidence to support your opinion when … the news.
  a you hear b you will hear
2 The managers will notice positive results before … negative ones.
  a they notice b they will notice

B Choose the correct options.

1 We use / don't use the future tense in a time clause.
2 We use the simple present / simple past in the time clause.

For more practice, go to page 144.

C Complete the sentences.

1 I ___will call___ (call) you as soon as I ___get___ (get) home.
2 From now on, I ___won't share___ (not share) a story on social media until I ___check___ (check) it.
3 I think the problem ___will get___ (get) worse before it ___gets___ (get) better.
4 ___Will you meet___ (you / meet) me at the airport when I ___arrive___ (arrive)?
5 After I ___watch___ (watch) the movie, I ___will tell___ (tell) you whether I like it or not.

D IN PAIRS Ask and answer the questions.

1 What will you do when this lesson ends?
2 What will you do as soon as you get home tonight?

MAKE IT REAL

We also use time clauses with *the minute* or *the instant*, meaning "immediately," e.g., *Call me **the minute** you get there.*

GO TO page viii for **GRAMMAR** step-by-step instructions.

SPEAKING

A Make notes. You do not need to write complete sentences.

1 Do you and your online friends always agree about things or do you sometimes disagree? What do you disagree about?

2 In what ways do you think confirmation bias is a problem?

3 Now that you've read about confirmation bias, will you do anything different when you are online?

B IN PAIRS Ask and answer the questions in A. Use the Confident Communicator box to help you.

CONFIDENT COMMUNICATOR
KEEP TALKING

Use the following phrases to give yourself time to think when asked a question.
That's a good question.
Let me think about that for a minute.

GO TO page xii for **SPEAKING** step-by-step instructions.

GRAMMAR

Explain that a future time clause is the part of the future sentence after *when, as soon as, after, before,* or *until.* This part of the sentence doesn't take *will.* What is really happening is that two sentences are being joined together by conjunctions. There are two events. One happens first.

SPEAKING

Get students to try being active listeners to those whose opinions they don't agree with. They can use the phrase *Tell me more about that* or ask *Why do you feel that way?* rather than immediately formulating an opposing viewpoint. A good listener strives to hear others' viewpoints calmly and openly.

CONFIDENT COMMUNICATOR

Remind students to always look at the *Confident Communicator* box before they start a speaking exercise. The *Confident Communicator* box has speaking strategies that students can practice right away during their discussion.

GO TO page xi
for **LISTENING** step-by-step instructions.

GO TO page 139
for **AUDIO SCRIPT**.

LESSON 2 Artificial Intelligence

LISTENING

A Do you think machines will be able to think in the future?

B 3.02 LISTENING SKILL—Listen for attitude Listen to a radio call-in show. Match the callers (1–4) to the statements (a–d).

1 Julia: c
2 Rafael: a
3 Megan: d
4 Victor: b

a This person is confident that AI makes the world safer.
b This person is afraid that AI will change the economy.
c This person is doubtful that machines will ever be intelligent.
d This person is worried that AI might get out of control.

C 3.02 Listen to the call-in show again. Then complete the sentences.

1 Julia says that machines are just following rules when they play games such as chess.
2 Julia says that humans are good at thinking because they have been doing it for 200,000 years.
3 Rafael says that humans make mistakes because they get tired and bored.
4 Megan says that no human understands how some computer systems work and that's dangerous.
5 Victor says that machines may do 47% of American jobs in the future.
6 Victor says that people who work in services may lose their jobs.

D THINKING SKILLS—Evaluate Consider and describe other ways we use AI today.

Suggested answer: AI is used in, for example, digital voice assistants (Alexa, Siri, etc.), video games, and the travel and banking industries.

VOCABULARY word formation

A Complete the table with the different forms of the words. Check your ideas in pairs.

Verb	Adjective	Noun (abstract)	Noun (person)
create	1 creative	5 creativity 6 creation	11 creator
power	2 powerful 3 powerless	power	
solve	solvable	7 solution	solver
think		8 thought	thinker
	4 dangerous	danger	
employ	employable	9 employment 10 unemployment	12 employer 13 employee

B IN PAIRS Discuss the questions.

1 As computers get more powerful, is there a danger to employment from AI?
2 Will computers ever be powerful enough to understand emotions?

GO TO page ix
for **PRONUNCIATION** step-by-step instructions.

PRONUNCIATION *say, says, said*

A 3.03 How do we say each of the words in bold? Listen, check, and practice.

1 Some people **say** that AI is a danger.
2 My mom **says** that she'll never lose her job to a robot.
3 My dad **said** the same thing and then lost his job!

GRAMMAR present perfect progressive

A Read the sentences from LISTENING B and complete the explanation.

Scientists have been researching artificial intelligence since the 1950s.
Humans have been thinking and solving problems for 200,000 years.
I've been thinking about AI a lot recently.

We form the present perfect progressive with *has/have* + been + *–ing form*.

LISTENING

LISTENING SKILL—Listen for attitude

If students listen for attitude, they should be able to identify it. They should listen for tone, speed, volume, and intonation. Have students work in pairs and say a phrase in four different ways: confidently, fearfully, doubtfully, and worriedly. Ask if they can discern each other's attitudes.

VOCABULARY

Tell students that word formation is a great way to expand their vocabulary. Simply using prefixes and suffixes to change the forms of words they know will give them access to many more related words, including verbs, nouns, and adjectives.

PRONUNCIATION

The middle sound in *says* and *said* are the same: /e/. However, they are different from the /ai/ sound in *say*. Students commonly make the mistake of rhyming *says* with *say*. Have students listen carefully to the pronunciation. Once they are able to hear it, they will be able to reproduce it.

B **Read the sentences in A again and choose the correct option.**

1 We use the present perfect progressive to talk about …
 a an activity that started in the past and is still in progress now.
 b an experience at a particular time in the past.
2 We also use the present perfect progressive to talk about …
 a the result of a recent continuing action.
 b an experience at any time in the past.
3 To talk about a finished action in the past that has results in the present, we use …
 a the present perfect.
 b the present perfect progressive.
4 When we mention the point the action began, we use for / since.
5 When we mention the duration of the action, we use for / since.

For more practice, go to page 145.

C **Complete the sentences.**

Expert Systems

An expert system is a computer program that uses AI to solve problems. People in various professions have **1** __been__ using expert systems **2** __for__ a number of years. An expert system uses a database of knowledge together with rules for using that knowledge. Scientists **3** __have__ been using them **4** __since__ 1965, when the first expert system was developed. Many health professionals, such as doctors and nurses, use expert systems. Health professionals **5** __have__ been recording our health data **6** __since__ the day we were born. Perhaps your doctor **7** __has__ been using one **8** __for__ some time to help decide what is wrong with his or her patients. Expert systems are just one of the ways in which AI **9** __has__ been helping people in the workplace. Where else do you think expert systems are used?

D **IN PAIRS Ask and answer the questions.**

1 How have people been using AI recently?
2 What have you been doing in another class / at work recently?
3 How long have you been living where you live now?

SPEAKING

A **Think about your chosen career and answer the questions.**

1 Are expert systems used in your chosen career now? In what ways?
2 Do you think expert systems will be used more in your chosen career in the future? In what ways?
3 Do you think your chosen career is in danger from expert systems or AI? Why or why not?

B **IN PAIRS Ask and answer the questions in A.**

A: I'm planning to be a lawyer in future. I think that lawyers have been using expert systems for years to research past cases.

B: Do you think that lawyers will use expert systems more in the future?

CONFIDENT COMMUNICATOR
START TALKING

To start your conversation, use the following phrases:
I'm planning to be a doctor.
I'm hoping to work as an engineer.
I want to work in accounting.

GRAMMAR Alternative Activity

Play *Keep the Conversation Going*. Using the questions in D, students ask as many follow-up questions as they can to keep talking for as long as possible. They can't repeat a question, and the conversation has to make sense. The pair that keeps talking the longest wins. This is a good way to improve active listening and speaking.

SPEAKING

Have students research how machine learning is used in their chosen field. Give them thinking and planning time to prepare what they are going to say about it. After the speaking activity, ask volunteers to report back to the class about the most interesting thing they learned from their partner.

LESSON 3 Get Creative

VOCABULARY phrasal verbs

A Match the phrasal verbs in bold (1–6) to the definitions (a–f).

1 How do you **come up** with all your amazing ideas? d
2 You should never **give up** if you want to achieve your dreams. a
3 Why don't you **look up** the word in an online dictionary? b
4 Don't **make up** excuses! I know you broke my phone! c
5 You can **rely on** this smartphone. It'll never break down or stop working. f
6 I might **take up** a new sport to try to get in shape. e

a stop making an effort
b find information in a book or online
c write or say something that isn't true
d think of, create
e start doing a regular activity, a hobby, etc.
f trust someone or something to do what they should do

MAKE IT YOURS
There are many different ways to describe how you have ideas. How could you describe the way you have ideas?

B IN PAIRS Choose the answers that are true for you. Talk to your partner about your choices.

1 I find it easy / hard to come up with ideas.
2 I often / sometimes / never give up if I find things hard.
3 I often / sometimes / never look things up to check information.
4 I often / sometimes / never make things up and I always / don't always tell the truth.
5 I often / sometimes / never rely on other people.
6 I often / sometimes / never take up a new activity.

LISTENING

A Discuss when it is important or useful to think creatively.

B 3.04 Listen to Part 1 of a talk and choose *True* or *False*.

GO TO page 140 for AUDIO SCRIPT.

1 Some people always find it easy to be creative. True / False
2 Some people will never be creative. True / False
3 Knowledge stops you from being creative. True / False
4 Feeling like a new learner helps creativity. True / False

Answers: 1 False, 2 False, 3 False, 4 True

C 3.05 LISTENING SKILL—Listen for main ideas Listen to Part 2 of the talk. Make notes about the three creative exercises the speaker describes.

GO TO page 140 for AUDIO SCRIPT.

Exercise 1: You try to think of lots of ways to use a common object.
Exercise 2: You write two lists of very different objects, and ways the objects are the same.
Exercise 3: You ask questions about what famous people would do with a problem.

GLOSSARY
fictional (adj): invented for a book, play, or movie

D THINKING SKILL—Apply Record as many different ways to use a paper clip as you can. You have three minutes.

Suggested answers: clean your nails / make holes in paper / make a necklace / play a guitar / scratch your name / hold clothes together / etc.

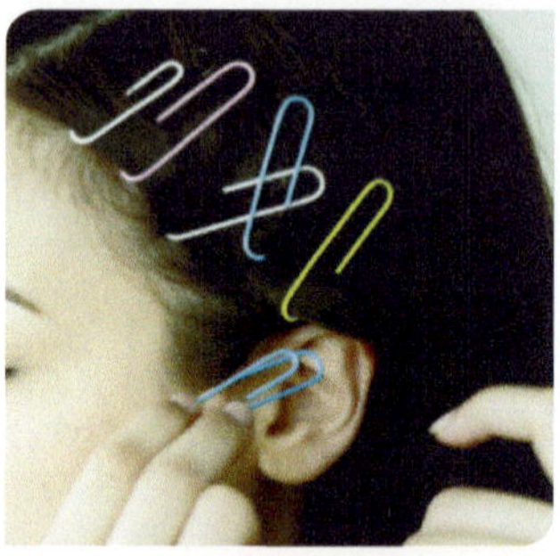

VOCABULARY

Phrasal verbs go a long way toward helping students sound like native speakers. Phrasal verbs consist of verbs and particles and can often have more than one meaning. They may be transitive (with a direct object) or intransitive (with no direct object). They may be separable or inseparable. If a phrasal verb is separable, you can separate the two words and put the direct object in the middle. If it is inseparable, you can't separate the words.

LISTENING

Have students preview the statements in B before they listen. This way they can use the strategies they have used in previous units, like using key words to predict meaning. Play the talk as many times as needed. The listening passages are for language input.

THINKING SKILL—Apply

Students have the chance to use the ideas they have learned about being creative right away. Once they have recorded as many ways to use a paper clip as they can, have them share their ideas in groups. Extend the activity by asking volunteers to share other creative activities they know about.

WRITING an informal email

A Read the email. Then answer the questions.

New Message

To: Cc Bcc

Subject:

a Hi Alex,

Sorry I didn't reply to you sooner. **b** I've been working a lot, but it isn't so bad now.

We had a talk at work about being productive, and **c** I thought you would be interested in it. The speaker said we can all be productive, and he gave us a few tips.

d First of all, it's a good idea to have a to-do list. It really helps you to keep going when you just feel like giving up! And it also helps you to focus on what you're doing.

e The second thing he mentioned is the 2-Minute Rule. When you can't start something, choose a task that will take two minutes. Everyone has two minutes to do something. And when you start, it's easy to continue!

f Hope you find this useful.

g Regards,

h Grace

Send

1 What reason does Grace give for not writing?
2 What did Grace do at work?
3 How does a to-do list help?
4 How does the 2-Minute Rule help?

B Match the descriptions (1–8) with the correct parts of the email in A (a–h).

1 the second main point __e__
2 a closing expression such as *Love*, *Best wishes*, etc. __g__
3 a piece of personal news __b__
4 a general description of the rest of the email __c__
5 the writer's first name __h__
6 a short wish or hope __f__
7 a greeting with *Hi* or *Dear* __a__
8 the first main point __d__

C Write an email to a friend. Describe the talk in LISTENING B. Use the email in A as a model.

GO TO page xiv for **WRITING** step-by-step instructions.

1 She has been busy at work.
2 She heard a talk about being productive.
3 It helps you to keep going when things are hard. It lets you focus on what you're doing.
4 It helps you start something and then it's easy to continue.

SPEAKING

A Write one more object in each list. Make sure that the objects you add are different from the ones already listed.

List A	List B
a pineapple	a guitar
a fork	a ladder
a cell phone	a clock
______	______

B IN PAIRS At random, choose one thing from List A and one thing from List B. How are those two things the same? Discuss and make a list of as many ways as you can.

A: We've got a cell phone and a guitar. They can both play music. Anything else?
B: You use both of them with your fingers!

CONFIDENT COMMUNICATOR
KEEP TALKING

To ask for further suggestions, use the following expressions:
What else do they have in common?
Are there any other ways that they're the same?
What other ideas do you have?

WRITING

Replay audio tracks 3.04 and 3.05 again. Have students take more notes and review what they wrote in LISTENING **B**. Advise them to read the email again before they start writing. With the model writing and the content from the talk, they have a starting point for their writing. Once they have written their email, allow students to read each other's work, and have them give each other kind and constructive criticism.

SPEAKING

Tell students to look around the room or think of things in their home or things they see in the street on the way to school to give them ideas for the objects on the list. Tell them to use the questions in the *Confident Communicator* box in their discussion. Finally, have students share their results with another pair and share creative connections with the class.

GO TO page xv

for LANGUAGE AND LIFE step-by-step instructions.

Language and Life

Design Thinking – An App

A 3.06 Read the article. Then answer the questions.

The Trouble With Social Media

Social media companies have been feeling worried recently. People have realized that there are a few problems connected to social media. One is the problem of confirmation bias. Our online friends make comments and share posts that we already agree with. We accept them as true and we never see any evidence of other opinions. This can mean that we share and like false stories more easily because they match what we already believe.

There are other problems, too. Some people spend too much time on social media. They update their status many times a day and their phones show notifications of other people's posts. This often means they waste time, or they ignore their real-life family and friends. They might also become anxious about how many shares or likes their posts get. Other people experience cyberbullying, where people make up comments about them. That can have an effect on people's lives and their health.

Another issue is our digital footprint. Every time we post, share, or comment, we leave a digital record. It often follows us for a very long time. When you apply for a job or when you meet someone new, they might check your social media. What will they see? Are you sure that you want them to see everything you've posted?

Finally, people share a lot of information on social media. They share their location, when they're on vacation, and what they do every day. That can leave the person vulnerable to crime or other problems.

Many people agree that we need to find ways to help people be safer on social media and to think more about the information they see and share.

1 What five problems with social media are mentioned? ______

1 problems created by confirmation bias / people spending a lot of time on social media / anxiety caused by reaction to posts / cyberbullying / sharing too much information

2 Have you or anyone you know ever had those problems with social media? Students' own answers

B You work for a company. Read the email from your manager. What does she want you to do?

She wants you to come up with ideas for an app to deal with problems created by social media.

New Message

Subject: app idea

Hi all,

We see a gap in the market for an app to help people deal with problems created by social media. It might fact-check stories in the media. Or it might help delete your social footprint. It could be anything, really. See if you can come up with a few ideas and we'll meet to discuss them.

Regards,

Rose

Send

OBJECTIVE

The prevalent use of social media has given rise to problems of confirmation bias, addiction to gadgets, self-image issues, safety, and privacy. The objective is that students learn how to understand the problems and brainstorm solutions. They will question and test their solutions to these problems. Then, they will see if their solutions stand up to scrutiny.

PROCESS OPTIONAL 3.06

Students read about troubles associated with social media. They identify problems and share personal anecdotes. Then, they read an email that calls for ideas for an app to address one of the problems. Alone, students think of apps. Then, they form groups and read about the starbursting technique. They choose one app idea and apply the starbursting technique to it. They use the *Wh–* question prompts to generate open questions for the app and discuss possible answers. Then, they report to the class about their app, the questions, and possible solutions. Finally, they reflect on using the starbursting technique and discuss other situations where it might be useful.

C **On your own, think of an app to suggest to your manager. Make a short note of what your app does.**

an app that immediately checks the facts in any story you see online

My suggested app: ______________________________

D **IN GROUPS** **You are going to use a method called starbursting. Read the description. Have you used starbursting or a similar technique before?**

Starbursting is a way of brainstorming good questions to ask about a suggestion. In the middle of a star, you write the suggestion. On the points of the star are the words *What, Who, Where, When, How,* and *Why*. You use these to come up with questions to ask about the suggestion. For example, you might ask: "Who will use this app?" By asking and answering the questions, you provide more detail on the suggestion and highlight key considerations.

E **IN GROUPS** **Write your app from C in the middle of the star. Use the starbursting method to write questions to ask about the app. Then ask and answer the questions for each person's app.**

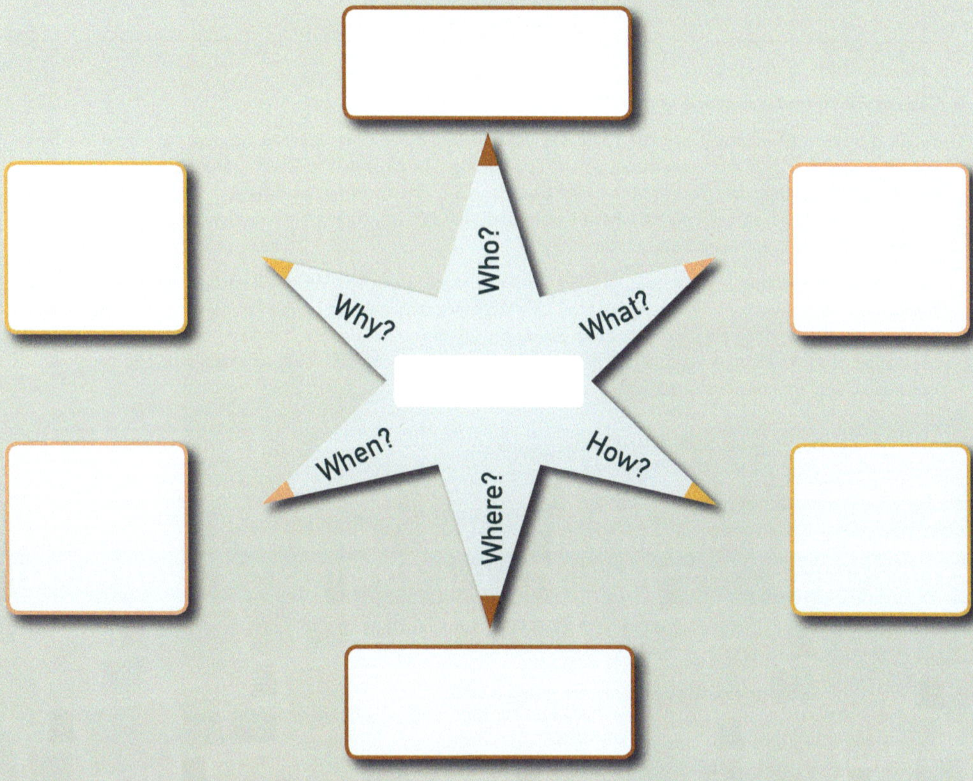

F **Compare the different apps from each group and choose which you like the best. Tell the class about the apps and about the answers to the questions in E.**

G **Discuss the questions.**

1. How useful did you find the starbursting method?
2. What key issues did the process highlight?
3. In what other situations do you think starbursting would help?

MAKE IT DIGITAL

Research the most popular apps in your country on different online app sites. Why do you think they are popular?

CLASSROOM MANAGEMENT

Think about the physical arrangement of groups in your classroom. Can everyone see each other? Can everyone in the group reach any charts or diagrams they are working on? Is there enough space for students to sit around a table or in a circle?

CULTURE NOTE

Since 2010, some people believed one should have a registration or license to use the internet just like we do for a car so that we can be identified online. The purpose of this legislation would be to make the perpetrators of cybercrime and cyberbullying identifiable.

Have students research global cybersecurity to find out which countries have the best security. Ask them to look into what actions countries are taking to protect themselves against cyberattacks. Ask students if they have experienced a hack, and discuss what they have done to protect themselves.

GO TO page xvii
for UNIT REVIEW step-by-step instructions.

UNIT 3

VOCABULARY review

SCORE: / 10

A Complete the sentences.

1 I'll create a fantastic design for your website. You can rely ___on___ me!
2 I wonder how great writers make ___up___ such wonderful stories.
3 I find it hard to concentrate ___on___ my work with all this noise!
4 When did you take ___up___ running in your spare time?
5 You'll remember more if you pay attention ___to___ what the speaker is saying.

B Complete the sentences using forms of the words in parentheses.

1 After brainstorming ideas, we finally found a ___solution___ (solve) to the problem.
2 Many people have lost their jobs recently and ___unemployment___ (employ) is a big problem.
3 It takes a lot of ___creativity___ (create) to produce beautiful works of art.
4 Do you think AI will be ___dangerous___ (danger) in the future?
5 Computers are becoming more and more ___powerful___ (power) every year.

GRAMMAR review

SCORE: / 10

A Choose the correct words and phrases.

People **1** were / have been using AI in different ways for some time now. Recently, however, some people have been **2** raised / raising questions about where it's all going. The people who **3** will / have been asking these questions include important figures such as Bill Gates and Elon Musk. When we **4** have / will have machines that can think for themselves, will they do what we want them to? Will intelligent machines learn right from wrong before we **5** learn / will learn how to control them?

Machines **6** have getting / have been getting more and more intelligent. What will happen when our machines **7** become / will become more intelligent than us? And that point may not be too far in the future. Researchers **8** has made / have been making huge progress recently in developing AI that can learn and can design the next generation of AI. As soon as a machine **9** realizes / will realize we can turn it off, what will it do? Perhaps we won't know until that day finally **10** comes / will come.

16–20 correct: You can use phrasal verbs and form word derivatives. You can use future time clauses and the present perfect progressive.
0–15 correct: Look again at the Vocabulary and Grammar sections in the unit.

TOTAL SCORE: / 20

WHAT DO YOU KNOW NOW? Look back at page 27 and add the words you know now to the box.

GO TO page xviii
for STUDY SKILLS step-by-step instructions.

STUDY SKILLS — MAKING A PRESENTATION OR GIVING A TALK

Take the quiz about making a presentation or giving a talk. Go to **Study Skills** on page 129 to find the answers. Then learn more about the topic.

1 Why should you arrive early when you are giving a talk?
a to make last-minute changes to your talk **b** to have time for tea or coffee **c** to meet the audience members as they arrive

2 When you are giving a talk, where should you look?
a at one person in the audience **b** into the eyes of a few different people **c** at your notes

3 It's best if your slides don't contain a lot of text.
a True **b** False

4 What should you wear when you are giving a talk?
a professional-looking clothing that you have worn before **b** comfortable old clothing that you would wear to relax in **c** fashionable new clothing that you would wear to a special event

36 Unit 3 Think About It

CLASSROOM MANAGEMENT

For an added challenge, give students a time limit to complete the review activities. Fifteen minutes for both the vocabulary and grammar exercises ought to be challenging. Before checking the answers, ask students to circle the items they have doubts about.

GRAMMAR

Have students review the grammar boxes from lessons 1 to 3. Tell them to put one question mark next to those they still have some questions about and two question marks next to the grammar explanations they have no idea about. In pairs, have students help each other with their doubts. Answer questions if needed.

FURTHER DISCUSSION

Write the following questions on the board. Then have students form groups of three and ask each other:

- Do you think you have confirmation bias sometimes?
- What machines do you depend on?
- Can you imagine using more machines in the future?
- What do you think creativity is?
- How have you been creative recently?

UNIT 4

Beyond Words

GO TO page vi
for UNIT OPENER step-by-step instructions.

WHAT DO YOU ALREADY KNOW?

1 Think about words you know about communication. Write the words.

2 IN PAIRS Share and compare your ideas. Add more words to your lists.

Personal communication

Digital communication

STUDENTS MAY ALREADY KNOW:

- **Personal communication:** talk, speak, listen, gesture, face-to-face, facial expression, voice, conversation, message, understand, misunderstand, letter, send a signal, send flowers.
- **Digital communication:** phone, computer, tablet, app, text message, voice call, video conference, cell phone, chat, smartphone, instant message.

DISCUSS & SHARE

VIDEO

3 IN GROUPS Watch the video and answer the question.
SYM Would you rather call someone or text them?

GO TO page xx
for VIDEOS IN SYM step-by-step instructions.

In this unit, you will …

- present a subject you know, ask questions and assess someone's body language, and decide on the best means of communication for different situations.
- use thinking skills: evaluate, apply, and predict.
- read about how to be a good communicator.
- learn strategies to use eye contact, use language to ask for more information, and to make your meaning clearer.
- use reasoning skills to discuss the pros and cons of a company proposal.
- follow a PR professional to learn about this job and the skills needed for this industry.

Unit 4 Beyond Words 37

WHAT DO YOU ALREADY KNOW?

If students are struggling to understand what to do, you can ask them some questions to prompt their thinking:

- Who do you communicate with the most?
- How do you communicate?
- Do you like talking to people?
- Do you prefer text messaging or a phone call?
- Is all communication done with words?

VIDEO

Before viewing, ask:

What is an advantage of texting?
texting is silent, you don't bother other people
What is an advantage of phone calls?
they are more personal, it is faster

After viewing, put the continuum on the board.

phone call —— text

Have students mark the continuum and explain their preferences.

DISCUSS & SHARE

Have students think about whether they call people or text them. With texting, you can set up group chats and everyone gets the message at the same time, but you may have to wait for replies. Calling is immediate—you can get a reply right away if someone answers. Students should place themselves on a continuum of opinion. They should choose one viewpoint and defend it with examples.

LESSON 1 Good Communicators

GO TO page x
for **READING** step-by-step instructions.

READING

A Do you think you are a good communicator? Why or why not?

B 4.01 **READING SKILL—Read for gist** Read the article quickly. Then choose the best summary.

Being a Good Communicator

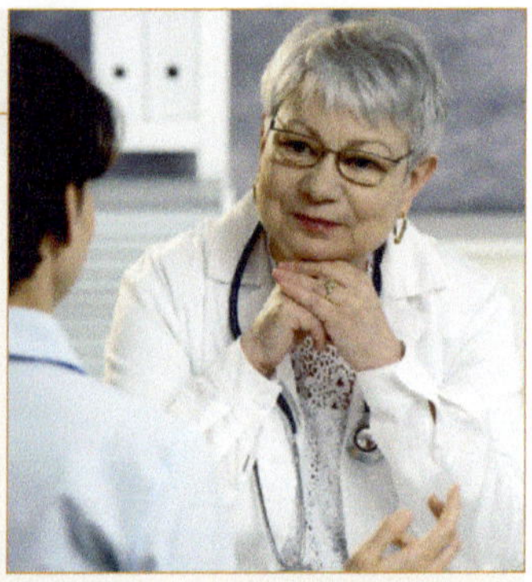

Many of us find it hard to communicate. You may know what you want to say but not know how. What makes a good communicator? You might think a good communicator is someone who can speak well and explain his or her ideas. You might think a good communicator can **persuade** people to do what he or she wants. However, there's a lot more to communication than expressing yourself well. Communication is an important skill in our personal, academic, and professional lives. And it's easy to learn a few simple communication techniques.

The first is active listening. Good communicators listen carefully to understand the other person's thoughts. They repeat ideas back to the other person to show they understand. They also encourage the person to say more by asking relevant questions. For example, a good communicator might say: "I hear you saying that you're unhappy with your major. How, exactly?"

Good communicators are **honest**. In an argument with a friend, you don't help communication when you pretend that everything is fine. Good communicators talk honestly about how they feel.

Finally, good communicators make a personal **connection** with people. They try to find something they **have in common** with the person they are speaking to. That helps them to understand what the other person wants from a situation. Or they might try to put themselves in the other person's position and ask: "If I were him or her, what would I want to hear?"

Using these techniques will help to improve your relationships with other people at home, at school, and at work.

1 Communication is a way of getting other people to agree with you. You do this by asking them questions and talking about your feelings.

2 You can become a better communicator by listening carefully, telling the truth, and building relationships with people.

C Read the article in B again and choose the correct options.

1 What point is the writer making in the first paragraph?
  a It isn't right to try to change other people's opinions.
  b Communication isn't just about explaining things well.

2 According to the writer, active listening is a way of …
  a understanding someone's opinion.
  b getting people to understand you.

3 According to the writer, good communicators …
  a pretend they feel the same way as the other person.
  b tell the truth about their emotions.

4 It can help you understand what people want when you …
  a look for things that are true for both of you.
  b help them understand a situation correctly.

the ability to express complicated ideas simply / being clear / knowing when to speak / being confident

D **THINKING SKILL—Evaluate** Decide what other things make someone a good communicator.

GO TO page vii
for **VOCABULARY** step-by-step instructions.

VOCABULARY

A Complete the sentences using the words in bold in READING B.

1 You need to explain your ideas clearly to __persuade__ other people to do what you want.
2 I find it easy to communicate with you because we __have__ a lot __in common__.
3 I have a very strong __connection__ with my twin brother and I know what he's thinking.
4 Be __honest__. You don't like my new hairstyle, do you?

READING OPTIONAL 4.01

Some famously good communicators include John F. Kennedy, Martin Luther King Jr., Oprah Winfrey, and Emma Watson. During the opening discussion, ask for some anecdotes. What makes someone a bad communicator? Can you share an example of poor communication?

THINKING SKILL—Evaluate

Things that make someone a good communicator are: connection, being passionate and compassionate, knowing your audience, speaking clearly, loudly, and with good rhythm and intonation, speaking at the right pitch and pace, knowing your subject, being prepared, making eye contact, and rehearsing.

VOCABULARY

Have students expand their vocabulary by looking up synonyms and antonyms of the vocabulary words (e.g., *persuade: encourage, dissuade; honest: reliable, dishonest; connection: association, disconnection*). You may want to encourage students to look for more word formations (e.g., *persuade–persuasion, honest–honesty, connection–connect*).

GRAMMAR infinitives with *to*

A Match the sentences (1–4) to the correct explanations (a–d).

1. Many of us find it hard to communicate. d
2. You may know what you want to say but not know how. c
3. You might think a good communicator can persuade people to do what he or she wants. b
4. ... listen carefully to understand the other person's thoughts. a

We use the infinitive with *to* ...

- **a** to express a purpose
- **b** after some verbs (*advise, tell, warn, persuade*, etc.) + direct object
- **c** after some verbs (*agree, like, prefer, want*, etc.)
- **d** after some adjectives (*easy, happy, hard, ready*, etc.)

For more practice, go to page 146.

B Circle one more example of each use in READING B.

1. to express a purpose
2. after a verb + direct object
3. after a verb
4. after an adjective

C Complete the sentences with the correct forms of the words from the box.

agree	appear	communicate	learn
make	see	understand	

Good Public Speakers

All public speakers try **1** to communicate their message to their audience. Good ones plan their presentation carefully **2** to make sure their message is clear. They know that it's hard **3** to understand a complicated speech, so they make it as simple as they can. Then, they start **4** to learn the material. Many practice in front of a mirror **5** to see how confident they appear. Appearing confident is very important in getting your audience **6** to agree with your ideas. Everyone gets nervous, but successful speakers try not **7** to appear nervous to the audience.

D IN PAIRS Have you ever given a presentation?

MAKE IT DIGITAL

People in many careers need to give presentations. Watch expert presenters online and learn from them. Look for opportunities to give short presentations in class.

SPEAKING

A Think of a subject you know something about. It could be an academic subject, a famous person, a kind of music, etc. Make notes for a short presentation to a small group.

Subject: ______

Main points: ______

B IN GROUPS Take turns giving a short presentation (2–3 minutes) on your chosen subject. Use the Confident Communicator box to help you.

CONFIDENT COMMUNICATOR — KEEP TALKING

To be a good communicator, make eye contact with the person or people you are talking to. When you are talking to a group of people, try to make eye contact with each of them equally.

GO TO page viii for **GRAMMAR** step-by-step instructions.

1 Good communicators repeat ideas back to the other person to show they understand. **2** They also encourage the person to say more by asking relevant questions. **3** They try to find something they have in common with the person they are speaking to. / Using these techniques will help to improve your relationships with other people at home, school, and work. **4** And it's easy to learn a few simple communication techniques.

GO TO page xii for **SPEAKING** step-by-step instructions.

GRAMMAR

Some more commonly used adjective + infinitive combinations are: *difficult, impossible, important, possible, exciting, likely, a good idea*, and *a pleasure*. For example, *His name is difficult to remember. It's important to be polite. It's exciting to travel. It's a good idea to prepare your presentation well. It's a pleasure to meet you.*

MAKE IT DIGITAL

Some good presenters your students may want to watch are Sir Ken Robinson, Amy Cuddy, Simon Sinek, Brené Brown, and Julian Treasure. Have students think about giving a presentation in their future chosen field. What might they have to give a presentation about?

SPEAKING

A simple outline for a presentation is:

1. Say what you are going to talk about: *Today, I'd like to talk about ...*
2. Talk about it: *First, ...; Then, ...; Next, ...*
3. Review what you talked about: *I hope you learned something interesting about ...*

LESSON 2 What Do You Really Mean?

VOCABULARY ways to communicate

A Complete the sentences with words from the box.

distance	position	speed	touch
tone	space	volume	

1 Your ___tone___ of voice is the way you say something and it shows how you feel.
2 Some people talk at a fast ___speed___, which can be hard to understand.
3 How much personal ___space___ do you need when you are talking to someone?
4 The ___volume___ of your voice is how loud or quiet it is.
5 The ___distance___ from New York to London is 5,567 kilometers.
6 The ___position___ of your arms can mean you are friendly or it can mean you feel uncomfortable.
7 In some countries, ___touch___ is a part of communication and people often put their hands on each other's arms.

B IN PAIRS Think about your country compared to other countries. Choose and then talk about your choices with a partner.

	Strongly agree	Agree	Neither agree nor disagree	Disagree	Strongly disagree
1 People talk at high speed and high volume.	☐	☐	☐	☐	☐
2 People need a lot of personal space.	☐	☐	☐	☐	☐
3 Touch is a part of communication.	☐	☐	☐	☐	☐

GO TO page xi for **LISTENING** step-by-step instructions.

GO TO page 140 for **AUDIO SCRIPT**.

LISTENING

A Look at the picture. What do you think they are talking about? What does their body language tell you?

B 4.02 LISTENING SKILL—Listen for specific information Listen to Part 1 of an interview and label the diagram and key.

Three Parts of Communication

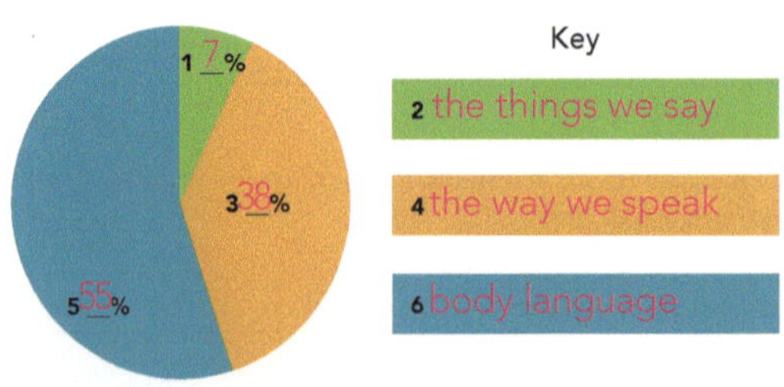

GO TO page 141 for **AUDIO SCRIPT**.

C 4.03 Read the sentences and predict what the missing words or short phrases could be. Then listen to Part 2 and complete the sentences.

1 It's easy to misunderstand when communicating ___by email or text message___ because there's no tone of voice.
2 People in Romania want almost twice as much personal space as people in ___Argentina___.
3 We often have our arms ___open___ when we are interested in another person's opinion.
4 You need to be careful when someone's body language means ___the opposite___ of their words.

GLOSSARY
verbal (adj): connected to words

VOCABULARY

Encourage students to complete the sentences with their best guesses before looking in a dictionary. Often, the meaning of a word can be worked out from the context. Before checking answers, have students compare with a partner.

LISTENING Extra Practice

Extend LISTENING **A** by asking students to be aware of body language and personal space when they are in the street and report back to the class. Have them be observers of body language. They should see how many messages they can figure out simply by watching people from a distance.

THINKING SKILL—Apply

Ask students to guess the personal space for the activity. Then have them stand up and test it out for real. Finally, ask them to measure how far the distances really were and if their guesses were accurate.

D **THINKING SKILL—Apply** How close you would stand to (a) a stranger, (b) someone you know, and (c) a close friend? Record your answer on the diagram and compare with a partner.

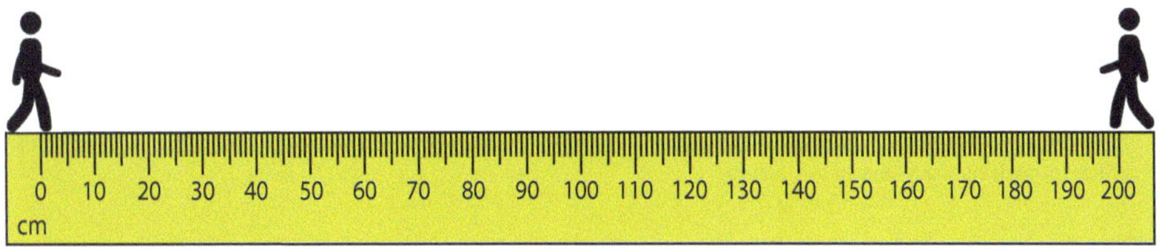

GRAMMAR separable and non-separable phrasal verbs

A Check (✓) the correct sentences.

1
- [✓] I looked up "body language" online.
- [✓] I looked "body language" up online.
- [✓] I looked it up online.
- [ ] I looked up it online.

2
- [✓] You can **rely** on Ruby to give a good talk.
- [ ] You can **rely** Ruby on to give a good talk.
- [✓] You can **rely** on her to give a good talk.
- [ ] You can **rely** her on to give a good talk.

B Choose the correct options.

With separable phrasal verbs, you **1** can / can't put a noun between the verb and the particle. With non-separable phrasal verbs, you **2** can / can't. With separable phrasal verbs, we **3** always / never separate the verb and the particle when the object is a pronoun (*you, it, them*, etc.). Phrasal verbs with a particle plus a preposition (e.g., *come up with*) are **4** always / never separable.

For more practice, go to page 147.

C Choose the correct options. Both may be correct.

1. Her body language told me she was making the story up / making up the story.
2. Her body language told me she was making it up / making up it.
3. I told Matt you would call back him / call him back.
4. You should take up psychology / take psychology up to learn more about body language.
5. I ran into Alice / ran Alice into outside class yesterday and we had a good chat.

D **IN PAIRS** Do you know when someone is making a story up? Discuss.

SPEAKING

A Write three statements about yourself. Two of the statements should be true and one should be false. Don't tell anyone which one is false.

I once went to New York. I'm thinking of taking the violin up. I have a cat named Dog.

B **IN PAIRS** Follow the instructions. Use the Confident Communicator box to help you.

Find someone in class who doesn't know you very well. Ask each other questions about your statements. As your partner talks, watch his or her body language carefully. Can you tell which statement is false?

CONFIDENT COMMUNICATOR
KEEP TALKING

To ask someone to provide more information, use the following phrases:
Tell me more about taking up the violin.
What happened when you went to New York?
What else can you tell me about your cat?

GRAMMAR

Some common separable phrasal verbs are *figure it out, pick (someone) up, spell it out, write it down, think it over*, and *figure it out*. Tell students to look them up in a dictionary. Remind students that phrasal verbs often have more than one meaning. The best way to learn them is to commit them to memory as chunks. Once they are aware of phrasal verbs, they will hear them everywhere.

SPEAKING

Remind students to ask each other a lot of questions before guessing the false statement.

Alternative Activity

Give students new words that they don't know the meaning of. Each student should choose a word and look up its meaning. They should then invent two other meanings. In groups, each person says their word and three meanings. Group members have to guess the correct meaning.

LESSON 3 From Words to Pictures

LISTENING

GO TO page 141 for AUDIO SCRIPT.

A Discuss how communication has changed in your lifetime.

B 4.04 **LISTENING SKILL—Listen for the order of events** Listen to a lecture. Write an event which took place in each of the years listed below.

1971	1973	1992	1999	2007	2009	2011
email was invented	the first cell phone appeared	the first text or SMS message	emojis were invented	the first mass-marketed smartphone/ iPhone	WhatsApp appeared	Snapchat appeared

C 4.04 Listen again and answer the questions.

1 How many emails are sent each day? over 280 billion
2 What percentage of people have a cell phone? 67%
3 How many emojis are there today? over 2,800
4 How many apps are there for the iPhone? over 2 million
5 How many messages are sent through WhatsApp each day? 55 billion
6 How many people use Snapchat? 188 million

D **THINKING SKILL—Predict** Calculate how many messages of different kinds (emails, text messages, etc.) you send each year. Compare with a partner.

PRONUNCIATION electronic communication

GO TO page ix for PRONUNCIATION step-by-step instructions.

A 4.05 How do you say each of the phrases in italics? Discuss with a partner. Then listen and check.

Go to www.macmillan.com
My email is lisa_jackson3@emailtoday.org
Under the picture, it says #selfie and #mybestlook
My email is carrie-smith@fly.org

MAKE IT YOURS

Think about other types of electronic communication you use. How do you say the phrases associated with those types of communication?

B Practice saying the sentences in A.

VOCABULARY emojis

A Write a word or phrase from the box under each emoji.

clap point punch shake hands smile thumbs up wave

 1 wave
 2 shake hands
 3 thumbs up
 4 clap
 5 point
 6 punch
 7 smile

B **IN PAIRS** Do you use emojis? Why or why not? Discuss.

LISTENING

Ask students how communication has changed. Have them think about how gadgets were used when they were children. What is their first memory of using the phone or sending a text? Ask them to discuss how they communicate now and how communication has changed.

THINKING SKILL—Predict

In order to predict the number of messages sent in a year, have students calculate approximately how many they send in a day and multiply that by 365. Remind students that on special occasions, people send more messages. Find out who in the class sends the most messages a year.

VOCABULARY

Discuss the most common emojis that students are using at the moment: *Which emojis are in fashion? Which have gone out of fashion? What do the ones you use say about you?*

Extra Practice

Have students create messages for each other using only emojis and symbols. Tell them to be as creative as they can.

WRITING text message and email

A Read the text message. Match each informal phrase (1–8) with a more formal phrase (a–h).

[1] Hi Pedro. [2] Come to my party next Friday. [3] It's at the Sunrise Café, 7pm. [4] It's for my 21st birthday. [5] Hope you can be there. [6] Don't worry about a present. [7] Can you come? [8] ♥ Alexa

1 g	5 f		
2 c	6 h		
3 a	7 b		
4 d	8 e		

a The party is taking place at the Sunrise Café at 7 p.m.
b Please let me know if you are able to attend.
c I would like to invite you to my party next Friday.
d The event is to celebrate my 21st birthday.
e Best wishes,
f I hope you will be able to come.
g Dear Pedro,
h Please don't feel you need to bring a gift.

B Read the email and underline two sentences that are informal. Rewrite the sentences more formally.

New Message

Dear Amelie,

Come to my house-warming party. I have just moved into a new apartment and I thought it would be a good chance to get to know everyone in the office. The party is taking place on the 15th after work. I hope you will be able to come. Don't bring any gifts.

Please let me know if you are able to come so that I know how many people to expect.

Sincerely,
Millie

Send

1 ______
2 ______

Suggested answers:
1 I'd like to invite you to my house-warming party. / I'm writing to invite you to my house-warming party.
2 Please don't feel you have to bring any gifts. / There's no need to bring any gifts.

C Read the information. Then write an email to a colleague you don't know very well inviting him or her to the event.

Event: a party to celebrate my birthday
Time and place: my home, 4th, 8:30 p.m.
Comments: no gifts, I need to know who's coming

D Swap emails with a partner. Check for the correct spelling and punctuation and the right level of formality.

GO TO page xiv for WRITING step-by-step instructions.

SPEAKING

A Which is the best way to communicate in each situation?

	Text message	Email	Phone call
1 telling a friend some bad news	☐	☐	☐
2 congratulating a friend on success	☐	☐	☐
3 wishing your grandparents a happy anniversary	☐	☐	☐

B IN PAIRS Why would you use different means of communication in different situations? Discuss.

CONFIDENT COMMUNICATOR — KEEP TALKING

To make your meaning clearer, use the following phrases:
I ***mean****, you can't give someone bad news in a text message.*
In other words*, you need to speak to someone in person when it's serious.*

Unit 4 Beyond Words 43

WRITING

These activities compare formal and informal language. Draw students' attention to the examples, and show them that generally the more polite the language, the longer the expression.

When checking each other's work, encourage students to use a technique where they say something positive about what they read before they suggest corrections. Sharing your work with others can be intimidating, so we want to create a culture of mutual support and respect.

SPEAKING Extra Practice

Extend the activity by asking students to discuss whether they have been in any of the example situations. For example, *Has anyone ever broken up with you via text message? How do you like to be congratulated on your success? Do you communicate with your grandparents via text message?*

Have students role-play a situation of their choice using a means of communication they think will be dramatic in that situation.

GO TO page xv

for **LANGUAGE AND LIFE** step-by-step instructions.

Language and Life

Reason Effectively – An International Company

A 4.06 **Read the article. Then answer the questions.**

Communication Problems

Businesses and other organizations succeed when the people communicate well with each other. There needs to be a free flow of information and instructions. Unfortunately, communication often goes wrong.

One reason for communication problems is that in large, multinational corporations, people often come from different cultures and speak different languages. They may use a common language to communicate, often English, but that doesn't remove the possibility of misunderstandings. People from some cultures, such as the US and Western Europe, may think it's important to clearly express their ideas and say how they feel. They might not see a problem in correcting a colleague or criticizing an idea. However, this can make people from some *other* cultures feel very uncomfortable. Similar problems can happen when people are from the same culture but have different life experiences.

Another reason for problems is communication technology. Many of us work from home at least some of the time these days. We communicate with colleagues through software such as Skype or Google Hangouts, and it doesn't always work perfectly. When we don't completely understand something and we are not able to check our understanding, it can lead to problems.

You might be surprised to hear that another possible reason for communication problems is friendships at work. Normally, we think of friends as people we communicate well with. However, mixing personal and professional communication isn't a good idea. It makes some people feel uncomfortable and it can start arguments.

Many organizations work hard to improve communication, for example, organizing diversity training sessions for employees. Another idea is a no-email day. One day a week, no one sends emails. Instead, they speak to people on the phone or meet in person. Small changes like that can make a big difference.

1 Why might there be misunderstandings in a multinational corporation?
People from different cultures might have different ways of expressing ideas or feelings.

2 Why can there be misunderstandings between people from the same culture?
They might have different life experiences.

3 How can communication technology cause communication problems?

4 Why does the writer say "You might be surprised"?

5 What happens on a no-email day?
People don't send emails. Instead, they make phone calls or meet in person.

6 What difference do you think a no-email day has on the people in a company?

44 Unit 4 Beyond Words

3 It doesn't always work perfectly, if you misunderstand something, you don't have the chance to check your understanding.

4 We think friendship means good communication, but it can cause communication problems at work.

OBJECTIVE

The objective of this lesson is to have students consider breakdowns in cross-cultural communication at work and discuss solutions. They suggest solutions to problems of miscommunication and debate the pros and cons of those suggested solutions. This activity replicates a real-life situation in which advantages and disadvantages are considered and suggestions are questioned and defended.

PROCESS OPTIONAL 4.06

Students first read an article about communication problems in business and other organizations. Then, they answer a series of questions about misunderstandings and what might cause problems. Next, students are presented with a scenario in which a communication problem needs to be solved. Students are given some suggested solutions and asked to debate the advantages and disadvantages of those solutions. They must narrow down the suggested solutions to two or three based on their group discussion. Students will present their solutions and the pros and cons of each one. Finally, students will discuss how successfully they communicated their explanations.

B **Read and evaluate the information. Think about what you need to do. What are your next steps?**

Students' own answers

You work for a large corporation with offices in different countries. Managers have noticed some communication problems recently. They feel that people from different countries seem to misunderstand each other, although they all speak English well. They are looking for ideas to improve everyone's communication skills and they have asked you and your team for suggestions.

C **IN GROUPS** **Analyze each of the ideas and identify the pros and cons. Add more ideas of your own. Use the phrases to discuss your thoughts.**

One good thing about diversity training is ...

Overseas visits are useful because ...

One problem with language training is ....

1. Diversity training

Advantages: ______________________

Disadvantages: ______________________

2. Overseas visits

Advantages: ______________________

Disadvantages: ______________________

3. Language training

Advantages: ______________________

Disadvantages: ______________________

4. Other idea

____

____

D **Decide which ideas you are going to suggest. Choose one or two.**

E **Tell the class which ideas you have chosen. Explain how you made your choice.**

F **Discuss the questions.**

1. What reasoning skills did you use to form an opinion and select an idea?
2. In what other situations do you think this process would be useful?

MAKE IT DIGITAL

Go to your college or company's website. Do they have a diversity and inclusion policy? Do they offer any training for this?

CLASSROOM MANAGEMENT

Have students try a technique called *devil's advocate* during their discussions. For each idea that someone comes up with, someone in each group must make a contradictory statement. This is a strategy for looking at all sides of a problem without anyone getting upset.

CULTURE NOTE

Ask students to share experiences they have had in cross-cultural situations, especially misunderstandings. They may have personal anecdotes or secondhand stories. Have they seen a foreign person making etiquette mistakes in their country?

GO TO page xvii
for **UNIT REVIEW** step-by-step instructions.

1 It is hard to persuade people to do what you want them to do.
2 It's important to try to relax if you want your audience to agree with you.
3 I always advise public speakers not to speak too fast.
4 Speak to people in person to avoid communication problems and to see their body language.
5 I prefer to speak to small groups because it's possible to see if they're listening.

UNIT 4

VOCABULARY review

SCORE: / 10

A Complete the sentences with words from the box.

common	express	shake	thumbs	volume
connection	persuade	smile	tone	wave

All human cultures have at least two things in **1** common. First of all, we all use language to **2** express ourselves. Exactly how we speak may change. We may speak at a higher **3** volume when we are excited or use a different **4** tone of voice when we are angry. We may speak in a certain way when we want to **5** persuade somebody to do something. But all of us use words to try to make a **6** connection to other people every day. Second, we all communicate non-verbally through gestures. Interestingly, a **7** thumbs up gesture generally means something good in Western countries, but it isn't a polite gesture in West Africa. People in many countries **8** shake hands when they meet, but the strength used might be different. And in some countries people just **9** wave at each other to say hello. There are even differences in how often people **10** smile to show they are happy!

GRAMMAR review

SCORE: / 10

A Use the prompts to write sentences in your notebook.

1 It is hard / persuade people / do / what you want them / do.
2 It's important / try / relax / if you want your audience / agree with you.
3 I always advise public speakers / not speak too fast.
4 Speak to people in person / avoid communication problems and / see their body language.
5 I prefer / speak to small groups because it's possible / see if they're listening.

B Check (✓) the correct responses. Rewrite the incorrect responses in your notebook.

1 "When did you take up karate?" ☑ "I took it up about a year ago."
2 "How did you come up with the idea for your app?" ☐ "I came it up with when I was at work."
3 "Is your story based on real life?" ☐ "No. I just made up it."
4 "Do you use your smartphone every day?" ☑ "Oh, yes! I rely it on for everything!"
5 "What does *irrelevant* mean?" ☐ "Why don't you look up it in the dictionary?"

16–20 correct: You can talk about communication and gestures. You can use infinitives with *to* and separable and non-separable phrasal verbs.
0–15 correct: Look again at the Vocabulary and Grammar sections in the unit.

TOTAL SCORE: / 20

WHAT DO YOU KNOW NOW? Look back at page 37 and add the words you know now to the boxes.

GO TO page xix
for **FOLLOW A PRO** step-by-step instructions.

2 I came up with it when I was at work.
3 No, I just made it up.
5 Why don't you look it up in the dictionary?

FOLLOW A PRO COMMUNICATION

Take the quiz about communication. Go to Follow A Pro on page 130 to find the answers. Then learn more about working in communication.

1 Where do companies spend the most money on advertising?
a television b newspapers c the internet

2 What percentage of the world's population can access the internet?
a 30%–35% b 55%–60% c 85%–90%

3 When was writing invented?
a 3,000 BCE b 500 BCE c 500 CE

4 When was the first radio program broadcast?
a 1906 b 1922 c 1935

CLASSROOM MANAGEMENT

Have students work individually to complete the vocabulary and grammar reviews. Then, before checking answers, ask them to work in pairs to check each other's work. If they have a different answer for something, they should discuss it.

ALTERNATIVE ACTIVITY

In groups, have students invent the name of a country and 10 rules of etiquette. They should concentrate on rules for communication, giving presentations, body language, and use of gadgets. Have them share their rules with another group, which should give them positive feedback but suggest they change one.

FURTHER DISCUSSION

Write the following questions on the board. Then have students form groups of three and ask each other:

- When was the last time you gave a presentation?
- Who is your favorite public speaker?
- What, for you, would be the ideal gadget for communication?
- Have you ever had to tell someone bad news?

GO TO page vi
for UNIT OPENER step-by-step instructions.

UNIT 5 One Planet

WHAT DO YOU ALREADY KNOW?

1 Think about the words you know for weather. Write the words.

2 IN PAIRS Share and compare your ideas. Add more words to your lists.

Weather

Severe weather

STUDENTS MAY ALREADY KNOW:

- **Weather:** rain, wind, storm, snow, sunny, windy, rainy, hot, cold, temperature, Celsius, Fahrenheit.
- **Severe weather:** hurricane, tornado, twister, cyclone, named storm, typhoon.

VIDEO

DISCUSS & SHARE

3 IN GROUPS Watch the video and answer the question.

SYM Do you think the changes in severe weather are natural or caused by people?

GO TO page xx
for VIDEOS IN SYM step-by-step instructions.

In this unit, you will ...

- discuss global warming problems, talk about solutions, and brainstorm products.
- use thinking skills: summarize, analyze, and categorize.
- read about climate change.
- use strategies to start speaking for a group, talk about problems and solutions, and comment on ideas.
- use global-competence skills to explain your ideas about environmental projects.
- learn strategies to improve reading speed.

WHAT DO YOU ALREADY KNOW?

If students are struggling to understand what to do, you can ask them some questions to prompt their thinking:

- What's the weather like today?
- What kind of weather do you like?
- Have you ever been caught in a storm? What was it like?
- How is the weather changing in the world?

VIDEO

Before viewing, ask:

What creates bigger storms? *the oceans are warmer because of the greenhouse effect*
What can we do to reduce carbon dioxide? *plant trees or a garden*

After viewing, put the continuum on the board.

natural causes —— caused by people

Have students mark the continuum and explain their preferences.

DISCUSS & SHARE

Ask students if they believe changes in severe weather are natural or caused by people. Are severe weather patterns cyclical? Or are humans impacting the weather? Students should place themselves on a continuum of opinion. They should choose one viewpoint and defend it with examples.

GO TO page vii
for **VOCABULARY** step-by-step instructions.

VOCABULARY

A Match the words in the box with the definitions.

climate degree forest fire melt trap weather

1 degree: a unit to measure temperature
2 trap: to keep something like air or gas in one place
3 weather: conditions in the atmosphere like temperature, rain, clouds, etc.
4 forest fire: a large area of trees burning
5 climate: the type of weather that a country or region has
6 melt: to change a solid material to a liquid

MAKE IT YOURS

Do these words used to describe climate change describe the changes where you live?

B IN PAIRS Test your partner. Take turns reading definitions from A and saying the correct word.

GO TO page x
for **READING** step-by-step instructions.

READING

A 5.01 IN PAIRS Choose *True* or *False*. Then read the article to check your answers.

1 Global warming and climate change are the same thing. True / **False**
2 Global warming is caused by the greenhouse effect. **True** / False
3 If the Earth's temperature rises just a little, there won't be any problems. True / **False**
4 If the polar ice caps melt, the seas will rise. **True** / False
5 If we do nothing, some coastal cities may disappear. **True** / False

FAQs About Climate Change

Followers

1 Are climate change and global warming the same thing? 1
Global warming refers to the general rise in the Earth's temperatures that has happened since the beginning of the Industrial Revolution. Climate change refers to
1 all of the changes in weather and climate that are caused by global warming, such as hotter summers, more severe storms, and more forest fires. 2

2 What causes global warming?
Global warming began with the Industrial Revolution when we started using fossil fuels—
3 carbon-based fuels like oil and gas—but most global warming has happened since the 4
1970s. When we burn fossil fuels, they produce carbon dioxide. The carbon dioxide in the atmosphere traps heat and holds it near the Earth. Other types of gases, like methane, also trap heat near the Earth. This is called the greenhouse effect.

3 Does it really matter if the Earth is only a few degrees warmer than it was?
It is true that the Earth is only about 0.99°C warmer than it was in the mid-20th century, but if temperatures go up even a small amount, big changes take place. Sea levels rise and more severe weather events happen. The United Nations predicts that if temperatures rise more than 1.5°C, the effect on our lives will be extreme. If we didn't burn so many fossil fuels, the effects of global warming wouldn't be so serious.

4 What are the effects of global warming and climate change?
Unless we stop global warming, the polar ice caps will melt and sea levels will rise. This will affect Arctic and Antarctic species like polar bears and penguins, and it will mean more floods in coastal cities. Some areas will have hotter summers with long droughts and terrible fires. Other areas will have colder winters with bad ice and snowstorms. There will be more severe weather events like tornadoes and hurricanes. 5

If we don't do anything about global warming, there will be terrible consequences. Some coastal cities like Miami, Osaka, and parts of Rio de Janeiro may disappear. Many species of animals may also disappear, and this will change the Earth's ecosystems. One thing is certain: our planet will not be the same place it is today.

GLOSSARY
drought (n): a long period of time when there is little or no rain and plants die

VOCABULARY Extra Practice

Extend the activity by allowing students to use dictionaries to add words to their personal vocabulary lists. Remind students that dictionary apps say the words for you, which is great for pronunciation practice. Grammar mistakes don't matter so much if you have an extensive vocabulary. More words related to climate change are *precipitation*, *sea levels*, *impact*, *region*, *area*, *phenomenon*, *drought*, *poles*, *extinct*, *pollution*, *gases*, *cause*, *effect*, *variation*, and *weather patterns*.

READING OPTIONAL 5.01

Tell students to read the statements and guess if they are true or false before reading the article. This kind of preview will allow students to become familiar with the language and content they will encounter in the article. Previewing leads to active reading.

Extra Practice

As an additional exercise, have students ask each other the questions in the paragraph headings and summarize the paragraphs in their own words.

B READING SKILL—Identify explanations, definitions, and examples Find and underline the following things in the text in A.

1 definitions of global warming and climate change (Question 1)
2 three examples of changes caused by global warming (Question 1)
3 an explanation of what fossil fuels are (Question 2)
4 an explanation of what the greenhouse effect is (Question 2)
5 two examples of severe weather events (Question 4)

C THINKING SKILL—Summarize **Explain why scientists say that today's climate change and global warming are primarily caused by human activity.**

Suggested answer: Climate change is happening much faster than it did at other times in the Earth's history. Global warming started with the Industrial Revolution, and it has increased very quickly since the 1970s. Scientists know that it is caused by gases in the atmosphere, and human activity produces enormous amounts of those gases.

GRAMMAR review of conditionals

A Match the conditionals (1–3) to the verb forms (a–c) to complete the rules.

If temperatures go up even a small amount, big changes take place.
If that happens, the effect on our lives will be extreme.
Unless we stop global warming, the polar ice caps will melt.
If we didn't burn so many fossil fuels, global warming wouldn't happen so quickly.

1 (zero conditional) *If/Unless* + simple present verb, c
2 (first conditional) *If/Unless* + simple present verb, a
3 (second conditional) *If/Unless* + simple past verb, b

a + *will/won't* + base verb
b + *would/wouldn't* + base verb
c + simple present verb

For more practice, go to page 148.

B Label the sentences *zero*, *first*, or *second* according to the rules in A.

1 If we stopped using fossil fuels, there would be less carbon dioxide. second
2 If sea levels rise, some cities will be in danger. first
3 Ice melts if the temperature goes above 0°C. zero
4 If you watch a program about global warming, how do you feel? zero
5 If you buy a new car, will you buy an electric one? zero
6 If you could change one thing in your town or city, what would it be? second

C IN PAIRS Discuss questions 4, 5, and 6 in B.

GO TO page viii for GRAMMAR step-by-step instructions.

SPEAKING

A IN PAIRS Discuss which of the effects of global warming are affecting your country. Make some suggestions about what will happen and possible solutions. Make notes in your notebooks.

- Rising sea levels
- Drought
- Severe rainstorms
- Hurricanes
- Tornadoes
- Severe winters

If sea levels continue to rise, we will probably lose three of our major coastal cities.

There are already more droughts in the center of the country, and they will get worse. This will affect our food supply because ...

If we changed to electric cars, we would produce less pollution.

B IN GROUPS Work with another pair. Compare your ideas from A. Do you all agree? Use the Confident Communicator box to help you.

A: We think that if sea levels rise, we'll lose ..., ..., and ... .
B: We agree about ... and ... . We might not lose ... because it's higher.

CONFIDENT COMMUNICATOR
START TALKING

To start the conversation when speaking for a group, use the following phrases:
We think ... / We believe ... / As we understand it, ... / As far as we know, ... / Our view is ... / We decided ...

GO TO page xii for SPEAKING step-by-step instructions.

GRAMMAR

Ask about climate change: *How do you feel when you see a program about the environment on TV? Would you buy an electric car? Why or why not? What things about the environment would you change in your town or city?* Make a list of the things students would change on the board. The list will come in handy for the following speaking activity.

SPEAKING

Students should read the examples carefully and underline language they can use for their suggestions. For example, *If ... we will ...; This will affect ... because ...* Have them choose an effect of global warming that is affecting their town and make notes. Prompt by asking questions like *Are you being personally affected by climate change? Do you see any effects in your town or city?*

LESSON 2 Time to Act

VOCABULARY taking action

A Complete the sentences with words and phrases from the box.

create laws	pay a fine	reduce
don't allow	provide	require

Air and water pollution: Make companies that produce pollution **1** pay a fine. Have lower taxes for people and companies that use clean energy.
Trash: 2 Provide free recycling services. **3** Reduce the use of plastic. Make people pay for plastic bags in stores and grocery stores. Make products that **4** require less packaging.
Overfishing: Limit fishing of certain types of fish. **5** Don't allow certain types of fishing nets.
Endangered species: 6 Create laws to protect species that are disappearing.

GO TO page ix for PRONUNCIATION step-by-step instructions.

PRONUNCIATION word stress in verb phrases

A 5.02 Listen to the phrases and underline the stressed word in each phrase. What type of word is stressed?

Nouns are stressed.

verb + noun	verb + adjective/adverb + noun
1 reduce pollution	4 pay for plastic bags
2 provide recycling	5 require less packaging
3 create laws	6 use clean energy

B IN PAIRS Practice reading the sentences with stress on the correct words.

1 They should create a law that requires less packaging.
2 The city should provide recycling and support businesses that use clean energy.

GO TO page xi for LISTENING step-by-step instructions.

GO TO page 142 for AUDIO SCRIPT.

LISTENING

A Discuss the questions as a class.

Do you think young people in your country are very concerned about environmental problems? Why or why not?

B 5.03 LISTENING SKILL—Listen for main ideas Listen to four short radio interviews. Which four environmental problems do the speakers talk about?

C 5.03 Choose the correct options. Then listen again and check.

1 The first person thinks the main cause of global warming is companies using …
a fossil fuels. b taxes. c clean energy.
2 According to the second person, … of the people in the world don't have clean water to drink.
a thousands b millions c billions
3 The third speaker is worried about trash, especially …
a glass. b plastic. c metal.
4 The fourth speaker says that overfishing could destroy her country's …
a oceans. b ecosystems. c economy.
5 The host says that he hopes … are taking environmental problems seriously.
a governments b all countries c young people

D IN GROUPS THINKING SKILL—Analyze Prioritize the environmental issues mentioned in B. Which two are the most important?

VOCABULARY

Tell students to read the whole text before completing the activity. Have them try to complete it first without a dictionary, as they will be able to figure out the meaning from context. It's important they learn to trust themselves before resorting to looking up every single word they don't know.

PRONUNCIATION

Breathing out is an important factor in the pronunciation of English. Have students take a breath in before saying a sentence and release it as they talk.

A fun activity is to have students snap their fingers on the stressed words in a sentence. For example, *They should create a **law** that requires less **pack**aging.*

LISTENING

Ask students to give examples to support their opinions in **A**. They may think people don't care about the environment because they see people continuing to dump trash. Or they may think people do care about the environment because there is much less single-use plastic.

GRAMMAR present and future hopes and wishes

A Write whether the sentences refer to the present (*P*) or the future (*F*).

1 I hope our generation is taking environmental problems seriously. P
2 I hope our generation makes a lot of changes to help save the planet! F
3 I hope all cities will provide free recycling soon. F
4 I wish fossil fuels didn't exist! P
5 I wish every country had stronger laws against water pollution. P
6 I wish my government would make fishing companies reduce certain types of fishing. F

B Match the structures (1–4) with the functions (a–d).

1 *wish* + *would* or *could* d	**a** something that you want and expect to be true in the present
2 *hope* + simple present, present progressive, or *can* a	**b** something that you want and expect to happen in the future
3 *hope* + *will*, *can*, or simple present b	**c** something that you would like to be true in the present but isn't
4 *wish* + simple past c	**d** something that you would like to happen in the future but probably won't

For more practice, go to page 148.

C Complete the conversations with the correct forms of the words in parentheses.

A: I hope it **1** doesn't/won't rain (not rain) this weekend!
B: Let's see … My phone says it will be clear on the weekend. I hope that it **2** is (be) correct!
A: I wish I **3** had (have) more time to do volunteer work.
B: Me, too. I hope I **4** can (can) do some volunteer work next semester.
A: I wish my brother **5** would/could help (help) me with my ecology project, but he says he can't.
B: I wish I **6** didn't have (not have) so much work because I would help you with it.
A: I hope the government **7** creates/will create (create) a new soda tax law.
B: Yeah. I wish they **8** would create (create) a tax on plastic bottles, too!

D IN PAIRS Change the underlined information in C to make new conversations with your own ideas.

SPEAKING

A Think about the answers to these questions. Make notes.

1 Which environmental issues are most important in your country? Why?
2 What do you wish your country would do about these issues?
3 What do you hope your generation will do about environmental problems in the future?

A: I think global warming is the most important issue for us because we have two coasts.
B: I agree. If the seas rise, we'll lose some of our cities, and also, we'll have a lot of hurricanes and other bad storms. I wish we had stronger air pollution laws.
C: I hope young people will help educate the public about the problem of global warming.

B IN GROUPS Discuss your answers to the questions in A. Do most of you have similar ideas? Use the Confident Communicator box to help you.

CONFIDENT COMMUNICATOR
KEEP TALKING

To talk about problems and solutions, use the following phrases:
Problems
One problem/issue is …
The biggest/main problem/issue is…
… is a big/major/serious problem.
Solutions
If we had stronger laws, we wouldn't have so much pollution.
What if we had stronger pollution laws?
I think we need / should have stronger pollution laws.

GRAMMAR

Tell students that the language of hopes and wishes is useful for talking about issues. We use the conditional to talk about regrets or things we wish were different.

As students create new conversations in **D**, walk around the room and listen. After students have finished, write the sentences you heard on the board and have volunteers pick out the correct ones and correct the mistakes in the others.

SPEAKING

Ask for three volunteers. Tell them to read the examples in **A** out loud. Then ask students to read the questions and think about their answers individually. Give students thinking time and talking time. Monitor and help out where needed during the planning stages.

In **B**, before students work in groups, draw everyone's attention to the *Confident Communicator* box to look at the language that will be useful for them for the group discussion.

LESSON 3 **Hope for the Future**

LISTENING

A Match the environmental solutions (1–8) with the photos (a–h).

a

England

b

Chile and Peru

c

US

d

Singapore

e

Indonesia

f

Kenya

g

Japan

h

Mexico

1 plant pots made from tires c
2 recycled paper flip-flops e
3 super trees d
4 recycled plastic houses h
5 fog catchers b
6 school desks made from recycled materials f
7 living walls a
8 green roofs g

GO TO page 142 for AUDIO SCRIPT.

B 5.04 **LISTENING SKILL—Listen for details** Listen to a class discussion. Under the photos a–h in A, write the name of the country where each environmental solution is taking place.

C 5.04 **THINKING SKILL—Categorize** Listen again and decide who should do each of the eight projects. Categorize the projects as *private companies, the government,* or *either*. Give reasons for your opinions.

I think the government would have to ... because it would be very expensive.

MAKE IT REAL

Informal ways to say strange or unusual: *weird, bizarre, wild*

VOCABULARY materials and products

A Match the descriptions with words from the box.

coconut flip-flop net pot roof rubber steel tire

1 a material with spaces made of string, rope, or metal wire: net
2 the part of a wheel that is filled with air: tire
3 a container used to cook or to plant flowers or other plants: pot
4 the fruit of a kind of palm tree: coconut
5 a strong metal made of iron and carbon: steel
6 the top of a house or other building: roof
7 a type of sandal with a V-shaped strap: flip-flop
8 a flexible material similar to plastic that comes from a tree: rubber

B IN PAIRS Think of other things that can be made from recycled materials. Discuss.

LISTENING Alternative Activity

Play *Hot Potato* with country names. In groups of four, have students arrange themselves in a circle and stand up facing each other. Each group needs a ball or a crumpled-up piece of paper. Set a timer for 30 seconds. The object of the game is to be the last one out. Students toss the ball from student to student around the circle. Each time they receive the ball, they say the name of a country. The person holding the ball when the timer goes off sits down. If someone repeats the name of a country, they sit down.

VOCABULARY

Some products made from recycled materials are shoes and bags made from plastic bottles, children's toys made of recycled material, bags made from car airbags, and tablet or phone covers made from wetsuit material.

You may also want to have students think about other everyday materials that can be recycled—things like batteries, computers, furniture, and appliances.

WRITING

GO TO page xiv for WRITING step-by-step instructions.

A Read the essay. Does the writer have a generally positive or generally negative opinion of his country's actions on the environment? Tell a partner.

My country has changed a lot since I was a small child. Twenty years ago, air pollution was terrible in big cities, and water pollution was very bad, too. The government has given tax breaks to industries that moved to new locations, and they have created strong anti-pollution laws. Companies that pollute the air or water have to pay big fines. My city has built new parks and other green spaces, and it has created new pollution laws for vehicles.

The results from the changes have been positive, but I wish we would do more to help with problems like deforestation and global warming. If universities offered programs to train people in rural areas to do different jobs, they wouldn't have to cut down trees to get money. Also, my city gives people free trees to plant in their yards. There will be a lot more trees if all of the cities do that. Another thing that helps with the problem of air pollution and global warming in general is roof gardens. If companies put gardens on their roofs, the plants would put oxygen into the air and take out carbon dioxide. I believe that my country is doing some good things for the environment, and I hope we will do many more things in the near future.

Generally positive—he says that pollution was bad 20 years ago and lists things that have been done to help the environment. He says the changes have been positive, and he believes his country is doing some good things for the environment.

B IN PAIRS Find and underline actions and their results in the second paragraph of the text in **A**. Say which is the action and which is the result in each case.

If universities offered programs to train people in rural areas to do different jobs (action), they wouldn't have to cut down trees to get money (result).

There will be a lot more trees (result) if all of the cities do that (action).

If companies put gardens on their roofs (action), the plants would put oxygen into the air and take out carbon dioxide (result).

C Think about environmental projects in your country. Make a list of actions your government or companies have taken and the results for the environment. Make another list of actions you recommend and the results.

Action	*Result*
Reduced taxes for companies that move to new locations	*Less air pollution in big cities*
Recommended action	*Result*
Plant more trees in the cities	*More oxygen in the air*

D Use your notes from **C** to write a short essay similar to the one in **A**.

SPEAKING

A IN PAIRS Brainstorm new ideas for programs or products to help the environment in your country.

B IN GROUPS Discuss which ideas are practical. Use the Confident Communicator box to help you.

A: The government could create a law that requires all buildings to have living walls.
B: If they did that, it would be too expensive for a lot of people.
A: That's true. What if just big companies had to do it?
C: I think that's an awesome idea! It wouldn't be too hard, and it would help with air pollution.

CONFIDENT COMMUNICATOR
KEEP TALKING

To comment on good or unusual ideas, use the following phrases:
Good ideas: *What a* **cool** / **awesome** / **brilliant** *idea!*
Unusual ideas: *That's a* (**very**) **weird** / **bizarre** / **different** / **strange** *idea!*

WRITING

If possible, invite guest speakers in to talk about environmental projects so students can learn about environmental projects in the local context. You might invite a member of the staff to talk about what your institution does to help the environment, such as recycling programs the school initiates. You could invite a city employee to talk about the city's initiatives, or a local business might send someone to talk about their company's environmental programs.

SPEAKING

Tell students to brainstorm as many ideas as they can to help the environment. They can make notes as a vertical list or as a mind map. Invite them to use the starbursting method used in Unit 3 to dig further into one of their ideas.

When working in groups, encourage students to use expressions from the *Confident Communicator* box to keep talking about their ideas for programs or products to help the environment in their country.

GO TO page xv

for **LANGUAGE AND LIFE** step-by-step instructions.

Language and Life

Global Competence – Environmental Issues

A 5.05 **Read the blog. What is the blogger's main point?**

a Governments should do more to help the environment.
b Individual people and communities can only help the environment in very small ways.
c Individual people and communities can help the environment a lot.

Evan the Eco Guy—Micro-Ecology

How often have you heard or said this about a problem: "Why don't *they* do something?" Who is *they*? In the case of environmental problems, *they* probably refers to the government or to the world in general. But what if we stopped saying *they* and started saying *we*? There are many things that we, the people, can do to reduce global warming and to help the environment in general.

First, there are many small things that individual people and families can do. If we all tried to save energy, we would use less oil and gas, and there would be less carbon in the atmosphere. There are some very easy ways to save energy. Turn off lights when you are not in a room. Turn off your computer at night. Do several errands when you go out in your car, and offer to do errands for other people in your family. Share rides to school or work with family or friends. Try to buy locally produced food and other products. There are also many things that we can all do to produce less trash. Use reusable shopping bags for all types of shopping. When you buy fast food, don't take too many napkins, and don't take plastic forks if you are going to eat the food at home.

Neighborhoods and communities can also do many things to help the environment. Community gardens help in several ways. First, plants put oxygen into the air and use carbon dioxide. Second, if people eat food from local gardens, they are not eating food that was transported by trucks or planes. Third, flowers attract insects and birds that pollinate plants. Communities can also set up neighborhood websites to share rides, recycle things like clothes or toys, or organize volunteers to pick up trash in local parks and recycle it. If we did a little more as individuals and communities, we could have a very positive effect on our environment.

B IN PAIRS **Answer the questions about the blog in A.**

1 According to the blogger, who does the word *they* usually refer to?
2 What would happen if everyone did a few small things to save energy?
3 How do you think sharing rides and doing errands for other people can help save energy?
4 Why do you think buying local products helps the environment?
5 How many reasons does the writer give for having community gardens?
6 How can people use neighborhood websites?

1 the government or the world in general
2 There would be less carbon in the atmosphere.
3 It would mean that fewer people were using cars, so carbon emissions would be reduced.
4 Local products don't have to be transported long distances, so there are fewer planes, trains, and trucks producing carbon emissions.
5 three
6 to share rides, give away things like clothes or toys, or organize volunteers to pick up trash in local parks and recycle it

OBJECTIVE

Students think about their own habits for helping the environment. It is easy to presume that problems have to be solved by government or big business. However, there are many small actions individuals can take to reduce waste and save energy. Students consider what they would be willing to do and try to persuade others to change their habits, too.

PROCESS OPTIONAL 5.05

Students read a blog and answer questions about what can be done to help the environment at a grassroots level. They look at a chart with suggestions for individual projects and check things they already do or would be willing to try and note why they wouldn't do others. They discuss the ideas in groups with the goal of convincing others to try some of the suggestions. Next, the groups come up with more ideas for environmental projects. As a class, they analyze how effective the ideas would be in their community. Students vote on the top three ideas. Finally, students discuss the questions about persuasion.

C Look at some ideas for individual environmental projects. Check (✓) the *Yes* column for the ones that you already do or think you would do. For the ones that you would not do, write the number of the reason in the *No* column.

	Yes	No	Reason Not to Do It
Use a carpool to go to work or school.			1 I don't think it works.
Plant trees or flowers.			2 It's expensive.
Use my own coffee cup or water bottle.			3 It takes too much time or effort.
Combine errands with friends and neighbors.			4 I don't know how/where to do it.
Use my own shopping bags.			5 I won't remember to do it.
Use energy-efficient light bulbs.			6 I don't want to do it.
Take shorter showers.			7 It isn't possible in my area.
Have a vegetarian day once a week.			
Save gift wrapping and use it for other gifts.			
Buy locally produced food and products.			

D **IN GROUPS** Discuss your answers to C. Encourage your classmates to take action and try some of the ideas.

A: It's easy to buy local products. For example, you can shop at the farmer's market.
B: We should take shorter showers. Why? Because it saves water, and it also takes less time!
C: It doesn't matter if you don't know how. If you look online, you can find out how to …
D: It's really important to … because …

E With your group, think of more ideas to take action and help the environment. Make a list of ideas.

____
____
____
____
____

F Share your ideas with the class and discuss whether you think they would work in your community. Agree on the top three ideas.

A: I think a community garden is a great idea.
B: Me too. We could sell the vegetables we grow.
C: I'm not sure. You would need lots of volunteers.

G Discuss the questions.

1 Was it easy or difficult to encourage people to try your ideas? Why or why not?
2 How can we encourage people to change their every day habits?
3 What global impact would there be if we made these changes?

MAKE IT DIGITAL

Go online to find out what town or neighborhood programs already exist in your community and volunteer to help. If there are no initiatives, use social media to organize one.

Unit 5 One Planet 55

CULTURE NOTE

According to different sources, Germany and Austria are leaders in recycling. They send less of their waste to landfills than other countries. However, they incinerate waste, which may cause other environmental issues. In some countries, people work in an informal industry as garbage pickers and collect recyclables from landfills to sell to recyclers. This practice reduces landfills and increases recycling rates. It's good for the Earth.

MAKE IT DIGITAL

There are a number of green bloggers out there like the one featured in the lesson. Additionally, there are some sites that give suggestions for community environment programs.

GO TO page xvii
for **UNIT REVIEW** step-by-step instructions.

UNIT 5

VOCABULARY review

SCORE: / 10

A Complete the sentences with words from the box.

fines	melts	provide	rubber	traps
fog	nets	reduce	steel	weather

1 We need to ___reduce___ our use of fossil fuels.
2 ___Fog___ is a cloud close to the ground.
3 We're having bad ___weather___ this week—a lot of storms.
4 Cities ___provide___ many services, such as trash collection and electricity.
5 The greenhouse effect happens when carbon dioxide ___traps___ heat in the atmosphere.
6 Companies that pollute should have to pay ___fines___.
7 ___Nets___ are often used to catch large numbers of fish.
8 If the ice in the Arctic and Antarctic ___melts___, sea levels will rise to dangerous levels.
9 ___Rubber___ is a natural material used to make things like tires and flip-flops.
10 ___Steel___ is a type of very strong metal.

1 reads / will read
2 don't do
3 will be
4 would be
5 would be
6 created
7 act
8 won't have
9 could understand / understood
10 would work

GRAMMAR review

SCORE: / 10

A Complete the blog entry with the correct forms of the verbs in parentheses.

Earth Citizen

I hope everyone **1** ________ (read) this. If we **2** ________ (not do) something about climate change in the near future, it **3** ________ (be) too late. Years ago, scientists told us that if we didn't stop using so much fossil fuel, there **4** ________ (be) terrible consequences. It isn't too late yet. If we used less fossil fuel, there **5** ________ (be) less carbon in the atmosphere. Climate change would happen more slowly if we **6** ________ (create) stronger laws, but unless we **7** ________ (act) soon, we **8** ________ (not have) our beautiful planet anymore! I wish everyone **9** ________ (understand) the importance of this problem, and I wish world leaders **10** ________ (work) together in the future to save our planet.

16–20 correct: You can talk about environmental issues and offer solutions. You can use conditionals for present and future hopes and wishes.
0–15 correct: Look again at the Vocabulary and Grammar sections in the unit.

TOTAL SCORE: / 20

WHAT DO YOU KNOW NOW? Look back at page 47 and add the words you know now to the boxes.

GO TO page xviii
for **STUDY SKILLS** step-by-step instructions.

STUDY SKILLS IMPROVING READING SPEED

Take the quiz about improving reading speed. Go to **Study Skills** on page 131 to find the answers. Then learn more about improving reading speed.

1 It is always important to read things quickly.
a True **b** False

2 Reading aloud is always beneficial for reading.
a True **b** False

3 Which two of the following are active reading strategies?
a scanning **b** questioning **c** skimming **d** predicting

4 Moving your finger down the page as you read can help you read faster.
a True **b** False

CLASSROOM MANAGEMENT

Before starting the review activities, give students some time to glance over the unit and review the vocabulary and grammar sections in each lesson. Once they have looked over the material, they will be ready for the review exercises.

ALTERNATIVE ACTIVITY

Write the following prompts on the board. Have students finish the statements for themselves.

- I remember … about the article on page 48.
- I remember … about the environmental problems mentioned in the radio interviews on page 50.
- New words I remember are …
- The grammar I learned is …

FURTHER DISCUSSION

Write the following questions on the board. Then have students work in groups of three and ask each other:

- Why is the topic of climate change in the media these days?
- Do you wear sunscreen?
- Who recycles at your house?
- Are you using anything made from recycled material right now?

UNIT 6 Moments in Time

GO TO page vi
for UNIT OPENER step-by-step instructions.

WHAT DO YOU ALREADY KNOW?

1 Think about events, inventions, and people in history. Write the words.
2 IN PAIRS Share and compare your ideas. Add more words to your lists.

The past

STUDENTS MAY ALREADY KNOW:

- **Past events:** wars, space exploration, elections.
- **Inventions:** personal computer, electricity, train, car, airplane, microprocessor, fire, wheel, telephone, printing press, medicine, vaccines, smartphone.
- **People in history:** Ana Frank, Mahatma Gandhi, Steve Jobs, Malala.

VIDEO

DISCUSS & SHARE

3 IN GROUPS Watch the video and answer the question.
SYM Do you wait for inspiration or do you do your work step by step?

GO TO page xx
for VIDEOS IN SYM step-by-step instructions.

In this unit, you will ...

- compare different generational use of technology, share your opinions about inventions, write quiz questions about people in history.
- use thinking skills: predict, evaluate, and question.
- read about technological change.
- use strategies to keep a conversation going when you do not know a word, interrupt politely, and express interest and surprise.
- use decision-making skills to make judgments about UNESCO sites.
- follow an archaeologist to learn about this job and the skills needed for this industry.

WHAT DO YOU ALREADY KNOW?

If students are struggling to understand what to do, you can ask them some questions to prompt their thinking:

- What historical events are important in your country?
- What inventions are important?
- What has been invented in your lifetime?
- What was invented in your grandparents' lifetimes?
- What would you like to invent?

VIDEO

Before viewing, ask:

How long did Kevin work in the café design? *a month*
How long did Jessica work in the café design? *two weeks*

After viewing, put the continuum on the board.

inspiration —— step by step

Have students mark the continuum and explain their preferences.

DISCUSS & SHARE

Students should place themselves on a continuum of opinion. Ask students to think about whether they believe inventions are the result of inspiration or hard work. Do new discoveries happen after years of trial and error, or are they the result of a bolt-of-lightning type of idea? Students should choose one viewpoint and defend it with examples.

LESSON 1 Decades of Change

GO TO page x for READING step-by-step instructions.

READING

A 6.01 **READING SKILL—Scan** **Check (✓) the commercial technology events that you think happened before 1900. Then scan the first paragraph of the magazine article to check your answers.**

- [x] the first electric taxis
- [ ] the first commercial flight
- [x] the first commercial telephone company
- [ ] the first movie theater
- [x] the first locomotive passenger train
- [ ] the first radio station

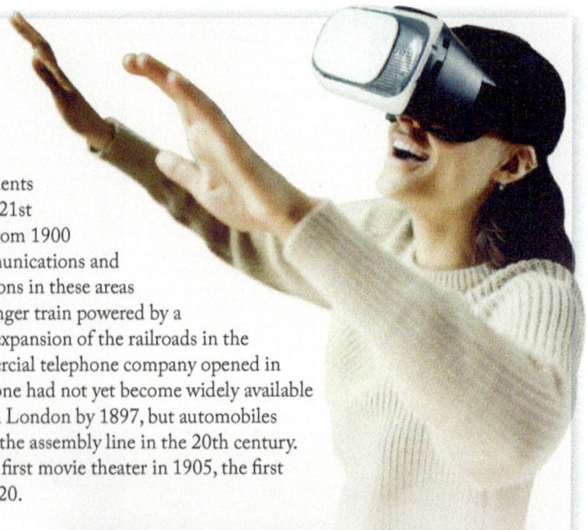

In Just 20 Years...

By the end of the 19th century, the Industrial Revolution had changed the world forever, and technology has continued to make many improvements since then. The first two decades of both the 20th and the 21st centuries brought life-changing progress in technology. From 1900 to 1920, there were enormous changes, especially in communications and transportation. Of course, there had already been innovations in these areas when the 20th century began. For example, the first passenger train powered by a locomotive had started in 1825 in England, but the huge expansion of the railroads in the US and Europe came in the 20th century. The first commercial telephone company opened in 1878, but at the beginning of the 20th century, the telephone had not yet become widely available to the public. Most surprisingly, there were electric taxis in London by 1897, but automobiles became available to ordinary people with the invention of the assembly line in the 20th century. The first two decades of the 20th century also brought the first movie theater in 1905, the first commercial flight in 1914, and the first radio station in 1920.

In the first two decades of the 21st century, progress in information technology was particularly important. This "Digital Revolution" included two of the most important developments in communications since the telephone—smartphones and the creation of social media platforms. The first social media network was Friendster in 2002, and the first modern smartphone was the iPhone in 2007. Entertainment technology also changed enormously from the close of the 20th century to the first decades of the 21st century. Some of the major 21st-century inventions so far have been wireless headsets in 2002, YouTube and internet radio in 2005, e-readers in 2007, and virtual reality headsets in 2016. It is hard to imagine where digital technology will take us by the end of the 21st century!

1 the Industrial Revolution in the 19th century and the Digital Revolution in the 21st century
2 three: 19th, 20th, 21st
3 communications and transportation
4 social media platforms and smartphones
5 Entertainment technology changed with the invention of wireless headsets, YouTube, internet radio, e-readers, and virtual reality headsets.
6 the first

B **IN PAIRS** **Read the article. Then answer the questions.**

1. What two types of revolution does the article mention? When did they happen?
2. How many centuries are mentioned in the article?
3. What types of technology are mentioned in the first paragraph?
4. What were two important developments in communications in the 21st century?
5. How did entertainment technology change in the 21st century?
6. Did most of the progress in IT mentioned in the article happen in the first or the second decade of the 21st century?

GLOSSARY

innovation (n): a new idea, method, or object
assembly line (n): a system for making things in a factory in which each worker or machine adds one part
decade (n): 10 years

C **IN GROUPS THINKING SKILL—Predict** **The writer says it's hard to imagine where digital technology will take us by the end of the 21st century. Predict what technology you think will exist by the end of this century.**

A: I think people will have ... *B: I don't think so, but I think ... / Maybe there will be ...*

READING OPTIONAL 6.01

Before starting, ask students to quickly look at the article and say any numbers, years, or dates they can see. Write a list on the board, and practice saying them as a class—for example, *nineteenth century, twenty-first century, nineteen hundred, nineteen twenty, eighteen twenty-five, two thousand (and) seven.*

Tell students the first reading is a scanning exercise. They do not have to read carefully but just read enough to find the details for **A**. The second reading, **B**, should be a more careful one. Students will need to answer comprehension questions. If time allows, tell students to add any words to their glossaries that are new for them.

THINKING SKILL—Predict

You may want to help students predict how technology will change the world by writing some categories on the board to prompt their thinking (e.g., *transportation, medicine, communications, space exploration, home, work, our brains*).

VOCABULARY

A Scan the article in READING A and write a word with a similar meaning for each of these words.

1 close (n): end [para. 1]
2 progress (n): improvement [para. 1]
3 huge (adj): enormous [para. 1]
4 especially (adv): particularly [para. 2]
5 invention (n): creation [para. 2]
6 important (adj): major [para. 2]

GRAMMAR past perfect

A Label the underlined times or events *1* or *2* to indicate which happened first.

1 By the end of the 19th century, the Industrial Revolution had changed the world forever …
2 1
2 Of course, there had already been innovations in these fields when the 20th century began.
1 2
3 …, but at the beginning of the 20th century, the telephone had not yet become widely available to the public.
2 1

B Choose the correct options.

1 Use the simple past / **past perfect** to talk about an action that happened before another action in the past.
2 Use the **simple past** / past perfect to talk about an action that happened after another action in the past.
3 Form the past perfect with *have* / ***had*** + a past participle.

For more practice, go to page 149.

C Complete the paragraph with the simple past or past perfect forms of the verbs in parentheses.

I was born in 1980, so I've seen a lot of changes in technology in my life. When I **1** started (start) college in 1998, I **2** had used (use) a computer, but I **3** hadn't sent (not send) an email because I didn't have internet. I **4** got (get) internet service at home in 2000, and by 2002, when I **5** graduated (graduate) from college, I **6** had learned (learn) to use email, and I **7** had even joined (join) the Friendster social media network! I **8** thought (think) I was very modern!

D Think about technology the year you became a teenager. Write three things you had already done and three things you hadn't done yet at that time. Share your sentences with a group or a partner. Who used more technology as a preteen?

I had already learned to use the internet.
I hadn't bought a tablet yet.

SPEAKING

A IN PAIRS Make a list of as many things as you can think of that people in the 21st century frequently do online, such as make plane reservations, buy things, or ask for advice about problems. Use the Confident Communicator box to help you.

B Make a list of things you think your parents had and had not done online by 2000.

C IN GROUPS Compare your lists. Whose parents had already done a lot of things online by 2000? Which things have they now done online that they hadn't done in 2000?

CONFIDENT COMMUNICATOR
KEEP TALKING

To continue the conversation when you don't know a word, use the following phrases to communicate what you mean:
I can't think of the exact word, but It's similar to … / It's a kind of …
What's the word I'm thinking of? It means …

GO TO page vii
for **VOCABULARY** step-by-step instructions.

GO TO page viii
for **GRAMMAR** step-by-step instructions.

GO TO page xii
for **SPEAKING** step-by-step instructions.

VOCABULARY

Alternative Activity

Play *Find It First*. In groups of three, have one person say a word from VOCABULARY **A** and have the other two race to find the synonym in the text. The person who finds and says the word first wins a point. The first person to score three points wins the game.

GRAMMAR

To demonstrate the past perfect, plot the example sentences on timelines. Tell students to think about the events in relation to each other. Both events are in the past. Past perfect is used when something happened before something else. The form is *had* + past participle.

SPEAKING

Allow students to interview their parents or other adults in order to be able to talk about what they had and hadn't done online before the year 2000.

Alternative Activity

Talk about innovations that had or hadn't happened by a certain point in time.

GO TO page xi
for **LISTENING** step-by-step instructions.

LESSON 2

Inventions Big and Small

LISTENING

A **IN PAIRS** **Look at these 21st-century inventions. Match each picture (a–f) to a category (1–6), according to your opinions.**

a car that drives itself

a waterproof notepad for the shower

a hammock for feet

a light that creates a bike lane

a camera that takes 360° photos

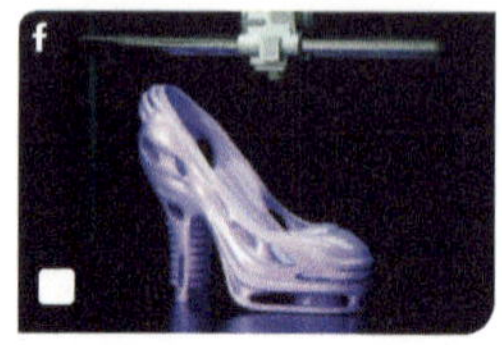

a printer that makes 3-D objects

1 the most unusual invention ____
2 the most amusing invention ____
3 the most exciting invention ____
4 the most worrying invention ____
5 the most useful invention ____
6 the most useless invention ____

3-D printers—worrying; 360° cameras—exciting; a hammock for feet—amusing; a car that drives itself—amazing and worrying

GO TO page 143
for **AUDIO SCRIPT**.

B 6.02 **Listen to the street interviews. Check (✓) the things in A that the speakers mention. Make notes of words the speakers use to describe each invention.**

C 6.02 **IN PAIRS LISTENING SKILL—Listen for supporting details** **Listen again. Then answer the questions.**

1 Why is the first man worried about 3-D printers? It will change business forever.
2 Why is the first woman excited about 360° cameras? They're totally changing professional photography.
3 How does the second man feel about many 21st-century inventions? He feels amused.
4 What is the second woman worried about with driverless cars? safety in big cities with a lot of traffic

D **IN GROUPS THINKING SKILL—Evaluate** **Assess the opinions of the people who were interviewed in B. Do you agree or disagree with their opinions? Discuss.**

VOCABULARY *–ed* and *–ing* adjectives

A **Read the examples from LISTENING B. Then choose the correct options to complete the rules.**

A: I'm pretty worried about some of the recent inventions.
B: To me, the invention that is the most worrying so far is the 3-D printer.
A: I'm really amused by some of the things that have been invented.
B: Yes, I guess some inventions are more amusing than useful.

1 Adjectives like *worried* and *worrying* are formed from nouns / verbs.
2 Adjectives with *–ing* are used to describe something or someone / a feeling about something or someone.
3 Adjectives with *–ed* are used to describe something or someone / a feeling about something or someone.

LISTENING

Play the interviews all the way through on the first listen, and then check the answers with the class. On the second listen, stop after each speaker and let students take notes. A short pause will give them time to recall what they have heard and process the information.

THINKING SKILL—Evaluate

You may want to have an open-class discussion about which of the speakers they agree or disagree with, or you could have students work in pairs and assign them roles. Assign them an opinion, either to agree or disagree, and they have to think of reasons to support that view.

VOCABULARY

Some more *–ed* and *–ing* adjectives are: *amused–amusing, annoyed–annoying, confused–confusing, disappointed–disappointing, excited–exciting, exhausted–exhausting, frightened–frightening, satisfied–satisfying,* and *shocked–shocking.*

B Choose the correct adjective forms.

I'm not sure about driverless cars. Personally, I think driving is **1** amazed / amazing, so I would be **2** disappointed / disappointing if I couldn't do it anymore. I understand that there are many people who would like to have a driverless car. How **3** relaxed / relaxing to sit in your car and read or sleep! I definitely get **4** bored / boring driving in traffic, and it would be very **5** entertained / entertaining to watch a video or play a game on your phone while your car drives, but we need to be patient and wait until the technology is more advanced.

MAKE IT YOURS

Some people think technology is amazing. Others are terrified. How do the different types of technology around you make you feel?

GRAMMAR defining relative clauses

A Underline the word or phrase that each relative pronoun in bold refers to.

1 I'm on a street **where** lots of young people hang out on Saturday evenings. ___place___
2 If there's a time **when** people can make most of their own products, ... ___time___
3 There are some inventors **who** are creating some pretty amusing things! ___person___
4 ... to me, the invention **that** is the most worrying so far is the 3-D printer. ___object___
5 The 21st-century device **which** does everything is the phone. ___object___

B Now label the sentences in **A** *person*, *place*, *time*, or *object* according to what the relative pronoun refers to. Then choose the correct option in the rule.

You can use *that* / *when* instead of *who* or *which*.

For more practice, go to page 150.

C Complete the sentences with relative pronouns. Then think of a response to each sentence.

1 Give an example of a time ___when___ you bought something that you were disappointed with.
2 Name the main places ___where___ you shop, apart from online.
3 Give examples of some recent innovations ___that/which___ you have used lately.
4 Think of a person ___who/that___ has been very important in the first decades of the 21st century.

D IN PAIRS Share your responses in **C** with your partner.

SPEAKING

A Answer the questionnaire.

Opinion Poll on 21st-Century Innovations and Inventions

1 What recent invention or innovation is the most exciting to you?
2 Are there any modern inventions that you find confusing and hard to use?
3 Was there a time when you were disappointed by a new product?
4 Is there an inventor or innovator who is a role model to you?
5 What possible future inventions are you interested in or excited about?

B IN GROUPS Share your opinions about the poll in **A**.

CONFIDENT COMMUNICATOR
KEEP TALKING

To interrupt someone politely, use these phrases:
Excuse me, can/may I interrupt?
Just a second. Can I ask you a question?
Sorry, can you repeat that?

GRAMMAR

Let students know they can use clauses to extend the length of their sentences when speaking in English. At this level, that should be one of their goals.

Extra Practice

You may want to hand out copies of the scripts of the street interviews from LISTENING **B** and have students find and underline examples of defining relative clauses.

SPEAKING

Have students answer the questionnaire individually first. Tell them to use vocabulary and grammar from the lesson to give longer answers and as much detail as possible. Have them work in groups to share their opinions from the poll in **A**. One of the objectives of the activity is to have students interrupt each other. If students are not inclined to interrupt others, give each student three tokens. Tell them they have to put one in the middle each time they interrupt effectively, and their goal should be to use all of their tokens by interrupting at appropriate moments.

L E S S O N 3 **Game Changers**

LISTENING

A Match the people in the pictures (a–d) with the things they did (1–4).

a 
Michel Krieger

b 
Mario Molina

c 
Dr. Christiaan Barnard

d 
Mary Anderson

1 identified the danger of chlorofluorocarbons in the atmosphere. b
2 performed the first heart transplant. c
3 co-founded Instagram. a
4 invented windshield wipers. d

GLOSSARY

transplant (n): a medical operation to take an organ from one person's body and put it into another person's body
cardiac surgeon (n): a doctor who operates on human hearts
defect (n): a fault or problem in something
pneumonia (n): a serious illness of the lungs and respiratory system

Suggested answers:
1 Christiaan Barnard
2 Where was he from? South Africa
3 When was he born? In 1922
4 What did he do? / Why was he famous? He was a heart surgeon, and he performed the first successful heart transplant.

B 6.03 **THINKING SKILL—Question** **Predict the types of information in the podcast about a famous person. Write questions to ask about that information. Then listen and write the answers to your questions.**

Questions	Answers
1 What was his name?	________
2 ________	________
3 ________	________
4 ________	________

GO TO page 144 for AUDIO SCRIPT.

1 1922—Christiaan Barnard was born.
2 1967—Dr. Christiaan Barnard performed the first heart transplant.
3 54—the age of the man who received the first transplant
4 18—the number of days the man lived after his transplant
5 7,000—the number of heart transplants performed every year now

C 6.03 **LISTENING SKILL—Listen for numerical information** **Listen again and write information about each number in your notebook.**

1 1922 2 1967 3 54 4 18 5 7,000

D IN PAIRS Compare your notes in C. Explain in your own words the importance of each number.

VOCABULARY adjective suffixes

A Add the suffixes *–ful*, *–less*, *–able*, and *–ible* to form adjectives from LISTENING B. Then check your work with a partner. Some words can go in more than one column.

	–ful	–less	–able	–ible
1 success–	*successful*			
2 cap–			capable	
3 hope–	hopeful	hopeless		
4 incred–				incredible
5 thank–	thankful	thankless		

LISTENING

Remind students to think of open-ended questions for their predictions. These are *who*, *what*, *where*, *when*, and *how* questions.

LISTENING SKILL—Listen for numerical information

We use numbers in every aspect of our lives, in practical everyday activities at home and beyond. Good numerical information is essential for students to understand what they are learning. Decisions in life are so often based on numerical information; to make the correct choices, we need to be numerate.

VOCABULARY Extra Practice

Have students use the words in a sentence to check that they understand the meaning and usage. You may also like to direct students to look up synonyms for the adjectives to broaden their vocabulary.

B Match the adjectives in A with the definitions below.

1 thankful: grateful or happy about something
2 hopeless: unlikely that a situation will succeed or improve
3 successful: achieving the result you want
4 hopeful: believing that something good will happen
5 incredible: very, very good
6 capable: able to do something

PRONUNCIATION stress in multisyllable adjectives

A 6.04 **Listen and underline the stressed syllable in each word.**

hopeful capable thankful successful preventable incredible

GO TO page ix for PRONUNCIATION step-by-step instructions.

WRITING

A **Read the short biographical essay. What was unusual about Valentina Tereshkova?**

She was the first woman to travel in space.

GO TO page xiv for WRITING step-by-step instructions.

Valentina Tereshkova

a In 1960, the idea of humans in space was still a dream. By the end of 1961, the dream had become reality with Soviet cosmonaut Yuri Gagarin. In that decade, science and space travel were dominated by men. **b** However, on June 16, 1963, cosmonaut Valentina Tereshkova became the first woman to travel into space.

c Valentina Tereshkova was born in 1937 in a small town about 277 km. from Moscow. In 1954, she started working at a textile factory, and around that time, she learned to parachute. Because of her parachuting experience, in 1962 she was chosen to train as a cosmonaut. On her space flight in 1963, Tereshkova orbited the Earth 48 times in a little less than three days. When she returned to Earth, Tereshkova parachuted over 6,000 meters from her spacecraft to Earth! **d** As the first woman in space, Valentina Tereshkova was a pioneer for women in space travel and for professional women in general.

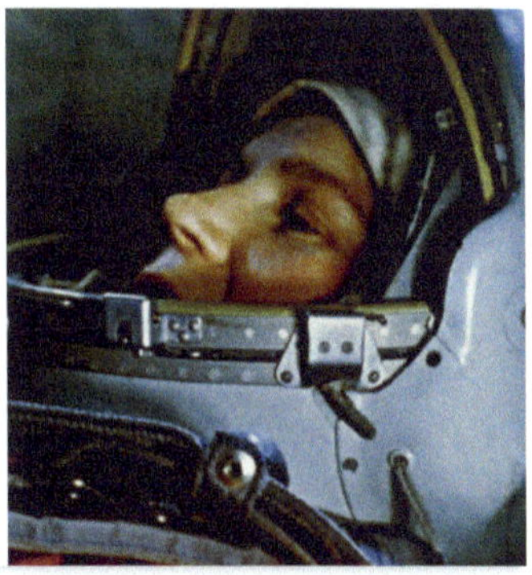

B **Read the tips for writing a biography. Match the underlined parts (a–d) of the text in A to the tips (1–4).**

1 Choose a specific angle, e.g., the first to do something, and present it in your introduction. b
2 Write an interesting first sentence to introduce the topic. a
3 Restate your angle in the conclusion of your essay. c
4 Give basic biographical facts about the person's life. Include some interesting details. d

C **Make notes to prepare to write a short biographical essay. Use the tips in B as a guide.**

D **Write your biography. Then share it with a partner. Help each other with ideas for improvements.**

SPEAKING

A IN PAIRS **Match the historical facts (a–d) with the people (1–4).**

1 Roger Bannister (UK) b
2 Junko Tabei (Japan) a
3 Gabriela Mistral (Chile) d
4 Leonardo da Vinci (Italy) c

a the first woman who climbed Mt. Everest
b the first person who ran a mile in less than four minutes
c the first to understand the circulation of blood in the body
d the first Latin American author to win the Nobel Prize for Literature

B IN PAIRS **Write a quiz similar to the one in A. Your quiz should have four to six items.**

CONFIDENT COMMUNICATOR
KEEP TALKING

Use these phrases to express interest:
Really? *Oh, I didn't know that.* *That's interesting.* *Huh.*
Use these phrases to express surprise:
Seriously?! *That's so cool!*

PRONUNCIATION

Before having students find the stressed syllable, ask them to count the syllables in each word. First, your students need to be able to identify the syllables and then identify stressed syllables. Tell them that word stress and sentence stress are important for sounding natural in English.

WRITING

Have students research a person in history. An angle for their writing might be similar to the one in the article. Remind students to use the tips for writing a biography in **B** when they start planning their work. Have them write a plan and the first draft and then check each other's first draft. Finally, have them write the final draft.

SPEAKING Alternative Activity

Tell students to choose four historical facts and the people related to the facts. They can be ancient, modern, or recent historical facts. They should be able to name four historical facts without researching. Tell them to use what they already know.

GO TO page xv

for **LANGUAGE AND LIFE** step-by-step instructions.

Language and Life

Decison Making – UNESCO Sites

A 6.05 Read the information about UNESCO sites. Then choose *True* or *False*.

UNESCO: Preserving Our Heritage

The main role of the United Nations Educational, Scientific, and Cultural Organization (UNESCO) is to encourage international collaboration, and to promote global security and peace. One way that UNESCO achieves this is through the preservation of sites of great cultural or national importance. This develops respect for those sites among the citizens of those countries. It also educates tourists about those sites and encourages them to discover the beauty of that country's culture.

Tourists can find out more about all of the UNESCO's sites by going to the World Heritage List, which can be found on the official UNESCO website. Currently, there are almost 1,100 sites on this list, including national parks, forests, islands, temples, and houses. Some of the sites are very well-known, like the Great Wall in China and Machu Picchu in Peru, but there are many sites that are well-known only within the countries where they are located. It is possible to use the World Heritage List as a way to find out more about your own country, or to inspire future vacations.

To be included on the World Heritage List, a site needs to be considered of universal importance. UNESCO has created a set of criteria to select World Heritage sites. These criteria examine the site's cultural importance, as well as its natural beauty. There are a total of ten criteria that UNESCO considers in the site selection process, and a site has to have at least one of them to be selected. Some of the criteria are:

1 Be an example of an important cultural tradition of the past or present
2 Be an example of amazing human creativity
3 Be an example of a culture's use of land or sea that is positive for the environment
4 Have incredible natural beauty
5 Represent an important period in the Earth's history
6 Represent great achievements in technology, architecture, the arts, town planning, or landscape design

Khajuraho Temple, Madhya Pradesh, a UNESCO World Heritage site

1 One purpose of UNESCO is to educate people about different cultures. **True** / False
2 All UNESCO sites are buildings. True / **False**
3 All UNESCO sites are very famous. True / **False**
4 A site has to have most of the criteria to be chosen by UNESCO. **True** / False
5 Human creativity is important to UNESCO. True / **False**
6 Ecology and the environment are factors in UNESCO selections. **True** / False

OBJECTIVE

Students learn how to choose a United Nations Educational, Scientific, and Cultural (UNESCO) site using a rating system based on criteria. There are many ways to make decisions, and a rating system is one way to include a set of standards. In this case, the set of standards are factors to consider when choosing a UNESCO site.

PROCESS OPTIONAL 6.05

Students read an article about the purpose of UNESCO and the criteria used for choosing UNESCO sites. They read about a recent UNESCO selection and identify the criteria applied to the site. Next, students work in pairs to choose a possible UNESCO World Heritage site. They rate and score their proposal against the criteria. Then, groups share their proposals and decide which proposal they will share with the class. Finally, the class can respond during an open discussion to the final reflection questions, or have students write their reflections in a learning journal.

B IN PAIRS **Read about a recent UNESCO selection. Decide which of the criteria in A you think UNESCO applied to this site.**

Suggested answers: Chiribiquete criteria: 1, 2, 4

Chiribiquete National Park, Colombia—The Maloca of the Jaguar

The Chiribiquete National Park is the largest protected area in Colombia. The flat, table-top mountains are an unusual geological feature, and they give the park its dramatic beauty. There are rock shelters at the base of the mountains that have over 75,000 paintings dating from 20,000 BCE to the present. The paintings represent the powerful jaguar, and this is a sacred region for indigenous communities.

C IN PAIRS **You are going to choose a site in your country to propose as a UNESCO World Heritage Site. Follow the steps to help you make a good decision.**

Making Decisions with Criteria and Weight

1. Rate the six UNESCO criteria in column 1 from 1 to 3 points—3 being very important to you and 1 being the least important to you.
2. Think of a site or region in your country that might qualify for UNESCO. Add it to the table in column 2.
3. Rate your site from 1 to 3 for each of the six criteria (3—completely matches the criterion; 1—does not match the criterion very well).
4. Multiply each criterion by the rating. Add up the total points for each option.

1 UNESCO Criteria (1–3 points)	2 Site/Region: ______ (rating 1–3)	3 Weighting (criterion x rating)
1: ______ pt(s).		
2: ______ pt(s).		
3: ______ pt(s).		
4: ______ pt(s).		
5: ______ pt(s).		
6: ______ pt(s).		
	Total weighting score: ______	

D IN GROUPS **Present your UNESCO proposal to your group. Compare and evaluate weighting scores and decide which proposal is best for a UNESCO site. Present your proposal to the class.**

E **Discuss the questions.**

1. Do you think this is a useful way to help make decisions? Why or why not?
2. In what other situations might you use this ranking and rating system?

MAKE IT DIGITAL

Find out if there are any UNESCO World Heritage Sites in your country and if there are any sites proposed for the future.

CLASSROOM MANAGEMENT

When working in groups, have each member take a role. These roles could be captain, scribe, timekeeper, and motivator. The captain is the leader and drives the activity, the scribe takes notes or fills in charts, the timekeeper keeps everyone on track, and the motivator supports and encourages the groups to find solutions.

CULTURE NOTE

UNESCO is a cultural organization. Ask students if they know of any other cultural organizations, either international groups or organizations in their countries. Have those who know something about an organization share it with the class.

MAKE IT DIGITAL

Have students research online on UNESCO's website for a list of countries and their designated sites. Countries are listed alphabetically.

GO TO page xvii
for **UNIT REVIEW** step-by-step instructions.

VOCABULARY review

SCORE: / 10

A Choose the correct words.

I'm **1** thankless / thankful that there are so many **2** capable / hopeful people who invent useful things! Some are famous and **3** successful / entertaining people like Bill Gates, but many are not famous at all. There are people who work at companies all over the world to give us **4** amazing / amazed things like 3-D cameras and driverless cars. It's very **5** entertained / entertaining to play video games or watch online videos, and someone had to invent that technology. However, being an inventor can be **6** boring / bored because an inventor has to focus on very small details, and it takes a long time to invent something. Inventors are **7** disappointed / disappointing when their inventions don't work very well, but sometimes an invention becomes a **8** capable / huge success. A **9** huge / particularly important invention in recent years was HD (high-definition) TV. This was an enormous **10** improvement / creation in TV technology.

GRAMMAR review

SCORE: / 10

A Complete the sentences with the simple past or past perfect forms of the verbs in parentheses.

1 My dad ________ (not have) a smartphone before I ________ (give) him one for his birthday.
2 After I ________ (save) enough money, I ________ (buy) a small car.
3 When my dad ________ (buy) his first car, he ________ never ________ (drive) a car!
4 At the beginning of the 21st century, many people ________ (not use) the internet.
5 No one ________ (hear) the term *social media* when the first social media network ________ (begin) in 2002.

1 hadn't had / gave
2 had saved / bought
3 bought / had / driven
4 didn't use / hadn't used
5 had heard / began

B Complete the sentences with *who, that, where, when,* and *which.*

1 Driverless cars are an innovation which/that may change the transportation industry.
2 Tech companies are places where there are a lot of creative people!
3 An AI specialist is a person who/that works in artificial intelligence technology.
4 My dad was born in a decade when a lot of important technology was invented.
5 There are millions of people in the world who/that use the internet every day.

16–20 correct: You can talk about events in history and changes in the modern world. You can use defining relative clauses and adjective suffixes.
0–15 correct: Look again at the Vocabulary and Grammar sections in the unit.

TOTAL SCORE: / 20

WHAT DO YOU KNOW NOW? Look back at page 57 and add the words you know now to the box.

GO TO page xix
for **FOLLOW A PRO** step-by-step instructions.

FOLLOW A PRO ANCIENT CIVILIZATIONS

Take the quiz about ancient civilizations. Go to Follow A Pro on page 132 to find the answers. Then learn more about archeologists.

1 Cleopatra was …
a Greek. b Egyptian. c Roman.

2 According to a Roman legend, Rome's founder, Romulus, was raised by a …
a Greek woman. b goddess. c wolf.

3 The oldest civilization in the Americas was the …
a Olmec in Mexico. b Caral Supe in Peru. c Cherokee in the US.

4 One of the first medical centers was in …
a Persia (Iran), in the 6th century. b Athens, Greece, in the 12th century. c London, England, in the 16th century.

CLASSROOM MANAGEMENT

Tell students to read the whole text before they start answering VOCABULARY **A**. You might want to give them a six-minute time limit for this exercise. Give five minutes each for the GRAMMAR **A** and **B** activities.

ALTERNATIVE ACTIVITY

Play *Race to the Board* when you do the feedback for GRAMMAR **A**. Split the class into four teams. Give each team a marker and a designated space on the board. Read the sentences out loud up to the blank. Teams send a runner to the board to write the answer. The first correct and well-written answer wins a point. The first team to score five points wins.

FURTHER DISCUSSION

Write the following questions on the board. Then have students form groups of three and ask each other:

- Do you think time is passing quickly or slowly?
- Do you know someone who likes to invent things?
- What's a game changer in your city?
- What's a silly invention you haven't tried yet?

UNIT 7

Looking Back

GO TO page vi
for UNIT OPENER step-by-step instructions.

WHAT DO YOU ALREADY KNOW?

1 Think of words about things people sometimes regret. Write the words.
2 IN PAIRS Share and compare your ideas. Add more words to your lists.

STUDENTS MAY ALREADY KNOW:

- Regrets: buying a useless object, throwing something away, not calling someone, quitting a team, quitting a job, not visiting someone, not telling someone you loved them, not studying hard, missing a test.

Regrets

VIDEO

DISCUSS & SHARE

3 IN GROUPS Watch the video and answer the question.
SYM Do you think it's good to have regrets, or is it better to focus on the future?

GO TO page xx
for VIDEOS IN SYM step-by-step instructions.

In this unit, you will ...

- talk about things that a business should have done differently, discuss things you should not have bought, and recall events you regret.
- use thinking skills: evaluate, analyze, and apply.
- read about famous mistakes in history.
- use strategies and language to introduce an anecdote, give reasons for opinions and decisions, and set the scene for a story.
- use interpersonal communication skills to plan and give a presentation.
- learn skills to structure your writing.

WHAT DO YOU ALREADY KNOW?

If students are struggling to understand what to do, you can ask them some questions to prompt their thinking:

- Have you ever done anything you later regretted?
- Do you think about the past much?
- Has anything happened that you thought about later?

VIDEO

Before viewing, ask:

What does Andrea regret? *not practicing enough music, she wasn't sure she could make a living as a musician*
What is Sean looking for in the future? *his deam job*

After viewing, put the continuum on the board.

have regrets —— focus on the future

Have students mark the continuum and explain their preferences.

DISCUSS & SHARE

Ask students to think about whether regrets are worth spending time on or if people should move on and think about the future. Maybe people can learn from their mistakes, or perhaps we can't learn anything from thinking about the past. Students should place themselves on a continuum of opinion.

GO TO page x for READING step-by-step instructions.

The Reese's story could be considered an example of the butterfly effect. The fact that Mars Inc. refused permission to use their candy in a movie in the 1980s may have led to Reese's candy being the number one candy in the US now.

1 2 (The spacecraft was using one system, but the computers on the ground were using another.)

2 1 (Hershey made a lot of money when people saw Reese's Pieces in a major movie.)

GO TO page vii for VOCABULARY step-by-step instructions.

LESSON 1 Famous Mistakes

READING

A IN GROUPS THINKING SKILL—Evaluate Assess a description of the "butterfly effect." Do you think the statement is true, partly true, or false? Explain.

A butterfly moves its wings in Brazil, and it creates a storm in Texas.

B 7.01 Read the article about famous mistakes. Is either of the mistakes an example of the butterfly effect?

Famous Mistakes in History

1. Expensive Decision

In the 1982 mega-hit movie *E.T.* there is a scene where the little boy uses candy to convince *E.T.* the extraterrestrial, to follow him. The filmmakers had planned to use M&Ms for this scene, but Mars, Inc. did not give them permission to use their candy. They then asked Hershey for permission to use Reese's Pieces, and Hershey agreed, so it **turned out** that Reese's Pieces candy was used in the movie. Two weeks after the movie opened, sales of Reese's Pieces **went up** by around 65%. Today, a Reese's product is the number one candy in the US! Mars Inc. shouldn't have missed this opportunity!

2. Lost in Space

The Mars Climate Orbiter was a small spacecraft built to orbit Mars and record information about the surface and atmosphere of the planet. It went into space in December 1998, and it disappeared in September 1999. When researchers **looked into** why the Orbiter was lost, they **came across** an important mistake. They **found out** that the system on the spacecraft had used the metric system, while the computers on Earth had used the imperial system. Because of this mistake, the Orbiter went too close to Mars and **burned up**. Someone should have noticed that the two systems used different measurements!

GLOSSARY

metric system (n): a system of measurement that uses meters and kilograms
imperial system (n): a system of measurement that uses yards and pounds
orbit (v): the path of an object moving around a larger object in space
measurement (n): the exact size of something, expressed in numbers of standard units

C READING SKILL—Synthesize Match the descriptions below to the famous mistakes in B. Write the numbers.

1 a mistake caused by different people using different systems ____
2 a mistake that was very lucky for a competitor ____

VOCABULARY phrasal verbs

A Match the phrasal verbs in bold in READING B to the definitions (1–6). Write the base form of each phrasal verb.

1 look into : to investigate an event or situation
2 turn out : to have a certain result
3 find out : to discover information
4 come across : to meet someone or discover something by chance
5 burn up : to be destroyed by fire or heat
6 go up : to increase

68 Unit 7 Looking Back

READING OPTIONAL 7.01

THINKING SKILL—Evaluate

The butterfly effect is a theory that explains how a very small difference in a physical system can make a significant change at a later time. *The butterfly effect has become a metaphor for the existence of seemingly significant moments in time that alter history and shape destinies.*

CULTURE NOTE

Draw students' attention to the glossary. Ask them where in the world the measurements *yards* and *pounds* are used and in which countries *kilometers, meters, centimeters,* and *kilograms* are used. Review measurements and weights in both metric and imperial systems. Ask students about conversion rates.

VOCABULARY Extra Practice

Have students ask each other questions about the information in the article using phrasal verbs. For example, *Did the mistake turn out well for Mars? Did the sales of Reese's Pieces go up? Who looked into why the Orbiter was lost? What did they come across?*

B Choose the correct phrasal verbs.

When companies have poor sales, they have to **1** come across / look into the reasons why a product doesn't sell. When they do research, they sometimes **2** find out / turn out that the problem is with the marketing, but sometimes it **3** finds out / turns out that the problem is the product itself. The company may have to stop developing that product and develop a new product. This is not always a problem. Sometimes a series of mistakes can result in new products that make the company's sales **4** look into / go up a lot.

GRAMMAR *should/shouldn't have*

A Choose the correct options.

Someone should have noticed that the two systems used different measurements!
Mars Inc. shouldn't have missed this opportunity!

1 *Should have* and *shouldn't have* are used to express …
- **a** recommendations for the past.
- **b** recommendations for the present.
- **c** recommendations for the future.

2 *Should have* and *shouldn't have* are followed by the … form of a verb.
- **a** base form
- **b** simple past
- **c** past participle

For more practice, go to page 151.

B Complete the responses using *should have* or *shouldn't have* and the correct form of the verb in parentheses.

1 A British couple asked a lottery official to check their lottery ticket numbers. The official checked the numbers and told the couple that they had not won any money. The official tore the ticket in two pieces and threw it away. However, the couple later received a message to keep their ticket. They got the torn ticket from the lottery official, and it turned out that they had won 57.9 million euros!

The official *should have checked* (check) the numbers more carefully. / The official *shouldn't have thrown away* (throw away) the ticket.

2 In 1999, a company called Excite had the opportunity to buy Google. The heads of Google wanted one million dollars, but then they changed the price to $750,000. Excite thought it was too expensive and turned down the offer. Today, Google is worth billions of dollars.

Excite ______ (buy) Google. / Excite ______ (turn down) the offer.

3 J. K. Rowling's first book, *Harry Potter and the Philosopher's Stone*, was turned down by 12 publishers before it was published by Bloomsbury. One reason why Bloomsbury decided to publish the book was that the chief executive officer's eight-year-old daughter read part of the book and loved it.

The 12 publishers ______ (turn down) the book. / The 12 publishers ______ (accept) the book.

C **IN PAIRS** Take turns reading the responses in B. Do you have similar opinions?

SPEAKING

A Think of a mistake that a person or a company made and consider what they should have done differently. Use the questions as a guide and make notes.

1 Who was the person or what was the company?
2 What mistakes did the person or company make?
3 What should they have done differently?
4 How did the situation turn out?

B **IN GROUPS** Tell your group what happened. Say what you think the person or company should have done differently. Discuss other possible options with your group. Use the Confident Communicator box to help you.

CONFIDENT COMMUNICATOR
START TALKING

To introduce an anecdote or a short true story, use these phrases:
Here's something that happened to (person/company) in (date).
Listen to this. In (date), (name) made a really bad decision.

GO TO page viii
for **GRAMMAR** step-by-step instructions.

Suggested answers:
2 should have bought / shouldn't have turned down
3 shouldn't have turned down / should have accepted

GO TO page xii
for **SPEAKING** step-by-step instructions.

GRAMMAR

As the form is *should/shouldn't have* + past participle, it would be a good idea to review past participles. Have three students test each other—one student says an irregular verb, and the other two compete to say the past participle.

Some past participles for regrets are: *gone, broken, built, checked, done, driven, drunk, eaten, fought, forgotten, hit, hurt, lent, paid, said, sold, stolen, shot, slept, spoken,* and *written*.

SPEAKING

Being able to tell or share an anecdote is an excellent speaking activity. Remind students that an anecdote is a short, personal story. It could be funny and/or interesting. Have a volunteer student read the *Confident Communicator* box. Some more phrases to introduce an anecdote are *You are not going to believe this, but …, I'll never forget the time when …, Did I ever tell you about …*

LESSON 2 Why Did I Buy That?

VOCABULARY *spend, lose, waste*

A Write *spend, lose,* or *waste.*

1 lose : to have less money because of mistake
2 spend : to use money or time to get something
3 waste : to use money or time in a careless way

B Choose the correct words.

1 Many people **waste** / **lose** a lot of money buying unnecessary things.
2 Making a financial plan can help you **waste** / **spend** your money carefully.
3 If you buy lottery tickets, you are probably just **wasting** / **spending** your money.
4 Many people **lost** / **wasted** a lot of money when stock prices fell.
5 My uncle started a small company, but it failed. He **spent** / **lost** all of his money.

GO TO page xi for **LISTENING** step-by-step instructions.

GO TO page 145 for **AUDIO SCRIPT**.

Suggested answers: People think that things like swimming pools, kitchen gadgets, exercise equipment, or timeshares will make their lives better. They think they will enjoy their free time more, and they think they will change their habits and become healthier, thinner, or smarter if they buy something that will help them do it. This is almost never the case.

LISTENING

A IN PAIRS Which of these things do you think people often regret buying? Discuss.

1 
vacation homes

2 
a desktop computer

3 
exercise equipment

4 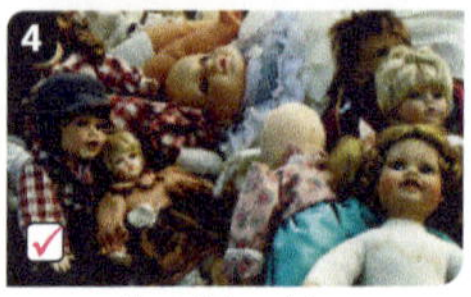
collectible objects

5 
a new car

6 
a swimming pool or a hot tub

B 7.02 Listen to the radio interviews. Check (✓) the items in A they discuss.

GLOSSARY

regret (v): to feel sorry or sad about something that happened
regret (n): a feeling of sadness about something that happened

MAKE IT YOURS

What things do your family and friends regret spending money on? How do you feel about the ways you spend money?

C 7.02 LISTENING SKILL—Listen for reasons Listen to the panel discussion again. Answer the questions.

1 For what two reasons does Steve regret getting a swimming pool? expensive and don't have much time
2 According to Monica, what are the problems with vacation homes? expensive, boring to always go to the same place; they are hard to sell
3 Why does Omar regret buying a desktop computer? almost always uses his laptop
4 Why does Sarah say she wishes she hadn't spent money on dolls? daughter isn't interested anymore

D IN GROUPS THINKING SKILL—Analyze After listening to the panel discussion, what can you infer about people's reasons for buying things that they later regret? Why do so many people waste money on those things?

GO TO page ix for **PRONUNCIATION** step-by-step instructions.

PRONUNCIATION /s/ and /z/

A 7.03 Do the letters in bold make an /s/ sound or a /z/ sound? Listen and check. Then practice saying the words.

lose waste tools use exercise house desktop objects

VOCABULARY

More words and phrases for spending, losing, and wasting money are *squander, splurge, drop, forget, leave behind, fritter away, misspend, misuse, be lavish,* and *use up.* Antonyms are *save, keep, hoard, find,* and *conserve.*

Ask students if they spend, lose, or waste money or if they save, keep, or hoard money.

LISTENING

Before listening to the panel discussion again in **C**, have students read through the questions. Then have them listen for the answers without writing anything down. When they hear the answer to each question, they should silently put their right index finger on their nose. This is a physical response that frees them from the stress of listening and writing simultaneously.

PRONUNCIATION Extra Practice

Tell students to write the sounds /s/ and /z/ on a piece of paper. In pairs, one student should say the sounds and the other point to what they hear. Have them say words containing either /s/ or /z/ and ask their partners to point to the sounds they hear. The /s/ sound is found in *waste, house, desktop, objects* and the /z/ sound is found in *lose, tools, use,* and *exercise.*

GRAMMAR past perfect for wishes about the past

A Choose the correct options.

1 "We really wish we had never bought that vacation home!" means …
  a "We bought a vacation home."
  b "We didn't buy a vacation home."
2 "I really wish I had saved that money instead" means …
  a "I saved money."
  b "I didn't save money."
3 The correct form of the verb for a wish about the past is *had* (*not/never*) + …
  a past participle.
  b base form.

For more practice, go to page 152.

B Write what the person probably wishes in each situation. You may want to write more than one sentence.

1 Justin bought a motorcycle two years ago. Since then, he has had three accidents and a lot of hospital bills.
a He wishes he hadn't *bought the motorcycle*.
b He wishes he had *been more careful*.

2 Karen sold her house and moved to another town. It's expensive there, and she is paying more for rent than she was paying for her mortgage loan.
a Karen wishes she had ________.
b Karen wishes she hadn't ________.

3 Paul got a good job offer, so he quit college and took the job. Now he is worried that he won't be able to move forward in his career.
a Paul wishes he had ________.
b Paul wishes he hadn't ________.

4 Leo is 45, and he is losing his hair. He saw an ad on TV for a machine that makes hair grow. It was expensive, but he ordered it immediately because he didn't want to waste any time. He didn't read any reviews of the product. He has been using the machine for several months, but the machine doesn't work.
a Leo wishes he had ________.
b Leo wishes he hadn't ________.

C IN PAIRS Read your sentences from B. Did you have similar ideas? Discuss.

Suggested answers:
2 a stayed in her old town
  b sold her house / moved
3 a stayed in college / finished his college degree
  b quit college
4 a read the reviews first
  b bought the machine

SPEAKING

A Think of two or three things you wish you hadn't bought. Use the cues to make notes about each thing.

Object or service bought: ________
Reason(s) you bought it: ________
Reason(s) why you regret buying it: ________

B IN GROUPS Tell your group about the things you regret buying. Use the Confident Communicator box to help you.

CONFIDENT COMMUNICATOR
KEEP TALKING

To give reasons for opinions and decisions, use the following phrases:
One reason why I wish … is that …
I should/shouldn't have … because …
The problem is/was that …
I wish I had … before I …

GRAMMAR

Using the past perfect for wishes about the past is very useful, and it's actually quite similar in structure to other languages. Once students gain confidence using the past participle easily in speech, they should master it. Let students know that the past perfect is used for wishes that didn't come true and things that turned out differently than had been hoped.

SPEAKING

Share with students something you have bought, the reasons you bought it, and why you later regretted it. For example, *I bought a waffle maker because an ad kept popping up on my social media feeds. Mixing the batter takes too much time. It was heavy and took up a lot of space. I put it away. It's not convenient, so I never use it. I shouldn't have bought it. I regret buying it.*

LESSON 3 Life's Regrets

LISTENING

A THINKING SKILL—Apply **As a class, predict five things you think people often regret when they get older.**

1 ______
2 ______
3 ______
4 ______
5 ______

GO TO page 145 for AUDIO SCRIPT.

B 7.04 Listen to a talk about regrets. Which of your ideas in A does the speaker mention? Did any of the regrets surprise you?

GO TO page 146 for AUDIO SCRIPT.

C 7.05 LISTENING SKILL—Listen for main ideas **Listen again to three segments of the talk about types of regrets. Then choose the main idea of each segment.**

1 Professional Lives
- **a** People wish they had earned more money.
- **b** People wish they had not worked so much.

2 Friendships
- **a** People wish they hadn't lost touch with old friends.
- **b** People wish they hadn't made old friends angry.

3 Children
- **a** People wish they had taught their children to do more things.
- **b** People wish they had had more children.

VOCABULARY collocations

A Match the parts of the verb phrases.

1 turn down <u>a</u>	**a** a job / an invitation / an opportunity / a chance
2 miss <u>c</u>	**b** a boyfriend / girlfriend
3 get in / stay in / lose <u>d</u>	**c** an opportunity / a chance
4 spend / waste <u>e</u>	**d** touch (with someone)
5 break up with <u>b</u>	**e** time or money

B Complete the paragraph with the correct forms of verb phrases from A.

I'm 84 years old, and I've had a wonderful life, but I have a few regrets. I've **1** <u>missed</u> some <u>chances</u> to do exciting things and make my life even better. I also have a professional regret. I **2** <u>turned down</u> an <u>opportunity</u> to go to an excellent art school because I didn't want to move to New York, and I really regret that. I stayed in my small town and lived with my parents. I **3** <u>wasted</u> some <u>time</u> (about three years) doing small jobs before I finally went to college. I wish I had gone to college and started my studies earlier. Finally, one of my biggest regrets is that I didn't **4** <u>stay in touch</u> with my best friend from college, but I'm trying to **5** <u>get in touch</u> with her now. I hope I can find her.

MAKE IT REAL

There are many ways to describe the end of a relationship. People can *split up with* or *part ways with* their partners.

LISTENING

In **A**, students apply previous knowledge about a topic. When doing an open-class discussion, pose the question or problem and give everyone thinking time. Then start to call on people randomly.

Areas in which older people might have regrets are family, work, medical issues, health, money, relationships, and travel.

VOCABULARY

Collocations are the way words naturally go together. As students progress in their language learning, they'll be able to use idiomatic expressions and more natural phrasing if they continue to expand their vocabulary and pay attention to how words are combined.

MAKE IT REAL

For this section, put students into pairs. Have them role play how they end up a relationship. Tell students they should use some collocations from VOCABULARY **A**. Then swich roles.

WRITING

A **IN PAIRS** **Read the blog entry. Why does the writer have mixed feelings about the messages?**

NO REGRETS? Really?

There are many messages on posters and on the internet that tell us that we should never regret things we think we should or shouldn't have done. **They say that** we should follow our hearts, take chances, and do the things we really want to do. That way, when we are older, we will not think "I wish I had done X," or "I wish I hadn't done Y." **Another argument is that** we should only regret the things we *wanted* to do but didn't do.

I have mixed feelings about these messages. **I think** people sometimes have to take chances in order to reach their goals. **I believe that** people often waste time regretting decisions they made and thinking about what they should have done differently. However, it is unrealistic to think that people can live their whole lives with no regrets. We all have regrets about something.

GO TO page xiv for WRITING step-by-step instructions.

He thinks people sometimes spend too much time having regrets and thinking about the past, but he also thinks it's normal to have regrets, and we can learn from them.

B **Write the phrases in bold in A in the correct columns in the table.**

Stating Your Opinion	Stating Other People's Opinions
In my opinion, …	Some people say that …
In my experience, …	Other people believe that …
I feel that …	Others feel that …
I have mixed feelings about …	They say that …
I think …	Another argument is that …
I believe that …	

C **Think about the posters and blog in A. Make notes in your notebook.**

1. What is your opinion of the first poster? Why?
2. What is your opinion of the second poster? Why?
3. What is your opinion of the blog? Do you agree or disagree with the blogger's ideas? Why?

D **Write a blog about your opinion on regrets. Include phrases from B.**

E **IN GROUPS** **Read your blog to your group. What are your group members' opinions about your ideas?**

SPEAKING

A **Make notes to tell an anecdote about a small thing that you regret. Try to think of something funny if possible. You do not have to talk about any regrets that you feel uncomfortable about.**

- What did you do or say?
- What was the result?
- What do you wish you had done differently?
- What did you learn from the experience?

B **IN GROUPS** **Tell your anecdotes. Give your classmates further advice about what they should or shouldn't have done. Use the Confident Communicator box to help you.**

Last week, I was at a restaurant with some friends. We ordered so much food! For dessert, I asked for a "chocolate bomb." It was a huge slice of chocolate cake with a massive serving of chocolate ice cream. I ate all of it, but felt so sick later. I definitely wish I hadn't eaten that dessert! I should have ordered some fruit.

CONFIDENT COMMUNICATOR
START TALKING

To start a story, set the scene.
Place: *I was at / in / on my way to …*
People: *I was alone / with …*
What was happening: *I was / We were … -ing …*

WRITING

Students will write a blog entry giving their opinions about regrets. You might like to ask some questions to give them ideas to get started:

- Do you think regrets are good or bad?
- Are regrets useful or useless?
- Do regrets have something to teach us?
- Does everyone have regrets?

They can use phrases stating their opinions and phrases stating others' opinions from WRITING **A** and **B**.

SPEAKING

Some small things people might regret are not having breakfast because now they are hungry, or not going to bed early because now they are tired. They might regret a time they were late to an appointment or a meeting recently. Ask your students if they have been in trouble recently and whether they have any regrets about what led to that.

GO TO page xv
for **LANGUAGE AND LIFE** step-by-step instructions.

Language and Life

Interpersonal Communication – A Presentation

A 7.06 **Read the case study. Then choose the correct options on the next page.**

Case Study:

The Edsel

INTRODUCTION

In 1957, the Ford Motor Company introduced the Edsel, a car that they were promoting as "the car of the future." However, the Edsel turned out to be one of the greatest mistakes in business history.

BASIC IDEA AND RESEARCH

- In the early 1950s, the US economy was extremely strong, and Ford wanted a new car in the medium-price range. Unfortunately, they did not pay attention to research that showed the US would soon experience a recession.
- Ford did not do enough research to find out what customers really wanted in a car. Instead, they based most of their decisions on the opinions of Ford executives, the people who managed the company.
- The executives spent a lot of money on research to help them decide on the name of the car, but they decided to use the name of Henry Ford's son, Edsel. It turned out that people hated the name.

DESIGN

- Ford wanted to design a car that looked very different from existing cars, but the company did not do research to find out if people liked the design. They didn't show the design to sales people or the public before the car was produced.
- The company wanted to produce a car that many different types of people would buy, so they made 18 different models of the Edsel.
- The Edsel had many new features that hadn't been used in cars before, but those new things did not always work well.

MARKETING

- Ford started promoting the Edsel as "the car of the future" in advertisements a year before the car was produced. There was a lot of excitement about it, and people even waited in line to see it. Unfortunately, many people did not like the new design when they saw it. They decided that it was an ugly, expensive car with a terrible name.

1957 Edsel

1964 Mustang

LESSONS LEARNED

Ford learned from its mistakes with the Edsel. They did excellent research for the Ford Mustang, which they produced in the 1960s. The Ford Mustang became one of the greatest successes in business history. It was exactly the right car for the right customers at the right time, and the Mustang is still a very popular car today.

OBJECTIVE

Students plan a presentation about a failed product. Companies spend a lot of time and money doing market research on products. Generally, they can predict how well their product will do once it is released. This was not always the case. Students will research other failed products, present the product's history, and suggest what should have been done instead.

PROCESS OPTIONAL 7.06

Students first read a detailed case study about a car the Ford Motor Company released in the 1950s. The case study is about how and why the car failed to sell well. Students then discuss what the company should have done differently. They compare and contrast the failed Edsel car to a successful car, the Ford Mustang that came afterward. Then, students plan a presentation about a failed product of their choice following clear steps. Next, students assign roles to members of the group, prepare notes, and practice their presentation. Finally, they give their presentation about a failed product to the class.

1 The basic idea for the Edsel was based on ...
   a existing cars. b Ford executives' opinions. c a lot of research.
2 Ford wanted to sell the Edsel to ...
   a young people. b wealthy people. c many types of people.
3 To sell the Edsel, Ford used the idea that it was ...
   a modern and different. b inexpensive. c attractive.
4 People thought the Edsel was ______ it had appeared in the advertisements.
   a better than b not as good as c the same as
5 Ford used ______ process for designing the Mustang.
   a exactly the same b a similar c a completely different

B IN PAIRS Discuss the questions.

1 What should Ford have done differently when it designed, promoted, and produced the Edsel?
2 Why was the Mustang a great success?

C IN GROUPS You are going to work together to plan a presentation about a product that was a failure. Follow the steps. Think about each person's skills and what each person can do to prepare and deliver the presentation. Look at the different points below and decide who in your group should be responsible for each part.

Step 1
Research the product—who likes investigating new facts?
- name and type of product
- company that made it
- target customers
- where it was advertised
- what the advertising promised
- design or quality
- how it was promoted
- the product
- how it was advertised
- what the company and others can learn from this experience

Step 2
Structure the presentation—who likes organizing information in an interesting and logical way?
- Decide the basic structure of the presentation.
- Plan what information there should be in each part.
- Agree on the key point you want to communicate.

Step 3
Give the presentation—who likes talking to groups and communicating their ideas?
- Decide who will say what.
- Discuss how you can engage your audience.
- Give the presentation!

D Discuss the questions.

1 How did you communicate your reasons for choosing each person's responsibility?
2 Did everyone agree with the reasons? Why or why not?
3 In what other situations might you have to communicate with a group of people?

MAKE IT DIGITAL

Before you buy a product, go online and read customer reviews. This can help you decide whether or not to spend money on the product.

CLASSROOM MANAGEMENT

When students are working in groups, it is important that all members have a role. Failure to distribute the work evenly may leave a few members of the group doing all the work. Make sure all members of the groups are participating equally.

MAKE IT DIGITAL

Have students go online and read the reviews of a product they are thinking of buying. Tell them that the most useful reviews are the bad ones and that they should first read the reviews with one and two stars. This will give them a realistic overview of the product.

CULTURE NOTE

Ask students if they know of any American products or businesses that have failed in other countries, particularly their country. Do they know about Walmart's failure in South Korea or Starbucks's inability to establish itself in Australia?

GO TO page xvii
for **UNIT REVIEW** step-by-step instructions.

Suggested answers:

1 a He shouldn't have bought the phone. / He should have read the reviews.
b He wishes he hadn't bought the phone. / He wishes he had read the reviews.

2 a I should have gone to the party.
b I wish I had gone to the party.

3 a She should have helped him study.
b She/He wishes she had helped him study.

4 a I shouldn't have lost touch with them. / I should have stayed in touch with them.
b I wish I hadn't lost touch with them. / I wish I had stayed in touch with them.

5 a They shouldn't have bought the tickets. / They shouldn't have wasted their money.
b They wish they had won. / They wish they hadn't bought the tickets. / They wish they hadn't wasted their money.

GO TO page xviii
for **STUDY SKILLS** step-by-step instructions.

VOCABULARY review

SCORE: / 10

A Complete the text with the correct forms of the verbs from the box.

find out	look into	lose touch	spend	turn out
go up	lose	miss	stay in touch	waste

My dad's business wasn't growing, so he **1** __looked into__ why that was happening, and he **2** __found out__ that the main problem was customer service. When the company started, my dad personally **3** __stayed in touch__ with all of the customers, but as the company grew, he had many other things to do. He said he couldn't **4** __waste__ time visiting or talking on the phone to customers. It **5** __turns out__ that if you don't take care of your customers, you **6** __lose__ their business! So he hired some people to help with other parts of the business, and he spoke directly with customers. Now he doesn't **7** __miss__ an opportunity to talk to a customer. He **8** __spends__ a lot of time each day making phone calls, and he often visits customers. He never **9** __loses touch__ with them! Now my dad's business is growing again! Profits have **10** __gone up__ and he is happy.

GRAMMAR review

SCORE: / 10

A For each situation, write two sentences: one using *should / shouldn't have* and another using *wish*. Use your notebook.

1 My dad's new cell phone isn't very good. He didn't read any reviews before he bought it.
2 I didn't go to Sam's party last Friday. I heard it was great!
3 Monica didn't help her brother study for his math exam, and he failed it.
4 I moved to another town and lost touch with my old friends.
5 Carol and Steve bought 20 lottery tickets, but they didn't win. They wasted a lot of money!

16–20 correct: You can talk about past mistakes and regrets. You can use *should/shouldn't have* and the past perfect for wishes about the past.
0–15 correct: Look again at the Vocabulary and Grammar sections in the unit.

TOTAL SCORE: / 20

WHAT DO YOU KNOW NOW? Look back at page 67 and add the words you know now to the box.

STUDY SKILLS STRUCTURING YOUR WRITING

Take the quiz about structuring your writing. Go to **Study Skills** on page 133 to find the answers. Then learn more about structuring your writing.

1 When we use the word *argument* to talk about essay writing, what do we mean?
a a disagreement between the writer and the reader
b the point the writer makes (which also gives the essay its structure)

2 Put the essay outline in order.
_c_ main argument
_d_ conclusion
_a_ title
_e_ introduction
_b_ objections to main argument

3 Which of the following are linking words?
a although **b** in spite of **c** consequently **d** outline

CLASSROOM MANAGEMENT

Before starting the review activities, give students some time to glance over the unit and review the vocabulary and grammar sections in each lesson. Once they have looked over the material, they will find the review activities more relevant.

Give those students who have had trouble time to look back at the relevant sections.

For fast finishers, tell them to write sentences similar to those in GRAMMAR **A**.

FURTHER DISCUSSION

Write the following questions on the board. Then have students form groups of three and ask each other:

- What do you do to save money?
- Do you like to spend money?
- What has been your most costly mistake?
- Have you done anything today that you shouldn't have?
- Do you spend much time on regrets?
- Have your regrets taught you anything?

GO TO page vi
for UNIT OPENER step-by-step instructions.

UNIT 8 A New Home?

WHAT DO YOU ALREADY KNOW?

1 Think of words you know about space. Write the words.
2 IN PAIRS Share and compare your ideas. Add more words to your lists.

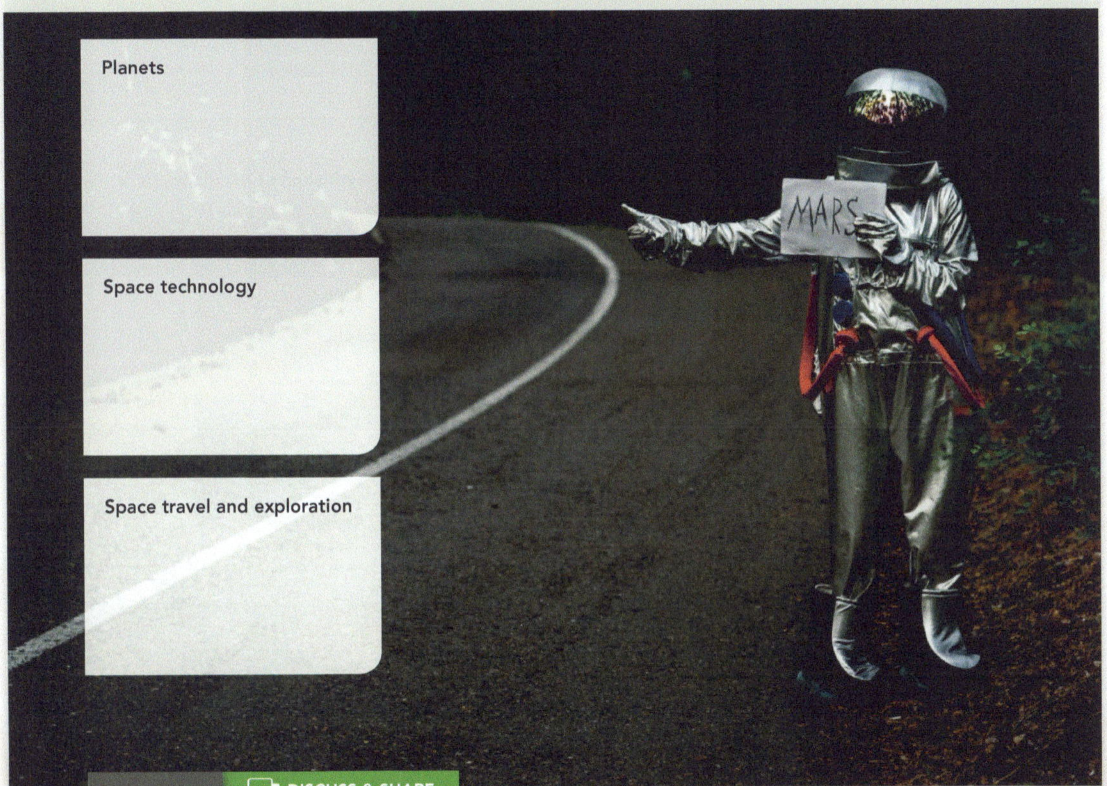

Planets

Space technology

Space travel and exploration

STUDENTS MAY ALREADY KNOW:

- **Planets:** Mercury, Venus, Earth, Mars, Jupiter, Saturn, Uranus, Neptune.
- **Space technology:** satellite, exploration, atmosphere.
- **Space travel and exploration:** spaceship, rocket, astronaut, scientist, pilot, the Sun, stars, universe.

VIDEO

DISCUSS & SHARE

3 IN GROUPS Watch the video and answer the question.
SYM Should we focus on problems on Earth before we explore other planets?

GO TO page xx
for VIDEOS IN SYM step-by-step instructions.

In this unit, you will …

- talk about hypothetical events in history, role play an interview with an astronaut, and discuss your opinions of space exploration.
- use thinking skills: analyze, question, and recall.
- read about the extinction of the dinosaurs.
- use strategies and language to express possibility or probability, use indirect questions to sound more polite, and clarify reasons for opinions.
- use reasoning skills to make decisions about a space team.
- follow an astrobiologist to learn about this job and the skills needed for this industry.

WHAT DO YOU ALREADY KNOW?

If students are struggling to understand what to do, you can ask them some questions to prompt their thinking:

- When you look into the night sky, what can you see?
- What if you look through a telescope?
- Do you ever think about what's out there in space?
- Do you think people will live on Mars one day?

VIDEO

Before viewing, ask:

Where does digital imagine come from? *from space technology that has led to new medical technology*
Who used wireless headphones first? *astronauts*

After viewing, put the continuum on the board.

problems on Earth —— other planets

Have students mark the continuum and explain their preferences.

DISCUSS & SHARE

Students should place themselves on a continuum of opinion. Ask students to think about whether we should focus on problems here on Earth before we explore other planets. Space exploration may be an exciting prospect, but it is costly. Space exploration has led to many scientific discoveries.

GO TO page vii
for **VOCABULARY** step-by-step instructions.

GO TO page x
for **READING** step-by-step instructions.

LESSON 1 What If ...?

VOCABULARY

A Match the words to the definitions.

asteroid debris crater tidal wave extinction soot herbivore carnivore

1 tidal wave: a very large wave
2 soot: a dirty black substance from a fire
3 herbivore: an animal that eats only plants
4 asteroid: a mass of rock that moves in space
5 extinction: when a species disappears
6 crater: a large round hole in the ground
7 carnivore: an animal that eats other animals
8 debris: small pieces left when something is destroyed

READING

A IN PAIRS READING SKILL—Predict Number the events leading up to the extinction of the dinosaurs in the order you think they happened.

5 Plants died, and the herbivores didn't have food.

3 Burning debris caused forest fires.

4 Soot blocked the sunlight.

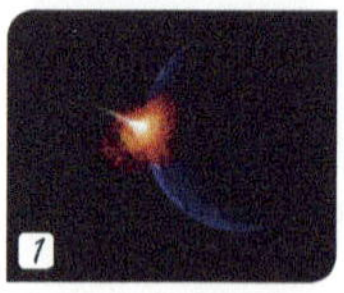
1 An asteroid hit the Earth and made a crater.

6 The carnivores didn't have food, so they died.

2 The impact caused tidal waves.

B 8.01 Read the article and check your predictions.

WHAT ON EARTH HAPPENED?

Sixty-six million years ago, during the time of the dinosaurs, something happened that changed our planet forever. A meteorite hit the Earth near the Yucatan Peninsula of Mexico and created a crater that was 185 km wide. The impact caused an explosion equal to about 10 million Hiroshima bombs. This caused a chain of events that resulted in mass extinctions of life on Earth.

Scientists almost all agree that the meteorite was the main cause of these mass extinctions. They now think they understand what happened after the meteorite hit. First, if you had been within 1,000 km. of the impact site, you would have been killed by a massive ball of fire. Almost immediately after the impact, there were earthquakes and 300-meter-high tidal waves all over the planet. About eight minutes after the impact, debris from the explosion would have started to fall out of the sky. A lot of the debris was on fire, and this caused massive forest fires. A few minutes later, there would have been 965-km-per-hour winds caused by the quickly heating air. These winds would have destroyed everything they came into contact with.

Common theories suggest that if you had been far enough away, you would have survived the explosion. However, in a few days, you would have seen the sky get very dark because of the carbon soot that filled the atmosphere. The soot blocked the sunlight for months and perhaps for years. Without sunlight, plants began to die. When the plants died, there was no food for the herbivores, so they died, too. When the herbivores died, the carnivores didn't have food, so they also died.

It is interesting to try to imagine what would have happened if the meteorite had *not* crashed into Earth. Some scientists think dinosaurs might have survived. They believe they could have adapted to slow changes in climate over many years. Just imagine ...

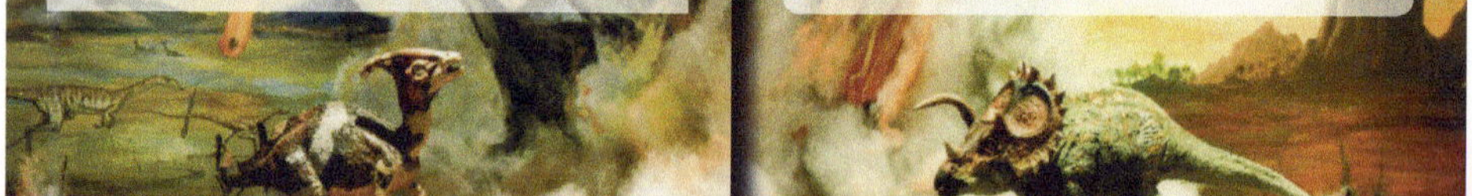

VOCABULARY

Before checking the answers, have students put a check mark next to the definitions they are certain they have matched correctly to the words and a question mark next to the ones they are still unsure of. This kind of self-assessment will help students reflect on their learning.

READING OPTIONAL 8.01 Extra Practice

As an additional activity, after completing the reading exercise, have students go back and prepare five varied comprehension questions about the contents of the article. Ask them to write down their five questions and exchange them with a partner who should answer them.

C IN GROUPS THINKING SKILL—Analyze Infer the answers to these questions. Explain the reasons for your answers.

1 Did all life on Earth disappear after the asteroid crashed?
2 Do all scientists agree on what caused the dinosaurs to become extinct?

GRAMMAR third conditional

A Choose the sentences with the same meanings. Then choose the correct options in the rule.

1 First, <u>if you had been within 1,000 km of the impact site</u>, ...
  a You were not within 1,000 km of the impact site.
  b You were within 1,000 km of the impact site.
2 If you had been far enough away, <u>you would have survived the explosion</u>.
  a Your survival in the past was certain.
  b Your survival in the past was not certain.
3 .... others think <u>dinosaurs might have survived</u>.
  a The dinosaurs' survival in the past was certain.
  b The dinosaurs' survival in the past was not certain.
4 ... <u>they could have adapted to slow changes</u> in climate over many years.
  a Their adaptation was certain.
  b Their adaptation was not certain.

To make the third conditional, use *if* + present / past perfect and *would/might/could have* + present / past participle.

For more practice, go to page 152.

B Write third conditional sentences for the situations.

1 A meteorite hit the Earth. The dinosaurs didn't survive.
If a meteorite hadn't hit the Earth, the dinosaurs might have survived.
2 There were no humans on the Earth at that time. They didn't die from the meteorite crash.
If there had been humans on the Earth at that time, they would have died from the meteorite crash.
3 The soot in the air blocked the sun. Temperatures became much cooler.
4 Dinosaurs didn't have food after the meteorite crashed. They disappeared in a few years.

C IN PAIRS Take turns reading your sentences. Did you have similar ideas?

SPEAKING

A IN PAIRS How would history have been different if certain events had or had not happened? Write down three examples in your notebook.

If the 1969 moon landing hadn't been successful, people might not have gone to the moon again.

B IN GROUPS Share your ideas. Discuss whether you agree with your classmates' speculations. Use the Confident Communicator box to help you.

CONFIDENT COMMUNICATOR
KEEP TALKING

To express possibility or probability, use *maybe* or *probably*:
***Maybe** humans wouldn't have gone to the moon again if the moon landing hadn't been successful. (possibility)*
*Humans **probably** wouldn't have gone to the moon again if the moon landing hadn't been successful. (probability)*

GO TO page viii
for **GRAMMAR** step-by-step instructions.

1 No. If life had disappeared, there might not be higher life forms on Earth today. Many mammals and sea animals survived because they lived in burrows underground or under the water and were protected from the explosion.
2 Scientists think the meteorite was the main cause of the mass extinctions. Actually, most scientists think the extinctions would have happened anyway, due to changes in climate. However, it is unlikely that the dinosaurs would have disappeared so quickly and they might have been able to adapt and survive if the meteorite had not caused such extreme consequences. Not fully accepted yet, the latest theories suggest that dinosaurs were eliminated on the same day as the meteorite impact.

GO TO page xii
for **SPEAKING** step-by-step instructions.

3 If the soot in the air hadn't blocked the sun, temperatures (probably) wouldn't have / might not have become much cooler.
4 If dinosaurs had had food after the meteorite crashed, they wouldn't have / might not have disappeared in a few years.

GRAMMAR

Point out the underlined phrases in GRAMMAR **A** and ask students to find them in the article in READING **B**. Tell students to read the sentences in which the phrases appear and the surrounding sentences. Reading grammar in context will help students understand the grammar's usage.

In **C**, have students read the sentences aloud. Remind them to pause at the comma.

SPEAKING

Before asking students to write examples in their notebooks of how history would be different, brainstorm a list of historic events with the class and write them on the board. It will be interesting to see which historic events your students consider important. According to the Pew Research Center, in a 2016 survey in the United States, the September 11 attacks on the World Trade Center in New York overshadow other modern events.

1 4

2 1

3 tie yourself to a chair

4 because long hair would float

5 to space stations and other planets

6 a beautiful blue, green, and brown ball

GO TO page xi for LISTENING step-by-step instructions.

GO TO page 146 for AUDIO SCRIPT.

Suggested answers: The fact that you can't see countries makes you realize that it's all one planet, and we are all one species on the planet. We worry too much about artificial boundaries and about our differences.

GO TO page ix for PRONUNCIATION step-by-step instructions.

VOCABULARY space

A Complete the sentences with the words from the box.

outer space	International Space Station	space capsule	spacecraft	space shuttle	zero gravity

1 People have been traveling into space on ___spacecraft___ for over fifty years.
2 The first person who traveled to ___outer space___, the area outside Earth's atmosphere, was Yuri Gagarin, in 1961.
3 In the 1970s, the first ___space shuttle___ was developed, a vehicle that could go to space and return several times.
4 A ___space capsule___ is a compartment or cabin where the astronauts live during a space flight.
5 In the 1990s, the US, Russia, Japan, and Europe built the ___zero gravity___ (ISS) to discover more about human life in space.
6 One of the effects of living in ___International Space Station___ is that people get taller!

LISTENING

A IN PAIRS What do you think the challenges of living in a space capsule would be? Discuss.

B 8.02 Listen to an interview about life in space. Were your ideas correct?

C 8.02 LISTENING SKILL—Listen for specific information Listen again and complete the notes.

1. *Number of times Karen has flown into space:*
2. *Number of times she has been to the International Space Station (ISS):*
3. *How you sit down in space:*
4. *Why Karen has short hair:*
5. *Where spacecraft may go in the future:*
6. *What the Earth looks like from outer space:*

D IN GROUPS THINKING SKILL—Question Decide what the astronaut meant when she made this statement about observing Earth from outer space.

"You can see the oceans and the continents, but no countries, of course, and that can make you think differently about our world."

MAKE IT REAL

The International Space Station is often referred to as the *ISS*. It is common in English to refer to companies and institutions by their initials. Can you think of any more examples?

PRONUNCIATION consonant clusters with /s/

A 8.03 Underline the consonant cluster with /s/ in each word. Listen and practice.

1 host 2 guest 3 space 4 sleep 5 just 6 school 7 student 8 desk

VOCABULARY Alternative Activity

Have a competition to see who can use the most words from the word box in a sentence. Tell students the sentence has to be contextual and descriptive. Have students read each other's sentences and then nominate some to go to the final judging by you, the teacher.

LISTENING

After **A**, elicit open-class feedback and write some notes on the board in preparation for the first time they listen to the interview.

Before **C**, have students listen for the numbers they hear and write them down on a piece of paper. Then have them listen again and complete the notes.

PRONUNCIATION Extra Practice

Pronouncing consonant clusters is hard for some learners with Spanish-speaking backgrounds. For additional practice, tell them to say the consonant sounds in isolation and then say the words (e.g., *sl–sleep*, *st–guest*).

GRAMMAR indirect questions

A Read the examples of direct and indirect questions and complete the rules with the correct options.

Direct questions	Indirect questions
What is life like at zero gravity?	Can you tell us what life is like at zero gravity?
How do you drink water?	Could you explain how you drink water?
Will the US have space shuttles again in the future?	Do you know if/whether the US will have space shuttles again in the future?

1 Direct questions have the verb *be* or the auxiliary (*will*, *did*, etc.) **before** / **after** the subject.
2 Indirect questions have the main verb **before** / **after** the subject.
3 Indirect questions in the simple present or simple past **have** / **don't have** the auxiliary *do*/*did*.

For more practice, go to page 153.

B Rewrite the direct questions as indirect questions.

1 How big is the International Space Station?
Could you tell me how big the International Space Station is?
2 What do astronauts in the ISS do?
Can you explain what astronauts in the ISS do?
3 Will the ISS ever return to Earth?
Do you think the ISS will ever return to Earth?

C IN GROUPS Take turns asking and answering the questions from B.

SPEAKING

A IN PAIRS Read the facts and look at your notes from LISTENING C. Use the information in the web page and your own ideas to think of questions to ask an astronaut. Include indirect questions.

ZERO GRAVITY FACTS

- You lose muscle mass, so you have to exercise a lot to build muscles.
- You breathe in things that are floating in the air, so you have to be careful about things like crumbs from food, drops of water, or hair from shaving.
- It's hard to sleep. You have to sleep in a special sleeping bag with arm bags so that your arms don't float.

B IN PAIRS Role-play your interview for another pair. Use the Confident Communicator box to help you.

A: Can you tell me what you like and don't like about life in space?
B: Well, I really like … I don't like … or … very much because … .
A: That's interesting. And do you know if you will go to space again?

CONFIDENT COMMUNICATOR
KEEP TALKING

To make a question sound more polite, especially in a formal situation like an interview, use at least some indirect questions: *Can you tell me why you didn't like the experience?* Instead of *Why didn't you like the experience?*

GRAMMAR

Indirect questions are used to sound more polite. They are often used with strangers and in professional situations. This is a natural and useful way to ask for information. For example, *Excuse me, do you know where the bathroom is?* Rather than *Excuse me, where's the bathroom?*

SPEAKING

Indirect questions are often used in news programs when the host is interviewing an expert. For the role-play, suggest one student play an interviewer and one student a space company executive, scientist, or astronaut. They can use questions from GRAMMAR **B** or questions of their own. Tell them to use notes from LISTENING **C** as well. Students may want to do some research to answer the indirect questions posed. You could have students work in groups and do the role-play as a panel interview with different experts. Then have them present the role-play as a TV show.

GO TO page 147 for AUDIO SCRIPT.

Suggested answers:

The space program helps us learn about our own planet.

It gives us new technology that can be used on Earth.

There is a lot of medical research on astronauts' health, and some of the medical developments can be used in normal medicine.

We may discover new elements or bacteria that can be used in medicine, technology, or energy.

We use space technology like satellites to learn more about weather and climate.

The space program may be able to invent technology to save Earth from another event like an enormous asteroid impact.

We may discover a new planet where humans can live.

LESSON 3 Do We Need Space Exploration?

LISTENING

A IN GROUPS Discuss the reasons for space exploration. How many different things do space programs do?

B 8.04 LISTENING SKILL—Listen for main ideas Listen to a panel discussion about space exploration. Then answer the questions.

1 Are the people on the panel in favor of or against space exploration?
in favor of

2 What does Seth, the astronaut, say space exploration is mainly about?
learning about our own planet

3 What does the second guest, Lauren, say that satellites do?
give us information about the weather

4 What does the third speaker, Cristina, focus on in her comments?
technology for everyday inventions

5 What does the last speaker, Mike, say the space program is like?
a giant science teacher

C 8.04 THINKING SKILL—Recall Choose the speaker who discussed each point. Compare with a partner. Then listen and check.

1 The space program encourages young people to study. — Seth / Lauren / Cristina / **Mike**
2 The space program gave us cell phone cameras. — Seth / Lauren / **Cristina** / Mike
3 The space program makes us safer. — **Seth** / Lauren / Cristina / Mike
4 The space program is not only about astronauts. — Seth / **Lauren** / Cristina / Mike

VOCABULARY space program inventions

A Label the pictures with words from the box.

cordless vacuum	foil blanket	home insulation
memory foam	water filter	wireless headset

1

cordless vacuum

2
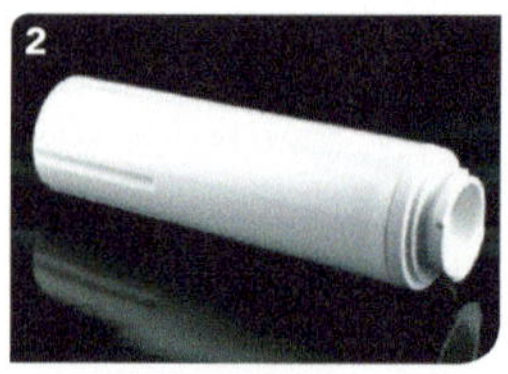
water filter

3

wireless headset

4
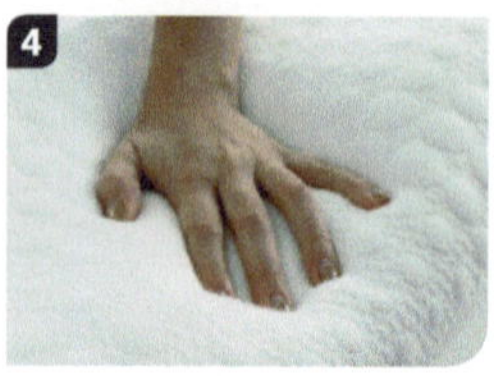
memory foam

5

home insulation

6

foil blanket

B IN GROUPS Discuss which of the contributions from space exploration you have used.

LISTENING

Reasons for space exploration might be to study the Sun, explore the solar system and other planets, discover life on other planets, investigate if we can live in space or on Mars, or study the weather on Earth. These days, space exploration is done by both humans and robots.

THINKING SKILL—Recall

Recall means to bring something to mind or simply remember it. Recall is vital to language learning. Have students practice remembering words and phrases again and again after they have seen them for the first time.

VOCABULARY

When students are talking about things they have used that have come into use through space exploration programs, have them give more details so as to give longer answers. Ask them to talk about how, where, and when they use them or have used them.

WRITING

GO TO page xiv for WRITING step-by-step instructions.

A Read the opinion posted on a blog site. Then choose the statements that best reflect the writer's opinion.

Stop Exploring Space!

It's time to stop exploring space. It is true that space exploration has developed technology that is used in many ways on Earth. However, I feel certain that if the technology hadn't been invented for the space program, it would have been invented anyway. The main problem with space exploration is the cost. If we hadn't spent billions of dollars on space exploration, we could have already stopped world hunger. In addition, space travel is dangerous. Astronauts become ill from a number of health problems from being in zero gravity for long periods of time. Furthermore, we don't know what dangerous viruses might be in space—it could be dangerous for Planet Earth. Also, some kinds of rockets use enormous amounts of fossil fuel.

Many people argue that we need to learn about our universe. Nevertheless, I am convinced that we should spend our energy and our money on ways to make our lives better here on Earth.

1 **a** He thinks that we wouldn't have had some technologies if we hadn't had a space program.
  b He thinks we would have developed our technologies even without a space program.
2 **a** He thinks we should spend money to stop world hunger instead of on space exploration.
  b He thinks we have almost stopped world hunger.
3 **a** He thinks being in space is very dangerous.
  b He thinks people will live in space in the near future.
4 **a** He thinks we should look for new sources of fossil fuel on other planets.
  b He thinks space exploration uses too much fossil fuel.

B Look back at the blog. Find words and phrases that connect ideas.

To add ideas: *and*, In addition, Furthermore, Also
To contrast ideas: *but*, However, Nevertheless

C You are going to respond to the blog with the opposite point of view. Write notes to plan your response.

Opening statement: ____
Arguments from the blog you disagree with: ____
Other reasons to support space exploration: ____
Closing statement: ____

D Write your blog post. Use connecting words and phrases from B to structure your response.

E IN PAIRS Read each other's blog posts. Did you use similar arguments?

SPEAKING

A Decide whether you are for or against space exploration in the future. Make a list of your arguments. Use ideas from this lesson or your own ideas.

B IN GROUPS Discuss your opinions from A. Ask questions to clarify your classmates' reasons for their opinions. Use the Confident Communicator box to help you.

A: I think space exploration is a waste of time.
B: Can you tell me why you think that?

CONFIDENT COMMUNICATOR
KEEP TALKING

To ask someone to clarify the reasons for their opinions, use these phrases:
Can you tell me why you think …?
Why do you think …?
What makes you believe …?

WRITING

Students will write an opinion blog post in support of space travel to refute the post that is against it. They will use *and*, *also*, *in addition*, and *furthermore* to connect ideas and *but*, *however*, and *nevertheless* to contrast ideas. Have them listen to the panel discussion from LISTENING **B** again. Tell them to check their answers in LISTENING **B** and the statements in LISTENING **C** for ideas for their blog entry.

They will use phrases stating their opinions and opening and closing statements, pinpoint parts of the former argument they disagree with, and use reasons to support their own arguments.

SPEAKING

Now that they have heard both sides of the argument, students will decide how they feel about space exploration in the future and discuss their own point of view on the matter. Students can find more information about future space missions online.

GO TO page xv
for LANGUAGE AND LIFE step-by-step instructions.

Language and Life

Reason Effectively – Space Team

A IN PAIRS What challenges/problems/difficulties would people living on Mars face? Discuss.

B 8.05 Read the description of what life would be like on Mars. Does it include any of your ideas from A? What other challenges does it include?

Life on Mars

Artist's rendition of an ecosystem on Mars.

Traveling to Mars is hard. Living on Mars is even harder. First, there are serious environmental issues. One problem is radiation. Astronauts on the International Space Station get 10 times more radiation than on Earth, and the radiation in deep space could be even stronger. One possible solution is ice-covered domes because ice partly blocks radiation. The second problem is the effects of low gravity on the human body. People's bones and muscles become weaker if they are in low gravity for a long time. It is necessary to use weights and do heavy exercise to prevent this. A third problem is that people will have to live in a closed ecosystem. They have to stay inside a dome or a spacesuit at all times. There is no fresh air, so there is a danger of pollution or contamination by bacteria or viruses.

Life on Mars will also have psychological difficulties. First, there will be very few people on Mars, at least at the beginning, so there will not be many choices of friends. There will be no restaurants, cafés, or parks, so there will be few options for social activities, and life could be very boring. Second, the living spaces will be very small. People will be living very close to each other. Life will not be very comfortable. Water will be very limited, so people will have to take 30-second showers and almost never wash their clothes. Plants cannot grow on Mars, so all food will be dried or in cans. Also, most food tastes the same at low gravity. Finally, communication with Earth will be very hard. Cell phones and other voice communications will be impossible, so the only communication will be through email. It will take 20 minutes for an email to reach Earth, and another 20 minutes to get a reply, and most of us are used to very fast communication with our friends and families.

C IN GROUPS You are going to choose the first three people who will live on Mars for two years. What characteristics and experience are important? Make a list.

Characteristics	Experience
calm	*background in science*

OBJECTIVE

Students learn to choose a candidate for a special mission: traveling to Mars. In choosing the right people, companies must define the needs and challenges of a project and analyze the candidates. The abilities and experience of the candidates must match with the project. Students must convince their groups of the suitability of candidates they think are right for a Mars mission.

PROCESS OPTIONAL 8.05

Students brainstorm challenges they think people will face living on Mars. They read an article about life on Mars and the problems new settlers would face. There would be environmental (high levels of radiation, low gravity) and psychological challenges (cramped living quarters, no friends, poor communication with Earth). Once students understand the challenges, they complete a chart with characteristics and experience they think the first three candidates should have. Next, students read the profiles of five candidates and debate the pros and cons of each person. They choose the best three. Finally, they discuss which factors influenced their decisions the most.

D **IN GROUPS** **Read the descriptions of the candidates for the Mars mission. Analyze and evaluate each description. Discuss the characteristics and experience you listed in C and relate them to each candidate. Consider the candidates' pros and cons and choose the best candidate.**

MARTIN
MALE, 28
USA
COMEDIAN
NOT MARRIED

Competes in sports competitions and marathons. Now doing a TV show where he uses humor to teach people about nutrition. Very friendly, but friends say he talks too much!

Specializes in rare tropical diseases. Has lived in the jungles of northern Colombia and central Africa. Lived by herself for a year on a remote Pacific island. No time to do sports or socialize with people because her work is so important.

SUSANA
FEMALE, 45
COLOMBIA
MEDICAL RESEARCHER
NOT MARRIED

ARI
MALE, 35
RUSSIA
DOCTOR
MARRIED

Works at a family medicine clinic in Moscow. Practices general medicine, but specializes in respiratory diseases in children. Grows vegetables and rides his bicycle in his free time. Work and city living make him feel stressed; he relaxes by walking and bicycling in the countryside on weekends. Wife and two children support his decision to go to Mars for two years.

Designs large urban office buildings and specializes in green buildings with solar energy, rainwater collection systems, and air pollution cleaning systems. Loves decorating; skilled at house repairs. Loves living in Nairobi because it's an exciting city with many things to do. Has many friends and a very active social life. Married for two years; hopes to have children in the future.

ASHA
FEMALE, 32
KENYA
ARCHITECT
MARRIED

CLAUDIA
FEMALE, 50
BRAZIL
PSYCHIATRIST
MARRIED

Specializes in stress disorders. Uses herbs, meditation, and exercise therapy to help her patients. Works well with patients because she has had a lot of stress in the past. Grows her own herbs. Learned about herbal medicine when she lived in a small village in the Amazon where there was no electricity, running water, or communication with the outside world.

E **IN GROUPS** **As a class, discuss which candidates you chose and which factors—experience, skills, other factors—most influenced your group's decision about the candidates.**

A: Can you explain why you think Susana is better than Ari?

B: Susana has more experience with unusual diseases. If Ari had done more research on those types of diseases, he would have been a better candidate than Susana, but I think her experience is important.

F **Which factors most influenced your group's decision about the candidates—experience or skills? Did any other factors, such as gender, age, or nationality influence your decision? If so, which ones?**

G **Discuss the questions.**

1. What process did your group use to evaluate and select the three candidates? Were you happy with the process?
2. What steps are necessary in order to reason effectively?
3. How do reasoning skills help you at college or at work?

MAKE IT DIGITAL

Do research to find out about someone who went on a space mission. What skills did they have?

MAKE IT DIGITAL

Here are some skills an astronaut must have: intelligence, adaptability, physical conditioning, mental endurance, and education.

Students can do a search online using key words like *famous astronauts* or *space missions*. They can also follow the International Space Station (ISS) on social media sites.

CULTURE NOTE

Astronauts who work on the ISS come from all over the world. The ISS is an international project involving the United States, Russia, Canada, Europe, and Japan. In the year 2015, 220 people from 17 countries have visited the ISS. The first crew was made up of three astronauts from the United States, Russia, and Ukraine.

GO TO page xvii
for **UNIT REVIEW** step-by-step instructions.

UNIT 8

VOCABULARY review

SCORE: / 10

A Complete the sentences with words from the box.

asteroid	cordless vacuums	debris	extinction	ISS
outer space	soot	spacecraft	tidal waves	zero gravity

Millions of years ago, a/an **1** asteroid hit the Earth and caused the **2** extinction of many species of animals and plants. The impact caused giant **3** tidal waves from the ocean and fires that filled the air with black, smoky **4** soot.

People started traveling into **5** outer space in the 1960s, and now people from different countries live on the **6** ISS for months at a time. Astronauts travel there in a Russian **7** spacecraft. It is hard to live at **8** zero gravity because everything floats. If there is any **9** debris in the air, it can get into the air filters and damage them. Space programs have given us many everyday inventions, like memory foam, home insulation, and **10** cordless vacuums.

GRAMMAR review

SCORE: / 10

A Write the correct verb forms to make third conditional sentences. More than one answer may be possible.

1 If a meteorite hadn't/wouldn't have hit (not hit) Earth, maybe the dinosaurs might not have lived (live) for longer.
2 If the meteorite had hit (hit) the Earth more recently, people would have died (die).
3 My uncle would/might have been (be) an astronaut if he had grown up (grow up) in the US.
4 If I had known (know) about last night's TV show on space programs, I would/might have watched (watch) it.

B Rewrite the direct questions as indirect questions in your notebook.

1 Are there any good documentaries about space exploration?
2 How big is the International Space Station?
3 Where did the meteorite hit?
4 Why did mammals survive after the meteorite?
5 Have other meteorites hit the Earth?
6 Will we live on other planets in the future?

Do you know …
1 … if there are any good documentaries about space exploration?
2 … how big the International Space Station is?
3 … where the meteorite hit?
4 … why mammals survived after the meteorite?
5 … if other meteorites have hit the Earth?
6 … we'll live on other planets in the future?

16–20 correct: You can talk about events in the past and their impact on today. You can ask questions and discuss space exploration. You can use the third conditional and make indirect questions.
0–15 correct: Look again at the Vocabulary and Grammar sections in the unit.

TOTAL SCORE: / 20

WHAT DO YOU KNOW NOW? Look back at page 77 and add the words you know now to the boxes.

GO TO page xix
for **FOLLOW A PRO** step-by-step instructions.

FOLLOW A PRO SPACE

Take the quiz about space. Go to Follow A Pro on page 134 to find the answers. Then learn about astrobiology.

1 The hottest planet in our solar system is …
a Mercury. **b** Venus. **c** Mars.

2 Scientists think there may be a planet made of …
a diamonds. **b** gold. **c** silver.

3 One day on Venus is longer than one … on Earth.
a week **b** month **c** year

4 A NASA space suit costs about … dollars.
a five hundred thousand **b** one million **c** twelve million

86 Unit 8 A New Home?

CLASSROOM MANAGEMENT

Give students time to glance over the unit's vocabulary and grammar sections in each lesson. Once they do this, they will find the review activities more relevant.

Remind students to read the whole paragraph before starting to answer VOCABULARY **A**. For GRAMMAR **A**, allow students to check answers with a classmate before doing open-class feedback. Write answers to GRAMMAR **B** on the board for students to check their work.

FURTHER DISCUSSION

Write the following questions on the board. Then have students form groups of three and ask each other:

- Have you ever wondered about the disappearance of ancient cultures?
- What events led up to the Inca and the Maya abandoning their kingdoms?
- Did you know the Mayan people charted the stars and watched the sky?
- How does space influence the weather?
- Would you like to be a tourist in space?

GO TO page vi
for UNIT OPENER step-by-step instructions.

UNIT 9 The World of News

WHAT DO YOU ALREADY KNOW?

1 Think of words you know about media and the news. Write the words.

2 IN PAIRS Share and compare your ideas. Add more words to your lists.

Media/News

STUDENTS MAY ALREADY KNOW:

- Media/News: TV, radio, podcasts, broadcast, 24-hour news cycle, announcer, reporter, journalist, headlines, article, breaking news, newsflash, notification, viral, listen, read, check, hear, app, big story, trending news, fake news.

VIDEO

DISCUSS & SHARE

3 IN GROUPS Watch the video and answer the question.

SYM The news—how much is too much?

GO TO page xx
for VIDEOS IN SYM step-by-step instructions.

In this unit, you will ...

- give your opinions on fake news, journalists and citizen journalists, compare real and fake news stories, and role-play a job interview for a news career.
- use thinking skills: analyze, apply, and deduce.
- read about developments in news.
- use strategies and language to ask for an opinion, interrupt politely, and introduce new information about your skills and experience.
- use problem-solving skills to discuss the pros and cons of solutions to a problem.
- learn tips to make notes.

WHAT DO YOU ALREADY KNOW?

If students are struggling to understand what to do, you can ask them some questions to prompt their thinking:

- How do you get your news?
- Are you interested in the news and current affairs?
- Do you read a newspaper? If so, is it in print or online?
- Do you use an app to find out about breaking news?

VIDEO

Before viewing, ask:

What does Dave think about the news? *too much news is a distraction*
What does Ellen think about the news? *She needs to know what is going on in the world.*

After viewing, put the continuum on the board.

less news —— more news

Have students mark the continuum and explain their preferences.

DISCUSS & SHARE

Students should place themselves on a continuum of opinion: less news is better or more news is better. Ask students if they think we have too much information about what is happening in the world. With the 24-hour news cycle, we are being constantly bombarded with news. Should people limit their intake of news?

GO TO page x
for **READING** step-by-step instructions.

LESSON 1 News in the 21st Century

READING

A How interested are you in the news? Share your view with the class.

1 Very interested. I like to know what's happening in the world.
2 Pretty interested. Some things interest me more than others.
3 Not interested at all. Events in the news aren't really part of my life.

B 9.01 READING SKILL—Identify text types Read the texts. Write the correct text type from the box next to each text. There is one text type you do not need.

blog post | email | online article | review | tweet

Changing Times

It's no surprise that newspaper sales have fallen in recent years and TV news audiences are smaller because of the **effect** of 24/7 online news sites. It's too early to say how this will affect the way we present the news, but it's such an important **industry** that it's likely to survive technological change. There will always be journalism and a need for good journalists.

1 an online article

I never buy newspapers these days. What's the point? News is reported so quickly because it changes all the time. I'm not that interested in current affairs, but I read news stories online, and sometimes I watch the news on TV if something "big" is happening somewhere in the world. I see some news items on social media, but the majority are **human-interest stories**, and that kind of story is not interesting enough for me to repost. I'd like to know if anyone here does repost those stories in their newsfeed.
posted by jamiek 12:23

follow

2 a blog post

Citizen Journalists: The Word on the Street
by Amos Hadfield

A must-read for all journalism students is *Citizen Journalists: The Word on the Street* by Amos Hadfield. Citizen journalism is where ordinary people collect, report, share, and comment on news stories via their social media newsfeeds or tweets. It's an interesting **trend** because it's so hard to control. A positive point is that ordinary people can get involved. However, there are some problems. "It isn't easy to limit the spread of fake news" he writes. "**Governments** want more power, but that is also dangerous."

3 a review

Amber Spratt @ The Ark

Breaking news! People are here in the thousands—there's such an amazing atmosphere right now. No word from the president yet, but we expect more information soon. #excitingtimes

4 a tweet

GLOSSARY

journalism (n): the activity of reporting the news
fake (adj): not real or true
current affairs (phrase): events that are happening now and that are discussed in news reports

C Read the texts in B again. Complete the sentences with the correct text types.

1 The writer of the blog post is not interested in the news.
2 The writer of the tweet is reporting events as they happen.
3 The writer of the online article believes that journalism is an important profession.
4 The writer of the review mentions a new way of reporting news.

D THINKING SKILL—Analyze Read text 3 in B again. Compare the arguments in favor of citizen journalism and the arguments against it.

READING OPTIONAL 9.01

READING SKILL—Identify text types

We read many different kinds of texts each day; these might be emails, text messages, articles, magazines, fiction books, nonfiction books, labels, websites, newspapers, textbooks, tweets, social media posts, blog posts, and reviews. Have students think about their day. Can they name the different kinds of things they have read today?

THINKING SKILL—Analyze

Comparing and contrasting strengthens students' analytical skills. In READING **C**, students will compare *for* and *against* arguments.

Comparing and contrasting is how our brain naturally interacts with the world. We find differences and similarities around us and organize the information according to our experiences. Comparing promotes the analysis of both new and known information and leads to making connections between them. Comparing and contrasting can be done between concrete objects or concepts and ideas.

VOCABULARY

A Match the definitions to a word or phrase in bold in READING B.

1. news reports about a person's life or experiences human-interest stories
2. a change that is the result of another action effect
3. a specific trade or service industry
4. the groups of people who control a country governments
5. something popular at a specific time trend

MAKE IT YOURS

Go online and look at a website where you can read the news in English. What news sections does the website have? Look up any words for the sections that you don't know.

GO TO page vii for VOCABULARY step-by-step instructions.

GRAMMAR *so, such, too, enough*

A Complete the sentences from the texts in READING B. Then match with the correct forms.

1. It's an interesting trend because it's so hard to control.
2. … there's such an amazing atmosphere right now.
3. … that kind of story is not interesting enough.
4. It's too early to say how this will affect …

a *such* + adjective + noun 2
b (*not* +) adjective/adverb + *enough* 3
c *so* + adjective/adverb 1
d *too* + adjective/adverb 4

Can you find any more examples in the texts?

GO TO page viii for GRAMMAR step-by-step instructions.

More examples:
News is reported so quickly because it changes all the time.
… but it's such an important industry that it's likely to survive technological change.

B Match the words (1–4) with their meanings (a–d).

1. *such/so* d
2. *too* a
3. *enough* c
4. *not enough* b

a more than needed
b less than needed
c the right amount
d very

For more practice, go to page 154.

C Rewrite the sentences correctly in your notebook.

1. Some news reports are such shocking I can't watch them.
2. Jake is enough shy to succeed as a journalist.
3. My journalism teacher said I don't have to rewrite my report. It is enough good.
4. I think being a journalist must be so an interesting job.

1 Some news reports are so shocking I can't watch them.
2 Jake is too shy to succeed as a journalist.
3 My journalism teacher said I don't have to rewrite my report. It is good enough.
4 I think being a journalist must be such an interesting job.

D IN PAIRS Discuss sentences 1 and 4 in C. Are they true for you?

SPEAKING

A Make notes about how young people see the news in the 21st century. Think about the questions.

- What types of news stories are young people interested in?
- Are there are too many news sources?
- Are journalists professional enough?

B IN PAIRS Write three opinion questions about these topics. Use *too, so, such,* or *enough* in your questions.

- Fake news
- Journalists
- Citizen journalists

Do you think there is too much fake news?

C Go around the class. Ask different students your questions. Encourage them to give reasons for their opinions. Use the Confident Communicator box to help you.

CONFIDENT COMMUNICATOR — KEEP TALKING

Use these phrases to ask for someone's opinion:
Hi, can/could I ask you some questions about …?
Do you mind if I ask you about …?
Could you answer some questions about …?

GO TO page xii for SPEAKING step-by-step instructions.

VOCABULARY

More words and phrases related to news are: *breaking news, read the news, watch the news, follow the news, report the news, informed, disaster, local news, politics, front page, headlines, article, advertising, crossword puzzle, accident, murder, war, coup, national news, international news, lifestyle section,* and *sports section*.

GRAMMAR

In order to complete the sentences in **A**, students have to find them in READING **B**. This encourages noticing the grammar in context. In the reading section of the lesson, students were reading for meaning and identifying texts; now they are reading for another purpose—to notice the grammar.

SPEAKING

Encourage students to speak to classmates they don't usually work with. Have them change partners after asking their questions. Remind them that each person should ask and answer questions. Students will find that, as they have more practice answering the same questions, they will speak more fluently and feel more confident.

LESSON 2 **News Reporting—Who Do You Trust?**

VOCABULARY news stories

A Match the underlined words to the correct definitions (a–f).

1 It can be hard to figure out what is fake news. c
2 If a news headline makes you laugh, it's probably not true! d
3 We get news from many different sources – newspapers, TV, news websites and social media, for example. b
4 To prove that a news story is true, compare it to other reports of the story. a
5 Fake news is not accurate and can be dangerous. f
6 You should only trust news websites that have a good record of telling the truth. e

a show that something is true
b people or places we get information from
c understand; find the answer
d the title of a newspaper story
e believe is honest, fair, and reliable
f true; correct; without mistakes

B Complete the sentences with an underlined word from A.

1 The headline is "Dangerous Tigers Escape From Zoo!"
2 Which websites do you trust for the world news?
3 Can scientists prove that there is life on other planets?
4 We need to include information from three sources in our report.
5 How do you know this information about national exam results is accurate?
6 It can be difficult to figure out how to tell a fake news story from a real one.

GO TO page xi
for **LISTENING** step-by-step instructions.

LISTENING

A 9.02 Listen to Part 1 of a lecture on fake news. Then answer the question.

Why is fake news a "hot topic"? Give two reasons. There is a lot of fake news out there.
We are not that good at recognizing fake news.

GLOSSARY
rumor (n): information that may or may not be true

GO TO page 148
for **AUDIO SCRIPT**.

GO TO page 148
for **AUDIO SCRIPT**.

B 9.03 LISTENING SKILL—Listen for information order Listen to Part 2 of the lecture. Put the steps in the correct order (1–5).

a Research the person who wrote the story. 2
b Question everything you read online. 5
c Check links to other news stories. 3
d Research where the story comes from. 1
e Check if the story is on other websites. 4

C THINKING SKILL—Apply Think about a news item you saw on social media. Use the information you heard in B to establish if the news was real or fake.

GRAMMAR modals of deduction

A Read the sentences from LISTENING B. Choose the correct option in the rule.

If they haven't written anything else for a source you trust, the article **could** spread fake news.
Think to yourself, "This story **might** be true, but it **may not be** 100% accurate."
Or, "This story **can't be** true because certain details don't seem right."

When talking about deductions in the present, use a modal (+ *not*) + the base infinitive / infinitive with *to* form of the verb.

VOCABULARY

Ask students about reputable news sources in their country. What are the news sources they trust? Do they fully trust the news they read, hear, or see? What do they do to get accurate information? Have they ever been tricked by a fake news story?

LISTENING

LISTENING SKILL—Listen for information order

To listen for information order, play the audio all the way through once. Then play it again, stopping briefly after each point. Once they have put the steps in the correct order, have students circle the three points they think are the most important.

THINKING SKILL—Apply

Students immediately use the steps they learned from the audio to check the quality of a news article. For research purposes, the ability to question the veracity of information is vital. These skills will serve your students well in future.

B Complete the sentences with words from the box.

can't	could	may	might	must

You're 99% sure the news is fake.	The news **1** ___must___ be fake.
You aren't sure if the news is fake or not.	Do you think that story **2** ___may___ / **3** ___might___ / **4** ___could___ be fake?
You're 95% sure the news is true.	The news **5** ___can't___ be fake.

For more practice, go to page 154.

C Complete the sentences with the correct modal of deduction. More than one answer may be possible.

1. Your friend Lola said she would visit you today. There's a knock at the door. "That ________ be Lola."
2. You see someone in a store who looks like your cousin Martha. But Martha works abroad as a journalist. "That ___can't___ be Martha."
3. You look out of the window. People are carrying open umbrellas. "It ___must___ be raining."
4. You're sure TV news ends at 11 p.m. "It's midnight. The news ___can't___ be on TV."

1 may/might/could

D IN PAIRS Look at these pictures. What do you think they show? Use modals of deduction to discuss.

a 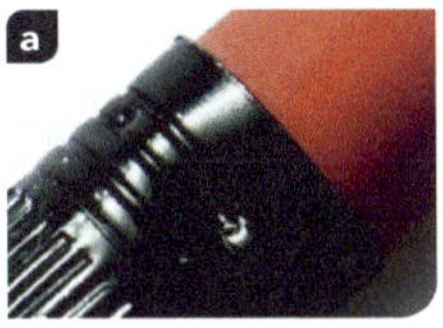
b 
c 
d 

This picture must be a …
This might be a …

MAKE IT REAL

You can use *maybe* and *perhaps* instead of *may be*, *could be*, and *might be*:
Maybe it's a/an … *Perhaps they're …*

SPEAKING

A Read these two news story summaries. Have you heard about them or seen them in the news?

Story 1:
Some cities around the world now use "silent fireworks" in displays to make the shows more enjoyable for children and less stressful for pets.

Story 2:
A group of penguins is living on an island of ice and plastic waste in the Pacific Ocean.

B IN PAIRS Work together to decide which might be fake news and which might be true.

This one can't be a true news story, because …
That one must be fake news, because …

C IN GROUPS Talk about how you worked out which news story was fake. Use the Confident Communicator box to help you.

Story 1 is an example of a "true" news story.
Story 2 is an example of a "fake" news story.

CONFIDENT COMMUNICATOR
REPAIR IT

To interrupt politely, use the following phrases:
Excuse me, can I just interrupt here and say …
Do you mind if I interrupt?
Sorry, can I just add that …

GRAMMAR

The modals *can*, *could*, *may*, *might*, and *must* help us make deductions. The modal we use depends on the amount of certainty. The verb following the modal is in base form and doesn't change in the third person.

Another common use of modals is deducing what things are in the distance. If possible, point out a distant building or landmark and have students guess what it might be using modals of deduction.

SPEAKING Additional Activity

Have students write two short news accounts of their own—one real and one fake. In pairs, ask them to read each other's news stories and guess which one is fake. Remind them of the structure of an opening paragraph for a news story—who was involved, what happened, where it happened, and when it happened. Their partner should use modals of deduction when guessing the fake story.

LESSON 3 A News Career

VOCABULARY news careers

A Look at the pictures. Match the careers from the box with the correct pictures.

foreign correspondent	investigative journalist	news anchor	newspaper editor
photojournalist	reporter	sports journalist	translator

1  photojournalist

2  translator

3  newspaper editor

4  sports journalist

5  news anchor

6  investigative journalist

7  foreign correspondent

8  reporter

B IN PAIRS Talk about what skills a person needs to do each of the jobs.

A: I think a news anchor needs to feel confident in front of a camera.
B: True. And an investigative journalist must not be afraid to ask hard questions.

GO TO page ix
for PRONUNCIATION step-by-step instructions.

PRONUNCIATION /ə/ versus /r/

A 9.04 There are differences in the pronunciation of certain sounds in British English and American English. Listen and notice the difference between the sounds /ə/ and /r/ at the end of these words.

1 anchor 2 translator 3 editor 4 reporter

B 9.05 Listen and choose the sound you hear.

1 anchor — a the /ə/ sound — b the /r/ sound
2 translator — a the /ə/ sound — b the /r/ sound
3 editor — a the /ə/ sound — b the /r/ sound
4 reporter — a the /ə/ sound — b the /r/ sound

LISTENING

A What do you think the job of foreign correspondent is like? How about a translator in a different country?

GO TO page 148
for AUDIO SCRIPT.

B 9.06 Listen to the interview and choose the correct answers.

1 What is Dana McDonald's job?
  a foreign correspondent b translator c professor
2 Where does Dana McDonald live?
  a England b the US c India
3 What did Peter Marsden study at college?
  a Arabic b English and French c journalism
4 Where is Peter from?
  a the US b Algeria c India

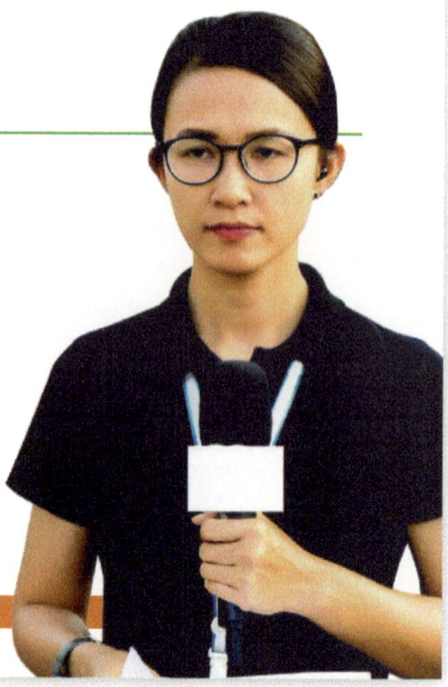

VOCABULARY

Some more words related to news media are: *journal, magazine, tabloid, editorial, column, review, breaking news, news bulletin, 24-hour news cycle, business, opinion, technology, science, health, arts, style, food, travel, music,* and *celebrity*. Ask students what kind of news they are interested in. Are they interested in celebrity news, science, or technology?

PRONUNCIATION

Remind students that besides differences in American and British pronunciation, each country has its regional differences. Just like there are regional differences in pronunciation in their country, each region of each country can display variations of pronunciation. Ask students if they can identify different English pronunciations.

LISTENING

Ask students what they think a job as a foreign correspondent or a translator would be like. Before listening to the interview, write the ideas that students brainstorm on the board. Then remind students to read through the options and questions in **B** and **C** before listening.

C 9.06 **LISTENING SKILL—Listen for opinions** Listen again and decide who expresses the following opinions. Write *D* for Dana, *P* for Peter, or *B* for both.

Who …

1. worked in a different career in the beginning? P
2. finds their job quite hard? D
3. doesn't really speak the language of the country they live in? D
4. is away from home for long periods of time? B
5. works for themselves? P

MAKE IT REAL

To talk about a job that would/wouldn't suit you, use:
I'd make a good/terrible … because I …
e.g., *I'd make a terrible photojournalist because I can't take good pictures!*

D **THINKING SKILL—Deduce** Decide what you would find challenging about being a foreign correspondent or a translator in a different country.

WRITING

GO TO page xiv for **WRITING** step-by-step instructions.

A Read this fact file about a person who works as an undercover investigative journalist. Would you like to do a job like this?

> **FACT FILE:** Undercover investigative journalist
> **NAME:** Faye Garcia [not her real name]
> **AGE:** 32
>
> 
>
> I work as an undercover journalist. I hide my real identity as a journalist so that I can find out about things. Right now, I'm investigating people in the Congo who illegally trade wild animals. My job is to collect as much accurate information as I can and give that information to the local police. I love it, but it's a hard job. It's essential that the criminals don't figure out who I am. I find that it's hard because my life might be in danger. I have the feeling that other people would hate this job. As for me, I think it's very exciting. In my opinion, it's the most amazing job in the world.

B Underline four examples in **A** where the writer gives her opinion.

C Choose another news career from this lesson. Write about 100 words on whether you think you would like the job. Use the phrases from **B** to give opinions.

SPEAKING

A **IN PAIRS** Choose a news career from this lesson. Decide what skills and experience a person needs to do this job. Write five questions that an interviewer would ask someone who was applying for the job.

B **IN PAIRS** Role-play an interview for the job. Change roles after two or three minutes. Use the Confident Communicator box to help you.

A: So, why do you think you would make a good reporter?
B: Well, I'm very interested in current affairs and …

C **IN GROUPS** Talk about how the interview went and who you think did well in the interview.

CONFIDENT COMMUNICATOR
KEEP TALKING

To introduce important skills and experience that an interviewer hasn't asked about, use the following phrases:
Did I mention that I have experience in / know how to …?
Although I don't have much experience in …, I'm very good at …
I think my experience in … could help in my role as a/an …

WRITING

Students will write a paragraph giving their opinion about a job from the lesson or a related job. They choose a job similar to the job of investigative journalist and write why they would like to do it. Students use **A** as a model for their own writing. If students choose war correspondent, they should say which wars and which countries they would like to work in. If they choose translator, have them give details about the languages they would like to work in. Would they like to be an undercover food writer? Where would they like to do it?

SPEAKING

Some more questions an interviewer might ask are:

- What skills do you possess that would make you a good …?
- What experience have you had as a …?
- What personal qualities do you think a … needs?
- Do you know anyone who works as a …?
- What do you already know about the job?

GO TO page xv

for **LANGUAGE AND LIFE** step-by-step instructions.

Language and Life

Problem Solving – Local News

A IN PAIRS **Discuss the questions.**

1 Do you ever read a local newspaper (in print or online)?
2 If not, how do you get information about what's happening in your local area?
3 Do you think local newspapers are important? Why or why not?

B 9.07 **Read the article about a new local newspaper. Then answer the questions.**

No Story Is Too Small

With the rise of social media and online news sites, local newspapers have had a hard time. However, in a group of small towns in the Midwestern United States, print news is fighting back. Gene Nightingale and Matt Emerson, two journalists who were worried about local journalism, decided to start up their own micro newspaper. The newspaper goes on sale once a month and sells around 4,000 copies.

The newspaper is based on the idea that "no story is too small" because they write about small stories, such as how a farmer's field was flooded with water after a pipe burst, and how a new sandbox has been installed in a children's play area.

But it is these "small stories" that are the building blocks for any community. If people are aware of what is happening in their local area, they feel more connected to their community. This connection helps to create strong relationships between people who live in villages, towns, or cities. Whether it is good news, such as a local student winning a national debating competition, or bad news, such as the closure of the town library, the point is that it is news—it is something to discuss and debate and bring people together. Gene and Matt's newspaper provides that essential link.

Local newspapers are in danger. A recent report by the US Bureau of Labor Statistics found that the number of newspaper jobs fell from 458,000 in 1990 (considered to be the start of the internet age) to about 183,000 in 2016. That's a fall of almost 60%. This has an effect on local newspapers in that local news stories are not investigated in the same way. "People depend on Facebook and social media, so what's going on close to home can be ignored by larger newspapers," says Emerson. Local businesses have been very helpful and paid for the first copy of the newspaper. Nightingale and Emerson hope there might be the chance to start up other "micro newspapers" in other small towns over the next few years.

Burst pipe floods local field

Jenny McGill's winning argument

Town library in danger of closing

Read more

1 How often is the paper published? once a month
2 What idea is the newspaper based on? No story is too small.
3 How many people were working in newspaper jobs in 2016? 183,000
4 Who helped to pay for the first copies of the newspaper? local businesses

94 Unit 9 The World of News

OBJECTIVE

Students learn how to make suggestions for improving the sales of a small newspaper. They discuss the advantages and disadvantages of various strategies. This is a realistic scenario that students will most likely face in their work lives at some point. When they are called on for ideas to improve sales figures, they will have a template for putting forward the advantages and disadvantages of any single approach.

PROCESS OPTIONAL 9.07

First, students will discuss what they already know about local newspapers. Then, they will read an article about a successful new local news paper. After answering questions to show they understand the article, students read suggestions for improving sales. They choose the best five suggestions and then discuss the advantages and disadvantages of each one. After that, they have the opportunity to add their own ideas for boosting circulation.

C IN PAIRS **Imagine that you work for a local daily newspaper that has lost sales. Your boss has some suggestions on how to improve sales. Choose the five best suggestions and write them in note form in the first column of the table.**

My tips for improving business

1. *Include more human-interest stories and more photos.*
2. *Encourage citizen journalism where local people write stories that are important to them.*
3. *Include live-blogging on the website to cover breaking news stories. Readers can add audio and video posts.*
4. *Make online stories more personal. Allow readers to choose the news and the area that they are interested in. They receive notifications when news that's important to them happens.*
5. *Have an online-only news service. Readers join and pay a monthly fee as they would with Spotify or Netflix.*
6. *Offer reader discounts at other local businesses, e.g. a discount on a Valentine's Day meal in a local restaurant if you buy the newspaper every day for a week, for example.*
7. *Go from being a daily newspaper to a weekly newspaper.*
8. *Increase the price of the newspaper.*

	Suggestions	Advantages	Disadvantages
1			
2			
3			
4			
5			

D IN PAIRS **Discuss the advantages and disadvantages of each of your choices. Write them in the table.**

A: One advantage of using citizen journalists is that they do it for free. We can save money.

B: Yes, that's true, but they might not be very good at writing news stories.

E **Compare your ideas and agree on the best five. Make some other suggestions for ways to improve sales.**

F **Discuss the questions.**

1. Why is it useful to identify the advantages and disadvantages of a solution?
2. What other approaches to solving problems can you think of?

MAKE IT DIGITAL

Go online and find a local news website. Share some examples of interesting or amusing local news with the class.

CLASSROOM MANAGEMENT

Write your lesson objective in bullet points in a corner of the board. As the lesson progresses, quietly check off the objectives as you cover them. You don't have to announce anything to the class, but this practice will help show your planning and their progress.

MAKE IT DIGITAL

Have students read local news in their first language and then report back to the class in English. This will give them practice explaining local issues to English speakers. If possible, invite a native English speaker to class to whom your students can report local news they have researched online.

CULTURE NOTE

Ask students to name some reliable and unreliable news sources in their countries. Tell students that they should generally try to look for news from sources with professional, ethical, unbiased journalistic practices. They should question any news outlet's political viewpoint and judge how this may influence reporting.

GO TO page xvii
for **UNIT REVIEW** step-by-step instructions.

VOCABULARY review

SCORE: / 10

A Complete the sentences with the correct words. The first letter is given.

1. Right now, I'm working as a s<u>ports journalist</u> on the magazine *Soccer Special Weekly*.
2. Your facts must be accurate, or your readers won't t<u>rust</u> you to tell the truth.
3. Whenever there is b<u>reaking news</u> around the world, I get an update on my newsfeed.
4. This is a great picture for our article, but will people be able to f<u>igure out</u> what it is?
5. I read the news online, but I'm not interested in h<u>uman-interest</u> stories about people I don't know.
6. In some countries, the g<u>overnment</u> controls the media, especially television and newspapers.
7. One of the e<u>ffects</u> of online news is that newspaper sales have fallen.
8. Do you speak Spanish, or would you like a t<u>ranslator</u> to help you?
9. As an investigative journalist, my job is to try to p<u>rove</u> that the story I'm investigating is true.
10. Have you seen today's h<u>eadline(s)</u>? They've found water on Mars!

GRAMMAR review

SCORE: / 10

A Choose the correct words.

My hero is Nellie Bly. She was **1** so / **such** an amazing woman. She became one of the world's first investigative journalists, writing articles about female factory workers. Male readers were **2** enough / **so** shocked to learn that the writer was a woman that Nellie was moved to the women's section of the paper. Nellie thought that writing about fashion and gardening wasn't **3** **interesting enough** / enough interesting for her. In 1888, her editor suggested she travel around the world in 80 days—something that people thought was **4** such / **too** dangerous for a woman to attempt. It is **5** **so** / such amazing that she returned in just 72 days!

B Complete the sentences with the correct modals of deduction.

1. I can't open my email. There ________ be a problem with my wi-fi.
2. The news report says it's cold, but it ________ be snowing. It almost never snows in Los Angeles!
3. My phone shows I have one missed call. ________ it be about the reporter's job I applied for?
4. That newspaper ________ be mine. My copy is in my briefcase.
5. I'm sure I know that woman. I think she ________ be the news anchor on our local news channel.

1 must
2 can't
3 May/Might/Could
4 can't
5 may/might/could

16–20 correct: You can talk about news stories and news careers. You can use *so*, *such*, *too*, and *enough* and modals of deduction.
0–15 correct: Look again at the Vocabulary and Grammar sections in the unit.

TOTAL SCORE: / 20

WHAT DO YOU KNOW NOW? Look back at page 87 and add the words you know now to the box.

GO TO page xviii
for **STUDY SKILLS** step-by-step instructions.

STUDY SKILLS — MAKING NOTES

Take the quiz about making notes. Go to Study Skills on page 135 to find the answers. Then learn more about making notes.

1 When taking notes from a book, it's a good idea to write down every word you read without changing anything.
a True b **False**

2 What is plagiarism?
a writing so fast that you can't read what your notes say
b **including someone else's ideas in your essay without mentioning the source**

3 You can use your own symbols and abbreviations in both your notes and assignments.
a True b **False**

4 How many sets of notes should you aim to have?
a **one** b two c three

3 Use symbols and abbreviations in notes, but not in assignments.
4 Visual familiarity will help you to remember the content of your notes.

CLASSROOM MANAGEMENT

For a cooperative approach, have students work in pairs to complete a different section each. One student completes the vocabulary section, while the other student completes the grammar section. They come together to explain their answers to their partner. Then, they can discuss the vocabulary and grammar they have learned in the unit.

FURTHER DISCUSSION

Write the following questions on the board. Then have students form groups of three and ask each other:

- Do you know anyone who works as a journalist?
- Do you read your news in print or online?
- How do different newspapers in your city report news differently?
- Which TV channels have reliable news, in your opinion?

GO TO page vi
for UNIT OPENER step-by-step instructions.

UNIT 10 Got It?

WHAT DO YOU ALREADY KNOW?

1 Think about the things you are good at in different areas of your life. Write the things.

2 IN PAIRS Share and compare your ideas. Add more words to your lists.

At home

At school or work

Sports and art

DISCUSS & SHARE

VIDEO

3 IN GROUPS Watch the video and answer the question.

SYM Would you use your talent to express your creativity or make money?

In this unit, you will ...

- talk about your talents and abilities, ask and answer questions for a talent show audition, and share advice on how to succeed in the music industry.
- use thinking skills: question, analyze, and evaluate.
- read about what causes talent.
- use strategies and language to talk about your achievements politely, control your nerves when speaking to a group, and use idioms in informal contexts.
- use communication skills to make judgments and choose winners of a talent contest.
- follow a talent scout to learn about this job and the skills needed to be in this industry.

STUDENTS MAY ALREADY KNOW:

- **At home:** communication, organization, cooking, gardening, fixing things, hobbies, cleaning, washing, fixing the car.
- **At school or work:** school subjects, punctuality, friendships, relationships, mentoring.
- **Sports and art:** drawing, painting, sketching, soccer, basketball, running, athletics.

GO TO page xx
for VIDEOS IN SYM step-by-step instructions.

WHAT DO YOU ALREADY KNOW?

If students are struggling to understand what to do, you can ask them some questions to prompt their thinking:

- Do you organize your time and activities well?
- Do you help out at home?
- What's your favorite subject at school?
- Do you play sports?
- What are your hobbies?
- What new things are you learning?

VIDEO

Before viewing, ask:

Why does Andrea sing in a local band? *She loves when everyone is clapping and singing along.*
What does Sean do with his talent? *teaches, do design work, and pay bills*

After viewing, put the continuum on the board.

creativity —— make money

Have students mark the continuum and explain their preferences.

DISCUSS & SHARE

Students should place themselves on a continuum of opinion. Ask students to think about whether they believe talent equals success or not. Is having an amazing talent going to mean you'll be successful? Can one be successful without talent? What else is needed to be successful besides talent?

GO TO page x
for **READING** step-by-step instructions.

LESSON 1 Born with Talent?

READING

A Think about different kinds of great artists. What talents do they have?

B 10.01 Read the text. Then choose what type of writing you think it is.

a a blog entry b a newspaper article c a popular science magazine article

Ask an Expert

Petra Waterhouse from Berlin asks: Are great artists born or made? In other words, is **talent** genetic or is it learned?

Professor Anna Felix answers: **1** I think the short answer is both. Musical ability is a good example here because some people are born with greater **potential** than others, but without hard work and practice, they don't achieve it. **2** A study of 1,211 sets of **identical twins** born between 1959 and 1985 found that even when one twin practiced music regularly and one didn't, it made no difference. In one case, one man practiced for over 20,000 hours more than his twin, but their musical ability was about the same. This goes some way to showing us that at least some talents are genetic. **3** I believe they are part of our DNA and we probably inherit them from our parents. So, thank you, Mom and Dad!

4 A different study by Professor Zach Hambrick investigated 14 studies of top chess players and musicians: could their level of ability be explained by their hours of practice? The answer was "no." **5** Practice only made about a 30% difference to how good these people were. In previous research, Hambrick argues that what is important is the ability to remember things. Having an excellent **memory** can mean the difference between just being smart and being a genius.

6 One **theory** is that it takes 10,000 hours of practice to become an expert at something. There is possibly a degree of truth in this (although this will probably depend on what you are practicing). But if your DNA gives you a love of chess, languages, music, or soccer, I'd **assume** that would make you more likely to be prepared to put in those long hours of practice anyway.

GLOSSARY

genetic (adj): related to chemicals in a cell that are passed from one generation to another
inherit (v): get something (e.g., a talent, a medical condition) from one's parents
genius (n): a very intelligent person

C **READING SKILL—Recognize fact and opinion** Read the text in READING B again. Are the underlined sentences (1–6) facts or opinions? Write *F* (fact) or *O* (opinion).

1 O 2 F 3 O 4 F 5 F 6 F

D **THINKING SKILL—Question** Do you think great artists are born or made? What has helped the artists you know become famous?

GO TO page vii
for **VOCABULARY** step-by-step instructions.

VOCABULARY

A Match the words with their definitions.

1 assume (v): f
2 potential (n): e
3 memory (n): c
4 talent (n): d
5 identical twins (n): a
6 theory (n): b

a brothers or sisters born at the same time that look exactly the same
b an idea that explains how something happens
c the ability to remember things
d a natural ability for something
e an ability that may be developed in the future
f believe that something is true without proof

MAKE IT DIGITAL

Go online to find profiles of talented people. Make a note of the adjectives that are used to describe them.

READING OPTIONAL 10.01

Some famous artists are Pablo Picasso, Claude Monet, Rembrandt, Frida Kahlo, Kandinsky, Andy Warhol, and Salvador Dalí. Some famous singers and bands are the Beatles, Madonna, Elton John, Elvis Presley, Janet Jackson, Freddie Mercury, and Pink Floyd. Some talented actors are Meryl Streep, Cate Blanchett, Julia Roberts, Halle Berry, Nicole Kidman, Robert De Niro, Al Pacino, Tom Hanks, and Tom Hardy. Some famous writers are Ernest Hemingway, Maya Angelou, Virginia Woolf, and Stephen King.

Ask students to name great writers, artists, singers and bands, and actors of their era or country.

VOCABULARY

More phrases to describe talent are: *to be good at math, to be a good cook, a natural runner, a talented singer, an awesome dancer, a first-rate skier, the best teacher ever, a gifted storyteller, an accomplished artist, a brilliant soccer player, an expert driver, a top-notch inventor,* and *an ace carpenter.*

GRAMMAR reported speech: statements

A We use reported speech to report something a person has said or written. Read the example from READING B. How does the tense change between direct speech and reported speech?

"I think the short answer is both." (direct speech)
She said she thought the short answer was both. (reported speech)

1 Simple present becomes simple past.

B Complete the table.

Tense	Tense Change	Direct Speech	Reported Speech (note reporting verb)
simple present	simple past	"Jack is very talented."	She said (that) Jack was very talented.
present progressive	1 past progressive	"I'm learning the saxophone."	She told me (that) she was learning the saxophone.
present perfect	past perfect	"I have never seen *The X Factor*."	She admitted (that) she 2 had never seen *The X Factor*.
simple past	past perfect	3 "My dad was good good at singing."	She explained (that) her dad had been good at singing.
future with *will*	*will* becomes 4 would	"Macy will be a genius one day."	She mentioned (that) Macy would be a genius one day.

C Choose the correct options for the rules.

1 Use quotation marks for **direct speech** / reported speech.
2 In reported speech, the verb tense in the noun clause changes to the **past** / future form.

For more practice, go to page 155.

D Rewrite the statements in your notebooks using reported speech.

1 "Lyndon is a very talented soccer player." (the coach, say)
2 "I don't really like abstract art." (Alessandro, admit)
3 "We will practice the dance routine this weekend." (the class, promise)
4 "I learned how to draw by watching video clips online." (Alicia, tell me)

GO TO page viii for **GRAMMAR** step-by-step instructions.

1 The coach said (that) Lyndon was a very talented soccer player.
2 Alessandro admitted (that) he didn't really like abstract art.
3 The class promised (that) they would practice the dance routine this weekend.
4 Alicia told me (that) she had learned how to draw by watching video clips online.

SPEAKING

A Think about something that you have learned to do well. Make notes.

- what you learned
- how you learned it
- how you felt about it

B IN PAIRS Take turns talking about the thing you learned in A. Ask and answer questions to find out more. Use the Confident Communicator box to help you.

C IN PAIRS Now work in a different pair. Report what your first partner told you.

Nina said she had learned to windsurf when she was 15 …,

GO TO page xii for **SPEAKING** step-by-step instructions.

CONFIDENT COMMUNICATOR
KEEP TALKING

To talk about your own achievements without sounding overconfident, use the following phrases:
It took a lot of hard work, but I managed to learn …
I was really lucky, because I found it easy to …
I had a really good teacher/tutor/friend who helped me to …

GRAMMAR

The change in tenses from direct to reported speech is called *backshift*. Ask students to think about whether backshift occurs in their own language. Sometimes, analyzing one's own language can put the second language into perspective. The modal verbs *might*, *could*, *would*, *should*, and *ought to* do not change in reported speech.

SPEAKING

Remind students that when they are reporting what their partner said, they do not have to report everything that was said in the original conversation. They should choose the most interesting parts to share.

Alternative Activity

Play *Gossip*. Put students in groups of five or six. One student says something in direct speech in secret to the student next to them—for example, *I'm learning to play the piano*. The second whispers it to the next student and so on. The last student has to say what they heard out loud in reported speech—for example, *She said she was learning …* Is it close to the original?

GO TO page xi
for **LISTENING** step-by-step instructions.

GO TO page 150
for **AUDIO SCRIPT**.

LESSON 2 TV Talent Shows

LISTENING

A **Which TV talent shows are popular in your country? Do you like watching them? Why or why not?**

B **10.02 Listen to short excerpts from a TV talent show. Match the speakers (1–3) with their acts (a–d). There's one act you don't need.**

1 Noel _d_
2 Caitlyn _c_
3 Bobby _a_

a a ventriloquist
b a magician
c a comedian
d a singer

GLOSSARY

audition (n): a short performance so someone can decide if you are good enough to perform at an event

GO TO page 150
for **AUDIO SCRIPT**.

C **10.03 LISTENING SKILL—Identify attitude Listen to the same speakers talking about their experience after the TV talent show auditions. Choose how they think they did.**

1 Noel
a very well **b** OK **c** badly
2 Caitlyn
a very well **b** OK **c** badly
3 Bobby
a very well **b** OK **c** badly

MAKE IT REAL

If you don't do something you were planning to do because you're too nervous or scared, you can use the phrasal verb *chicken out.*
I was supposed to go to an audition for The Big Break, but I ***chickened out*** *at the last minute.*

D **THINKING SKILL—Analyze Discuss this statement: "Only a small number of people who appear on TV talent shows are really talented." Do you agree or not?**

VOCABULARY phrasal verbs

A **Match the phrasal verbs in bold (1–5) with the definitions (a–e).**

1 Bridget's dance classes are not easy, but she plans to **keep on going**. _e_
2 The director **turned down** a lot of people who auditioned for the play. _d_
3 When will you **come back** from the audition? _b_
4 Please **fill out** this form with your name and contact information. _c_
5 Over 100 people **showed up** at the movie studio for the audition. _a_

a to arrive at a place
b to return to a place
c to complete a form
d to say no to an offer or request
e to continue doing something

PRONUNCIATION stress in phrasal verbs

A **10.04 Listen to the sentences. Underline the stressed word in each one. Can you notice the difference?**

1 **a** He filled out the form. **b** He filled it out.
2 **a** She turned down the job. **b** She turned it down.
3 **a** I gave up dance classes. **b** I gave them up.

LISTENING

American Idol, America's Got Talent, The Voice, and *The World's Best* are some talent shows in the United States and United Kingdom. Local versions of these shows have been made all over the world. Ask students if their country has a version of these talent shows or if they have their own. What other kinds of talent competition shows do students like to watch?

VOCABULARY

Other phrasal verbs and idioms related to talent and TV talent shows are: *keep it up, keep smiling, give up, drop out, sign up for, warm up, take part in, show off, cool down, join in, be cut out for, show up, measure up,* and *believe in.* Have students look up the meanings of these.

PRONUNCIATION

Students should notice how the stress shifts when the phrasal verb is separated. In the first set of sentences, the particle (out, down, up) isn't stressed, but in the second set of sentences, it is.

GRAMMAR reported speech: questions

A Read the direct questions and reported questions from LISTENING B. Notice how the tense changes are the same as in reported statements.

1 He asked, "Do you need some water?" → He asked whether I needed some water.
2 He asked, "Are you feeling confident?" → He asked if I was feeling confident.
3 He asked, "How long have you been doing your act?" → He asked how long I'd been doing my act.
4 He asked, "Who are you?" → He asked who I was.

B Choose the correct options to complete the grammar rules.

1 Use *if* or *whether* in **reported *yes/no* questions** / reported information questions.
2 Use a question word in reported *yes/no* questions / **reported information questions**.
3 Use / **Don't use** auxiliary verbs in reported questions.
4 The word order in reported questions is **the same as** / different from word order in affirmative sentences.
5 Use / **Don't use** a question mark at the end of reported questions.

For more practice, go to page 156.

C Rewrite the direct questions as reported questions.

1 She asked, "Do you ever watch TV talent shows?" → She asked ______.
2 She asked, "What are you wearing to the audition?" → She asked ______.
3 She asked, "How long have you been waiting?" → She asked ______.
4 She asked, "Who is the best candidate?" → She asked ______.

1 if/whether I ever watched TV talent shows
2 what I was wearing to the audition
3 how long I had been waiting
4 who the best candidate was

D IN PAIRS Think about the last time you spoke to a close friend. What did he or she ask you about? Report it to your partner.

Last night, I spoke to my friend Estefan. He asked me if I had done anything interesting ...

SPEAKING

A Imagine you are going to an audition for a TV talent show.

Would you ...

- sing a song?
- dance?
- do something else?
- tell jokes?
- do a magic trick?

B Write questions that an interviewer might ask you at the audition.

C IN PAIRS Ask and answer the questions from B.

A: Have you been in any other talent shows?
B: No, this is the first time I've auditioned.
A: And how long have you been doing magic?
B: I've been doing magic since I was six.

D IN GROUPS Report what your partner told you using reported speech. Use the Confident Communicator box to help you.

CONFIDENT COMMUNICATOR
KEEP TALKING

You might feel nervous talking to a large group of people or the whole class. To help in these situations, you can try the following things:

- Control your breathing; breathe in and out slowly before you begin.
- Focus on what you are saying and not on your audience.
- Speak slowly.

GRAMMAR Alternative Activity

Play *What Would Grandma Ask?* Make a set of index cards with different kinds of talent shows on each card: magic show, singing competition, baking competition, and so on. On another set of cards, write the names of family members. Have pairs play against other pairs. The person whose turn it is takes one index card from each set and reports something the person would ask about the topic—for example, grandma / singing competition: *My Grandma would ask how much prize money the winner would get in the singing competition.* If they make a correct sentence, they win a point for their team and the turn passes to the other team. The first team to score five points wins.

SPEAKING

Have students listen to LISTENING **B** for questions an interviewer might ask at an audition. For example, *Why did you want to audition for the show? Have you filled out the application form? How long have you been doing your act? What are you going to do for us today?* Tell students to think of their own questions as well.

LESSON 3 Making It!

VOCABULARY idioms and sayings connected to success

A **Match the idioms (1–6) with the meanings (a–f). Use a dictionary or look online if you need help.**

1 be in the right place at the right time __c__
2 it isn't what you know; it's who you know __d__
3 set your sights on something __a__
4 have your heart set on something __b__
5 dream big __e__
6 be hungry for success __f__

a focus on something as your goal
b want something very much
c be lucky because of where you are and when
d make progress in life because of personal connections
e have goals or hopes that are difficult to achieve
f want to do very well

B **IN PAIRS Do you know any other idioms about success in English or another language? What are they?**

LISTENING

A **What special talents or abilities do you think you need to succeed in the music industry?**

GO TO page 150 for AUDIO SCRIPT.

B **10.05 Listen to this radio call-in show. What does Elsa Hardman do?**

a She runs a music website.
b She manages a music store.
c She owns a record company.

C **10.05 LISTENING SKILL—Listen to take notes Listen again and complete the notes. Remember that you don't need to write every word you hear.**

Tips to Make It in the Music Industry!

Starting a Record Company:
- *Dream big!*
- *Go out and* **1** __meet people__
- *Ask people with more experience for* **2** __help__

Finding Work as a Singer:
- *Keep goals* **3** __small__
- *Sing at a local show*
- *Think of yourself as a* **4** __business__
- *Be* **5** __professional__

D **THINKING SKILL—Evaluate How do people measure success in your country? Discuss the top three things that you think make a person successful.**

A: I think the three things that make someone successful are hard work, talent and the people you know.
B: What about luck? You need to be lucky too!
A: But is luck more important than hard work?

VOCABULARY

The saying related to success *If you've got it, flaunt it* is used for saying that you should be proud of your success, beauty, money, and so forth and not hide it. *Rags to riches* is used for describing a situation in which someone who has been very poor becomes very rich. *The sky's the limit* is used for saying that there is no limit to what someone can do.

LISTENING

THINKING SKILL—Evaluate

Write the following questions on the board as your students evaluate success. Tell them they do not have to answer the questions but, instead, they should consider them as they think about the task.

- Is success measured by money?
- Is it measured by happiness?
- Are the most successful people the most powerful or those that have the most meaningful lives?
- Can a person with little money be successful?

WRITING

GO TO page xiv for WRITING step-by-step instructions.

A Read the informal email. Match the items (a–e) with the underlined parts of the email (1–5).

- **a** informal greeting 1
- **b** informal closing 4
- **c** contraction 2
- **d** informal punctuation 3
- **e** signature 5

> New Message
>
> From: Delia Roberts — Cc Bcc
>
> To: Henri Martinez
>
> [1] Hi Henri,
>
> I hope [2] you're well. I'm writing to ask a favor. A friend has her heart set on working in the music industry. She's a fantastic singer, but she isn't very confident. I thought since you're a music producer you'd have some advice I can give her before she gives up. Any information welcome [3]!
>
> [4] Thanks for your help!
>
> [5] Delia
>
> Send

B Now read Henri's reply. How is the style of Henri's email different from the email in A?

It is more formal. Henri has used a more formal greeting and closing, and he hasn't used contractions or informal punctuation.

> New Message
>
> From: Henri Martinez — Cc Bcc
>
> To: Delia Roberts
>
> Dear Delia,
>
> Thank you for your email. I am pleased to hear that you are well. I have some advice for your friend. She will need to make a recording of her voice and send it to as many producers as possible. We are always looking for new talent, so send it to me, too. We will be able to decide if she has real musical talent.
>
> Yours sincerely,
>
> Henri Martinez
>
> Send

C Rewrite Henri's email giving advice to Delia, but in a more informal style. Use the points in A.

Suggested answer:

Hi Delia,

Thanks for your email. Great to hear that you're doing OK. I've got some advice for your friend. She'll need to make a recording of her voice and send it to as many producers as possible. We're always looking for new talent, so send it to me, too. We'll be able to decide if she has real musical talent.

Good luck!
Henri

SPEAKING

A IN PAIRS Read the emails you rewrote. Whose email sounded more informal?

B IN GROUPS Report the advice from your partner's email for making it in the music industry. Ask the group: whose advice is the most useful?

A: Jose said that she should use social media to advertise her talents.

B: And Francesca said she should practice at home to improve her confidence.

C IN GROUPS Discuss the statement. Use the Confident Communicator box to help you.

It isn't what you know, but who you know that matters in the music industry.

CONFIDENT COMMUNICATOR — KEEP TALKING

Use only a few, well-known idioms in your informal speaking and writing.
Make sure that you know the meaning of an idiom before you use it.

WRITING

Students compare and contrast emails written in an informal style and a formal style. They will look at aspects of the informal style of writing: informal greetings like *hi* and *hey*, informal closings like *bye* and *write soon*, contractions like *I'm* and *he's*, and informal punctuation such as exclamation points.

SPEAKING

Idioms are set phrases and must be used with the right wording or they sound strange. The word order cannot be changed. Words can't be added or subtracted.

The expression *It isn't what you know, but who you know* means that your contacts are more important than your skills.

CONFIDENT COMMUNICATOR

These are some idioms related to performance: *break a leg* means good luck; *the show must go on* means that whatever happens, everyone is committed to the performance; *get the show on the road* means to get started and can be used in any context.

GO TO page xv
for LANGUAGE AND LIFE step-by-step instructions.

Language and Life

Communication – Talent Contest

A **Have you or anyone you know ever taken part in a talent contest? What was the experience like?**

B 10.06 **Read the article about the beginnings of TV talent shows. Then answer the questions.**

Talent Contests

A TV talent show audition

The TV talent show *Got Talent*, started by Simon Cowell in 2004, has become a global success story. Viewers watch the shows in 58 countries. In 2014, *Guinness World Records* named it the most successful reality TV show ever. A number of other audition-based shows, such as *The Voice* and *The X Factor*, are also popular with audiences across the planet. And the reason? People love watching as the contestants go from nothing to huge success over a few weeks and months. But how did it all start?

Back in 1934, a radio show called *Original Amateur Hour* began in the US. After some success, it moved to TV in 1948. That show was similar to talent shows today. TV professionals traveled the country looking for entertainers who then went to New York for the auditions. The entertainers would audition for the judges on TV, and if chosen, they would come back and audition again. The audience would vote for their favorite act by phone or by mail. The final competition was at Madison Square Garden and the winners received a trophy and $1,500.

Original Amateur Hour helped to create a number of stars. Frank Sinatra performed on the radio show. Surprisingly, Elvis Presley wasn't successful when he auditioned for the show in Tupelo, Mississippi.

Another talent competition was *Star Search*. *Star Search* was different because entertainers competed in different categories, such as best male singer and best female singer. The prize money was $100,000 for each category. Many well-known pop stars and singing groups auditioned when they were younger, including Justin Timberlake, Destiny's Child, Christina Aguilera, Britney Spears, and Usher.

American Idol started on TV in 2002. Many more TV talent shows followed: *So You Think You Can Dance*, *The X Factor*, *Rockstar INXS*, *The Sing-Off*, *Dancing With the Stars*, and most recently, *The Voice*. Past winners of *Got Talent* include a performing police dog team, acrobats, ventriloquists, wheelchair dancers, and even Rubik's cube puzzle solvers.

1 What did the winners of *Original Amateur Hour* win? a trophy and $1,500
2 Who auditioned, but did not get a place, on *Original Amateur Hour*? Elvis Presley
3 What was different about the format of *Star Search*? There were multiple/different categories.
4 When did *American Idol* first appear on TV? in 2002
5 What talents do the past winners of *Got Talent* have?
6 Why might these talents be interesting to watch on TV? Students' own answer

5 a performing police dog team, acrobats, ventriloquists, wheelchair dancers, and even Rubik's cube puzzle solvers

C **IN PAIRS** **Talk to your partner and discuss what talents you have.**

A: I have a cool talent. I can play music using glasses of water!
B: Really? That's amazing. I can play guitar.
A: Maybe we could perform together!

OBJECTIVE

Students learn how to be a contestant or judge in a talent competition. They use critical thinking skills to consider the act they would like to perform or decide on the criteria for judging a talent show. They use teamwork skills to work with others and social skills to navigate the performance and to judge politely and constructively.

PROCESS OPTIONAL 10.06

Students read about the history of one of the most successful reality talent show of all time, *Got Talent*. After answering questions, students will prepare to hold their own talent contest. They decide if they want to be a contestant or a judge. The contestants decide on the act they want to do and think about what they will be asked by the judges. The judges decide on the criteria for judging and the questions they want to ask the contestants. Then, everyone reports back. Next, they hold the talent contest. Finally, they decide on a winner and give everyone positive feedback.

D **Your class is going to hold a talent contest. Choose three classmates to perform. Decide if you want to be a contestant or a judge and follow the instructions.**

Contestants: Get into groups. Explain what you want to do. Choose from one of the following:

- singing
- dancing
- playing an instrument
- reading a poem out loud
- acting out a scene from a movie or theater show
- another talent

Think about the questions you may be asked in the audition and work together to prepare clear and precise answers.

Possible Questions	Possible Answers
I think they might ask me how long I have been playing piano.	*I've been playing piano for five years.*

Judges: Get into groups. Discuss and agree how you are going to give scores for each contestant. Are you going to judge them on:

- talent?
- effort?
- appearance?
- a combination of these things?

Think about what you want to ask in the audition and work together to prepare clear questions.

Possible Questions
I'd like to ask why they want to be in the talent contest.

E IN PAIRS **Find a partner from the opposite group (contestants or judges). Report the questions that your group prepared and make sure they are the same.**

A: Our group thought you would ask us how long we had been playing an instrument

B: Our group had that question. We also decided to ask you why you wanted to be in the talent contest.

F **Return to your groups. Record your questions then hold the talent contest.**

Contestants: Perform in front of the judges. Answer any questions as clearly as possible.
Judges: Ask questions that you made a note of.

G **Decide on the winner(s) as a class. Explain what you liked about each performance and why.**

H **Discuss the questions.**

1 Were you happy with your questions and answers? Did they help you to communicate clearly?
2 In what other situations might you have to plan questions to ask someone or plan answers to give to someone?
3 What other factors contribute to effective communication?

MAKE IT DIGITAL

Record the talent contest. Decide whose performance was the best. Who definitely has talent?

CLASSROOM MANAGEMENT

Allow students ample time to prepare their performances. Have the criteria clearly established before judging begins. If the class is a large one, and it is hard to narrow down the number of contestants, have some elimination rounds before deciding on the final three classmates to perform.

MAKE IT DIGITAL

Students who show the least interest in being either contestants or judges could be the film crew. Have them record the performances. They should also decide on the ones in the group they believe have true talent. If possible, show edited versions of the performances to the class.

CULTURE NOTE

Be aware of gender equity in the classroom. Don't allow bullying based on gender or established gender roles. If a contestant wants to perform a piece that others deem outside their definition of being acceptable for a boy or a girl to do, don't allow bullies to change their minds.

GO TO page xvii
for UNIT REVIEW step-by-step instructions.

1 Kyle told Dan (that) he was doing a project about unusual talents. 2 Kyle asked (Dan) if/whether he knew anyone who had one. 3 Dan said (that) his cousin Elena had a cool talent. 4 Kyle wanted to know what she could do. 5 Dan explained (that) she could juggle. 6 Kyle asked where she had learned to do that. 7 Dan said (that) she had taken a circus class. 8 He asked (Kyle) if/whether he had ever taken a circus class. 9 Kyle admitted (that) he wasn't good at that kind of thing. 10 Dan said (that) most people were not.

UNIT 10

VOCABULARY review

SCORE: / 10

A Complete the sentences with the idioms from the box.

dream big | hungry for success | in the right place | set his heart on | set his sights on

1 Eliza works hard because she is hungry for success.
2 Be sure to dream big! Then you will have a goal to work toward.
3 Nat has set his sights on a singing career. He even has a manager!
4 I was in the right place at the right time, and I got a record deal while I was at music school.
5 Sam has set his heart on being a rock star when he leaves school!

B Complete the sentences with a phrasal verb from the box that means the same as the verb in parentheses.

come back | fill out | keep on going | make up | show up

1 If you forget the dance steps in the show, make up (invent) your own steps.
2 The theater doors don't open until 8 p.m., so you should come back (return) then.
3 To enter the talent show, you need to fill out (complete) an application form.
4 If you've failed your music exam five times, keep on going (continue) until you pass!
5 Auditions for the talent show start at 10 a.m., so please show up (arrive) just before then.

GRAMMAR review

SCORE: / 10

A Rewrite the numbered sentences in your notebook as reported speech. Use the verbs in parentheses.

Kyle: **1** I'm doing a project about unusual talents (tell). **2** Do you know anyone who has one? (ask)
Dan: **3** My cousin Elena has a cool talent. (say)
Kyle: **4** What can she do? (want to know)
Dan: **5** She can juggle. (explain)
Kyle: **6** Where did she learn to do that? (ask)
Dan: **7** She took a circus class. (say) **8** Have you ever taken a circus class? (ask)
Kyle: **9** I'm not good at that kind of thing! (admit)
Dan: **10** Most people aren't. (say)

16–20 correct: You can talk about your talents and abilities and use phrasal verbs and idioms connected to success. You can use reported statements and questions.
0–15 correct: Look again at the Vocabulary and Grammar sections in the unit.

TOTAL SCORE: / 20

WHAT DO YOU KNOW NOW? Look back at page 97 and add the words you know now to the boxes.

GO TO page xix
for FOLLOW A PRO step-by-step instructions.

FOLLOW A PRO ENTERTAINMENT

Take the quiz about entertainment. Go to Follow A Pro on page 136 to find the answers. Then read about the entertainment industry.

1 Which country has the most televisions, with approximately 400 million?
a Russia b China c the US

2 In what year was the first in-flight movie shown?
a 1925 b 1945 c 1965

3 Which Hollywood actor was first spotted by a talent scout having an argument in a bank?
a Jennifer Lawrence b Natalie Portman c Charlize Theron

4 How many boys auditioned for the leading role in the first Harry Potter movie?
a 160 b 1,600 c 16,000

106 Unit 10 Got It?

CLASSROOM MANAGEMENT

Before starting the review activities, give students some time to glance over the unit and review the vocabulary and grammar sections in each lesson. Once they have looked over the material, they will find the review activities more relevant.

ALTERNATIVE ACTIVITY

Play *In Which Lesson*. Have students work in pairs or small groups. One student looks over the unit and asks three review questions beginning with *In which lesson …?* For example, *In which lesson did we learn about writing an informal email?* The person answering has to guess the lesson number (Lesson 3). Then, students exchange roles.

FURTHER DISCUSSION

Write the following questions on the board. Then have students form groups of three and ask each other:

- Can you think of anyone famous now who will become a great artist in future?
- Can you think of a time when practice has paid off for you?
- Have you had any small successes lately?

UNIT 11 Money in the Bank

GO TO page vi
for UNIT OPENER step-by-step instructions.

WHAT DO YOU ALREADY KNOW?

1 Think about words you know related to money and finances. Write the words.

2 IN PAIRS Share and compare your ideas. Add more words to your lists.

Money/Finances

STUDENTS MAY ALREADY KNOW:

- **Money/Finances:** save, spend, cost, buy, cash, rich, poor, coins, bills, bank, stores, change, price, millionaire, billionaire, salary, own, rent, borrow, steal, invest, How much is it?

VIDEO

DISCUSS & SHARE

3 IN GROUPS Watch the video and answer the question.

SYM Is it better to save for the future or enjoy your money now?

GO TO page xx
for VIDEOS IN SYM step-by-step instructions.

In this unit, you will ...

- discuss who you would employ if you were a millionaire, share ideas about what to do with a fortune, and compare your budget with that of a partner.
- use thinking skills: question, apply, and recall.
- read about the gig economy.
- use strategies and language to talk about imagined future situations, collaborate on creative ideas, and politely refuse to answer a question.
- use collaboration skills to manage a budget.
- learn tips for personal development.

WHAT DO YOU ALREADY KNOW?

If students are struggling to understand what to do, you can ask them some questions to prompt their thinking:

- Do you get an allowance or have a part-time job?
- Is your income enough to meet your needs?
- What have you spent money on today?
- Do you save money?
- Do you invest your money?

VIDEO

Before viewing, complete with Kevin's answers:
Let's go to dinner tonight ... *We could eat at home for a lot less money.*
Movie? ... *We have streaming service.*
Let's go to a concert ... *Stream their music or watch the videos online.*

After viewing, put the continuum on the board.

save money —— enjoy money

Have students mark the continuum and explain their preferences.

DISCUSS & SHARE

Ask students if they think it's important to save for the future. Students should place themselves on a continuum of opinion. Do they need a nest egg for an unexpected event? Should people put money away for retirement? Alternatively, can they worry about that later and enjoy their money now?

GO TO page x

for **READING** step-by-step instructions.

A gig economy is a system where people get paid for short or freelance gigs, but they don't get a regular salary. The person in picture 1 is driving a taxi, the person in picture 2 is delivering food, and the person in picture 3 is renting part of their home to guests.

LESSON 1 The Gig Economy

READING

A Do you know what the "gig economy" is? Can you figure out what it is from the pictures?

B 11.01 READING SKILL—Read for the main idea Read the job ad, article, and business profile. Match a title with each one.

a Every Day is Different! **b** Calling All Computer Game Fans … **c** Changes to Our Working and Home Lives

1 _b_ We're **hiring** in your area! Would you like to earn some extra cash? Are you happy to do freelance work from home? If the answer is "yes," then give Reviews4U a call at 800-555-3210. We're a software company that needs gamers to test our new range of exciting PC games. We'll pay $40 for each gaming review you send to us. No **contract**, no stress, and hours that work for you.

2 _c_ Today's workers no longer expect to have the same job for life. The gig economy means that more and more people are working for themselves, offering their services and time **in exchange for** cash, but with no contract, no **pension**, and no vacation or sick pay. The way we take care of chores has changed at home, too. We have people take care of our gardens and yards, we make someone else walk our dogs because we're too busy to do it ourselves, and we get people to decorate our apartments. We have our groceries delivered and we get our houses cleaned. Interestingly, there are things that we used to get *others* to do in the past that we now do *ourselves* because of changes in technology. Now, we book our own flights online instead of getting a travel agent to do it for us. We also manage our own money online without the help of a bank clerk.

GigGetters

3 _a_ CeeCee Rogers, a tech worker in New York City, was **laid off** in 2018. She knew it might take a long time to find another job in her field.

"I wasn't sure what to do," explains CeeCee. "When I lost my job, it was a big shock. Luckily, I found out about GigGetters and I signed up with them. They have me do various gigs so I can make money while I'm looking for a more **permanent** job. I enjoy it. No day is the same!"

C Read the texts again. Write *True* or *False*.

1. The job at Reviews4U pays the same amount of money every month. _False_
2. Working for Reviews4U would mean working in an office. _False_
3. Text 2 includes information about disadvantages for workers in a gig economy. _True_
4. CeeCee wants to work for GigGetters for as long as possible. _True_

GLOSSARY

freelance (adj): not employed by a particular company, but working for them on a temporary basis

D THINKING SKILL—Question **What are the advantages of gig work? What are the disadvantages?**

108 Unit 11 Money in the Bank

READING OPTIONAL 11.01

gig economy (n): when there are more short-term contracts or freelance work than permanent jobs

READING SKILL—Read for the main idea

In *Speak Your Mind*, students practice many different reading skills and are given the opportunity to read for different purposes. When reading for the main idea, students can read the texts quickly. For READING **B** tell students to read the texts and match the titles with each one before listening to the audio.

THINKING SKILL—Question

Ask students if they do any gig work and what they like or dislike about it. What gig-work jobs are common in their areas? Would they prefer the flexibility of gig work, or would they prefer a permanent position?

Some advantages of gig work are flexibility of time, independence, and the ability to fit work in around another job or school. Some disadvantages are irregular income, no benefits, and loneliness.

VOCABULARY

A Complete the sentences with a word or phrase in bold in READING B.

1 My friend gave me a skirt that didn't fit her in exchange for a brown jacket that I never wear.
2 I was laid off a month ago, so I'm looking for another job.
3 When people retire from work, they usually get a regular amount of money called a pension from the company or government.
4 Did you sign a contract with your company when you started?
5 Dave has a temporary job, but he's looking for something permanent.
6 This restaurant is hiring chefs and servers.

MAKE IT YOURS

Go online or use a dictionary to find job advertisements in English for your chosen career. Are most companies hiring permanent workers, temporary workers, or gig workers?

GRAMMAR causatives with *have, get,* and *make*

A Underline examples in Text 2 in READING B of things we pay people to do for us and things we do ourselves.

B Complete the grammar rules with forms from the box.

base form of verb (x 2) infinitive past participle

1 Use *have* or *get* to talk about paying or asking someone to do something for you.
subject + *have/get* + object + past participle → I have/get my house cleaned.
2 Use *make* when you force or persuade someone to do something.
subject + *make* + object + base form of verb → I made my brother clean his room.
3 Use *have someone do something* to talk about someone who does a job for you.
subject + *have* + person + base form of verb → We had a mechanic fix the car.
4 Use *get someone to do something* when you ask, persuade, or pay someone to do something for you.
subject + *get* + person + infinitive → They got a vet to check their dog's health.

For more practice, go to page 156.

C Complete the sentences with the correct forms of the words in parentheses.

If you think being one of the world's wealthiest people sounds like fun, think about all the staff you'd need to hire just to keep your life in order! You'd need **1** ________ (get / housekeeper / clean) the house. You'd have to **2** ________ (have / nanny / take care of) your children and a private tutor **3** ________ (make / them / do) their homework. But think of the advantages! When you came home at the end of a long day, you could **4** ________ (have / your meal / cook) by your personal chef and **5** ________ (make / butler / bring) your slippers for you before you put your feet up in front of the TV!

D IN PAIRS Talk about things you have, get, or make other people do for you.

SPEAKING

A You have an unlimited amount of money. Make notes about what you would get these people to do for you.

- a hairdresser
- a mechanic
- a chef
- a dog walker

B IN PAIRS Talk about your ideas. Use the Confident Communicator box to help you.

C IN GROUPS What jobs would you like to have people do for you and what jobs you would prefer to do yourself?

CONFIDENT COMMUNICATOR
START TALKING

To start a conversation about things you dream of for the future, use:
You know what I'd do if I were …?
You know what I'd do if I had enough money? I'd have a chef cook all my meals.

GO TO page vii for **VOCABULARY** step-by-step instructions.

GO TO page viii for **GRAMMAR** step-by-step instructions.

1 take care of our gardens and yards / walk our dogs / decorate our apartments / deliver groceries / clean our houses
2 book vacations online / manage money online

1 to get a housekeeper to clean
2 have a nanny (to) take care of
3 to make them do
4 have your meal cooked
5 make the/your butler bring

GO TO page xii for **SPEAKING** step-by-step instructions.

VOCABULARY

Some more words and phrases related to the gig economy are: *sick leave, sick days, benefits, vacation pay, paid days off, fired, on call, orientation, insurance, medical benefits, license, training, steady job, short-term contracts, freelance work,* and *independent contractor.*

GRAMMAR

Here are some more things people have done. Getting things done might be habitual or once in a while. For example, *I get my nails manicured on Saturdays. I have the car washed once in a while. I get the lawn cut once a month. Last week, a plumber fixed a leak.*

SPEAKING

Have students share their lavish lifestyles with the class. Vote on the most creative, over-the-top lifestyles. Students may pretend they are a famous singer, actor, or other celebrity and share their extravagant habits.

Ask students to research the habits of someone rich. They might be surprised at how hard they work.

In 2017, George Soros donated $18 billion to charity foundations. This totals about 80% of his net worth.

In 2017, Bill and Melinda Gates gave away $4.6 billion in shares in his company Microsoft to fight against the spread of the disease malaria.

By 2012, Oprah Winfrey had given away $400 million to educational causes. In 2013, she donated $13 million to the Smithsonian National Museum.

In 2001, Alcario and Carmen Castellano won $141 million in the lottery. They set up The Castellano Foundation to help Latino communities and have donated over $1 million to help educate Latino children.

GO TO page xi

for **LISTENING** step-by-step instructions.

GO TO page 151

for **AUDIO SCRIPT**.

LESSON 2 Giving Away Money

VOCABULARY money verbs and nouns

A Read the definitions. Write the related nouns. Use a dictionary if needed.

Verb	Noun (thing)	Noun (person)
donate: to give something such as money to a charity	**1** donation: an amount of something such as money given to a charity	**2** donor: a person who donates something
contribute: to give something such as money to help achieve something	**3** contribution: a gift or payment you make to help achieve something	**4** contributor: a person who contributes something

B IN GROUPS Do you know individuals who have donated large sums of money to a particular cause in your country or abroad? Discuss.

Examples: George Soros   Bill and Melinda Gates   Oprah Winfrey   Alcario and Carmen Castellano

LISTENING

A IN PAIRS Do you ever donate money to charity? What kind of charities do you support?

1 animal charities

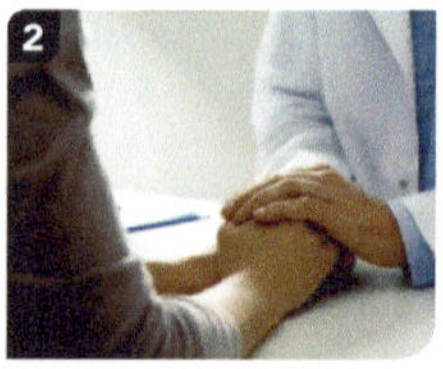
2 charities that help people with health problems

3 educational charities

4 environmental charities

5 charities that provide food, water, or housing

B 11.02 LISTENING SKILL—Listen for specific information Listen to an interview. Then complete the sentences.

1 The interviewer says that George Soros has donated over 18 billion dollars to charity.
2 The charity called *Rainbows* helps children.
3 Pat says that people can offer to work in the charity's thrift stores.
4 Danny says you can do online quizzes to help charities.
5 Danny says an organization called Free Rice helps people who need food.
6 Pat's charity has received 21 thousand dollars in foreign currency collected on planes.

GLOSSARY

campaign manager (n): a person who organizes ways to make money for a charity, organization, or political party
volunteer (n): a person who is not paid for the work they do
foreign currency (n phr): money from another country

C 11.02 IN PAIRS Compare your answers. Then listen again and check.

D THINKING SKILL—Apply Is it better to donate time or money to a charity? Give reasons.

VOCABULARY

Tell students they can read more about the foundations online.

For more information on George Soros' Open Society Foundations go to: https://www.opensocietyfoundations.org/

For more information on Bill and Melinda Gates foundation go to: https://gatesfoundation.org

For more information on Oprah Winfrey's foundation go to: https://charity.lovetoknow.com

For more information on Alcario and Carmen Castellano foundation go to: http://castellano-ff.org/

LISTENING

Give students a chance to think about the charities they support, or would like to support, and then ask for open-class feedback in the form of a show of hands to see what kinds of charities they are interested in. If students have ever donated their time, have them describe the experience.

GRAMMAR verbs with gerund, infinitive, or both

A **Read the examples from LISTENING B. Notice how some verbs are followed by the infinitive (*to* + base form of verb), the gerund (verb + *–ing*), or both.**

Many people decide **to give** cash …
Some people prefer **doing** these events
Have you considered **playing** games online?

B **Complete the rules with one of the verbs underlined in the examples from A. Then complete the example sentences.**

1 Some verbs (such as decide, *agree, want, offer*, etc.) are followed by infinitives.
EXAMPLE: Last year, my cousin did a 10k fun run and now, I really want **to do** one too.
2 Some verbs (such as consider, *suggest, deny, keep*, etc.) are followed by gerunds.
EXAMPLE: For a charity event, my friend suggest **raising** money by playing games online.
3 Verbs that describe feelings (such as prefer, *dislike, like, love, hate*, etc.) can be followed by both gerunds and infinitives.
EXAMPLE: I could never run a marathon! I absolutely hate **running**.

For more practice, go to page 157.

C **Complete the text with the infinitive or gerund form of the verb in parentheses. If both forms are possible, write both.**

Inheriting money can be hard, especially when the person who dies leaves instructions about what the person must (or mustn't) agree **1** to do (do) to get the money. Leona Helmsley, a hotel owner, left $12 million to her dog when she died. However, she gave instructions that two of her grandchildren would only inherit money if they promised **2** to visit (visit) their father's grave regularly. Henry Budd of London, who died in 1862, hated **3** seeing / to see (see) men with mustaches so much that he refused **4** to leave (leave) money to his two sons unless they avoided **5** growing (grow) facial hair. It seems some people just like **6** giving / to give (give) instructions even in death!

D **IN PAIRS Complete the sentences with information that is true for you. Discuss with your partner.**

1 I dislike ______
2 I sometimes help ______
3 I avoid ______
4 I really love ______
5 I always refuse ______

SPEAKING

A **Imagine that you have inherited $1 million. Would you spend it, save it, or give it to charity? Make notes.**

B **IN GROUPS Share your ideas. Give specific information about what you would do with the money. Use the Confident Communicator box to help you.**

CONFIDENT COMMUNICATOR
START TALKING

When you collaborate on creative ideas, it's good to start by going around the group, giving everyone the chance to talk about their ideas without interruptions. That way, everyone in the group can express their ideas with the full attention of everyone else.

GRAMMAR Additional Activity

Play *Basketball*. Find a bucket or box and a ball or crumpled-up piece of paper. Divide the class into two teams. Each team takes turns trying to make a shot. The team that makes a shot has a chance to win a point by making a correct sentence with a verb you supply from the grammar section. For example, *T: refuse S: He refused to go to school.*

SPEAKING

In order to speak for longer periods at a time, students should give as much detail as possible about their spending or charitable acts. If they want to spend their money, they should say what they are going to spend it on and why. If they are going to engage in charitable acts, they should say what organizations they want to donate to and why they chose that charity or area of work.

LESSON 3 Spending Money

VOCABULARY paying for things

A Label the pictures (1–6) with phrases from the box.

ATM / cash machine | cash | change | contactless payment | credit card | debit card

1 
cash

2 

debit card

3 

credit card

4 
ATM / cash machine

5 
contactless payment

6 
change

B **IN PAIRS** Talk about what you use to pay for different things.

A: I usually use cash to pay for lunch.
B: I sometimes use a debit card when I buy clothes.

GO TO page ix
for **PRONUNCIATION** step-by-step instructions.

PRONUNCIATION /tʃ/ versus /ʃ/

A 11.03 Listen to how these words are pronounced. Notice the difference between the /tʃ/ and /ʃ/ sounds.

change   cash machine

B 11.04 Practice saying these sentences. Then listen and check.

1 Do you have any change?
2 I'm going to use the cash machine.

LISTENING

GO TO page 152
for **AUDIO SCRIPT**.

A What do you spend money on? How do you manage your money?

B 11.05 **LISTENING SKILL—Listen for the main idea** Listen to a radio show. People are talking about the ways they manage their money. Match the speakers (1–4) with the ways to manage money (a–d).

1 Speaker 1 __d__
2 Speaker 2 __a__
3 Speaker 3 __c__
4 Speaker 4 __b__

a pays someone else to manage their money for them.
b says that they mostly use debit cards when they shop.
c uses traditional ways of managing their money.
d uses an app to help them manage their money.

C 11.05 Listen again and choose the correct speakers.

Which speaker …

1	isn't very good at managing money?	1	2	3	**4**
2	rarely uses a credit card?	1	2	**3**	4
3	would rather earn money than manage it?	1	2	3	**4**
4	likes to keep a physical record of her/his spending?	1	2	**3**	4
5	uses computer programs to manage her/his money?	**1**	2	3	4
6	uses their smartphone to manage her/his money?	1	**2**	3	4

MAKE IT REAL
To *splurge* means to spend a lot of money.
Maria used her birthday money to splurge on expensive new shoes.

D **IN PAIRS THINKING SKILL—Recall** Try to remember how much money you spent yesterday. What did you spend it on? How did you pay?

A: I really don't remember. I know I bought a soda and a sandwich.
B: Is that it? I'm sure you bought more than that.

VOCABULARY

Some more words related to money are *withdrawal, deposit, allowance, change, currency, money order, promissory note (IOU), pocket money, spending money, magnate, tycoon, billionaire,* and *earn.*

Some idioms related to money are the following: *to be as poor as a church mouse* means to be really poor; *to bring home the bacon* is to earn money.

PRONUNCIATION

Students should notice that although the word *machine* has a *ch* like the words *change* and *check*, it is pronounced /ʃ/,not /tʃ/.

Ask students why they think pronunciation activities are useful. Discuss the importance of pronunciation for being understood. The more they think about their pronunciation, the more quickly they will sound natural in English.

LISTENING

Have students discuss the tips that they liked the best or that have worked for them in the past. Ask them to share any other money management tips they have with the class. Students might want to think of someone they know who manages their money well and share what they do.

WRITING

A **A friend is visiting you from abroad. Read her email. What does she need advice about?**

1 restaurants 2 sightseeing 3 money

New Message

How are you doing? I'm really excited about seeing you in a few weeks. Can you give me some advice?

- Should I bring cash with me? If so, how much do you think I'll need per day for food, shopping, sightseeing?
- Should I change my dollars into the local currency here or wait until I'm there?
- Can I use my debit card or credit card at the ATMs?
- Please let me know what you think is best. A list of do's and don'ts would be great.

See you soon!
Amelia

Send

B **Think about Amelia's questions. Add advice to the table.**

Do's	Don'ts
change some money before you arrive	bring too much cash

C **Write an email to Amelia. Include the information from your table in B.**

D **IN PAIRS Share your emails. Did your partner answer all of Amelia's questions?**

SPEAKING

A **Find out what the average income is for people in your country per month. Write it in the table. Then fill in the amounts of money you think you would need to spend per month on these things.**

Item	Amount	Item	Amount	Item	Amount
rent/mortgage	1	food	2	clothes	3
entertainment/going out	4	travel/transportation	5	phone	6
household bills (water, gas, electricity, etc.)	7	other	8		

1 Total monthly income: ______________ 2 Total monthly spending: ______________

B **IN PAIRS Compare the amount of money you imagine you would spend on each thing.**

A: I think I would spend about $100 a month on food.
B: Really? I think I'd need to spend more than that. I wrote $150.

C **IN GROUPS Report to the group what you have learned about your partner's budget. What advice would you give to people who have spent too much? Use the Confident Communicator box to help you.**

Rico enjoys eating out. He thinks he'd spend between $60 and $100 a month. Maybe he should eat out less.

CONFIDENT COMMUNICATOR
KEEP TALKING

Money can be a hard topic to talk about. There are phrases you can use to refuse, politely, to answer questions you aren't comfortable with:
I'd rather not answer that question, if you don't mind.
That's a personal question. I'd rather not say.
I'm sorry, but that isn't information I want to share.

GO TO page xiv for WRITING step-by-step instructions.

Suggested answers:
Do's: use debit card or credit card at the ATMs
Don'ts: use ATMs at night

Students' own answers

WRITING

Students will write an email to a hypothetical friend giving her advice about how much money to bring on a trip to visit their country and some dos and don'ts related to money for her trip. Tell students to check they have given all of the information that Amelia asked for in their email.

SPEAKING

To find out the average income in countries around the world, tell students to use key words in their favorite search engine. If students can't find information they trust for their own county's average income, use your judgment and give them a figure to work with.

CONFIDENT COMMUNICATOR

It is helpful to be able to refuse to answer delicate questions politely. When talking about money, students might want to be able to do that. Have students ask some inappropriate questions as they walk around the room and politely refuse to answer each other's questions.

GO TO page xv
for LANGUAGE AND LIFE step-by-step instructions.

Language and Life

Collaborate – A Budget

A Are there any businesses near you that were set up by local people? What kinds of things do they sell? Are they popular?

B 11.06 Read the newspaper article about two friends who set up a business. Answer the questions.

Business Profile: KylieBelle's Bakery

Meet Annabelle Eggers and Kylie Howell, a pair of high school friends who recently set up KylieBelle's Bakery, a bakery and coffee shop on the North Shore. The pair both left successful careers in law to start their own business. But things didn't get off to a good start.

"It hasn't been easy," Kylie explains, when we meet up at the bakery on a Sunday morning. "I don't think we realized how much hard work it would be. We thought we'd be doing the jobs we love all day, which for us is making cakes and serving customers. But actually, there's a lot more involved, like accounting. Also, we had an awful first day." The pair had to close the bakery after a serious fire in their kitchen on the day they opened. "It was terrible," admits Annabelle. "We thought we might not be able to afford to open again after the accident. We were both in tears."

Luckily, a local resident, Marlene Parks, offered to help by investing over $10,000 in the business. "I was looking for a small business to invest some money in," says Marlene. "And who doesn't love a nice bakery in their local area? I hope the business does really well and I wish Annabelle and Kylie lots of luck." The women used the money to get builders to repair the kitchen, and the bakery reopened two weeks later.

"Thanks to Marlene, we were able to get the business open again. We need to pay her back, obviously, but it meant we could start making money. The business is doing really well. We're going to have a new seating area built outside so we can serve more of our cakes. People love our white chocolate cheesecake!"

1 What profession did Annabelle and Kylie use to work in? law

2 What happened on the first day the bakery opened? a fire started

3 How did the women get money for builders to repair the kitchen? Marlene Parks, a local resident, invested in their business.

4 What are they planning to build outside and why? a new seating area

OBJECTIVE

Students learn how to write a business plan for starting a new business. Students will learn how to think like entrepreneurs. They will approach a problem systematically. They will learn how to express themselves and defend their proposal. Importantly, they will consider starting a small company within the realistic boundaries of cost.

PROCESS OPTIONAL 11.06

Students will discuss pop-up shops. They will read a newspaper article about two friends who set up a business. Once students have understood the article, they work in pairs to think of a small business they might like to open. Then, they answer a series of questions about their new business. They do an exercise to consider how they can save money on start-up costs. Students think about the work they can do themselves and the work they will have to hire out. Finally, students present their business plan to the class. The class identifies the businesses that will be able to start on budget.

C IN PAIRS **Imagine you want to open a small business in your city or town with your partner. You have a budget of $10,000 to get the business started. Together, discuss the questions and reach an agreement for each point.**

1. What kind of small business will you open?
2. Where will it be located?
3. What is the rent?
4. What will you call it?
5. What product or service will you sell?
6. How much will the product or service cost?
7. What kinds of payment will you accept (cash, credit cards, debit cards)?
8. What kinds of problems do you think the business might have?
9. What can you do about these problems?

D IN PAIRS **Before you open the business, you need to decide which jobs you can do yourself and which you are going to get someone else to do for you. Decide together and write the jobs and the costs in the correct column.**

Jobs we can do ourselves	Jobs we need to get someone else to do	Expected costs for jobs other people will do
delivering leaflets	*installing new kitchen equipment*	

E **Underline the jobs in D that will cost a lot to have someone else do. Could you do any of them yourself? Negotiate with each other to decide who could do which job.**

F IN GROUPS **Share your ideas. Find out which businesses are within the $10,000 budget.**

G **Discuss the questions.**

1. Did you and your partner work well together? How did you overcome any disagreements?
2. In what other situations might you have to collaborate and agree on a solution?

MAKE IT DIGITAL

Find and read an online article about starting a new business. What other things should you consider that were not discussed in this lesson?

CLASSROOM MANAGEMENT

You may want to set up the sharing activity as a meeting with the small business association. Nominate three panelists to listen to each proposal. Tell the panelists to give students advice on their business proposal. They should share money management tips, product ideas, and marketing suggestions.

CULTURE NOTE

Some popular and profitable pop-up stores are seasonal. They set up just before Christmas and sell Christmas decorations, or they appear a few weeks before Halloween selling Halloween costumes. The success of these stores is timing and anticipating the kinds of products customers are looking for.

MAKE IT DIGITAL

Check online for articles about pop-up businesses. Students can search with key words such as *pop-up shop examples* or *pop-up shop ideas.*

GO TO page xvii
for **UNIT REVIEW** step-by-step instructions.

UNIT 11

VOCABULARY review

SCORE: / 10

A Complete the sentences with words from the box.

contract contribution donor pension permanent

1 In some countries, you can receive a pension from the government at the age of 60.
2 Did you sign a contract when you started your new job?
3 This is a permanent job, so you'll have a fixed schedule.
4 A generous celebrity donor has given $1 million to this charity.
5 Did you make a contribution to any charities last year?

B Choose the five correct answers to complete the sentences.

1 I don't like borrowing money, so I don't have any **credit** / debit cards.
2 Do you have any ATMs / **cash**? This machine doesn't accept change / **contactless payments**.
3 The credit card / **ATM** isn't working so I haven't got any **cash** / cash machines at all.

GRAMMAR review

SCORE: / 10

A Choose the correct words.

1 She is **having** / making her hair cut at the hairdresser at the moment.
2 Did you **have** / get a mechanic fix your car?
3 They are **getting** / making a painter to decorate their new bathroom.
4 Mom **made** / got the kids mow the lawn before they had lunch.
5 Will he **get** / have a taxi to take him to the airport at 3 a.m.?

B Complete the sentences with the correct forms of the verbs in parentheses. Write both forms where possible.

1 My manager has agreed to give (give) me time off when I move.
2 I've decided to save / saving (save) some money every month for a vacation.
3 Marcus promised not to spend (not/spend) a lot of money on his fiancée's Christmas gifts.
4 I prefer to pay / paying (pay) for things with my debit card rather than with a credit card.
5 I avoid wasting (waste) money buying things I don't need.

16–20 correct: You can talk about money and paying for things. You can use *have, make* and *get* and verbs with the gerund, infinitive, or both.
0–15 correct: Look again at the Vocabulary and Grammar sections in the unit.

TOTAL SCORE: / 20

WHAT DO YOU KNOW NOW? Look back at page 107 and add the words you know now to the box.

GO TO page xviii
for **STUDY SKILLS** step-by-step instructions.

STUDY SKILLS PERSONAL DEVELOPMENT

Take the quiz about personal development. Go to **Study Skills** on page 137 to find the answers. Then learn more about personal development.

1 Recording yourself answering questions is a useful study technique.
a True **b** False

2 Studying for short periods of time is not effective.
a True **b** False

2 It can be very effective.

3 What is overlearning?
a It's when you work too hard and get very tired.
b It's when you go over to a friend's house to study.
c It's when you continue learning something even when you think you've already learned it.

4 What percentage of students admit to studying for exams at the very last minute?
a 99% **b** 90% **c** 65% **d** 51%

CLASSROOM MANAGEMENT

Give those students who have had trouble with the review activities time to look back at the relevant sections. Allow them to do the review activities again. Also allow them to talk to peers about the things they found challenging.

FURTHER DISCUSSION

Write the following questions on the board. Then have students form groups of three and ask each other:

- What do you do to save money?
- Do you like to spend money?
- Is it better to start a business or invest your money?
- Are you careful with your money?

UNIT

12 Inside Advertising

GO TO page vi

for UNIT OPENER step-by-step instructions.

WHAT DO YOU ALREADY KNOW?

1 Think about ads you like. Write words to describe them.

2 IN PAIRS Share and compare your ideas. Add more words to your lists.

Ads:

STUDENTS MAY ALREADY KNOW:

- **Ads:** sell, buy, products, food, holidays, cars, pet food, cleaning products, TV, television, radio, ads.

DISCUSS & SHARE

VIDEO

3 IN GROUPS Watch the video and answer the question.

SYM Does advertising work?

GO TO page xx

for VIDEOS IN SYM step-by-step instructions.

In this unit, you will ...

- discuss the advertising of energy drinks, talk about ads that you like and dislike, and debate the effects of advertising.
- use thinking skills: evaluate, symbolize, and induce.
- read about advertising controls around the world.
- use strategies and language to make sure everyone has a turn in a discussion, get a discussion back on track, and paraphrase to clarify what someone has said.
- use media-literacy skills to make a TV ad.
- follow a digital copywriter to learn about this job and the skills needed to be in this industry.

WHAT DO YOU ALREADY KNOW?

If students are struggling to understand what to do, you can ask them some questions to prompt their thinking:

- Where do you see advertising?
- Is some advertising clever? Is some advertising annoying?
- What kinds of products are advertised? Where are things advertised?
- Who advertises the most?

VIDEO

Before viewing, ask:

What is advertising? *To be persuaded to buy something.*
How does advertising help Ellen? *It helps her find the products she like.*

After viewing, put the continuum on the board.

advertising —— no advertising

Have students mark the continuum and explain their preferences.

DISCUSS & SHARE

Students should place themselves on a continuum of opinion. Ask students to think about whether they believe advertising works or not. Are they motivated to buy something because of advertising? What kind of advertising works on them? Do they believe advertising doesn't have any influence on them?

LESSON 1 Advertising Regulations

GO TO page x
for **READING** step-by-step instructions.

READING

A **Are there any ads that you dislike? Why don't you like them?**

B **12.01 Read the article. Then answer the questions.**

Advertising Around the World: Who Controls What?

As you might expect in the modern world, more and more advertising is being controlled by strict rules. In the US, the Federal Trade Commission (FTC) makes sure that all ads are accurate. In the UK, this is done by the Advertising Standards Agency (ASA), which in 2017 received about 30,000 **complaints** about ads. The job of these agencies is to decide if certain rules are broken by advertisers. **1** _c_ The FTC and the ASA decide if the ad can be shown or if it has to be **removed**.

Ads that you might think aren't very offensive can cause lots of complaints. **2** _d_ People felt that this ad might encourage bad habits in children. In 2017, another TV ad for fried chicken that showed chickens dancing to rap music was **criticized** for being offensive to vegetarians and vegans. The request was turned down by the ASA.

Each country has different rules about what they allow. A famous series of billboard ads made by a fashionable Italian clothing company caused problems in countries where they appeared. One ad, showing a very young baby, shocked a lot of people. In Sicily, the company was ordered by the town officials to remove the ad. **3** _a_ It was given a prize by the Swiss General Poster Association, and a hospital in Bologna asked **permission** to display the ad on its walls.

Some ads have been **banned**, not for showing offensive images, but for the way they market the product. A well-known soft drink ad campaign, which had been seen by millions, was removed for showing a famous celebrity sharing her drink with a police officer at a protest event. **4** _b_

GLOSSARY

offensive (adj): causing people to feel upset or embarrassed
billboard (n): a large board for ads in an outside public space

1 What is the name of the organization that controls ads in the US? the Federal Trade Commission (FTC)
2 What did viewers not like about the fried chicken ad? offensive to vegetarians and vegans
3 What type of company produced an ad showing a newborn baby? a clothing company

C **READING SKILL—Identify missing sentences** **Match the sentences (a–d) to lines 1–4 in the article.**

a It is interesting that what shocks some people is loved by other people.
b The message is just as important as the image.
c These might include making false promises about the product or using offensive images.
d A TV ad showing people talking with their mouths full of food received the most complaints in the ASA's history.

D **THINKING SKILL—Evaluate** **Consider this statement: "Advertising doesn't really have an effect on the things I choose to buy." Is this statement true for you?**

GO TO page vii
for **VOCABULARY** step-by-step instructions.

VOCABULARY

A **Match the words in bold in READING B with the definitions.**

1 _banned_ (v): officially stated that people must not do or say something
2 _complaints_ (n plural): written or spoken statements in which someone says they are not happy with something
3 _criticized_ (v): said what you thought was bad or wrong about something
4 _permission_ (n): the right to do something that someone with power gives you
5 _removed_ (v): taken away from a place

MAKE IT DIGITAL

Research online for examples of ads that have been banned. Do you think that they should have been banned?

READING OPTIONAL 12.01

The Super Bowl, in the United States, offers some of the most expensive advertising in the world. Companies create advertisements specifically to be aired during halftime. These ads are usually innovative. For READING **B** make sure students read the article and answer the questions before listening to the audio.

THINKING SKILL—Evaluate

Have students give reasons for their opinions in **D**. Do they think advertising doesn't have an effect on the things they choose to buy? Or do they think it does? Are they immune to the messaging, the emotive music, the catchy jingles, and the rhyming slogans in advertising?

VOCABULARY Extra Practice

For further practice of the new vocabulary words, dictate synonyms to students. Tell them to write them down and write the target vocabulary word from READING **B** that matches the set.

- *authorization, consent* (permission)
- *prohibit, disallow* (ban)
- *objection, grievance* (complaint)
- *take away, take off, withdraw* (remove)
- *find fault with, disapprove of* (criticize)

GRAMMAR passive voice: other tenses

A Read the examples of the passive voice from READING B. Find five other examples of passive sentences in the article.

... more and more advertising is being controlled by strict rules. (present progressive passive)
The job of these agencies is to decide if certain rules are broken by advertisers. (simple present passive)
... was criticized for being offensive. (simple past passive)
Some ads have been banned ... (present perfect passive)
... which had been seen by millions ... (past perfect passive)

B Choose the correct options.

1 Use the passive voice to show that the action is **more** / **less** important than the person doing the action.
2 Use the passive voice when you **know** / **don't know** who did the action.
3 Only use the passive voice with **transitive** / **intransitive** verbs.

For more practice, go to page 158.

C Complete the text with the correct passive forms of the verbs in parentheses. More than one form may be possible.

An ad for an electronic device **1** ________________ (change) recently following a complaint. Alexa, as she **2** ________________ (know) around the world, tried to order cat food when she heard her name on a cat food ad. The ad, which shows the device **3** ________________ (use) in different situations by different people, confused Alexa into making the order. A complaint **4** ________________ (receive) by an advertising complaints organization. Amazon agreed that Alexa did place an order for the cat food, but the order **5** ________________ (cancel) by the customer. Customers now have to confirm their orders. The orders **6** ________________ (remove) immediately from their shopping carts if customers do not confirm them.

D IN PAIRS Think about a recent ad campaign that you like. Describe it to your partner. Can he or she guess the ad? Who is it made by? Where is it advertised? How long has it been advertised?

This ad is made by a fast food company. It's been shown on TV for about six months, but the actors have been changed recently.

GO TO page viii for GRAMMAR step-by-step instructions.

1 has been changed / was changed
2 is known
3 being used
4 has been received / was received
5 had been canceled / was canceled
6 are removed

SPEAKING

A IN PAIRS Should energy drinks be advertised on TV and in magazines? Complete the table and give reasons.

For	Against

B IN GROUPS Decide whether you are for or against advertising energy drinks on TV or in magazines. Take turns presenting your opinion and giving reasons. Use the Confident Communicator box to help you.

CONFIDENT COMMUNICATOR
KEEP TALKING

To make sure everyone in a group has a turn in a discussion, use phrases like this:
Can we hear someone else's opinion?
What do you think, [name]?

GO TO page xii for SPEAKING step-by-step instructions.

GRAMMAR

Many companies that do advertising campaigns are companies that sell insurance, cleaning supplies, toothpaste, medicine, cars, vacations, watches, food, toys, and beverages. Also, department stores and health care companies engage in advertising campaigns.

Demonstrate **D** by giving students another example of a commercial that appeals to you. For example, *This ad has been shown on channel … and channel … It was made by a famous … company. It shows …*

SPEAKING

Some studies have shown that the high levels of caffeine in energy drinks are harmful to people's health and can cause tachycardia or irregular heartbeat. If multiple energy drinks are drunk in a short period of time, it could be dangerous. However, the same could be said of coffee. Should we stop advertising coffee because, if abused, it could cause heart problems? What other stimulants do energy drinks contain?

LESSON 2 How Does Advertising Work?

VOCABULARY advertising campaigns

A Match the job responsibilities (1–6) with the meanings (a–f). Use a dictionary if needed.

1 come up with a slogan _a_
2 promote a product _c_
3 design the logo _f_
4 launch the product _d_
5 identify the target market _b_
6 manage the budget _e_

a think of words or phrases to sell a product
b figure out which groups of people will buy a product
c attract people's attention to a product
d start selling a new product
e control the money spent on a project
f create a memorable image connected to a product

GO TO page xi
for **LISTENING** step-by-step instructions.

LISTENING

A IN PAIRS Look at the magazine ads. What are they trying to tell you about the product? Who is the target market?

GO TO page 153
for **AUDIO SCRIPT**.

B 12.02 Listen to an excerpt from an interview with a marketing executive. What does he consider in ad campaigns? Choose the correct answers.

The man says that …
1 they identify their target market using **five** / **six** / **seven** different categories.
2 in ads for younger people, the music is **slower** / **faster** / **calmer** than in ads for older people.
3 ads for people over the age of **40** / **50** / **60** often have calmer music.
4 the more you write slogans, **the harder** / **the faster** / **the easier** it gets.

GO TO page 153
for **AUDIO SCRIPT**.

C 12.03 LISTENING SKILL—Listen for inference Listen to the ad. Then answer the questions.

1 What is the ad for? It's an ad for an energy drink.
2 Who is the target market? The target market is young, athletic men and women.
3 Why is the ad appropriate for this market? The man speaks dramatically and quickly, and the music is fast and energetic.

D THINKING SKILL—Symbolize Sketch as many logos as you can in two minutes. Why do you think these logos stick in your mind?

GRAMMAR comparative and superlative adverbs

A Look at the phrases in bold in the sentences from LISTENING B. Which adverbs are comparative? Which are superlative? Write C or S.

1 … one of the first things we have to **do the most carefully** is identify our target market. _S_
2 And in TV or radio ads directed at older people, the actors usually **speak more seriously** and less quickly. _C_
3 "These running shoes will help you **run faster**!" _C_

VOCABULARY

Write these slogans on the board: *Just Do It*, *I'm Lovin' It*, and *Have a Break, Have a Kit Kat*. Tell students they are three famous slogans in English. Ask if anyone can identify the companies and products (Nike, sportswear; McDonald's, burgers; Nestlé, Kit Kat). Do they know the logos for these companies? Ask students to think of slogans from local advertising campaigns. Ask them to think of any new products that have been launched lately.

LISTENING

Do an intensive-listening dictation. Read the sentence below five times at normal speed. Don't stop other than to pause at commas and take a breath at the colon and the period. Tell students to write down what they hear.

We identify our customers using six different categories: gender, age, occupation, relationship status, geographic location, and behavior.

B Choose the correct options to complete the grammar rules.

1 Most comparative adverbs are formed with ... + adverb.
   a *more* b *the most*
2 Most superlative adverbs are formed with ... + adverb.
   a *more* b *the most*
3 Most short adverbs, such as *fast* and *hard*, end in *–er* in the comparative and *–est* in the ...
   a superlative. b infinitive.
4 The verb usually goes ... the adverb.
   a before b after

For more practice, go to page 159.

C Complete the sentences with the correct forms of the words in parentheses.

1 In commercials for younger people, the actors talk more quickly (quick) than in commercials for older people.
2 Ad campaigns work the most successfully (successful) when they have a clear target market.
3 They're working more carefully (careful) on this ad campaign than the last one.
4 Our products are selling more slowly (slow) than we'd like them to.
5 The people in that ad sing worse (badly) than I thought possible!

MAKE IT REAL

There are different ways of talking about TV *ads*. You can talk about *ads* or *commercials* (all informal) or about *advertisements* (more formal).

D **IN PAIRS** Talk about ads.

Which ones ...
1 do you see most often?
2 work the most successfully?
3 make the product look better than it actually is?

SPEAKING

A Think about an ad you like and an ad you dislike. Complete the table with notes about them.

	Ad I Like	Ad I Dislike
Product		
Logo		
Slogan		
Target market		
Kind of ad (print, TV, billboard)		
People, activity, or music in ad		

B **IN GROUPS** Talk about ads you like and dislike. Suggest improvements for the ad you dislike. Use the Confident Communicator box to help you.

A: Why don't you like this commercial?
B: I think the people in the ad speak too quickly. I think they could speak more slowly.

CONFIDENT COMMUNICATOR
REPAIR IT

If a discussion goes "off topic," you can use the phrases to get the discussion back on topic:
Going back to what I was saying earlier about *advertising.*
Let's get back to talking about *how to improve this ad campaign.*
You were saying that *you didn't like this ad.*

GRAMMAR

Some comparative and superlative adverbs are: *well–better–best, fast–faster–fastest, hard–harder–hardest, late–later–latest, early–earlier–earliest, straight–straighter–straightest*, and *badly–worse–the worst*.

Lately is an adverb, but it means "recently." The adverb *badly* also has the meaning "to need something desperately." The adverb *wrongly* is acceptable but *wrong* is also used.

SPEAKING

Review *logo, slogan*, and *target market* from VOCABULARY **A**. Then brainstorm kinds of ads with the class. There are print ads, which appear in newspapers, magazines, journals, and fliers. TV ads are ever present. There are commercials on YouTube and streaming services. Billboards are plentiful along major highways in many countries. And don't forget radio.

Radio has massive coverage in Latin America. In Mexico, radio is considered a mass medium. It has a 98% national penetration and it has a wider diversity of owners and programming than on TV. This makes it a powerful advertising medium.

LESSON 3 The "Unreal" World of Advertising

VOCABULARY discourse markers

A Write the discourse markers from the box next to the correct functions.

although	as well as	for instance	such as
as a result	due to	in addition	whereas

Function	Examples
Adding information	also, too, and, furthermore, **1** as well as, **2** in addition
Giving examples	for example, **3** such as, **4** for instance
Giving reasons	because, so, therefore, **5** due to, **6** as a result
Contrasting different ideas	but, however, on the one hand, on the other hand, **7** although, **8** whereas

B Choose the correct options.

1 A: Do you always change channels when the commercials come on?
B: Not always, **because** / **although** I actually like watching some of them.

2 A: Did you know that this ad was banned in many countries?
B: I know. But **in addition** / **as a result**, the fast food chain became even more popular!

3 A: Ads for products **such as** / **due to** soft drinks shouldn't be shown during kids' movies.
B: I completely agree.

4 A: **As well as** / **Whereas** all the pop-up ads on Facebook, I get a lot of spam email, too.
B: Yeah, me too. It's really annoying.

LISTENING

A IN PAIRS **Compare the pictures. Which one has been photoshopped (changed to look different)? How do you know?**

GO TO page 153 for AUDIO SCRIPT.

B 12.04 LISTENING SKILL—Recognize discourse markers **Listen to four people giving their opinions about advertising. Then match each speaker with the discourse marker that he or she uses (a–d).**

1 Speaker 1: c
2 Speaker 2: d
3 Speaker 3: b
4 Speaker 4: a

a due to
b such as
c as a result
d although

GLOSSARY
edit (v): to make changes to a photo to make it look better

VOCABULARY

Learners sometimes ask about the word *although*, as they hear it often but are not sure how to use it. Generally, it means "in spite of." It is used to introduce a statement that modifies your main statement. Ask students for examples using *although* and check for pronunciation.

LISTENING Extra Practice

For further listening practice, have students work in groups of four for a jigsaw listening. Tell them to count off from one to four. Then have each member of the group make notes about what the speaker corresponding to their number says. Play the audio again. Each group member should listen more carefully to their speaker, take notes, and then share what they understood with their group.

C 12.04 Listen again and decide which speaker (1–4) has a positive opinion of advertising and which speaker has a negative opinion.

+ opinion Positive: 1

– opinion Negative: 2, 4

D THINKING SKILL—Induce Decide if people generally believe what companies say about their products.

PRONUNCIATION filler sounds and words

A 12.05 Listen to the sentences from LISTENING B. Underline the filler sounds and words that the speakers use. Why do you think they use them?

1 Situations that people can, um, understand and connect with.
2 I felt quite angry, hmm …
3 You might think ad companies would, you know, check the images carefully …
4 It's like, when I'm shopping, what makes me pick up certain things and buy them?

B Think about your language. What filler sounds and words do you use?

Speakers use filler sounds and words to give themselves a short time to think about what they are going to say.

GO TO page ix for PRONUNCIATION step-by-step instructions.

WRITING

A Read the essay prompt and one student's answer to it. Has the student answered the question? Why or why not?

PROMPT: "Photoshopped images should be banned in ads." Discuss the arguments for and against this statement.

In recent years, some advertising companies have been criticized for using photoshopped images in their advertising campaigns. For example, it's common for the pictures in ads for some products—beauty products, for instance—to be edited to make the people in the ads appear perfect. The ad companies use computer technology to change the shape of people's bodies. Due to this trend, young people can have health problems because they try to look like the people in the ads. As a result, photoshopping ads has already been banned in some countries. In France, for example, photoshopped images are not shown in magazines or on billboards. I agree that it should now be banned in the rest of the world, too.

B IN PAIRS Can you think of any arguments in favor of photoshopping images in ads? Make notes.

C Write a for-and-against paragraph about photoshopping. Use ideas from A and the notes you made in B. Try to include some discourse markers from VOCABULARY A.

GO TO page xiv for WRITING step-by-step instructions.

The student has not answered the question. The student has written about the arguments for banning photoshopped images but has not presented any arguments in favor of them.

Suggested answers:
Photoshopping is used all the time, not just on images of people, to make things seem brighter or clearer.
It's a useful tool for covering up small mistakes in pictures.
It isn't actually changing a person's appearance.
People can often tell that images have been edited, so they know the images are not realistic.

SPEAKING

A What is your opinion on the following question: "Do the images used in advertising have a positive or negative effect on people?" Make notes.

B IN GROUPS Discuss your ideas, giving examples and reasons. Use discourse markers to connect your ideas. Use the Confident Communicator box to help you.

CONFIDENT COMMUNICATOR
KEEP TALKING

Use the following phrases to paraphrase and clarify what someone else has said in a debate or discussion:
So, what you're saying is that these ads make people feel uncomfortable?
Am I right in thinking that you think ads do have a negative effect on people?
If I understand correctly, you're saying that ads don't have any negative effects?

PRONUNCIATION

Filler sounds and words go a long way toward helping your learners sound more natural when they speak. You don't want them to overdo it, but if they practice adding a couple of fillers to their speech, it will help give them thinking time and make them appear more natural and relaxed.

WRITING

Students will write a paragraph about photoshopping. They will mention points for and against photoshopping images for ads. A point against photoshopping is the influence it has on young people's health. One argument for why photoshopping shouldn't be banned is the entertainment value.

SPEAKING

Remind students to give reasons for their opinions and examples that will make their argument more convincing. For example, if they take the position that advertising has a positive effect, they should stick to it. To support this position, they could say that it promotes competition in business and informs people of their choices.

GO TO page xv for **LANGUAGE AND LIFE** step-by-step instructions.

Language and Life

Media Literacy – A TV ad

A 12.06 **When a company has an idea for a TV ad, they make a storyboard. Read the article and then choose the correct options.**

STORYBOARDS: WHAT YOU NEED TO KNOW

A Simple Guide

Have you ever come up with the most fantastic idea for an ad—or perhaps a home-made video—but had a problem getting your ideas down on paper? Then you need a storyboard!

WHAT IS A STORYBOARD?

A storyboard is a series of sketches, drawn in the style of a comic. It shows every scene of the ad. It shows what characters are in the scene, what they are doing, and what they are saying. A good storyboard will help you imagine the ad. It shows the production team what to photograph and in what order. It communicates ideas without long, wordy descriptions. As more people become involved in making the ad and give their opinions, the storyboard may develop and change.

HOW TO MAKE A STORYBOARD

A storyboard doesn't have to be complicated. Here's how to make one:

STEP 1: MAKE A TEMPLATE
Draw a series of **squares** or **rectangles** on a plain piece of paper, one for each scene. Leave room underneath the squares or rectangles for notes. You can also find free storyboards online.

STEP 2: DRAW THE STORY
Don't worry if you aren't very good at drawing. You can use **simple stick figures** in the boxes. Show any movement with an **arrow** or **short parallel lines**.

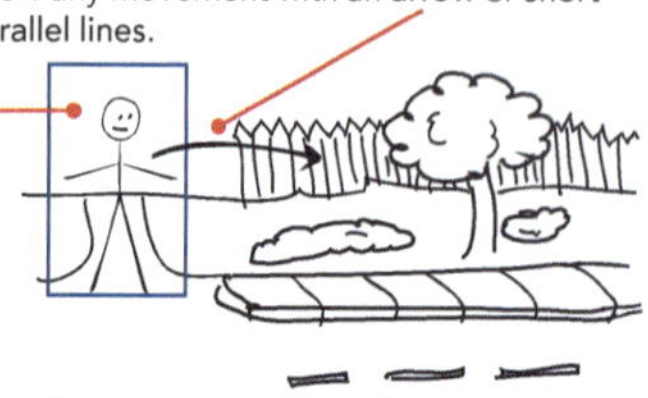

"Hey! Wait for me!"
Camera: Pans to the right from this angle as person walks. *Background music: Should have an upbeat tempo.*

STEP 3: ADD THE DIALOGUE
Write any dialogue underneath the pictures. You can also make a silent video where no dialogue is necessary.

STEP 4: ADD NOTES
These might include instructions for camera angles, descriptions of the actions in the scene, or ideas for music.

Good luck!

1 You make a storyboard at the start / end of an ad campaign.
2 A storyboard contains long / short written descriptions.
3 You need / don't need to be a good artist to draw a storyboard.
4 Storyboards have to / don't have to include dialogue.

124 Unit 12 Inside Advertising

OBJECTIVE

Students will learn how to create a storyboard for a TV ad. They will also pitch the idea for the ad represented by the storyboard. In this lesson, students will learn how an idea is brought to life in an ad through the use of storyboards.

PROCESS OPTIONAL 12.06

First, students will read an article about the theory behind storyboards and the practical steps in making one. Then, they look at an example and try to figure out what it is advertising. They discuss the example storyboard. Next, students take their own idea for an ad and make a storyboard for a TV ad. They don't have to be good at drawing. They should follow the instructions given in the article in **A**. They should identify how their ad will appeal to their target market. Groups should practice presenting their idea. Finally, groups will present their storyboards to the class.

B IN PAIRS **Look at the storyboard for an ad. Take turns describing what you think is happening in each of the scenes.**

The ad campaign could be for a new TV series or a new tablet.

C IN PAIRS **Discuss the following questions.**

1 What product do you think the ad is trying to sell?
2 Who is the biggest market?
3 What message is the ad trying to communicate?
4 Do you think the ad works? Why or why not?

D IN GROUPS **Make a storyboard for a TV ad.**

1 Choose a product. It can be real or imaginary.
2 Identify the target market.
3 Discuss your ideas and message for a TV ad.
4 Make a storyboard for a TV ad.

MAKE IT DIGITAL

Turn your storyboard idea into an ad. Decide which parts you are playing, practice any dialogue, and record your ad!

E **Present your storyboards as a class.**

F **Discuss the questions.**

1 Whose ad do you think would be the most successful. Why?
2 What are the key factors of a successful ad?

CULTURE NOTE

How does advertising change from country to country? Are the laws different? Are certain things advertised in some countries but not allowed in others? What are the rules surrounding advertising to children in your country? How do they compare to other countries? Encourage students to research rules for advertising in their country.

MAKE IT DIGITAL

Put students into groups, and ask them to check online for the best ads of the Super Bowl. Ask them to watch them and name the products being advertised. You may want to nominate different groups to research different years, watch the ads, and then describe them to the class. Or have groups check ads from the '80s or '90s and compare them to a more recent year. Finally, have them vote on the one they like the best.

CLASSROOM MANAGEMENT

Encourage students to go back over the units and check the *Confident Communicator* boxes for functional language that helps them work in groups, share ideas, negotiate with others, give suggestions, interrupt, and disagree politely.

GO TO page xvii

for **UNIT REVIEW** step-by-step instructions.

UNIT 12

VOCABULARY review

SCORE: / 10

A Complete the text with words or phrases from the box.

although | as a result | budget | comes up with | identify | in addition | launch | logo | such as | whereas

My job is to manage ad campaigns for a large grocery store. We need to develop an ad campaign for party food **1** ___such as___ snacks and drinks. **2** ___Whereas___ in the past, ads for food were designed to appeal mostly to women, nowadays we have to **3** ___identify___ our target market more carefully. **4** ___As a result___, we spend a lot more time researching who buys our products. The creative team **5** ___comes up with___ a slogan for the new ad and the design team makes the **6** ___logo___ that goes on our party food packaging. **7** ___In addition___, I have to manage the **8** ___budget___ to make sure we don't spend too much money. Today, we will have a meeting to discuss how we are going to **9** ___launch___ a new product in the market. **10** ___Although___ the different teams sometimes disagree about the best way to advertise a product, we usually produce a great ad!

1 This ad was shown for the first time this year.
2 That logo was designed by an artist.
3 That ad has been banned by some governments.
4 The product is being launched in the early fall.
5 The storyboard had been developed by the creative team.

GRAMMAR review

SCORE: / 10

A Rewrite the sentences using the passive voice in your notebook.

1 They showed this ad for the first time this year.
2 An artist designed that logo.
3 Some governments have banned that ad.
4 We are launching the product in the early fall.
5 The creative team had developed the storyboard.

B Choose the correct options.

1 Ed is the **harder** / **the hardest** worker on the design team.
2 The man in the soap ad sings **more beautifully** / **the beautifullest** than the woman.
3 Aiden draws **more slow** / **more slowly** than Mark.
4 Melanie presented her ideas **more confidently** / **most confidently** than Juan.
5 The ad campaign for cookies worked **most** / **more successfully** than that for brownies.

16–20 correct: You can talk about advertising and advertising campaigns. You can use the passive voice and comparative and superlative adverbs.
0–15 correct: Look again at the Vocabulary and Grammar sections in the unit.

TOTAL SCORE: / 20

WHAT DO YOU KNOW NOW? Look back at page 117 and add the words you know now to the box.

GO TO page xix

for **FOLLOW A PRO** step-by-step instructions.

FOLLOW A PRO ADVERTISING

Take the quiz about advertising. Go to Follow A Pro on page 134 to find the answers. Then learn about advertising.

1 What did the first ad shown on British TV advertise?
a dog food b toothpaste c hamburgers

2 Pepsi's TV ad campaign in 2002 was the most expensive ever. How much did it cost?
a $8.1 million b $81 million c $108 million

3 What event did the first billboard ad in New York advertise?
a a circus b a baseball game c a music performance

4 In most wristwatch ads, what time is shown on the watch?
a 8:40 b 10:10 c 12:00

126 Unit 12 Inside Advertising

CLASSROOM MANAGEMENT

Have students complete the exercises in 20 minutes, and then ask them to trade books with a partner. Hand out copies of the answers, and have them grade each other's work, count the score, and write in the result.

ALTERNATIVE ACTIVITY

Point out the activity types in the review activities. They are *complete the text*, *rewrite the sentences*, and *choose the correct option*. Encourage students to look over all of the review pages in all of the units and decide which activity types help them to review vocabulary and grammar and which ones they don't.

FURTHER DISCUSSION

Write the following questions on the board. Then have students form groups of three and ask each other:

- Which grammar points did you find the most difficult?
- How have you recorded your new vocabulary over the year?
- Which activities helped you more: listening or reading?
- Which Language and Life project did you enjoy the most?

UNIT 1

STUDY SKILLS

GO TO page xviii
for STUDY SKILLS step-by-step instructions.

A Read what students have to say about time management challenges. Which of the challenges do you face most often?

EFFECTIVE TIME MANAGEMENT

1 __a__ Radu I guess social media is my biggest obstacle to getting things done. It's just too easy to take time out and see what my buddies are doing. Before I know where I am, I've gotten myself involved in some kind of debate, or—and this happens more often—find myself scrolling through the vacation pictures of someone I barely know.

2 __e__ Deepali I find that I lose concentration too easily. I start off well, but after an hour I don't feel like I'm taking anything in anymore. How can I stay focused?

3 __d__ Katia Time just disappears. It's always the same—I start off feeling like I have all the time in the world. Then it gets to deadline time and I have no idea where the days and hours have gone! I wind up doing everything too fast and my grades aren't great as a result.

4 __c__ Roberto I feel like I spend a lot of time reading online. The internet's a huge place and it's easy to get lost. The problem is that I'm never sure if the stuff I'm reading is actually any good.

5 __b__ Simone I can focus on my studies if there are no distractions. The problem is that I get so many messages from friends, and they might think it's rude if I don't reply right away. Well, it is a bit rude, isn't it?

B Match the problems in A (1–5) to the pieces of advice (a–e).

a Turn your phone off when you are studying, or keep it on silent.
b Reward yourself with social media time at the end of a study session, but go offline when you are trying to complete a task.
c Before you start reading an article online, make sure that it comes from a source that you can trust.
d Be systematic in planning your schedule. Decide what needs to be done urgently and what is not so important. Be realistic about how long it takes you to complete tasks, and leave yourself enough time.
e Study in short periods (45 minutes is realistic), and reward yourself with 5 to 10 minutes of relaxation between study periods.

MAKE IT HAPPEN

Make a study plan for the coming month with your assignment deadlines and the exam dates. Write down the days and times you will be in class and decide how much time you need for independent study. Include time for hobbies, relaxation, and sleep in your schedule. Compare your schedule with that of your partner and give your partner feedback.

C Complete the tips with words from the box. Can you think of two more strategies for managing your time effectively? Write them below.

deadlines realistic schedule

Make a list of all your **1** __deadlines__. Write them on a calendar or in a planner so you can see how much time you have.
Be **2** __realistic__ about how long it takes you to do things. It's better to overestimate than underestimate.
Reward yourself for hard work by setting aside time for relaxation in your **3** __schedule__.
4 Students' own answers
5 Students' own answers

D IN PAIRS Talk about what you can do to become better at managing your time. Mention any specific challenges you face. Listen to your partner and offer advice based on what you have learned in this lesson.

E THINKING SKILL—Apply Explain why time management skills are so important in study, work, and life in general. Why does the "good time management skills" requirement appear so often in job advertisements?

Answers to the quiz on page 16
1 b and c 2 b 3 c 4 b

127

STUDY SKILLS TASK

Before reading the conversation, have students look up any of these expressions they are not familiar with: *to get things done; to take time out; to scroll through pictures; to lose concentration;* and *to stay focused.*

In activity **D** students will discuss how they can become better at managing their time based on what they have learned in this lesson.

THINKING SKILL—Apply

In this activity, students explain why time management skills are important for study, work, and life in general. Ask students to reflect on the statement *Time is money.*

MAKE IT HAPPEN

The activity suggests students make a study plan for the coming month. Tell them they can make the plan on paper or digitally. They may want to use an app, or they may prefer to use a notebook to record their activities. Sometimes the acts of writing, doodling, and coloring help with planning.

GO TO page xix

for **FOLLOW A PRO** step-by-step instructions.

1 because we all have phones with cameras and there are images all around us

2 where an animal is going to be and how it's going to act

3 because you may have to put yourself in an unusual position

4 business

5 because it takes a long time to build up a career in this area

UNIT 2 FOLLOW A PRO

A Read about a wildlife photographer's job. Answer the questions below in your notebook.

A WILDLIFE PHOTOGRAPHER

Jeff Richards works as a freelance wildlife photographer.

"These days, everyone has a camera on their phone, and there are images all around us. If you're going to make a living as a wildlife photographer, you need to be able to take pictures that are different and that really stand out. And that means getting into an animal's habitat to get close to it. A wildlife photographer needs to be an expert at using photographic equipment, but you also need to understand animal behavior. When you understand an animal, you can look ahead, know where it's going to be and how it's going to act, and be ready to take your shot. Physical fitness is very important, too, since you may need to put yourself in an unusual position to get the shot that is going to sell.

When I'm not on a shoot, the rest of my time is spent editing images, contacting clients, and planning future trips. It takes a long time to build up a career in this very competitive area, so you need to understand how to run a business as well as having a good eye for a picture. You need to be patient when you're trying to get the right shot of an animal, and you need to apply the same patience to your career. It's not necessarily the right career for someone who wants instant success."

1 Why do your pictures need to stand out and be different?
2 What does a wildlife photographer need to be able to predict?
3 Why does it help to be physically fit?
4 Apart from photographic skills and knowledge of animals, what other area does a wildlife photographer need to understand?
5 Why might this not be a good career for someone who wants instant success?

B Discuss the questions as a class.

1 What do you imagine is the hardest thing about being a wildlife photographer?
2 Do you think you have the right skills to be a wildlife photographer? What could you do or not do?

VIDEO WATCH THE VIDEO AND FOLLOW A MARINE BIOLOGIST.

C IN GROUPS Answer the questions.

1 What does the person do? marine biologist
2 Where does the person work? in a laboratory environment
3 What skills does the person need for the job? ______
4 What is the focus of the person's research? marine fish bahavior: fisiology and toxicology
5 On how many projects is the person currently working? 3
6 What is the most exciting part of the person's job? working with the fish hands-on in the lab

3 a general background in biology, chemistry, and math, scuba dive and snorkel

D IN GROUPS Check your answers to the quiz on page 26 and discuss the questions.

1 Do you know anyone who works with animals? Explain what you think his or her job is like.
2 What other jobs working with animals do you know about?
3 What do you think are the most enjoyable things about working with animals? What are the least enjoyable?
4 What skills does a veterinarian need? Is it a career you would consider?
5 Are there any opportunities to work with animals where you live? If so, what are they?

Answers to the quiz on page 26
1 b 2 c 3 c 4 a

128

ALTERNATIVE ACTIVITY

Have students look for collocations in the article about Jeff Richards, the freelance wildlife photographer. Collocations are words that naturally go together. Some examples of collocations in the text are *make a living, wildlife photographer, take pictures, stand out, photographic equipment, animal behavior, look ahead, physical fitness,* and *edit images.*

FURTHER DISCUSSION

- Besides wildlife photographer, what other types of photographers are there?
- What does it mean to make your business stand out?
- What other professions require you to edit images?
- Where do you imagine wildlife photographers work?
- Do you want to have your own freelance business one day?

VIDEO

Watch with sound off. Look for: *turtles, shark, gloves, laboratorie, fish, net, microscope.*

While viewing, listen for: *living things, underwater, scuba diving, biology, environment.*

After viewing, ask: *What else does Maria like to do? She likes teaching and giving lectures on Marine Science and do outreach projects.*

UNIT 3

STUDY SKILLS

GO TO page xviii
for **STUDY SKILLS** step-by-step instructions.

A **Read the conversation between Soren and Tania.**

MAKING A PRESENTATION OR GIVING A TALK

Soren: How's your talk going, Tania? Are you nearly ready?
Tania: It's going well, I think! I'm doing mine on the advantages and disadvantages of artificial intelligence.
Soren: Wow. That's really interesting. So, are there more advantages or disadvantages?
Tania: Whoa, hold on! I haven't gotten to that part yet. Right now, I'm just writing the history.
Soren: That's just the history? That's over 30 pages! How will you remember all that?
Tania: Ha, ha! I won't! I'll just type the information on my presentation and read it to the audience. It's much easier than remembering it all.
Soren: I see. But didn't Mr. Elmwood say the talk should be 10 minutes maximum?
Tania: Yeah, I know! Don't worry, though, I talk really fast when I get excited about something!
Soren: Well, be careful you don't write too much, or you won't have time to say it all. I mean, look—you've written 30 pages and you haven't even started writing about the advantages and disadvantages yet.
Tania: That won't take long. I mean, everyone knows that there are only advantages to artificial intelligence, right? No one thinks there are disadvantages.
Soren: Well, you certainly seem confident.
Tania: I don't really get nervous about talks, especially when I'm talking about my favorite subject. It'll be great!

B **Select four pieces of advice that you think would be most useful for Tania.**

Suggested answers: 1, 3, 4, 5

1 If possible, speak from notes written on note cards or from memory.
2 Choose a subject that you are interested in or feel strongly about.
3 Make sure your research and preparation are balanced.
4 Don't speak too fast. Pause and take a breath after each point you make.
5 Be aware and respectful of the fact that some audience members may not share your point of view.

C **Match the tips about oral presentations in B (1–5) to the explanations (a–e).**

a This means that your talk will flow better and that you will be able to make eye contact with your audience. 4
b Audience members are likely to stop listening if they feel their point of view is not being respected. 5
c This will make you seem calmer and more professional. Your voice will sound stronger, too. 1
d This will show that you are well prepared and not biased. 3
e This means that your enthusiasm will be noticeable and that people will enjoy listening to you. 2

D **IN PAIRS Discuss your experiences giving talks. Talk about your strengths and weaknesses and decide what further tips you would add to the list in B. Think about the following points.**

- Developing your main argument
- Providing a clear structure
- Opening and summing up
- Including effective visual aids
- Answering questions
- Engaging with the audience

E **THINKING SKILLS—Apply Think about a memorable talk you have listened to. Why was it memorable? What techniques did the speaker use to engage with the audience?**

MAKE IT HAPPEN

Prepare an oral presentation on something you are interested in. Use the tips from this lesson to help you plan, structure, and deliver your talk.

Answers to the quiz on page 36
1c 2b 3a 4a

STUDY SKILLS TASK

Students learn how to give a good presentation. They read a conversation about a bad presentation. Then, they match tips for a good presentation with explanations. In pairs, students discuss their experiences giving talks and identify their strengths and weaknesses. Finally, they add more tips to the list for giving a good presentation.

THINKING SKILL—Apply

If students can't think of a memorable talk they have listened to, have them search for a TED talk about a topic they are interested in. Searching for "TED in 3 Minutes" will bring up a list of short TED talks that the students can watch.

MAKE IT HAPPEN

Students apply what they have learned in the lesson about preparing and giving a good presentation to something they are interested in. Tell them to prepare thoroughly. Suggest they record themselves practicing and tell them to watch themselves to see what they need to improve.

GO TO page xix

for FOLLOW A PRO step-by-step instructions.

1 to communicate a company's messages to the public
2 They need a lot of contacts to communicate their messages.
3 when something negative happens
4 They need very good writing skills.
5 They give journalists the starting point for their articles and reports.

UNIT 4 FOLLOW A PRO

A Read about a PR professional's job. Answer the questions below in your notebook.

A PR PROFESSIONAL

Companies have messages about their brands that they want to communicate to members of the public. They use advertising for some of those messages. They also employ or hire PR (public relations) professionals. PR professionals work with journalists and other people in the media. They are responsible for communicating positive stories about a company and its products.

PR professionals need to be good at networking. They need contacts in many areas of the media. They need to know who they can persuade to run a story in a way that makes their business look good. This is particularly important when something negative happens to the company, such as people losing their jobs. The PR professional is the person who tries to explain the reason behind what is happening in a positive way.

Successful PR professionals have to express themselves clearly and have very good writing skills. They spend a lot of time producing press releases, fact sheets, and other documents that give journalists the starting point for their reports and articles. They can make a big difference to the stories that appear in the media. PR professionals also tell the stories behind their companies and brands through events such as press conferences or open houses. The PR professional is an important connection between a business and the public.

1 What is the main role of a PR professional?
2 Why does a PR professional need to be good at networking?
3 When is a PR professional's job particularly important?
4 What communication skills does a PR professional need to have?
5 How do PR professionals help journalists?

B Discuss the questions as a class.

1 What do you think PR professionals enjoy most about their job?
2 Would you be a good PR professional? Why or why not?

VIDEO **WATCH THE VIDEO AND FOLLOW A TRANSLATOR/INTERPRETER.**

C IN GROUPS Answer the questions.

1 What is the person's job? translator and interpreter
2 What skills does the person need for the job? ________
3 Where has the person worked as a translator? in an office or a quiet space
4 How many languages does the person speak? 3
5 What is the person's first language? Mandarin
6 Why does the person prefer doing interpretation instead of translation? she enjoys working with people

2 writting skills, accurate grammar, people skills, communicate effectively

D IN GROUPS Check your answers to the quiz on page 46 and discuss the questions.

1 What careers in communication do you know about?
2 Would you be interested in any of those careers? If so, which ones?
3 Do you know anyone who works in communication? If so, what do you think his or her job is like?
4 What personal qualities do you need to work in PR?
5 What qualifications do you need to work in PR?

Answers to the quiz on page 46
1 c 2 b 3 a 4 a

130

ALTERNATIVE ACTIVITY

Have students close their eyes and tell them to imagine they are a PR professional and their client is someone in the classroom. Write a press release to inform the public about him/her. It could be about something interesting they are going to do or an explanation about something interesting they did.

FURTHER DISCUSSION

- Can you think of a big company or important person that's in the news at the moment?
- Museums have PR officers. What do you think museums need to communicate to the public?
- What social media would a PR professional use to share information about their client?
- What tools or equipment would a person working in PR need?

VIDEO

Watch with sound off. Look for: *computer, office, books, notebooks.*

While viewing, listen for: *written formats, spoken languages, accurate, research, Spanish.*

After viewing, ask: *Why does Sonia loves her job? It could be financialy rewarding, she meets a lot of people, she likes challenge.*

UNIT 5

STUDY SKILLS

GO TO page xviii for STUDY SKILLS step-by-step instructions.

A Time yourself as you read this text as quickly as you can. What environmental problem is described in the text? What possible solutions are given?

Single-use plastic

Solutions: Using your own thermal flask, choosing items not wrapped in plastic when shopping, taking part in a "no single-use plastic" challenge, asking your college campus and local businesses to become "no single-use plastic" zones

IMPROVING READING SPEED

Let's imagine a typical morning. You leave your home for college or work. On the way, you stop and buy yourself a bottle of water. Perhaps you'll be given a plastic straw to drink it with. At lunch, you choose a nice healthy salad in a plastic box—or a sandwich wrapped in plastic. Maybe you'll eat the salad with plastic cutlery. On the way home, you'll stop off at the store for some groceries, probably also wrapped in plastic. All this plastic is used just once before you throw it away and forget all about it.

Here's the problem: plastic never fully biodegrades. It simply breaks down into smaller particles, which can be absorbed by our bodies. This has serious effects on our health; scientific research has linked plastic to cancer, birth defects, infertility, and a weakened immune system. Plastic is also a huge problem for marine animals, who can get tangled up in plastic rope or choke on pieces of plastic packaging. One million sea birds and 100,000 marine mammals are killed every year by plastic in our oceans.

In fact, 50% of plastic is used just once and then thrown away. Single-use plastic is probably one of the easiest things we could cut out of our lives to make a really big difference. Carry your own thermal flask for your coffee or hot drink, and carry your own water bottle. When shopping, try to choose as many items as you can that are not wrapped in plastic. There are lots of online challenges you can take part in to help you get motivated—or why not try a "no single-use plastic" challenge with a friend? You could also ask your college campus and local businesses to become "no single-use plastic" zones.

If each one of us committed to cutting out single-use plastic, we could fix one of the most serious environmental problems of our time.

B Match the sentence halves to make tips about improving reading speed.

1. Reading improves with practice, so you should __f__
2. If you move your finger down the page while you read, __a__
3. Active reading strategies such as predicting will __d__
4. Putting a colored filter over the page can __c__
5. Reading larger chunks of text at one time __e__
6. If a nonfiction text looks hard, you should __b__

a. you will train your eyes to move more quickly down the text.
b. start with something easier on the same subject.
c. make the words easier to read.
d. help you find the information you are looking for more quickly.
e. is less tiring for your eyes and will help you to read for longer periods.
f. look for subjects that interest you and read more for pleasure.

C Read the text in A again. This time, try to use as many of the tips from B as you can.

D IN PAIRS Which of the tips do you find most useful? Discuss your ideas with a partner.

Malin: I followed the tip about moving my finger down the page as I read. That definitely helped.

Theo: I tried reading larger chunks of text at one time, but I don't think it made a difference. I forgot what I had read!

Malin: I'm going to try that idea next time!

MAKE IT HAPPEN

Work with a partner. Look online and choose a text at an appropriate level that you think your partner would find interesting. Ask your partner to read the text using some of the tips outlined in these lessons. Share your findings in a group.

E THINKING SKILLS—Apply What makes a person a good reader? Apart from reading speed, what other ways can we use to measure our skills in this area?

Answers to the quiz on page 56
1 b 2 b 3 b and d 4 a

131

STUDY SKILLS TASK

Students learn about reading faster. They read a passage and some tips about how to improve their reading speed. Next, they read the passage again and apply the tips. Finally, they reflect on the most useful tips.

THINKING SKILL—Apply

Higher education requires students to read a lot of material both in print and online. A good reader can recall, summarize, infer, and give details about a passage. A good reader can also apply the information they learn in a passage to another situation.

MAKE IT HAPPEN

If students practice the tips from the lesson, they will improve their reading for work and study. Tell them to look for an article similar in length to the passage in the lesson and apply the strategies to it.

GO TO page xix for **FOLLOW A PRO** step-by-step instructions.

1 Archeology is a part of the larger field of anthropology, which is the study of human culture

2 Archeologists study structures and objects from ancient civilizations to try to understand what the ancient cultures were like and how ancient people lived.

3 Making a great discovery is what most archeologists dream of.

4 Research what an archeologist does online.

5 Most archeologists work at places like historic sites, national parks, museums, or universities.

6 Yes, because she can create something that has an impact in the world.

UNIT 6 FOLLOW A PRO

A Read about an archeologist. Answer the questions below in your notebook.

AN ARCHEOLOGIST

Many people think archeologists work outside, discovering the secrets of ancient civilizations in the mountains of Peru or the deserts of Egypt. Well, that's true, but is archeology really just about that? Archeology is a part of the larger field of anthropology, which is the study of human culture. Archeologists study structures and objects from ancient civilizations to try to understand what the ancient cultures were like and how ancient people lived. To be an archeologist, you will need a master's degree or a PhD. Your studies will include a large amount of research and probably some fieldwork. The chance of making a great discovery is what most archeologists dream of. However, even when it happens, archeologists have to carefully analyze their findings, to prove their importance. If you want to find out more about archeology before you spend a lot of time and money getting advanced degrees, research what an archeologist does online. You need to understand that archeologists do not all work in exciting places. Most of us work at places like historic sites, national parks, museums, or universities. We also often do not have regular working hours. We might work seven days a week for several weeks if there is an important project. We also have to work in all kinds of weather at all times of day. Archeology is an interesting job, and sometimes it's exciting, but you have to study a lot to become an archeologist, and you have to work very hard when you get a job!

1 What field is archeology a part of?
2 What do archeologists study? Why?
3 What do archeologists most want to achieve?
4 What is a good way to find out more about archeology before you decide to study it?
5 Where do archeologists work?

B Discuss the questions as a class.

1 In what ways is archeology a hard job?
2 Is archeology an important field in your country?

VIDEO WATCH THE VIDEO AND FOLLOW A MECHANICAL ENGINEER.

C IN GROUPS Answer the questions.

1 What does the person do? mechanical engineer
2 What skills does the person need for the job? problem-solving, computer skills, analytical skills
3 Where does the person often work? in an office with labs and capabilities for engineering work
4 What kind of special equipment does the person use? design and simulation software, 3D printers
5 Does the person work alone or in a team? in a team
6 Is the person happy with the job? Why? ______

D IN GROUPS Check your answers to the quiz on page 66 and discuss the questions.

1 What old or ancient civilizations were in your country? Have you ever visited any of their sites? If so, which ones?
2 What other archeological or historical sites in the world would you like to visit?

Answers to the quiz on page 66
1 a 2 c 3 b 4 a

132

ALTERNATIVE ACTIVITY

Before reading the article, write *archeologist* on the board and have students brainstorm about what this job might involve. Write students' ideas on the board.

FURTHER DISCUSSION

- Do you know anyone who works as an archeologist?
- Have you seen ever seen an active dig?
- Do you have any ancient ruins near your house?
- What tools does an archeologist use?
- Why do you think archeologists need higher degrees such as a master's or a PhD?

VIDEO

Watch with sound off. Look for: *computers, cables, whiteboard, office.*

While viewing, listen for: *policemen, firefighters, solutions, equipment, 3D printers, drills, success.*

After viewing, ask: *What is the biggest challenge of being a mechanical engineer? It is not a one straight path towards the final product.*

GO TO page xviii

for **STUDY SKILLS** step-by-step instructions.

UNIT 7 STUDY SKILLS

A Read the essay. Which of the questions is the writer trying to answer? What is your answer to that question?

b; Students' own answers

STRUCTURING YOUR WRITING

a Describe a time you made a serious mistake. What did you learn from it?
b If you don't make mistakes, you'll never learn. In your opinion, is this true?

Consider the achievements of the last hundred years. People have gone to space, invented the internet, and made incredible breakthroughs in medicine. Is it possible that in each of these attempts, the first try was successful? Of course not. We know that these achievements were only possible through trial and error—in other words, through making countless mistakes.

It's important to remember this in our own lives. Often, we believe that we need to do everything right the first time. This belief is generated by the images of perfection in magazines, on TV, and on social media.

However, this desire to get everything right the first time is dangerous. Take a man who has just started to play the violin, for example. How many wrong notes will he have to play before he plays something that is enjoyable to listen to? Or a woman who is learning to juggle? How many balls will she drop before she keeps them all in the air?

People who aspire to live a life free from mistakes will never take risks, never challenge themselves, and never learn anything new. They will turn down opportunities to avoid looking a fool. This will result in a safe life free from embarrassment and risk, but it will also result in regret at wasted opportunities.

Mistakes are seen as a form of failure but they can be really positive. Mistakes help us learn, and it is for this reason that I believe that they are not just important but desirable.

B Read the essay again. Check (✓) the correct sentences.

1 ☑ The essay is organized into paragraphs.
2 ☐ Each paragraph contains several different ideas.
3 ☑ The writer develops a clear argument, moving logically from point to point.
4 ☐ The writer doesn't provide any evidence to support her ideas.
5 ☑ The writer begins with an introduction and ends with a conclusion.

C Match the headings (1–4) to the tips for structuring essays (a–d). Then write your own tips under each heading in your notebook.

Students' own answers

1 Divide your main idea into topics __a__
2 Rearrange your notes __d__
3 Write an outline plan __b__
4 Organize the information into paragraphs __c__

a Use separate sheets of paper for each topic.
b Plan your introduction, conclusion, and the main body of your essay.
c Each paragraph should have one main idea with supporting details or evidence.
d Spread your notes out on the table so that you can easily see them.

D IN PAIRS Think about the last essay you wrote. Tell your partner about the process you went through to structure your essay. What would you do differently next time?

E THINKING SKILLS—Apply What do you find most challenging about structuring an essay? How can you develop this skill for future assignments?

MAKE IT HAPPEN

Choose one of the essay questions in **A** and write a short essay (500 words maximum) with your main idea divided into topics, each in their own paragraph.

Answers to the quiz on page 76
1 b 2 3, 4, 1, 5, 2 3 a, b, c

133

STUDY SKILLS TASK

Students learn how to structure their writing in an essay. They read an example essay and check it against a list of criteria. The essay has a clear argument and evidence to support the ideas. However, the essay is not organized into paragraphs—more linking words are required, and the essay lacks an introduction and a conclusion.

THINKING SKILL—Apply

Students reflect on how they can practice structuring their writing. Have students visualize working on their next essay. Have them imagine themselves applying the tips they learned in this lesson to their essay.

MAKE IT HAPPEN

Students will use the tips they have learned to write a short, well-structured essay in response to one of the essay questions in **A**. Remind them to follow the steps in **C**. Emphasize that the planning stage is the most important stage.

GO TO page xix for **FOLLOW A PRO** step-by-step instructions.

UNIT 8

FOLLOW A PRO

A Read about an astrobiologist. Then choose *True* or *False*.

AN ASTROBIOLOGIST

I'm an astrobiologist, which might sound like a job in a science-fiction movie! Actually, it's not science fiction. Astrobiologists study if life exists in other places in the universe besides Earth. We study how life originated, and how life could exist in extreme environments. There is an enormous variety in the jobs astrobiologists do. Some develop computer models to predict what life would be like on other planets. Others study life in extreme climates like the freezing Arctic, the Atacama Desert, or the deepest oceans. Some astrobiologists use high-tech radio telescopes to listen for signals from aliens. To be honest, I think that would be boring because so far, all the communication from outer space has come from our own satellites. Most astrobiologists work in an office or a lab and do research on elements like carbon, nitrogen, phosphorus, and iron. The results of the research help create the computer models that predict whether a specific planet or solar system could have life.

To work in astrobiology, you need a degree in a related field such as biology, chemistry, physics, astronomy, geology, mathematics, or information technology. You might think that all astrobiologists work at NASA in the US, but in fact, there are astrobiology jobs in many other parts of the world, including Europe, Australia, Mexico, and South America. There are jobs with NASA projects, at universities, or at private foundations. If you are interested in the origin of life, and the possibility of life on other planets, astrobiology might be the career for you.

1. Astrobiologists mostly work in science-fiction movies. True / **False**
2. Astrobiologists study the history of life. **True** / False
3. There are many different types of jobs in astrobiology. **True** / False
4. The writer thinks listening for alien communications is an exciting job. True / **False**
5. You have to live in the US to work in astrobiology. True / **False**

B Discuss the questions as a class.

1. Why do you think the writer says that astrobiology sounds like a job in a science-fiction movie?
2. Would any of the astrobiology jobs mentioned in the article interest you? If so, which ones?

VIDEO WATCH THE VIDEO AND FOLLOW AN ASTRONOMER.

C **IN GROUPS** Answer the questions.

1. What is the person's job? astronomer
2. Where does the person work? at the university observatory
3. What skills does the person need for the job? math, science, physics, patience
4. What specific subjects does the person study for the job? ______
5. Why does the person use special equipment in the job? to know how the universe works
6. What does the person say is the best part of the job? ______

4 science, math, physics, astronomy, astrophysics

6 being a kid again and see all the cool things that happend at night

D **IN GROUPS** Check your answers to the quiz on page 86 and discuss the questions.

1. If you had a lot of money, would you want to be a "space tourist"? Why or why not?
2. What do you think the most important reasons for space exploration are?

Answers to the quiz on page 86
1 b 2 a 3 c 4 c

134

ALTERNATIVE ACTIVITY

Before reading the article about an astrobiologist, write *subject* and *place* on the board. Ask students shout out as they scan the article for words describing subjects of study and places in the world and space. Have two volunteers write the words on the board as they are called. Allow students to check the meanings of words they don't know.

FURTHER DISCUSSION

- Have you ever observed a space event, like a meteor shower or an eclipse?
- How do you think events in outer space impact our everyday lives?
- Do you think we know enough about what is out there in space?
- Do you know anyone who works in a profession related to outer space?

VIDEO

Watch with sound off. Look for: *telescope, parks, screens, moon.*

While viewing, listen for: *stars, observatory, universe, planets, galaxies.*

After viewing, ask: *What does Simion looks through the telescopes?* *celestial objects, stars, planets*

UNIT 9

STUDY SKILLS

A **Esme and Marley are taking a course on the history of popular music. Read their notes about Motown music. Whose notes are more likely to be an effective study aid?**

Marley's notes are more effective.

MAKING NOTES

1 Esme

Motown is often described as "the sound that changed America." It was founded by an American songwriter called Berry Gordy (?) who got a loan of $800 (?) from his family to set the company up with. He wanted to set the record company up in recognition of the warm, soulful, and talented people he grew up with. Motown success stories included Smokey Robinson & The Miracles, Michael Jackson and the Jackson 5, Marvin Gaye, Diana Ross & The Supremes (?), and many more.

Motown was the first African American record label to achieve widespread recognition and acclaim.

2 Marley

From Billy Robson's "Sound of America," pps 35–37

Motown founded by Am. songwriter Berry Gordy from Detroit—1st Af/Am label to achieve widespread acclaim

Detroit called Motor City=name Motown

Acts: Smokey Robinson & Miracles, Michael Jackson & Jkson 5, Diana Ross & Supremes, etc.

B **Write *E* (Esme) or *M* (Marley).**

1. The writer has noted down the sources. M
2. The writer has tried to copy down every word. E
3. The writer has highlighted the most important information. M
4. The writer is not totally sure how correct the notes are. E

C **Match the sentence halves to make tips about taking notes.**

1. Before you start making notes, a
2. Make a list of questions you want to find answers to e
3. It's a good idea to label and number pages d
4. Use sticky notes so that you can b
5. Use abbreviations because this will c

a draw up a mind map so you can see what you already know about the subject.
b write down ideas as you think of them or add ideas to charts or posters.
c save you a lot of time.
d as this will make it easier to cross-reference your notes.
e as this will make your notes more focused.

D **IN PAIRS** **Think about notes you have taken from lectures or books. How could you improve your note-taking technique?**

E **THINKING SKILLS—Apply** **What do you find hardest about taking notes? How can you ensure that your notes are as effective as possible?**

MAKE IT HAPPEN

Go online and find a podcast on a subject that interests you. Take notes using the tips from **C**. When the podcast has finished, look at your notes. How can you make them clearer? How can you make the key information stand out?

Answers to the quiz on page 96
1 b 2 b 3 b; Use symbols and abbreviations in notes, but not in assignments. 4 a; Visual familiarity will help you to remember the content of your notes.

GO TO page xviii for STUDY SKILLS step-by-step instructions.

STUDY SKILLS TASK

Ask students about the last time they took notes in a lecture. Students read and explore ways to make notes. Once they see one good and one bad example, they read tips for good note-taking. Then, they reflect on what is hard for them and ways they can write effective notes.

THINKING SKILL—Apply

Students think about how they can apply to their own lives what they have just learned about making notes. The process of making notes is personal. It is the act of writing them that helps the brain organize the information—which is probably why students usually don't find it useful to borrow someone else's notes.

MAKE IT HAPPEN

Students find a lecture online that interests them and practice making notes. "TED in 3 Minutes" is a good site for finding lectures to help students practice taking notes.

GO TO page xix
for **FOLLOW A PRO** step-by-step instructions.

UNIT 10 FOLLOW A PRO

A Read about a talent scout's job. Answer the questions below.

A TALENT SCOUT

Meet Jeni Mills, a talent scout from Chicago.
Jeni says: "I started out working in theater production for musical shows on Broadway, which was a fantastic job to go to after college, where I majored in music and dance. But then I decided I wanted a change. I saw an ad for an international cruise ship company that was looking for a talent scout to find the best acts for their cruise ship shows. These shows are really popular, and the audience expects to see something special. While I know a lot of people in the entertainment industry from my work on Broadway, I want to find acts that are a little different, but still amazing. So, a few times a week I go to small gigs—shows at small theaters and local comedy and music clubs—and try to find the most talented people. I organize auditions and get the best acts to come back and try to impress a live theater audience before we offer them work on the ship. I've found wonderful magicians and amazing dancers, singers, and comedians. I've been doing the job for five years now and I love it. The only negative is that the hours are long, but I'm meeting interesting people all the time."

1. What job did Jeni do before she became a talent scout? worked in theater production
2. What did Jeni study in college? music and dance
3. Where does Jeni find the acts for her shows? small theaters, local comedy clubs, music clubs
4. How long has Jeni been working as a talent scout? five years
5. What does Jeni not like about her job? the long hours

B Discuss the questions as a class.

1. Would you like to be a talent scout? Why or why not?
2. What do you think it would be like to work on a cruise ship?

VIDEO

WATCH THE VIDEO AND FOLLOW A MUSICIAN.

C **IN GROUPS** Answer the questions.

1. What does the person do? musician
2. What skills does the person need for the job? musical skills, discipline, patience
3. What is the person's schedule? ___
4. How many instruments does the person play? 4
5. What is the person's favorite music style? jazz
6. What is the most exciting part of the person's job? ___

3 practice in the morning and then play in a show or have a 12-hour recording session

6 music can be a universal language and convey emotions

D **IN GROUPS** Check your answers to the quiz on page 106 and discuss the questions.

1. Do you know anybody who works in the entertainment industry? If so, what do they do?
2. What kinds of live entertainment are popular in your country?
3. What skills do you think a talent scout needs?
4. What type of acts (e.g., music, dance, comedy, magic) do you think require the most talent? Why?
5. Can you think of any professions other than the entertainment industry where talent scouts work? If so, what are they?

Answers to the quiz on page 106
1 b 2 a 3 c 4 c

136

ALTERNATIVE ACTIVITY

Before reading, write *Broadway* on the board. Elicit words that come to mind and write them. Do the same with *acts for cruise ships*.

- **Broadway:** theater, New York, actor, show, entertainment, musical, production, play, sing, dance, off-Broadway
- **Acts for cruise ships:** show, entertainment, music, singing, musical, jazz, live music, band

FURTHER DISCUSSION

- Can you think of any famous Broadway shows?
- Do you like theater?
- Do you enjoy magic shows, comedy, singing, or drama? Which do you prefer?
- Can you name any other forms of entertainment?
- What kinds of shows would you like to see if you were on a cruise ship?

VIDEO

Watch with sound off. Look for: *guitar, trumpet, microphone, base, CDs.*

While viewing, listen for: *jazz, language, recording session, drums, happy song, communicate.*

After viewing, ask: *What is the main instrument Sebastian plays?* the guitar

UNIT 11

STUDY SKILLS

GO TO page xviii
for **STUDY SKILLS** step-by-step instructions.

A **Read the conversation. Is this study session productive? What challenges are the friends facing?**

No, this study session is not productive. Marco is unmotivated, Jill is panicking, and Liz is struggling to manage her time.

PERSONAL DEVELOPMENT

Marco: Ah, I love study nights! It's so much more fun than reviewing my notes on my own. More pizza, anyone?
Jill: Yeah, it is good fun, Marco, but we need to focus now.
Liz: Sure, Jill. We can't let this delicious pizza get cold, though, can we?
Jill: I guess not … It's just that the exam is in only two weeks.
Marco: We're probably going to fail it, Jill. No one does well in Mr. Leaper's class.
Liz: Yeah. He's right. I guess we can try again next year, though, right?
Jill: Don't say that! I've been trying to study all month. This is my first night out of the house in weeks!
Liz: Hmm. You are looking really pale, Jill. Are you eating well?
Jill: I don't have time to eat! And I'm not hungry, to be honest. I'm way too stressed out.
Marco: Well, I studied all day yesterday. I sat at my desk for six hours. I'm not sure if I learned much, though. The view from my window is pretty cool …
Liz: Lucky you, having the time to look out the window! I'm just so busy … Getting the bus to work, working, looking after my brother. He's been sick this week, so I've been taking care of him …
Marco: Yeah, if only we had more time! Speaking of time, that new series everyone is talking about starts in 10 minutes. I know we haven't finished but we've done a lot, right?

B **Which student would benefit from each piece of advice? Write *M* (Marco), *J* (Jill), or *L* (Liz).**

1. Add your favorite TV shows to your timetable. Use TV shows as a reward for finishing a study session. M
2. Surround yourself with people who are positive and will encourage you. J
3. Seek help from a professional counselor at college if you feel you can't deal with things. J
4. Always carry your notes with you and study on the bus or while you wait. L
5. Study with friends if you struggle to study alone, but make sure you use the time constructively. For example, explain something to your friend and see how well your friend understands your explanation. M
6. Keep an exam question in your head and write points down as they occur to you. L

C **Match each piece of advice (1–4) to a way to follow it (a–d).**

1. Get organized and focused. d
2. Manage your time carefully. b
3. Stay healthy. c
4. Use exam papers from past years. a

a. Brainstorm answers to past questions.
b. Create a realistic schedule.
c. Include regular exercise in your schedule.
d. Make flashcards with key information.

D IN PAIRS **Role-play the study session in A. Make it more positive and productive.**

Lucille: Why don't we take a break and have some ice cream?
Rob: Why don't we wait until we've finished this chapter? Hey, can I try explaining what I've just read to see if I've understood it?
Lucille: Sure!

E THINKING SKILLS—Apply **What do you find hardest about studying for tests? What are your challenges, and how can you improve your study habits?**

MAKE IT HAPPEN

Talk about your study habits with your partner. Share what you think you are doing well and talk about the areas you need to improve.

Answers to the quiz on page 116
1 a 2 b; It can be very effective. 3 c 4 a

137

STUDY SKILLS TASK

Have students read the conversation out loud in groups of three and answer the opening question. Then, if necessary, they should read it again as they answer **B**. Allow students to work in the same group to match the advice to the ways to follow it.

THINKING SKILL—Apply

Have students write a list of five things they find hard about studying for tests and another list of five ways they can improve their study habits. Let them share their ideas with others. Tell them to take one idea from their partner and give their partner one of their ideas.

MAKE IT HAPPEN

Begin on a positive note. Have students say what they are already good at. This will give them confidence in their abilities and courage to implement strategies to improve. Have them work in different pairs or groups of three from the role-play.

GO TO page xix
for FOLLOW A PRO step-by-step instructions.

UNIT 12 FOLLOW A PRO

A **Read about a digital copywriter's job. Answer the questions below in your notebook.**

1 Because it's a job that happens behind the scenes, so not many people know about it.
2 checking all the online materials that go with an advertising campaign
3 two or three projects at the same time
4 journalist
5 He wants to become a creative director and be in charge of an advertising campaign.

A DIGITAL COPYWRITER

There are many different jobs in advertising. Bruno Torres is a digital copywriter. He tells us more about his career.

Bruno says: "People are always asking me what a digital copywriter's job is. I think it's because it's one of those "behind the scenes" jobs. It's a very important job—especially for the advertising industry. My team develops advertising campaigns. My main job is to check all of the online materials—the headlines, slogans, emails, and social media ads. I check spelling and grammar, obviously, but I also make sure that the advertising material is easy to understand and that it sells the product! I usually work on at least two or three projects for different campaigns at the same time, so I need to be focused and organized. It's also very important that I meet my deadlines and finish the work by a certain date. Advertising is about creating trends so I have to make sure I know what is important to young people—style, fashion, how things look—that's a major part of it. People don't just buy a product—they buy into a lifestyle. People also ask how I got started in my career. Well, I majored in media studies and worked as a journalist for three years. Then I changed to this career because it seems more interesting. I hope to become a creative director one day and be in charge of the whole advertising campaign from start to finish."

1 Why do people often ask Bruno what a digital copywriter's job is?
2 What is the main part of Bruno's job?
3 How many projects does Bruno usually work on?
4 What job did Bruno do before he became a digital copywriter?
5 What does Bruno want to do in the future?

B **Discuss the questions as a class.**

1 Would you like to work in advertising? Why or why not?
2 What would you like about being a digital copywriter? What would you dislike? Explain.

VIDEO

WATCH THE VIDEO AND FOLLOW A VIDEO EDITOR.

C **IN GROUPS Answer the questions.**

1 What is the person's job? video editor
2 Where does the person work? in an entertainment company and freelance
3 What skills does the person need for the job? creative and technical skills
4 What are the person's main responsibilities? ______
5 Has the person worked with someone famous? If yes, who? yes, professinal basketball players
6 What does the person say is the best part of the job? the final product

4 combining video, audio, and graphic elements to create a story

D **IN GROUPS Check your answers to the quiz on page 126 and discuss the questions.**

1 How important do you think good language skills are to a digital copywriter's job?
2 What other skills do you think a digital copywriter needs?
3 Would you be good at a job with deadlines? Why or why not?
4 What advertising campaigns have succeeded in your country? Why?
5 What is the most effective medium for advertising: TV, magazines, the internet, billboards, or something else?

Answers to the quiz on page 126
1 b 2 a 3 a 4 b

138

ALTERNATIVE ACTIVITY

Bruno looks happy in the photo. Have students discuss what they think makes a person happy in their job. What personal and professional needs have to be met for someone to feel satisfied at work? What happens when a person is not happy at work?

FURTHER DISCUSSION

- How do you feel when you see mistakes in an ad?
- Do you trust a product that has a poorly presented ad?
- What do you think a stylish fashion ad campaign should look like?
- Do you like international ad campaigns or local ads?
- What advantages do local advertising agencies have?

VIDEO

Watch with sound off. Look for: *screens, horns, office, images, street.*

While viewing, listen for: *graphic elements, television production, sports videos, story, basketball players.*

After viewing, ask: *What brings a lot of joy to Jason?* *knowing that millions of people are seeing somethig he worked on*

Grammar Review Answer Key

A **1** were watching **2** was playing **3** lit **4** ran **5** were coming **6** smelled **7** tried **8** called

B **1** a lot of **2** enough **3** somewhere **4** some **5** too much **6** everyone **7** a few **8** myself

C **1** laziest **2** riskiest **3** worst **4** most creative **5** kindest **6** best

D **1** You can't come in. **2** Would you like to go with me? **3** I may be late to the ceremony. **4** Could you book a hotel room for me? **5** I might not be able to come. **6** Our flight will land in 30 minutes.

E **1** has been **2** sold **3** established **4** published **5** have made **6** started **7** has done **8** has become

F **1** Jesse hasn't gotten his degree yet. **2** Has Lila ever gotten a promotion? **3** Peter has worked here since 2017. **4** Erica has already applied for the job. / Erica has applied for the job already. **5** I have just read about our benefits. **6** Tina has been team leader for a month.

G **1** cooking **2** to fly **3** making **4** cleaning **5** to see **6** Having **7** to go **8** to come

H **1** are not / aren't worn **2** eat **3** are made **4** were not / weren't **5** was sold **6** will not / won't have **7** is used **8** am / 'm meeting; am / 'm going to meet

Grammar Reference Answer Key

UNIT 1

Stative and dynamic verbs

A **1** D **2** D **3** S **4** S **5** D **6** S **7** D **8** S **9** D **10** S **11** D **12** S

B **1** know **2** Do … like **3** has **4** thinks **5** does not / doesn't understand **6** are … thinking **7** Are … reading **8** are not / aren't having

Expressing ability

C **1** can **2** was **3** in learning **4** to learn **5** play **6** was able to **7** to hear **8** manage to

D **1** I wasn't able to swim until I was a teenager. **2** He is able to name a hundred different kinds of fish. **3** Can you sing as well as your mother? **4** We couldn't take private music lessons. **5** I'm not able to explain the difference between a viola and a violin. **6** Were you able to speak English when you were young?

UNIT 2

Tag questions

A **1** e **2** h **3** b **4** f **5** a **6** d **7** c **8** g

B **1** aren't they **2** do you **3** does it **4** should they **5** haven't you **6** don't you **7** is it **8** don't we

Articles

A **1** a **2** an **3** The **4** a **5** the **6** the **7** the **8** –

B **1** a **2** the **3** – **4** the **5** an **6** –

Unit 3

Future time clauses (*after, as soon as, before, until, when*)

A **1** will have **2** comes **3** will not / won't be **4** finish **5** will get **6** will not / won't hire

B **1** After I get to work today, I will talk to my boss about a raise. **2** When she finishes this report, she will be a lot happier! **3** He won't provide feedback on my paper until he sees the final version. **4** I will help my colleague with her project before I leave the office today. **5** I will purchase a new computer as soon as I save enough money. **6** If you need help with your essay, I will be happy to help you.

Present perfect progressive

A **1** have / 've been trying **2** has not / hasn't been coming **3** has been researching **4** have not / haven't been getting **5** have been working **6** has been getting **7** has been studying **8** have not / haven't been going

B **1** What have you been doing lately? **2** Have they been playing video games? **3** Has Aaron been coming to class recently? **4** Why have they been learning how to code? **5** Have you been saving money for college? **6** How long has she been working here?

Unit 4

Infinitives with *to*

A **1** told **2** agree **3** prefer **4** persuaded **5** went **6** happy

B **1** to find **2** to see **3** to communicate **4** to listen **5** to be **6** to apply **7** to improve **8** to copy

Separable and non-separable phrasal verbs

A **1** a **2** a **3** b **4** a **5** b **6** b **7** b **8** b

B **1** You can always count on her. **2** I need you to fill it in now. **3** Who takes care of them? **4** Try to get them across. **5** Can you please turn it down? **6** It's hard to keep up with him. **7** It's not too late to call it off. **8** It's time to get rid of them.

Unit 5

Review of conditionals

A **1** HS **2** GT **3** PS **4** GT **5** PS **6** HS

B **1** push **2** will have **3** saw **4** won't be **5** reaches **6** would be **7** get **8** snowed

Present and future hopes and wishes

A **1** I hope you like my environmental poster. **2** She wishes they used fewer fossil fuels. **3** He hopes global warming will stop. **4** We wish you could help with our campaign. **5** I hope you can donate some money. **6** I wish you wouldn't reject our ideas.

B **1** get **2** would care **3** could change **4** are listening **5** had majored **6** can help **7** would appreciate **8** will participate

Student's Book Grammar Answer Key

Unit 6

Past perfect

A **1** a **2** a **3** b **4** b **5** a **6** b

B **1** knew, had tried **2** had saved, crashed **3** hadn't been, got **4** had left, got **5** had been, made **6** hadn't wanted, ate

Defining relative clauses

A **1** that **2** when **3** where **4** who **5** when **6** who **7** that **8** where

B **1** ~~when~~ where **2** ~~where~~ that **3** I know a guy who builds websites for free. **4** ~~who~~ that **5** ~~who~~ when **6** Do you know who the woman standing by the door is?

Unit 7

Should/shouldn't have

A **1** e **2** b **3** d **4** a **5** c **6** f

B **1** should have made **2** shouldn't have spent **3** should have tried **4** should have taken **5** shouldn't have refused **6** should have accepted **7** should have gotten **8** should have used **9** should have tested

Past perfect for wishes about the past

A **1** hadn't cut **2** had moved **3** had gotten **4** had ordered **5** hadn't lent **6** hadn't come **7** had bought **8** had worn

B **1** I wish I had lived off campus in college. **2** He wishes he hadn't gotten married so late. **3** She wishes her parents had allowed her to go to the party. **4** They wish they had gotten to know their old neighbors better. **5** I wish I hadn't sat at the back of the class. **6** We wish you had stayed at our party longer.

Unit 8

Third conditional

A **1** wouldn't **2** have learned **3** had **4** have found **5** had **6** hadn't used

B **1** would not / wouldn't have been, had not / hadn't worked **2** had not / hadn't abandoned, would have / would've been **3** would not / wouldn't have died out, had not / hadn't hit **4** would not / wouldn't have made, had followed **5** had not / hadn't invested, would not / wouldn't have gone **6** had crashed, would not / wouldn't have gotten

Indirect questions

1 Do you know who will go from Earth to Mars? **2** Can you tell us if/whether it's a one-way trip? **3** Do you have any idea how long it takes to get to Mars? **4** Could you explain what a colony on Mars will be like? **5** Do you happen to know if/whether Mars has seasons? **6** Do you know if/whether people on Mars can grow their own food? **7** Can you tell us how you became interested in Mars? **8** Could you please tell us if/whether you have ever seen a spacecraft?

Unit 9

So, such, too, enough

A **1** too **2** so **3** such **4** so **5** enough **6** too **7** enough **8** such

B **1** such **2** so **3** too **4** enough

Modals of deduction

A **1** f **2** e **3** h **4** b **5** c **6** g **7** a **8** d

B **1** must **2** could **3** can't **4** must **5** may **6** might

Unit 10

Reported speech: statements

A **1** Tina was thinking about doing a comedy routine **2** Les and Dina were very nervous **3** Maya had performed in Europe **4** Greg had been practicing his routine nonstop **5** Sebastian had performed a modern dance **6** Ken and Suzie would compete as a couple **7** Antonia wanted to make her parents proud **8** Greg and Maya would tie for the win

Reported speech: questions

A **1** what he had enjoyed most **2** if/whether she had watched the competition **3** if/whether she had ever sung live before **4** how long he had had a band **5** if/whether she would do magic tricks **6** if/whether I had much experience **7** how many instruments he played **8** who her greatest inspiration was

Unit 11

Causatives with *have, get,* and *make*

A **1** to drive **2** look **3** to give **4** checked **5** fixed **6** take **7** clean **8** installed

B **1** have my hair cut **2** get my jacket cleaned **3** have someone shop **4** makes me do **5** makes his son shop **6** get your teeth checked **7** have my friends tell **8** get your little brother to do

Verbs with gerund, infinitive, or both

A **1** G **2** I **3** B **4** B **5** I **6** G **7** G **8** I **9** I **10** B **11** B **12** G

B **1** giving **2** to volunteer **3** donating **4** to take **5** using **6** to become **7** to work / working **8** to save

Unit 12

Passive voice: other tenses

A **1** was **2** was **3** has **4** is **5** were **6** was **7** had been **8** has

B **1** The company's ads were criticized. **2** The ads have been called offensive. **3** The ads have now been discontinued. **4** A lot of money was lost. **5** Different ads are being used now.

Comparative and superlative adverbs

A **1** more easily **2** more often **3** worse **4** harder **5** more carefully **6** better **7** more quickly **8** later

B **1** the most carelessly **2** the best **3** the most generously **4** the worst **5** the hardest **6** the latest

Irregular Verbs

Infinitive	Simple past	Past participle
be	was/were	been
become	became	become
begin	began	begun
break	broke	broken
bring	brought	brought
build	built	built
buy	bought	bought
catch	caught	caught
choose	chose	chosen
come	came	come
cost	cost	cost
cut	cut	cut
do	did	done
draw	drew	drawn
drink	drank	drunk
drive	drove	driven
eat	ate	eaten
fall	fell	fallen
feed	fed	fed
feel	felt	felt
find	found	found
fly	flew	flown
get	got	gotten
give	gave	given
go	went	gone
grow	grew	grown
hang	hung	hung
have	had	had
hear	heard	heard
hit	hit	hit
hold	held	held
hurt	hurt	hurt
keep	kept	kept
know	knew	known
leave	left	left
let	let	let
lose	lost	lost
make	made	made
meet	met	met
pay	paid	paid
put	put	put
read	read	read
ride	rode	ridden
ring	rang	rung
rise	rose	risen
run	ran	run
say	said	said
see	saw	seen
sell	sold	sold
send	sent	sent
set	set	set
sing	sang	sung
sit	sat	sat
speak	spoke	spoken
stand	stood	stood
stick	stuck	stuck
take	took	taken
teach	taught	taught
tell	told	told
think	thought	thought
throw	threw	thrown
understand	understood	understood
wake	woke	woken
wear	wore	worn
win	won	won
write	wrote	written

Pronunciation Symbols

Vowels

ɪ	d**i**d
ɛ	b**e**d
æ	b**a**d
ʌ	c**u**p
ʊ	b**oo**k
ə	ban**a**na
i	f**ee**d
ɑ	f**a**ther, b**o**x
ɔ	t**a**ll
u	st**u**dent, f**oo**d
ɝ	sh**ir**t, b**ir**thday
eɪ	d**a**te, t**a**ble
aɪ	cr**y**, **eye**
ɔɪ	b**oy**
oʊ	c**o**mb, p**o**st
aʊ	ab**ou**t, h**ow**

Consonants

p	**p**ark, ha**pp**y
b	**b**ack, ho**bb**y
t	**t**ea
d	**d**ie
k	**c**ame, **k**itchen, **q**uarter
g	**g**ame, **g**o
f	**f**ace, **ph**otogra**ph**er
V	**v**egetable
θ	**th**ing, ma**th**
ð	**th**en, **th**at
s	**c**ity, **s**ummer
z	plea**s**e, goe**s**
ʃ	**sh**e, **sh**op
ʒ	lei**s**ure
h	**h**ot, **wh**o
tʃ	**ch**icken, wa**tch**
dʒ	**j**acket, oran**g**e
m	**m**en
n	su**n**, **kn**ow
ŋ	su**ng**, si**ng**er
w	**w**eek, **wh**ite
r	**r**ain, w**r**iter
l	**l**ight, **l**ong
j	**y**es, **u**se, m**u**sic

Unit 1

Track 01

Technology Creating an Accessible World

Through the use of technology, we are changing the world that is accessible to us. People such as Hugh Herr, co-director of the MIT Center for Extreme Bionics, are responsible for these changes. After losing both of his legs in a mountain climbing accident, Hugh Herr designed and developed new bionic legs. These new legs have a number of features that were previously impossible. The legs can be made longer or shorter. The feet can change depending on the surface of the mountain. It is even possible to attach different climbing equipment. All of these advances mean that Hugh Herr can achieve climbs that no one else has ever been able to do before. The MIT Center for Extreme Bionics is currently working on a digital nervous system which will connect the brain with a computer that can control artificial arms and legs.

Another area in which connections with computers are having a huge effect is communication. Facebook is currently working on a "silent speech" project: computers that can recognize what people are thinking so they can type messages with their brain. This system can help people who are disabled because of disease or injury. It can also help able-bodied people who want a faster way to type their ideas. Early tests in similar systems have used a person's thoughts to select letters and then write words. However, systems will get much faster. The aim of the silent speech project is for thoughts to be turned into text at a speed of 100 words per minute. How would you use technology to access a whole new world?

Track 02

Welcome to today's lecture in our Introduction to Psychology course. Over the last few lectures, we looked at the development of the brain, and this week I want to talk about abilities. Now, we all have various abilities, but I want to talk about two that some people have and others don't. These are perfect pitch and advanced language learning.

To begin with, people with perfect pitch can hear a musical note and tell you exactly what it is. According to the magazine *Psychology Today*, only 1 in 10,000 people has this ability. Mariah Carey has perfect pitch, and so did Mozart. As you probably know, Mozart could play the violin and the keyboard at the age of five. And he managed to write his first symphony at the age of eight. He wrote amazing music for the whole of his short life. He died of illness at the age of 35, but his music still brings happiness to people today. Interestingly, more people have perfect pitch in Asia. There is a possibility that this is because some languages in Asia use different tones.

Moving on to language learning, we all have the ability to learn a language. In fact, we all learn at least one language, our own, to a high level. And many of us have succeeded in learning one or two foreign languages. However, some people are able to learn languages with incredible speed. For example, Daniel Tammet, a writer from England, can speak 10 languages. For a TV program, he went to Iceland and gave himself one week to learn Icelandic. Amazingly, after a week, he could speak the language well enough to be interviewed on national TV. That was a real achievement.

Now I'd like to explore what is happening in the brains of people with these amazing abilities …

Track 03

1	able	ability
2	available	availability

Track 04

Host: Welcome to The Dave Goldstein Podcast. I'm your host, Dave Goldstein. On today's show, we're talking about amazing stories of survival. And with me is journalist and writer Ellen Delgado. Ellen, you've just written a book on people who have survived tough situations. Tell us about it.

Ellen: Thanks for having me on the show, Dave. Yes, while I was writing my book, I learned about some amazing survival stories.

Host: And do you have a favorite story?

Ellen: Yes. I think the person I respect the most was a very brave woman called Juliane Koepcke , who was born in Lima, Peru. When she was 17, in 1971, she was traveling by plane over the Amazonian rain forest when lightning hit the plane. The plane broke up at a height of 3.2 kilometers, and Juliane fell all that way in her seat!

Host: But she survived?

Ellen: Yes. People think that the seat she was in saved her when she crashed into the trees. When she woke up the following morning, she was alone in the rainforest, a long way from other people. The only food she had was a bag of candy. Luckily, Juliane was a calm, independent person. She found a stream and followed it. That was a good piece of logical thinking. After nine days, she found a boat and a small hut. She waited there, and the next day she was discovered by some men, who gave her food and then took her back to civilization.

Host: That's amazing. And what happened to her after that?

Ellen: She became a scientist and went back to the rain forests of Peru. She studied bats there. Later, she moved to Germany, and in 2011 wrote her autobiography, called When I Fell from the Sky, all about her amazing story of survival. If you're curious, you can read her story in her own words there.

Host: That's a great story of survival. We'll be back with more from Ellen after this break.

Track 05

Surviving in the Desert

It is 9 o'clock in the morning on a warm July day. You and your three colleagues were on a short flight to a conference in Southern California when your plane developed mechanical problems. The plane was forced off course by a few miles. Finally, the mechanical problems got worse, the pilot lost control of the plane, and you all crash-landed in the desert. You and your three colleagues find yourselves quite far from the plane. Although you keep looking, unfortunately it seems that the pilot is missing. You and your colleagues are on your own.

The nearest town, which you saw from the window when you flew over it half an hour ago, is about 30 kilometers away. That is an extremely long walk, and you know that it will be very difficult. None of you can get any signal at all on your cell phones, and without signal, none of the apps work. Daytime temperatures in this area can reach 40°C, and at night, they can fall below 0°C. It is already starting to get very warm, and you know that soon you will be in danger. One of your colleagues remembers reading an article about the desert, and he says it is better to move around during the evening, because it is less hot. He says that between late afternoon and sunset is the best time to move.

In different parts of the desert around you, you see a variety of different things, including a map, an empty lighter, and a few items of clothing. You discuss ideas with your colleagues and as you talk, you realize that you need to come up with a plan if you are going to manage to survive. Suddenly, there is a smell of smoke in the air. You look towards the plane and you see that it is beginning to catch fire. You know that this means that there is not much time to decide what to do because the fuel in the plane's tanks could explode. What do you do?

Unit 2

Track 01

The Mirror Test

Animals are interesting, aren't they? They can be cute, they can be fast, and they can be strong. But are they intelligent?

That isn't an easy question to answer. Animals all live in different habitats and their behavior is right for that situation. We need a standard way to test an animal's behavior. The mirror test, developed in 1970 by Dr. Gordon Gallup Jr., gives us that.

You recognize your own reflection in a mirror, don't you? But does an animal know that it's looking at itself when it looks in a mirror, or does it think it's a different animal? If an animal passes the mirror test, there's a good chance it is intelligent. We give the animal medicine so it goes to sleep. Then, we put a colored mark on the animal's body where it can't see it in a normal way, such as on its forehead or on its ear. When the animal wakes up and sees itself in a mirror, we watch how it behaves.

Animals that pass the mirror test see the mark and touch it or try to remove it. So far, the species that have definitely passed the test are great apes (chimpanzees, bonobos, and orangutans), elephants, dolphins, orcas, and Eurasian magpies. Some people say, though, that the test only works with animals that mainly use sight to explore the world, and it may not be a fair test of other animals, such as dogs, who use smell or sound more than sight and fail the test.

Track 02

Good morning, everyone, and thank you very much to the college for inviting me here today to speak to all of you. My name's Nancy Rubin, and I'm a career advisor. I'm here to talk about careers with animals and help you look at your options. I think everyone will be familiar with some professions, such as zookeepers and veterinarians, but there are many others, too. It's important to know what qualities employers are looking for, what exams you need to pass, and what experience is required. So, let's start by looking at a familiar career, and then one that's a bit more unusual!

Track 03

The first career I'd like to mention is marine biologist. Now, of course, *marine* refers to the sea, so a marine biologist is someone who studies animals that live in the sea. That can be anything from whales to tiny creatures called plankton. Marine biology is a large field and it covers many different careers. Many marine biologists are research scientists. They might spend the summer months doing research and the winter months teaching at a university. Marine biologists should be prepared for harsh conditions. They don't always work with dolphins in warm waters! If you choose this career path, you'll need a degree in biology or marine biology, and you'll probably then have to go to graduate school and possibly get a doctoral degree.

The second career I'd like to mention is a bit more unusual. It's a snake milker!

Now, you know that we milk cows, and sometimes sheep and goats, but how do you milk a snake? Snakes don't have milk. They have venom, the poison they use to kill the animals they eat. A snake milker takes venom from a snake. Why? The venom is very useful. First of all, it's used to make antivenom, which we need when a snake bites someone. The venom also has other medical uses. If you choose *this* career, you will need a degree in biology, chemistry, or biochemistry. And you will also need a lot of practical training!

Now let's look at another job related to animals—a zoologist …

Track 04

I have to take my dog to the vet.
My dog has to stay in the animal hospital.

Track 05

Thank you and hello everyone! Welcome to our open day here at Rashford Zoo. It's great to have the chance to speak to you about the work we do at the zoo. When you visit a zoo, you see animals in many different types of places. We try to provide an environment for each animal that is similar to where they live in the wild. That isn't always possible. We can't provide miles of ice and snow for the penguins, for example, but we try to get as close as we can. We want you, the visitor, to see the animals' natural behavior.

We also want to educate people about the dangers some animals face in the wild. We have posters around the zoo with information on them. Zookeepers also talk to members of the public about the threats to animals' habitats and what we can do about them. We have a responsibility to make sure that everyone knows the effects we humans have on nature.

Away from the public, we do a lot of work to help animals. Together with other zoos, we have breeding programs. When a species is endangered in the wild, we make sure there are enough animals in zoos to keep the species going. In some cases, for example wolves and pandas, we take animals from zoos and release them into the wild. That increases the numbers and helps the species to recover.

Now, if you'll all follow me, we'll go and see some of our zookeepers in action.

Track 06

The Trouble With Strays

Puppies are cute, aren't they? And kittens are adorable. But those puppies and kittens grow up to be adult dogs and cats. Often the demands of being a pet owner just get to be too much for people, and the cats and dogs end up on the street as strays. Sometimes it's the responsibility of looking after an adult animal that causes problems, and sometimes there are financial reasons. It's a growing problem. In the city of Detroit in the US, it is estimated that there are 50,000 stray dogs. The World Health Organization estimates that there are about 200 million stray dogs worldwide.

This situation causes a number of problems. First of all, the lives of stray animals are hard and stressful. Every day is a struggle to find enough to eat and a safe place to sleep. That means the animals are often in poor condition and get injured or die young. In addition to that, stray animals cause a number of problems for city residents. They can run into the road and cause traffic accidents. Stray animals can also carry diseases. They can pass these diseases on to people or to domestic pets. Last, packs of dogs can be dangerous and may attack people.

However, there may be a solution to the problem. One country that has reduced the number of stray dogs is the UK. In 2016, a new law was introduced. All dogs must be microchipped. This means that a small chip—the size of a grain of rice—is inserted under the dog's skin. It's a quick and painless procedure. Microchips contain a unique code that is connected to a national database. When the chip is scanned, it shows the owner's address. If your dog does not have a chip, you can receive a fine of up to £500. Microchipping is useful if your dog is lost or stolen, and it also encourages people to take more responsibility for their pets. According to the Dogs Trust's *Stray Dogs Survey Report*, in 2018 the number of stray animals in the UK was at its lowest level in 21 years—so this is a step in the right direction.

Unit 3

Track 01

Confirmation Bias

Scientists believe that the average person receives about 34 gigabytes of information and sees or hears 100,500 words every day. That's a lot of information, and no one can possibly concentrate on all of it. We choose what we pay attention to and what we think is important. That creates a problem: confirmation bias. We like to be right, and so we listen to evidence that supports what we already believe and we ignore evidence that goes against what we believe. For example, if you believe that the world is generally getting worse, you will see only evidence to support your opinion when you hear the news. You will pay attention to stories about rising crime and environmental problems. And you will ignore evidence that suggests people around the world are getting richer, becoming healthier, and living longer.

Confirmation bias means we see what we want to see. It can create problems. For instance, a business may try a new strategy. The managers will notice positive results, such as increased sales, before they notice negative ones, such as increased costs. That could be expensive for the business. Social media and other websites can make confirmation bias worse. Groups of online friends often agree with each other. They easily share information and news stories that support their opinions. They rarely hear the other side of the argument and miss relevant information. Some people are worried that this kind of "social media bubble" is bad for society.

Is there anything you can do to question your own confirmation bias? You can make an effort to listen to people with different views. You can visit websites that present a different opinion from yours. As soon as you do that, you will learn something about how other people think.

Track 02

Host: Hi, and welcome back to *Our World Today*. It's time once again for our weekly call-in. It seems that machines that can think, in other words, artificial intelligence, are becoming more common. Today's question is: What do you think of artificial intelligence? We've got Julia on line 1. Hi, Julia. What would you like to say?

Julia: I think there's no such thing as artificial intelligence. Scientists have been researching it since the 1950s. In that time, they've created machines that can play games like chess very well, but the machines aren't really thinking. They're just following rules. Only people can really think. Machines will never have the thinking power of a human. Humans have been thinking and solving problems for 200,000 years, and we've gotten very good at it!

Host: Thanks for that thought, Julia. And we've got Rafael on line 2. What's your opinion, Rafael?

Rafael: I disagree with the last caller. I think we already use artificial intelligence in different ways. Did you know that a commercial pilot only controls a plane for about seven minutes during a flight? The rest of the time it's controlled by the autopilot because humans get tired and bored and make mistakes. And driverless cars will all rely on AI to avoid accidents, and they'll probably be better at it than people. Some people think that it's only really AI if robots can fully communicate with us, but it isn't like that.

Host: Interesting points, Rafael. Thank you. Megan now on line 3.

Megan: Hello. I've been thinking about AI a lot recently, and I think there's something everyone has forgotten. Who is going to be in control of the machines in the future? I mean, when machines can think, will they be a danger to us? We create computer systems to control everything, and now some are really complicated. No human understands exactly what they are doing. I think that's a dangerous situation.

Host: Hmm … something to think about there. Thanks, Megan. Finally, Victor on line 4.

Victor: I'm worried about the effect on people's working lives. According to researchers at Oxford University, 47% of jobs in the US might be done by machines in the future. It'll have an effect on people who work in services: office workers, truck drivers and taxi drivers, and even people like receptionists and shop assistants. We won't need to employ people when AI becomes powerful enough. And what are we going to do then?

Host: Good question, Victor. Thanks to everyone for your views on this subject …
… some really interesting points. Next week we will be talking about …

Track 03

1 Some people **say** that AI is a danger.
2 My mom **says** that she'll never lose her job to a robot.
3 My dad **said** the same thing and then lost his job!

Track 04

Hello, everyone! It's great to be here to talk to you today about being creative. Now, I know that we all have times when it's hard to be creative. You're trying to solve a problem and you just don't have any ideas. It's easy to give up and think that you aren't a creative person. Or make up excuses and say that it was too hard, or you didn't have enough time. I'm here today to tell you that we can all be creative if we use the right methods. I've come up with a few easy ways to be more creative that we can all rely on.

One thing you can do is make sure you have the knowledge you need. Become an expert. Look up information online and learn about an area. Creative people get ideas by understanding other people's ideas. The more you know, the more your ideas grow.

Another thing you can do is take up a sport or hobby. When you do that, you put yourself in the position of being a beginner. When you get good at a sport, it's easy to stop learning and to think you know everything about it. Trying a new sport helps you remember what it's like not to know all the answers.

Track 05

Here are a few very simple exercises that people have been using for a long time to help them be more creative. The first is a way of coming up with lots of ideas. You take an ordinary object, such as a spoon or a paper clip, and you try to think of as many different uses for it as you can in three minutes. For example, a paper clip could be used to open a lock, or to eat cheese, or to tie your hair back!

For the second method, you need to write two lists of very different objects. It doesn't matter what they are, but you need to make them all different. Then you choose an object from the first list and an object from the second list. You have to find ways in which the objects are the same. For example, you might have an elephant and a flower. How could they be the same? Well, maybe you can see both at a zoo, or maybe an elephant's ears are like a flower's petals! Or maybe they both need water every day!

The third exercise uses famous people. Let's say you're coming up with ideas to solve a problem. You might ask: "What would the president do?" Or "What would Mickey Mouse do?" Or "What would my favorite singer do?" The answers to these questions might be silly, but they also might tell you something about the problem.

Another way to encourage creativity is to …

Track 06

The Trouble With Social Media

Social media companies have been feeling worried recently. People have realized that there are a few problems connected to social media. One is the problem of confirmation bias. Our online friends make comments and share posts that we already agree with. We accept them as true and we never see any evidence of other opinions. This can mean that we share and like false stories more easily because they match what we already believe.

There are other problems, too. Some people spend too much time on social media. They update their status many times a day and their phones show notifications of other people's posts. This often means they waste time, or they ignore their real-life family and friends. They might also become anxious about how many shares or likes their posts get. Other people experience cyberbullying, where people make up comments about them. That can have an effect on people's lives and their health.

Another issue is our digital footprint. Every time we post, share, or comment, we leave a digital record. It often follows us for a very long time. When you apply for a job or when you meet someone new, they might check your social media. What will they see? Are you sure that you want them to see everything you've posted?

Finally, people share a lot of information on social media. They share their location, when they're on vacation, and what they do every day. That can leave the person vulnerable to crime or other problems.

Many people agree that we need to find ways to help people be safer on social media and to think more about the information they see and share.

Unit 4

Track 01

Being a Good Communicator

Many of us find it hard to communicate. You may know what you want to say but not know how. What makes a good communicator? You might think a good communicator is someone who can speak well and explain his or her ideas. You might think a good communicator can persuade people to do what he or she wants. However, there's a lot more to communication than expressing yourself well. Communication is an important skill in our personal, academic, and professional lives. And it's easy to learn a few simple communication techniques.

The first is active listening. Good communicators listen carefully to understand the other person's thoughts. They repeat ideas back to the other person to show they understand. They also encourage the person to say more by asking relevant questions. For example, a good communicator might say: "I hear you saying that you're unhappy with your major. How, exactly?"

Good communicators are honest. In an argument with a friend, you don't help communication when you pretend that everything is fine. Good communicators talk honestly about how they feel.

Finally, good communicators make a personal connection with people. They try to find something they have in common with the person they are speaking to. That helps them to understand what the other person wants from a situation. Or they might try to put themselves in the other person's position and ask: "If I were him or her, what would I want to hear?"

Using these techniques will help to improve your relationships with other people at home, at school, and at work.

Track 02

Host: Hello, and welcome to the *Career Report*. This week's guest is Jayden Ross. Jayden's a psychologist who studies nonverbal communication. Jayden, welcome to the podcast.

Jayden: Good to be here.

Host: Now, we all know that communication skills are very important. What can you tell us about communication?

Jayden: There are three parts to it, really. The first is the things we *say*, the actual *words* we use. Researchers believe that words are only 7% of what we communicate.

Host: Is that all? That's amazing.

Jayden: Yes, it's much less than most people think. Then there's the *way* we speak. That's around 38% of what we communicate.

Host: OK. I'm guessing that includes tone of voice, speed, volume, things like that.
Jayden: That's right. And the rest, around 55%, is body language, all the things we do with our body when we are talking or when we are listening to someone else.

Track 03

Host: So, tell us about the way we speak.
Jayden: Your tone of voice plays a big part in communication. We all know that if you ask someone how they are, the *way* they say "I'm fine" can communicate a lot. It can communicate that the person really *is* fine, or it can communicate that the person *isn't* fine and wants you to ask how they really are! That's one reason why communicating by email or text message can create problems. There's no tone of voice, so it's easy to misunderstand someone's meaning.
Host: I see. And what about body language?
Jayden: First of all, there's personal space. There's usually a distance between you and the person you are talking to. And it changes in different cultures. Your listeners can look this up on the internet. People in Argentina, for example, want a distance of about 76 centimeters when they are talking to strangers. In Mexico, it's a meter, and in Romania, it's 1.4 meters.
Host: Interesting! What else?
Jayden: The expression on your face says a lot, and so does the position of your arms and hands. Open arms generally mean that you are open to another person's opinion, and arms across your body usually mean you don't want to listen. Touch is also important in some cultures.
Host: OK, so is there any general advice you can give our listeners about understanding body language?
Jayden: Don't rely on just a person's words or their body language. Look at them both together. Check when a person's words and body language *aren't* saying the same thing. If a person is saying something friendly but their body is saying the opposite, that's when you need to be careful!
Host: Jayden Ross, thanks for joining us today.

Track 04

We live in an age where communication is global and fast. You can contact anyone at any time through email, text message, or instant messaging. However, it wasn't always that way, and there are clear technological steps that have led us to where we are today.

These days, we all use email, and we send over 280 billion emails a day! Email has come a long way since it was invented in 1971. That was when a computer engineer named Ray Tomlinson sent the first email message—to himself! That was just a couple of years before the first cell phone appeared. Today, something like 67% of the world's population owns and uses a cell phone.

Many people use cell phones to send text messages, or SMS messages. SMS means "short message service," and the first SMS was sent in December 1992—it said "Merry Christmas." Today, we send text messages every day. Many people include emojis in their messages. Emojis were invented in 1999 by a Japanese designer, Shigetaka Kurita. He created 176 images, and today there are over 2,800 emojis. One of the most popular ones is the "face with tears of laughter."

The next big step in communication was the first mass-marketed smartphone, the iPhone. Apple brought it out in 2007. Today over 2 million apps are available for the iPhone. One of the most popular apps is WhatsApp, used for instant messaging. It first appeared in 2009, and today people send 55 billion messages a day through the service. A couple of years later, in 2011, a service began that allowed users to send pictures that disappear. Of course, this is Snapchat, and today 188 million people use it to communicate.

Now let's think about how different types of people use different means of communication.

Track 05

Go to www.macmillan.com
My email is lisa_jackson3@emailtoday.org
Under the picture, it says #selfie and #mybestlook
My email is carrie-smith@fly.org

Track 06

Communication Problems

Businesses and other organizations succeed when the people communicate well with each other. There needs to be a free flow of information and instructions. Unfortunately, communication often goes wrong.

One reason for communication problems is that in large, multinational corporations, people often come from different cultures and speak different languages. They may use a common language to communicate, often English, but that doesn't remove the possibility of misunderstandings. People from some cultures, such as the US and Western Europe, may think it's important to clearly express their ideas and say how they feel. They might not see a problem in correcting a colleague or criticizing an idea. However, this can make people from some *other* cultures feel very uncomfortable. Similar problems can happen when people are from the same culture but have different life experiences.

Another reason for problems is communication technology. Many of us work from home at least some of the time these days. We communicate with colleagues through software such as Skype or Google Hangouts, and it doesn't always work perfectly. When we don't completely understand something and we are not able to check our understanding, it can lead to problems.

You might be surprised to hear that another possible reason for communication problems is friendships at work. Normally, we think of friends as people we communicate well with. However, mixing personal and professional communication isn't a good idea. It makes some people feel uncomfortable and it can start arguments.

Many organizations work hard to improve communication, for example, organizing diversity training sessions for employees. Another idea is a no-email day. One day a week, no one sends emails. Instead, they speak to people on the phone or meet in person. Small changes like that can make a big difference.

Unit 5

Track 01

FAQs About Climate Change

1 **Are climate change and global warming the same thing?**
Global warming refers to the general rise in the Earth's temperatures that has happened since the beginning of the Industrial Revolution. Climate change refers to all of the changes in weather and climate that are caused by global warming, such as hotter summers, more severe storms, and more forest fires.

2 **What causes global warming?**
Global warming began with the Industrial Revolution when we started using fossil fuels—carbon-based fuels like oil and gas—but most global warming has happened since the 1970s. When we burn fossil fuels, they produce carbon dioxide. The carbon dioxide in the atmosphere traps heat and holds it near the Earth. Other types of gases, like methane, also trap heat near the Earth. This is called the greenhouse effect.

3 **Does it really matter if the Earth is only a few degrees warmer than it was?**
It is true that the Earth is only about 0.99 °C warmer than it was in the mid-20th century, but if temperatures go up even a small amount, big changes take place. Sea levels rise and more severe weather events happen. The United Nations predicts that if temperatures rise more than 1.5 °C, the effect on our lives will be extreme. If we didn't burn so many fossil fuels, the effects of global warming wouldn't be so serious.

4 **What are the effects of global warming and climate change?**
Unless we stop global warming, the polar ice caps will melt and sea levels will rise. This will affect Arctic and Antarctic species like polar bears and penguins, and it will mean more floods in coastal cities. Some areas will have hotter summers with long droughts and terrible fires. Other areas will have colder winters with bad ice and snowstorms. There will be more severe weather events like tornadoes and hurricanes.
If we don't do anything about global warming, there will be terrible consequences. Some coastal cities like Miami, Osaka, and parts of Rio de Janeiro may disappear. Many species of animals may also disappear, and this will change the Earth's ecosystems. One thing is certain: our planet will not be the same place it is today.

Track 02

1 reduce pollution
2 provide recycling
3 create laws
4 pay for plastic bags
5 require less packaging
6 use clean energy

Track 03

Host: Good afternoon. You're listening to KT Radio, and we're on the street today talking to young people about environmental issues. It's a little noisy here, so I hope you can hear me! Excuse me. What's your name, and what do you think is the biggest environmental problem today?

Eric: Uh, hi. I'm Eric Tyler. To me, the most important environmental issue is air pollution. Air pollution is caused by burning fossil fuels, and that causes global warming. If global warming continues, our planet will die. I wish fossil fuels didn't exist! We should have lower taxes for companies that use clean energy.

Host: Thanks, Eric. And how about you? Can you give me your name and tell us what you think?

Susan: Sure. My name is Susan Dyson. I think water pollution is the biggest problem. Millions of people in the world do not have clean water to drink. I wish every country had stronger laws against water pollution.

Host: Thank you, Susan. And what do you think? Sorry, what's your name?

Ali: I'm Ali Rahman. In my opinion, trash is the worst environmental problem. We are throwing away tons of trash, especially plastic. I wish we could completely stop using plastic bags and packages. I hope all cities will provide free recycling soon.

Host: Thanks, Ali. And … hi. What's your name?

Anh: My name is Anh Dao. I wish my government would make fishing companies reduce certain types of fishing. Fishing is very important for our economy, and if the fish populations were destroyed, it would be terrible for my country. I hope our generation makes a lot of changes to help save the planet!

Host: Thank you all, and Anh, that's a very good point. We're all young, and it's up to us. I hope our generation is taking environmental problems seriously, and I hope we will be more responsible.

Track 04

Tutor: Good afternoon, everyone. Now, as we discussed yesterday, there are many excellent government projects happening in countries around the world that aim to create solutions to environmental problems. There are also many new products invented by small or large businesses to address these problems. For example, several small companies here in the US are making plant pots from old automobile tires. The pots are attractive, and the tires don't go into the trash! So, I asked you to do some research. What did you find out?

Joe: I found a really interesting project that's kind of weird but cool. A company in Indonesia called Paper Flops is making flip-flops out of recycled paper, coconut shells, palm tree roots, and natural rubber. Also, they teach homeless children and disabled people to make the sandals, so they're helping people as well as the environment!

Tutor: Sounds great! Molly, what did you find?

Molly: Well, they're doing a lot of things to make Singapore green—planting a lot of trees and creating parks, for example, but my favorite thing is the giant structures called super trees. The trees are made of steel, but they have thousands of climbing plants and flowers. The trees also generate solar power and collect rainwater, so they help the environment in several ways. I hope other cities will put in super trees! How about you, Jorge?

Jorge: Wow … bizarre! I'd love to see them. OK. I'm from Chile, so I wanted to research environmental solutions in Latin America. I found a really interesting project in Mexico. A company called Eco Domum is making houses from recycled plastic. They use the plastic to make the walls and roof of the buildings. I think it's a great idea. Another project is producing water in very dry areas in Chile and Peru. They use giant nets to catch drops of water from fog. They hope that in the future, they can produce enough water for all of the people in the desert areas.

Tutor: Very interesting. And, finally, Asami, what can you tell us?

Asami: One of the biggest problems in the world is plastic trash, and in Kenya, a company called Eco Dawati is recycling plastic to make desks for schools. A lot of schools have never had desks, so it's great for the kids. It uses plastic trash in a practical way to help people. The next two things are kind of similar. The first one is living walls—walls that have plants growing on them. They look pretty, and they produce oxygen. They're using these living walls in many places, including England. The other one is green roofs. I was interested in this one because they're doing it in my country, Japan. When I go home, I hope I can live in a building with a green roof!

Tutor: You've all done a great job, and it's good to remember that many countries around the world are doing things to help the environment. If governments and companies in every country did just a few of these things, our planet would be a lot cleaner and healthier. Sometimes wild ideas are the best ones!

Track 05

Evan the Eco Guy—Micro-Ecology

How often have you heard or said this about a problem: "Why don't they do something?" Who is they? In the case of environmental problems, they probably refers to the government or to the world in general. But what if we stopped saying they and started saying we? There are many things that we, the people, can do to reduce global warming and to help the environment in general.

First, there are many small things that individual people and families can do. If we all tried to save energy, we would use less oil and gas, and there would be less carbon in the atmosphere. There are some very easy ways to save energy. Turn off lights when you are not in a room. Turn off your computer at night. Do several errands when you go out in your car, and offer to do errands for other people in your family. Share rides to school or work with family or friends. Try to buy locally produced food and other products. There are also many things that we can all do to produce less trash. Use reusable shopping bags for all types of shopping. When you buy fast food, don't take too many napkins, and don't take plastic forks if you are going to eat the food at home.

Neighborhoods and communities can also do many things to help the environment. Community gardens help in several ways. First, plants put oxygen into the air and use carbon dioxide. Second, if people eat food from local gardens, they are not eating food that was transported by trucks or planes. Third, flowers attract insects and birds that pollinate plants. Communities can also set up neighborhood websites to share rides, recycle things like clothes or toys, or organize volunteers to pick up trash in local parks and recycle it. If we did a little more as individuals and communities, we could have a very positive effect on our environment.

Unit 6

Track 01

In Just 20 Years …

By the end of the 19th century, the Industrial Revolution had changed the world forever, and technology has continued to make many improvements since then. The first two decades of both the 20th and the 21st centuries brought life-changing progress in technology. From 1900 to 1920, there were enormous changes, especially in communications and transportation. Of course, there had already been innovations in these areas when the 20th century began. For example, the first passenger train powered by a locomotive had started in 1825 in England, but the huge expansion of the railroads in the US and Europe came in the 20th century. The first commercial telephone company opened in 1878, but at the beginning of the 20th century, the telephone had not yet become widely available to the public. Most surprisingly, there were electric taxis in London by 1897, but automobiles became available to ordinary people with the invention of the assembly line in the 20th century. The first two decades of the 20th century also brought the first movie theater in 1905, the first commercial flight in 1914, and the first radio station in 1920.

In the first two decades of the 21st century, progress in information technology was particularly important. This "Digital Revolution" included two of the most important developments in communications since the telephone—smartphones and the creation of social media platforms. The first social media network was Friendster in 2002, and the first modern smartphone was the iPhone in 2007. Entertainment technology also changed enormously from the close of the 20th century to the first decades of the 21st century. Some of the major 21st-century inventions so far have been wireless headsets in 2002, YouTube and internet radio in 2005, e-readers in 2007, and virtual reality headsets in 2016. It is hard to imagine where digital technology will take us by the end of the 21st century!

Track 02

Host: Good evening everyone. I'm Melissa Warren and for today's show, I'm on a street where lots of young people hang out on Saturday evenings. I'm going to ask some people their opinions about inventions from the first two decades of the 21st century, and which inventions they think will be considered the most historic in the future. Excuse me, sir. I'm from Channel 9 TV, and I'm asking people to give their opinions about 21st-century inventions. Are there any that you think will have historic importance?

Man 1: Uh, yeah, maybe 3-D printers. Those could have historic importance. Actually, I'm pretty worried about several of the recent inventions, but to me, the invention that is the most worrying so far is the 3-D printer. If there's a time when people can make most of their own products, it will be very bad for business.

Host: That's an interesting point, thank you. What about you, ma'am? In your opinion, are there any historic 21st-century inventions so far?

Woman 1: Well, there are a lot of amazing new inventions. I'm a photographer, and I think one of the most exciting inventions is a camera that can take 360-degree pictures. I'm really excited because these cameras are totally changing professional photography. I don't know if it's a historic invention, but it's important in my career.

Host: I see, thank you for that. Excuse me, sir, which 21st-century inventions do you think are the most interesting or exciting?

Man 2: Well, I'm really amused by some of the things that have been invented recently. Apparently, somebody has invented a little hammock for feet, and I think that's really funny. There are some inventors who are creating some pretty amusing things!

Host: Yes, I guess some inventions are more amusing than useful. They probably won't have historic importance. Excuse me, ma'am, can I ask your opinion about 21st-century inventions?

Woman 2: Sure. Driverless cars are amazing, but are those cars going to be safe in big cities, where there is a lot of traffic? I'm worried about that. I guess there are a lot of people who want to read or check their text messages and let their car drive, but not me! Anyway, I think driverless cars will have a huge effect on transportation.

Host: Yes, I totally agree that driverless cars are a historic invention. I think there are some people who are worried about driverless cars, but I'm sure the technology will improve a lot before there are many of them on the streets.

Track 03

Today's subject on *Game Changers* is one of the most famous doctors in history. Before 1967, there had been transplants of several different human organs, but there had been no successful heart transplants. On December 3, 1967, South African heart surgeon *Christiaan Barnard* changed that forever.

Christiaan Barnard was born in South Africa in 1922, and he grew up in a poor family. Dr. Barnard got his medical degree at the University of Cape Town in South Africa and later studied cardiac surgery at the University of Minnesota in the US. Before he became a cardiac surgeon, Dr. Barnard had worked in medicine for several years, and he had found a cure for a fatal kidney defect.

Dr. Barnard was a very capable heart surgeon for 10 years before he attempted the first transplant. He introduced open-heart surgery to South Africa. Before he transplanted the first human heart, Dr. Barnard had practiced the operation on dogs, so he had had some experience with the procedure. In 1967, he felt that he was ready to do a human heart transplant, and he found a 54-year-old man with serious heart disease. The man's situation was hopeless, and he agreed to try a transplant. Dr. Barnard found a heart donor, and the operation was done. The transplant was successful, but the man died of pneumonia 18 days after the operation. Dr. Barnard went on to perform more heart transplants, and several of his patients lived for years after their transplants.

Today, over 7,000 heart transplants are performed every year, and deaths from heart disease are often preventable. The world is thankful to Dr. Christiaan Barnard for his wonderful contribution to heart patients everywhere. Before Dr. Barnard's incredible achievement, most people had not imagined that a heart transplant would ever be possible.

Track 04

hopeful	capable	thankful
successful	preventable	incredible

Track 05

UNESCO: Preserving Our Heritage

The main role of the United Nations Educational, Scientific, and Cultural Organization (UNESCO) is to encourage international collaboration, and to promote global security and peace. One way that UNESCO achieves this is through the preservation of sites of great cultural or national importance. This develops respect for those sites among the citizens of those countries. It also educates tourists about those sites and encourages them to discover the beauty of that country's culture.

Tourists can find out more about all of the UNESCO's sites by going to the World Heritage List, which can be found on the official UNESCO website. Currently, there are almost 1,100 sites on this list, including national parks, forests, islands, temples, and houses. Some of the sites are very well-known, like the Great Wall in China and Machu Picchu in Peru, but there are many sites that are well-known only within the countries where they are located. It is possible to use the World Heritage List as a way to find out more about your own country, or to inspire future vacations.

To be included on the World Heritage List, a site needs to be considered of universal importance. UNESCO has created a set of criteria to select World Heritage sites. These criteria examine the site's cultural importance, as well as its natural beauty. There are a total of ten criteria that UNESCO considers in the site selection process, and a site has to have at least one of them to be selected. Some of the criteria are:

1. Be an example of an important cultural tradition of the past or present
2. Be an example of amazing human creativity
3. Be an example of a culture's use of land or sea that is positive for the environment
4. Have incredible natural beauty
5. Represent an important period in the Earth's history
6. Represent great achievements in technology, architecture, the arts, town planning, or landscape design

Unit 7

Track 01

Famous Mistakes in History

1 Expensive Decision

In the 1982 mega-hit movie *E.T.*, there is a scene where the little boy uses candy to convince *E.T.*, the extraterrestrial, to follow him. The filmmakers had planned to use M&Ms for this scene, but Mars, Inc. did not give them permission to use their candy. They then asked Hershey for permission to use Reese's Pieces, and Hershey agreed, so it turned out that Reese's Pieces candy was used in the movie. Two weeks after the movie opened, sales of Reese's Pieces went up by around 65%. Today, a Reese's product is the number one candy in the US! Mars Inc. shouldn't have missed this opportunity!

2 Lost in Space

The Mars Climate Orbiter was a small spacecraft built to orbit Mars and record information about the surface and atmosphere of the planet. It went into space in December 1998, and it disappeared in September 1999. When researchers looked into why the Orbiter was lost, they came across an important mistake. They found out that the system on the spacecraft had used the metric system, while the computers on Earth had used the imperial system. Because of this mistake, the Orbiter went too close to Mars and burned up. Someone should have noticed that the two systems used different measurements!

Track 02

Host: Welcome to Money Talk. I'm Brad Watson, and our topic today is buyer's remorse. That's the bad feeling you have after you have bought something you may not need. We have a panel of people who have buyers' remorse. I'll start with caller 1, Steven. Steven, is there anything that you really wish you hadn't bought?

Steven: Oh, yeah. My worst decision was to get a swimming pool. We don't have much time to use the pool, and it's very expensive to take care of it. We really wish we hadn't decided to get a pool. We definitely wasted our money!

Host: I can understand why you might regret that—a lot of people say they regret getting swimming pools or hot tubs. Any other regrets, Steven?

Steven: Well, I work a lot, and I don't have much time to go to the gym, so I bought several expensive pieces of exercise equipment. Guess how often I use them? About once a month! So I spent a lot of money on exercise equipment I almost never use.

Host: Yep, exercise equipment is definitely one of the things people most regret buying. What about you, Monica?

Monica: Well, my husband and I decided to buy a vacation home in Florida. But they can be expensive, and when you have one, you really don't want to spend money going on vacation in other places. It can be boring to always go to the same place, but it's very hard to sell a vacation home. We finally sold it for less than we paid, so we lost a lot of money. We really wish we had never bought that vacation home!

Host: Yes, many people say they wish they hadn't bought vacation homes. Omar, any regrets about things you've bought?

Omar: Just one. I bought an expensive desktop computer, but I don't use it very much because I almost always use my laptop.

Host: That's something that has changed a lot recently. Most people now say they use only a laptop, or even just a tablet. OK. Sarah, what are your regrets?

Sarah: Well, my daughter and I started collecting dolls when she was young, and now we have over a thousand of them. I've spent thousands of dollars on them. She's a teenager now and not really interested in the collection anymore. I really wish I had saved that money instead!

Host: Thanks, Sarah. I should point out that our panel's answers are very similar to answers on questionnaires about things people regret buying. It seems that there are things that most, or at least many, people end up wishing they had not spent money on!

Track 03

lose	waste	tools	use
exercise	house	desktop	objects

Track 04

Good afternoon. My talk today is called "Everyone Regrets Something." It is a human characteristic to feel sad about things we wish we had or had not done. Most regrets are about small things that don't make a big difference in our lives: "I wish I hadn't bought this shirt. I really don't like it very much," or "I definitely shouldn't have eaten that big meal! I feel terrible." However, a lot of people also have regrets about at least one or two *big* things in their lives.

OK, so why talk about a sad topic like regrets? Well, if we know what people have regrets about, we can try to avoid those same mistakes in our own lives. There has been quite a lot of research about what older people say they regret in their lives. I'm going to tell you about some of the things that many people say they regret. I think you can probably predict what some of the top regrets are, but others may surprise you!

The first regret is connected to people's professional lives, but it isn't about turning down a job or earning money. It's about time. Most people, especially very successful people, say they wish they had spent less time working and more time with their family and friends.

Another common regret is about friendships. People say they wish they had stayed in touch with old friends. We all get busy and time moves forward. Then sometimes we are afraid to get in touch with someone after a long time. We think they will be angry or hurt. However, they're probably thinking the same thing about you!

The other top regret for many people is, of course, love! Many people say they wish they hadn't broken up with someone they really loved, or they wish they had married someone they loved long ago.

Now, here are some regrets that you probably *didn't* predict. The first is travel. Some people say they should have traveled more. Most people take a lot of short trips and a few big trips in their lives, but how many people really see the world, or even their own countries?

Another regret is about children, but it isn't about having or not having kids. People say that they wish they had taught their children to do more things. This includes practical things, like how to fix problems in your house, and fun things, like how to play a game or sport.

Finally, quite a few people, especially Americans, say that they should have learned another language. Learning a second language can help you with your career, but it's also interesting, and it helps you learn about other cultures.

So, before you make a decision, try to imagine what regrets you might have about it later in life. Don't miss opportunities to make your life better! Thank you.

Track 05

The first regret is connected to people's professional lives, but it isn't about turning down a job or earning money. It's about time. Most people, especially very successful people, say they wish they had spent less time working and more time with their family and friends.

Another common regret is about friendships. People say they wish they had stayed in touch with old friends. We all get busy and time moves forward. Then sometimes we are afraid to get in touch with someone after a long time. We think they will be angry or hurt. However, they're probably thinking the same thing about you!

Another regret is about children, but it isn't about having or not having kids. People say that they wish they had taught their children to do more things. This includes practical things, like how to fix problems in your house, and fun things, like how to play a game or sport.

Track 06

Case Study: The Edsel

Introduction

In 1957, the Ford Motor Company introduced the Edsel, a car that they were promoting as "the car of the future." However, the Edsel turned out to be one of the greatest mistakes in business history.

Basic Idea and Research

- In the early 1950s, the US economy was extremely strong, and Ford wanted a new car in the medium-price range. Unfortunately, they did not pay attention to research that showed the US would soon experience a recession.

- Ford did not do enough research to find out what customers really wanted in a car. Instead, they based most of their decisions on the opinions of Ford executives, the people who managed the company.
- The executives spent a lot of money on research to help them decide on the name of the car, but they decided to use the name of Henry Ford's son Edsel. It turned out that people hated the name.

Design
- Ford wanted to design a car that looked very different from existing cars, but the company did not do research to find out if people liked the design. They didn't show the design to sales people or the public before the car was produced.
- The company wanted to produce a car that many different types of people would buy, so they made 18 different models of the Edsel.
- The Edsel had many new features that hadn't been used in cars before, but those new things did not always work well.

Marketing
- Ford started promoting the Edsel as "the car of the future" in advertisements a year before the car was produced. There was a lot of excitement about it, and people even waited in line to see it. Unfortunately, many people did not like the new design when they saw it. They decided that it was an ugly, expensive car with a terrible name.

Lessons Learned
Ford learned from its mistakes with the Edsel. They did excellent research for the Ford Mustang, which they produced in the 1960s. The Ford Mustang became one of the greatest successes in business history. It was exactly the right car for the right customers at the right time, and the Mustang is still a very popular car today.

Unit 8

Track 01

What on Earth Happened?
Sixty-six million years ago, during the time of the dinosaurs, something happened that changed our planet forever. A meteorite hit the Earth near the Yucatan Peninsula of Mexico and created a crater that was 185 km. wide. The impact caused an explosion equal to about 10 million Hiroshima bombs. This caused a chain of events that resulted in mass extinctions of life on Earth.

Scientists almost all agree that the meteorite was the main cause of these mass extinctions. They now think they understand what happened after the meteorite hit. First, if you had been within 1,000 km. of the impact site, you would have been killed by a massive ball of fire. Almost immediately after the impact, there were earthquakes and 300-meter-high tidal waves all over the planet. About eight minutes after the impact, debris from the explosion would have started to fall out of the sky. A lot of the debris was on fire, and this caused massive forest fires. A few minutes later, there would have been 965-km.-per-hour winds caused by the quickly heating air. These winds would have destroyed everything they came into contact with.

Common theories suggest that if you had been far enough away, you would have survived the explosion, but in a few days, you would have seen the sky get very dark because of the carbon soot that filled the atmosphere. The soot blocked the sunlight for months and perhaps for years. Without sunlight, plants began to die. When the plants died, there was no food for the herbivores, so they died, too. When the herbivores died, the carnivores didn't have food, so they also died.

It is interesting to try to imagine what would have happened if the meteorite had *not* crashed into Earth. Some scientists think dinosaurs might have survived. They believe they could have adapted to slow changes in climate over many years. Just imagine ...

Track 02

Host: Welcome to *Our Universe*. I'm your host, Sam Maxwell, and my guest today is astronaut Karen Simmons. Karen is going to give us some inside information about what it's like to live in a space capsule. First, Karen, can you tell us how many times you have flown into space?

Karen: Yes, I've been four times. One of those times was to the International Space Station.

Host: Could you explain what life is like in zero gravity?

Karen: Sure. You float, of course, so you have to hold on to something to stay in one place. When you sleep, you use a special sleeping bag, and you tie it to the wall or the floor. If you want to sit down, you have to tie yourself to a chair.

Host: How do you drink water?

Karen: You have to drink water through a tube. If you used a glass, the water would float out of the glass and into the air!

Host: You have very short hair. Is long hair a problem in space?

Karen: Oh, yes. I cut my hair before I went to space for the first time. If I hadn't, it would have floated around my head the whole time!

Host: I had never thought about that! Karen, the purpose of the US space shuttles was to take astronauts to the space station. The last space shuttle trip was in 2011. Do you know if the US will have space shuttles again in the future?

Karen: There probably won't be space shuttles exactly like the old ones, but the government is working with companies like Boeing and SpaceX to create new types of spacecraft that can take astronauts to the space station and possibly other space destinations.

Host: Wow, and do you know where they will go, besides the space station?

Karen: No, I don't, but at some point in the future, maybe even to other planets.

Host: Finally, can you tell us how you felt the first time you saw Earth from outer space?

Karen: It's just incredible. It's a beautiful blue, green, and brown ball. You think about the fact that it's the only planet we have, and that it isn't really very big. You can see the oceans and the continents, but no countries, of course, and that can make you think differently about our world.

Host: Well, that sounds amazing, Karen. Thank you ...

Track 03

1 host
2 guest
3 space
4 sleep
5 just
6 school
7 student
8 desk

Track 04

Host: Welcome to *Science and Society*. Our discussion today is about the effects of space exploration on society. Some people say that it's a waste of money to explore space. My guests today have the opposite opinion of space exploration. They are going to tell us why they believe that the space program is very important to our everyday lives. We have with us Cristina Fares, an engineer; Seth Foreman, a retired astronaut; Lauren Young, a weather scientist; and Mike Bolton, a science teacher. I'll start with Seth. Seth, as an astronaut, can you tell us why you think space exploration is important?

Seth: Yes, of course. Space exploration is not just about finding life on other planets or finding planets that humans could live on. In fact, it's mainly about learning about our own planet. For example, we can study the Earth's atmosphere from space and learn more about climate change. Also, space exploration makes us safer. We have satellites that can track asteroids and predict if and when an asteroid will hit the Earth.

Lauren: That's right. Remember that space exploration is also not just astronauts going into space. Sorry, Seth! Satellites are also part of the space program, and weather satellites give us accurate information about weather conditions like hurricanes and other storms. They also help us predict long-term weather conditions like droughts or very cold winters.

Host: Just to remind our audience, Lauren is a weather scientist and Seth is an astronaut—thank you for your opinions. Now let's hear from Cristina, who is an engineer. Cristina, can you explain how space exploration helps in your field?

Cristina: Yes. I'm an electrical engineer, and a lot of the technology that was developed for the space program has been used in everyday inventions, such as solar panels, laptop computers, and even wireless headsets. How many times a day do you use the camera on your cell phone? Well, the technology for micro-cameras was developed in the 1990s for use on spacecraft.

Host: I didn't know that my wireless headset and my phone camera came from the space program. Thanks, space program! Finally, Mike, you are a science teacher. What does the space program mean to education?

Mike: The space program is like a giant science teacher. First, it teaches us about the universe, about our own planet, and about the weather. Second, it teaches us about new ways to do things through advanced technology. Finally, I think the space program gives a lot of students a reason to want to study math and science. Space is interesting to them, and some of them will even want to grow up to be astronauts like Seth.

Host: So if space exploration had never started, we might not have developed many of the things we use here on Earth every day, and we might have had more damage from hurricanes and other major weather events over the past several decades. Is that a good summary of what you guys have been saying?

Seth: Yes.

Lauren: That's right.

Cristina: Correct.

Mike: Definitely.

Track 05

Life on Mars

Traveling to Mars is hard. Living on Mars is even harder. First, there are serious environmental issues. One problem is radiation. Astronauts on the International Space Station get 10 times more radiation than on Earth, and the radiation in deep space could be even stronger. One possible solution is ice-covered domes because ice partly blocks radiation. The second problem is the effects of low gravity on the human body. People's bones and muscles become weaker if they are in low gravity for a long time. It is necessary to use weights and do heavy exercise to prevent this. A third problem is that people will have to live in a closed ecosystem. They have to stay inside a dome or a spacesuit at all times. There is no fresh air, so there is a danger of pollution or contamination by bacteria or viruses.

Life on Mars will also have psychological difficulties. First, there will be very few people on Mars, at least at the beginning, so there will not be many choices of friends. There will be no restaurants, cafés, or parks, so there will be few options for social activities, and life could be very boring. Second, the living spaces will be very small. People will be living very close to each other. Life will not be very comfortable. Water will be very limited, so people will have to take 30-second showers and almost never wash their clothes. Plants cannot grow on Mars, so all food will be dried or in cans. Also, most food tastes the same at low gravity. Finally, communication with Earth will be very hard. Cell phones and other voice communications will be impossible, so the only communication will be through email. It will take 20 minutes for an email to reach Earth, and another 20 minutes to get a reply, and most of us are used to very fast communication with our friends and families.

Unit 9

Track 01

1

Changing Times

It's no surprise that newspaper sales have fallen in recent years and TV news audiences are smaller because of the effect of 24/7 online news sites. It's too early to say how this will affect the way we present the news, but it's such an important industry that it's likely to survive technological change. There will always be journalism and a need for good journalists.

2

Jamie: I never buy newspapers these days. What's the point? News is reported so quickly because it changes all the time. I'm not that interested in current affairs, but I read news stories online, and sometimes I watch the news on TV if something "big" is happening somewhere in the world. I see some news items on social media, but the majority are human-interest stories and that kind of story is not interesting enough for me to repost. I'd like to know if anyone here does repost those stories in their newsfeed.
posted by jamiek 12:23

3

Citizen Journalists: The Word on the Street by Amos Hadfield

A must-read for all journalism students is *Citizen Journalists: The Word on the Street* by Amos Hadfield. Citizen journalism is where ordinary people collect, report, share, and comment on news stories via their social media newsfeeds or tweets. It's an interesting trend because it's so hard to control. A positive point is that ordinary people can get involved. However, there are some problems. "It isn't easy to limit the spread of fake news" he writes. "Governments want more power, but that is also dangerous."

4

Amber: Amber Spratt @ The Ark

Breaking news! People are here in the thousands—there's such an amazing atmosphere right now. No word from the president yet, but we expect more information soon. #excitingtimes

Track 02

OK everyone, so, now I'd like to talk about fake news. This is very much a "hot topic" right now for two reasons. One is because of the large amount of fake news that is out there. The other is we don't recognize it. Although we might be amazingly good at using social media sites, uploading selfies, and texting friends, we aren't so good at figuring out exactly what is fake news and what isn't.

A study of 1,045 adults between the ages of 18 and 34 by the Media Insight Project found that by the age of 18, 88% of young adults received their news from social media. A different study, by Stanford University, of 7,804 students found that 82% of middle-school students couldn't understand the difference between an ad and a real news story. So there is a real need for us to teach young people about fake news.

Track 03

I'd like to talk through some steps you can use to find the real stories among the fake news.

First of all, find out about the source. Look at the website that the story comes from. Then check the text. There might be spelling mistakes, or the text may not be well written. Look at the pictures. Are they clear? If you aren't sure, leave the website and research the organization and its history. Remember that you can trust some websites more than others.

Next, look at the authors. To check if they are authors you can trust, look for proof. What other articles have they written? Who have they written for? If they haven't written anything else for a source you trust, the article could spread fake news.

Check that the article contains links to other news headlines, articles, and authors. Click on the links and check if the sources are real.

Then see if the story you are reading about is shared on any other news websites or channels. If it is, there is a better chance that the story is true. But be careful, because some news websites just copy what others have reported already.

Finally, always question what you read on the internet. Think to yourself, "Some of this story might be true, but it may not show the complete picture." I'll be taking any questions you have in a few moments, so …

Track 04

Male Narrator:

1 anchor
2 translator
3 editor
4 reporter

British Narrator:

1 anchor
2 translator
3 editor
4 reporter

Track 05

British Narrator:

1 anchor

Male Narrator:

2 translator
3 editor

British Narrator:

4 reporter

Track 06

Host: In our special report tonight, we're talking about people working in the world of foreign correspondence. On the phone, I have Dana McDonald, a foreign correspondent based in Mumbai, India. And with me in the studio is Peter Marsden, a translator who travels the world translating from Arabic into English. Dana, can you give us some idea of what a foreign correspondent does?

Dana: Sure. Foreign correspondents write news reports on breaking news stories. Then they send their reports to the news agency that they work for, which is usually abroad. Often we report on what I call "unhappy news"—wars, political troubles, things like that. I wrote about the Mumbai floods in 2017, for example.

Host: It must be hard to do a job like that.

Dana: Well, yes, it can be. But I don't always write about breaking news events. Sometimes I write human-interest stories as well. I love writing about that stuff; I've written reports on a variety of different topics … um, on women getting to vote in villages, for example, and on an Indian professor who is using recycled plastic to make roads.

Host: And what do you like most and least about your job?

Dana: Well, it's definitely a 24-hour-a-day, 7-day-a-week job, which is really stressful. When there's important breaking news, we have to stop whatever we're doing and find out more. But I love that every day is different, and I love India, although I do miss my family and friends back home. I don't see them very often.

Host: Do you speak any Indian languages?

Dana: No, not really. That's why I often have to work with a translator … someone like Peter. I couldn't do the job without a translator.

Host: Yes, Peter. You're a translator from Arabic into English. What's a typical day like for you?

Peter: Well, I don't really have a typical day. One day, I might be working on a written text—perhaps translating a news article into English, for example. And the next day I might be at a United Nations meeting translating for a group of Arab leaders.

Host: And you're a freelance translator. Is that right?

Peter: Yes. That means I work for myself and not for an organization. Working for myself has advantages and disadvantages, but it gives me the ability to choose the work I want to do.

Host: How did you decide you wanted to be a translator?

Peter: I actually studied English and French at college, but then I went to live in Algeria and worked as a teacher for five years. I started learning Arabic, which I love, and then I became a translator.

Host: But you're actually from the US. Is that right?

Peter: Yes, I have a home there, although I don't spend a lot of time there. I travel for about nine months of the year.

Host: Great. Well, thank you to both my guests for their interesting comments. I'll be back at the same time next week with another edition of *Careers Today* and I'll be looking at jobs in …

Track 07

No Story Is Too Small

With the rise of social media and online news sites, local newspapers have had a hard time. However, in a group of small towns in the midwestern United States, print news is fighting back. Gene Nightingale and Matt Emerson, two journalists who were worried about local journalism, decided to start up their own micro newspaper. The newspaper goes on sale once a month and sells around 4,000 copies.

The newspaper is based on the idea that "no story is too small" because they write about small stories, such as how a farmer's field was flooded with water after a pipe burst, and how a new sandbox has been installed in a children's play area.

But it is these "small stories" that are the building blocks for any community. If people are aware of what is happening in their local area, they feel more connected to their community. This connection helps to create strong relationships between people who live in villages, towns, or cities. Whether it is good news, such as a local student winning a national debating competition, or bad news, such as the closure of the town library, the point is that it is news—it is something to discuss and debate and bring people together. Gene and Matt's newspaper provides that essential link.

And local newspapers are in danger. A recent report by the US Bureau of Labor Statistics found that the number of newspaper jobs fell from 458,000 in 1990 (considered to be the start of the internet age) to about 183,000 in 2016. That's a fall of almost 60%. This has an effect on local newspapers in that local news stories are not investigated in the same way. "People depend on Facebook and social media, so what's going on close to home can be ignored by larger newspapers," says Emerson. Local businesses have been very helpful and paid for the first copy of their newspaper. Nightingale and Emerson hope there might be the chance to start up other micro newspapers in other small towns over the next few years.

Unit 10

Track 01

Ask an Expert

Petra Waterhouse from Berlin asks: Are great artists born or made? In other words, is talent genetic or is it learned?

Professor Anna Felix answers: I think the short answer is both.

Musical ability is a good example here because some people are born with greater potential than others, but without hard work and practice, they don't achieve it. A study of 1,211 sets of identical twins born between 1959 and 1985 found that even when one twin practiced music regularly and one didn't, it made no difference. In one case, one man practiced for over 20,000 hours more than his twin, but their musical ability was about the same. This goes some way to showing us that at least some talents are genetic. I believe they are part of our DNA and we probably inherit them from our parents. So, thank you, Mom and Dad!

A different study by Professor Zach Hambrick investigated 14 studies of top chess players and musicians: could their level of ability be explained by their hours of practice? The answer was "no." Practice only made about a 30% difference to how good these people were. In previous research, Hambrick argues that what is important is the ability to remember things. Having an excellent memory can mean the difference between just being smart and being a genius.

One theory is that it takes 10,000 hours of practice to become an expert at something. There is possibly a degree of truth in this (although this will probably depend on what you are practicing). But if your DNA gives you a love of chess, languages, music, or soccer, I'd assume that would make you more likely to be prepared to put in those long hours of practice anyway.

Track 02

1

Host: Hi there, Noel. How are you doing?

Noel: Hi. I'm OK. A little nervous.

Host: Sure. Don't worry—that's totally normal. Do you need some water?

Noel: No, I'm fine now, thank you.

Host: So, why did you want to audition for the show?

Noel: Um … I didn't. It was my cousin, actually. He said he thought I had a great voice. And, uh … you know, he told me I should try to sing live in front of an audience.

Host: Have you filled out the application form?

Noel: Yes, I have it here.

Host: Great. Good luck!

2

Host: Hello, Caitlyn. How are you?

Caitlyn: Oh, I'm great. Very excited!

Host: Tell me—how long have you been doing your act?

Caitlyn: About two years. Well, I've been telling jokes and making people laugh since I was a kid, but this is the first time I've applied to be in a talent show.

Host: And are you feeling confident?

Caitlyn: Definitely! I'm here to win.

Host: Awesome! Go for it, Caitlyn.

3

Bobby: Hi? Can you hear me?
Host: Hi, yes, we can. Who are you?
Bobby: I'm Bobby Jones. I'm here for the talent show auditions.
Charlie: And I'm Charlie!
Host: Hello, both of you! What are you going to do for us today?
Charlie: We're going to make you laugh, aren't we, Bobby?
Bobby: Yes, Charlie. Hopefully!
Host: Fantastic. Looking forward to your act.

Track 03

Noel

Well, that wasn't as bad as I thought it would be. I was so nervous—I nearly chickened out! I'd turned up five minutes late and I thought I might miss the audition, but they were a little late starting, so it was fine. The interviewer asked me whether I needed some water at the beginning, but I was all right. And luckily my voice was OK. The big surprise is that they asked me to come back for the first show in three months! I knew I'd sung my best, but it was still a shock. I'm going to call my cousin and let her know.

Caitlyn

I'm glad that's over! Yeah, um … he asked me how long I'd been doing my act. And he asked me if I was feeling confident. Which I was in the beginning. But then I forgot some of the jokes and I had to make some stuff up. Everything went wrong after that. At one point I thought, "I might as well just give up," but I kept going until the end. There weren't many laughs, to be honest. They said they would let me know in a few weeks. I wish I could try again. Maybe I was just feeling a bit *too* confident …

Bobby

It was a bit strange at the beginning because I was on stage with these bright lights in my face, and I couldn't see anyone or anything! They asked me who I was. And I thought, "I'm going to let Charlie answer this." He said, "I'm Charlie!" and the guy laughed, which was good. And the guy asked what I was going to do, and I made Charlie answer again. I don't think I did too badly, but I don't think it was great, either. I mean, they turn down people all the time, don't they? I'd be quite surprised to hear that I have a place on the show. But who knows?

Track 04

1 a He filled out the form.
  b He filled it out.

2 a She turned down the job.
  b She turned it down.

3 a I gave up dance classes.
  b I gave them up.

Track 05

Andy: Good morning, and welcome back to *Music Matters*. I'm Andy Harvey. On today's five-minute call-in, we have Elsa Hardman, the owner of the successful independent music company Buster Records.
Elsa: Hi, Andy.
Andy: Elsa, your first job was manager of a record store. How did you go from that to starting your own record company?
Elsa: Well, I guess part of it was being in the right place at the right time. Obviously, I knew quite a lot about music, and by chance, I met a guy at a concert who ran a music website, and we became friends. Both of us had our hearts set on having our own record company, so after about 10 years that's what we managed to do. Buster Records was born!
Andy: OK, Elsa, let's talk to our first caller on line 2. Hi, is this Lisa?
Lisa: Yes, it is. Hi.
Andy: Hi. And what's your question for Elsa?
Lisa: Hi, Elsa. I wanted to know how I can start my own music company like you. Is it just an impossible dream?
Elsa: No, Lisa, not at all. You have to dream big! My advice is to go out and meet people. Remember that music industry success is not about what you know, but who you know. And remember to ask people with more experience for help if you need it!
Andy: OK, good advice there. Thanks, Lisa. Now on line 1, we have Gabe. What's your question, Gabe?
Gabe: Hi, yes, I'd like to ask Elsa how I can become a singer. I think I have a good voice, but I don't know where to start …
Elsa: Hi, Gabe. Yes, I get asked this question a lot. First of all, you need to think about your goals and remember to keep them small. If you haven't sung in front of an audience before, try to sing at a small local show and make that your goal for the next few months. Then think about the goals for the following few months and work toward those.
Gabe: OK, yes, that's a good idea. I can do that …
Elsa: Also, and this is important: Start thinking of yourself as a business. Be professional at all times. That shows people that you're hungry for success!
Andy: Well, unfortunately, that's all we have time for today, but I'd like to say a big thank you to Elsa …

Track 06

Talent Contests

The TV talent show *Got Talent*, started by Simon Cowell in 2004, has become a global success story. Viewers watch the shows in 58 countries. In 2014, *Guinness World Records* named it the most successful reality TV show ever. A number of other audition-based shows, such as *The Voice* and *The X Factor*, are also popular with audiences across the planet. And the reason? People love watching the contestants go from nothing to huge success over a few weeks and months. But how did it all start?

Back in 1934, a radio show called *Original Amateur Hour* began in the US. After some success, it moved to TV in 1948. That show was similar to talent shows today. TV professionals traveled the country looking for entertainers who then went to New York for the auditions. The entertainers would audition for the judges on TV, and if chosen, they would come back and audition again. The audience would vote for their favorite act by phone or by mail. The final competition was at Madison Square Garden, and the winners received a trophy and $1,500.

Original Amateur Hour helped to create a number of stars. Frank Sinatra performed on the radio show. Surprisingly, Elvis Presley wasn't successful when he auditioned for the show in Tupelo, Mississippi.

Another talent competition was *Star Search*. *Star Search* was different because entertainers competed in different categories, such as best male singer and best female singer. The prize money was $100,000 for each category. Many well-known pop stars and singing groups auditioned when they were younger, including Justin Timberlake, Destiny's Child, Christina Aguilera, Britney Spears, and Usher.

American Idol started on TV in 2002. Many more TV talent shows followed: *So You Think You Can Dance*, *The X Factor*, *Rockstar INXS*, *The Sing-Off*, *Dancing With the Stars*, and most recently, *The Voice*. Past winners of *Got Talent* include a performing police dog team, acrobats, ventriloquists, wheelchair dancers, and even Rubik's cube puzzle solvers.

Unit 11

Track 01

1

Calling All Computer Game Fans …

We're hiring in your area! Would you like to earn some extra cash? Are you happy to do freelance work from home?

If the answer is "yes," then give Reviews4U a call at 800-555-3210. We're a software company that needs gamers to test our new range of exciting PC games. We'll pay $40 for each gaming review you send to us. No contract, no stress, and hours that work for you.

2

Changes to Our Working and Home Lives

Today's workers no longer expect to have the same job for life. The gig economy means that more and more people are working for themselves, offering their services and time in exchange for cash, but with no contract, no pension, and no vacation or sick pay. The way we take care of chores has changed at home, too. We have people take care of our gardens and yards, we make someone else walk our dogs because we're too busy to do it ourselves, and we get people to decorate our apartments. We have our groceries delivered and we get our houses cleaned. Interestingly, there are things that we used to get *others* to do in the past that we now do *ourselves* because of changes in technology. Now, we book our own flights online instead of getting a travel agent to do it for us. We also manage our own money online without the help of a bank clerk.

3

Every Day is Different!

CeeCee Rogers, a tech worker in New York City, was laid off in 2018. She knew it might take a long time to find another job in her field.

"I wasn't sure what to do," explains CeeCee. "When I lost my job, it was a big shock. Luckily, I found out about GigGetters and I signed up with them. They have me do various gigs so I can make money while I'm looking for a more permanent job." I enjoy it. No day is the same!"

Track 02

Simon: Welcome to *Money Matters* with me, Simon Bagshaw. Now, we often hear about some of the world's largest donors—people such as Bill and Melinda Gates and George Soros. Their donations make an enormous difference in lives and communities around the world. George Soros, for example, has donated over $18 billion to charity.
But what can ordinary people do to help charities? Many people decide to give cash, but how do you help if you can't afford to donate money? With me in the studio are the local campaign managers for two charities: Pat Beresford, campaign manager for the children's charity Rainbows, and Danny Hamer, campaign manager for the environmental charity Action for Earth. They are the people whose job it is to think of new ways to raise money. Welcome to *Money Matters*, both of you.

Pat: Thank you.

Danny: Thanks.

Simon: Pat, let's start with you first. Let's say I want to help your charity, Rainbows, but I don't have any money to donate. What can I do?

Pat: Well, there are lots and lots of things you can do as an individual, Simon. What we say to people is, if you can't help us with money, you can help us with your time. You can become a volunteer in one of our thrift stores around the country. We love to see young people giving their time in this way.

Simon: But what if you work full-time and you can't do that?

Pat: Well, there are many one-day fundraising events. We organize lots of events throughout the year—bake sales, music events, spelling bees … Some people prefer doing these events because it's a great way to spend time with friends and family. Or, you can make a contribution by getting people to pay you for completing a fun run or a marathon.

Simon: I'm not very sporty! Anything else, Danny?

Danny: Sure. Some people hate doing sports. But have you considered playing games online? Nowadays, there are lots of online quizzes that you can do. For every correct answer, companies will pay a certain amount to a charity.

Simon: Sounds like a great idea.

Danny: Yes, it started about 10 years ago with an organization called Free Rice. Basically, you go online and answer vocabulary questions. For every question you get correct, they donate 10 grains of rice to feed hungry people. It became popular so charities keep using this technique.

Simon: I'll check it out.

Pat: Another thing you might consider doing if you travel abroad often is to donate all the foreign currency that you have left at the end of a trip. Sometimes this happens on airplanes. The crew will offer to collect all your foreign currency and give it to a charity. Last year, we received $21,000 this way.

Simon: Yes, I've done that at the end of a few flights. Well, some great ideas there. Thank you both for giving me an idea of the small ways we can all contribute and make a big difference. Next week, we'll be discussing what to do if …

Track 03

change cash machine

Track 04

1 Do you have any change?
2 I'm going to use the cash machine.

Track 05

Host: So, as a follow-up to last week's program about how to make your money go further, we thought we'd ask different people on the street how they manage their money. Here are some of their answers:

Speaker 1: My brother got me into using computer programs like Excel and Google Spreadsheets, actually. He showed me how you can add all the information about what you spend, and it tells you how much money you have remaining until the end of the month. I don't like borrowing money from the bank, so I don't have credit cards, but I use a debit card for most of the stuff I buy. These days, so many payments are contactless, which suits me because I'm always forgetting my PIN.

Speaker 2: I guess I'm part of the generation that controls everything through their smartphone. I use my phone for online banking and that works fine, and I also use my phone to move money between bank accounts and to make payments to people. I have an app that's really useful for my business account—it tells me what I'm spending, but also how much I should pay into my pension and into the business itself. It costs me about $100 a year, but it's worth the money.

Speaker 3: Well, I'm from the older generation, and I think one of the best ways to manage your money is to write down what you spend. That's my first rule. I have a notebook that I carry with me and I make a note of everything I spend and everything I earn. I still use checks, too, although not so many stores accept them anymore. I also have online banking, but personally, I think it's much better if I can have a written record of my money. Oh, and my other rule is to only use my credit card in emergencies. And I always pay all the money I owe every month! I think I'm very sensible in that way.

Speaker 4: I'm actually really bad at managing my money. I don't really splurge on stuff, but I just find money management a really boring thing to do. That's why I'm happy to get someone else to do it for me. I have a financial planner who does all the stuff that I don't like doing. She organizes and pays my bills and checks my bank account—that kind of thing. I used to do it myself, but now that I have a large, growing business, it has become too hard. And to be honest, if I can get someone to do the stuff I don't like doing, it gives me more time to actually make money!

Track 06

Business Profile: KylieBelle's Bakery

Meet Annabelle Eggers and Kylie Howell, a pair of high school friends who recently set up KylieBelle's Bakery, a bakery and coffee shop on the North Shore. The pair both left successful careers in law to start their own business. But things didn't get off to a good start.

"It hasn't been easy," Kylie explains, when we meet up at the bakery on a Sunday morning. "I don't think we realized how much hard work it would be. We thought we'd be doing the jobs we love all day, which for us is making cakes and serving customers. But actually, there's a lot more involved, like accounting. Also, we had an awful first day." The pair had to close the bakery after a serious fire in their kitchen on the day they opened. "It was terrible," admits Annabelle. "We thought we might not be able to afford to open again after the accident. We were both in tears."

Luckily, a local resident, Marlene Parks, offered to help by investing over $10,000 in the business. "I was looking for a small business to invest some money in," says Marlene. "And who doesn't love a nice bakery in their local area? I hope the business does really well and I wish Annabelle and Kylie lots of luck." The women used the money to get builders to repair the kitchen, and the bakery reopened two weeks later.

"Thanks to Marlene, we were able to get the business open again. We need to pay her back, obviously, but it meant we could start making money. The business is doing really well. We're going to have a new seating area built outside so we can serve more of our cakes. People love our white chocolate cheesecake!"

Unit 12

Track 01

Advertising Around the World: Who Controls What?

As you might expect in the modern world, more and more advertising is being controlled by strict rules. In the US, the Federal Trade Commission (FTC) makes sure that all ads are accurate. In the UK, this is done by the Advertising Standards Agency (ASA), which in

2017 received about 30,000 complaints about ads. The job of these agencies is to decide if certain rules are broken by advertisers. These might include making false promises about the product or using offensive images. The FTC and the ASA decide if the ad can be shown or if it has to be removed.

Ads that you might think aren't very offensive can cause lots of complaints. A TV ad showing people talking with their mouths full of food received the most complaints in the ASA's history. People felt that this ad might encourage bad habits in children. In 2017, another TV ad for fried chicken that showed chickens dancing to rap music was criticized for being offensive to vegetarians and vegans. The request was turned down by the ASA.

Each country has different rules about what they allow. A famous series of billboard ads made by a fashionable Italian clothing company caused problems in countries where they appeared. One ad, showing a very young baby, shocked a lot of people. In Sicily, the company was ordered by the town officials to remove the ad. It is interesting that what shocks some people is loved by others. It was given a prize by the Swiss General Poster Association, and a hospital in Bologna asked permission to display the ad on its walls.

Some ads have been banned, not for showing offensive images, but for the way they market the product. A well-known soft drink ad campaign, which had been seen by millions, was removed for showing a famous celebrity sharing her drink with a police officer at a protest event. The message is just as important as the image.

Track 02

Male marketing executive:

When we're thinking about our advertising campaigns, one of the first things we have to do is carefully identify our target market. If we don't know who we're marketing our product to, then it just won't sell. We identify our customers using six different categories: gender—so male or female; age; occupation or job; relationship status—so married, single, divorced, et cetera; geographic location; and behavior.

Once our target customer has been identified, we start to think about how we're going to promote the product, and how to make *our* product the most attractive product to that group of people. One thing that is different between marketing to young adults and marketing to older people is the type of music we use in the ad campaign. Young people want faster, more energetic music, whereas older people—and when I say older, I mean over 60—well, they want music that is calmer and less noisy. And in TV or radio ads directed at older people, the actors usually speak more seriously and less quickly.

Then we have to come up with a slogan. Let's say we're advertising a new face cream. The slogan has to say something about the product in a phrase or short sentence. It has to be clear and easy to remember. We can't just say, "Buy our face cream because it's the best!" or "These running shoes will help you run faster!" We work very hard to get the perfect slogan, but the more often you do it, the easier it gets.

Then, of course, we have to think about designing the logo for the product—and then launching the product in the most exciting way, so people become interested in it quickly. And at the same time, we have to manage the budget so we use the money we have …

Track 03

Ad announcer:

It isn't just about you. It's about your dreams. It's about not giving up. It's about knowing you only get one chance to be the best you can be. Push harder. Run faster. Set your goals higher. Be the best. Because you can. Lion Aid Energy Drinks. The choice of true champions.

Track 04

Speaker 1: Working in advertising means that I spend a lot of time thinking about image and appearance. It's important that we get the right look in our ads. But we try not to over-edit. By that, I mean we want to make sure our models look natural and healthy. And we try to set our ads in real situations. Situations that people can … um … understand and connect with. People in our ads should look the same as the people in our target market and … uh … I think in our latest ad campaign, we've managed to do that. As a result, sales so far have been very good.

Speaker 2: I'm a model, and recently my agent had a photographer take pictures of me for a commercial. They were for possible jobs with a famous fashion company. About three weeks later, my agent emailed me the pictures that the photographer had taken and the photoshopped pictures. I was shocked when I saw them. Although I knew it was me, it didn't look like me at all. They'd made my face look really thin and moved my eyes up and made my nose smaller. I felt quite angry … hmm … Well, I know it happens all the time, but when you see your face changed like that … I mean, do they need to have models anymore or can they just use computer images?

Speaker 3: My friends and I play this game sometimes. We look at … um … magazine ads and try to find the funniest photoshopped images. You might think ad companies would … you know … check the images carefully, especially when they go on the front cover. But there are lots of mistakes. Sometimes you notice things such as … such as an image where the model's leg is missing or the model has an extra finger. Or they've made someone's head look … um … too big for their body. It's so funny! That's why we love ads I guess!

Speaker 4: I don't think people pay that much attention to ads, do they? I never feel like I see an ad and think, "Oh, yes, I really *have to* get one of those" or "I *have to* have that!" It's like … when I'm shopping, what makes me pick up certain things and buy them? Do you think that's due to an ad? I don't think I buy things due to an ad. I think it's because I just want to try … um … *that* cheese or *that* new shampoo. Ads are a waste of time, in my opinion. I buy stuff because I want to, not because I've heard a slogan or seen a logo!

Track 05

Situations that people can … um … understand and connect with.
I felt quite angry … hmm …
You might think ad companies would … you know … check the images carefully …
It's like … when I'm shopping, what makes me pick up certain things and things and buy them?

Track 06

Storyboards: What You Need to Know

Have you ever come up with the most fantastic idea for an ad—or perhaps a home-made video—but had a problem getting your ideas down on paper? Then you need a storyboard!

What Is a Storyboard?

A storyboard is a series of sketches, drawn in the style of a comic. It shows every scene of the ad. It shows what characters are in the scene, what they are doing, and what they are saying. A good storyboard will help you imagine the ad. It shows the production team what to photograph and in what order. It communicates ideas without long, wordy descriptions. As more people become involved in making the ad and give their opinions, the storyboard may develop and change.

How to Make a Storyboard

A storyboard doesn't have to be complicated. Here's how to make one:

Step 1: Make a template

Draw a series of squares or rectangles on a plain piece of paper, one for each scene. Leave room underneath the squares or rectangles for notes. You can also find free storyboards online.

Step 2: Draw the story

Don't worry if you aren't very good at drawing. You can use simple stick figures in the boxes. Show any movement with an arrow or short parallel lines.

Step 3: Add the dialogue

Write any dialogue underneath the pictures. You can also make a silent video where no dialogue is necessary.

Step 4: Add notes

These might include instructions for camera angles, descriptions of the actions in the scene, or ideas for music.
Good luck!

Workbook Answer Key

Unit 1

Lesson 1

READING A c

READING B **1** b **2** a **3** b **4** c **5** c **6** a

VOCABULARY A **1** impossible **2** achieve **3** turn into **4** select **5** disease **6** able-bodied **7** recognize **8** disabled

VOCABULARY B **1** disease **2** select **3** recognize **4** turn into **5** able-bodied **6** impossible **7** disabled **8** achieve

GRAMMAR A **1** Stative, *believe* **2** Dynamic, *watch* **3** progressive **4** think

GRAMMAR B **1** are looking / look **2** is **3** has **4** working **5** feel / am feeling **6** is running

GRAMMAR C **1** True **2** False **3** False **4** False **5** True **6** True

GRAMMAR D **1** are recovering **2** are thinking **3** are **4** know **5** need **6** Are you having

Lesson 2

VOCABULARY A **1** achievement **2** development **3** impossibility **4** illness **5** kindness **6** argument **7** responsibility **8** possibility

VOCABULARY B **1** impossibility **2** achievement **3** development **4** argument **5** sadness **6** availability **7** responsibility **8** hardness **9** possibility **10** illness **11** kindness

LISTENING A **1** can't **2** more than one **3** worse **4** order **5** was given

LISTENING B **1** b **2** b **3** a **4** a **5** b **6** a

GRAMMAR A **1** general, present **2** particular, difficulty **3** general, past, present **4** particular, difficulty **5** general, past

GRAMMAR B **1** succeeded in **2** could **3** managed to **4** can **5** are able to / can

GRAMMAR C **1** ~~become~~ becoming **2** ~~could~~ can **3** ~~could~~ managed to / ~~could get~~ succeeded in getting **4** ~~be able to~~ can **5** ~~can~~ could

GRAMMAR D **1** can't / am not able to **2** succeeded in **3** manage to **4** could / was able to **5** could / was able to **6** succeeded in **7** manage to

Lesson 3

VOCABULARY A **1** c **2** a **3** c **4** c **5** b **6** b **7** a **8** b **9** a

VOCABULARY B **1** curious **2** calm **3** confident **4** creative **5** generous **6** reliable **7** independent **8** selfish **9** brave

LISTENING A **1** a climber who had an accident **2** didn't change

LISTENING B **1** False **2** True **3** False **4** False **5** True **6** True

WRITING A **1** f **2** c **3** b **4** e **5** g **6** a **7** d

WRITING B **1** f **2** e **3** d **4** g **5** b **6** a **7** c

Unit 2

Lesson 1

READING A **1** stick, mat **2** pick up, come, go **3** elephants

READING B **1** similar to **2** objects **3** on top of **4** off **5** cannot **6** your body affects things

VOCABULARY A **1** cute **2** behavior **3** smell **4** intelligent **5** sight

VOCABULARY B **1** cute **2** sight **3** intelligent **4** behavior **5** smell

GRAMMAR A **1** *be* **2** *do* **3** modal **4** negative **5** positive

GRAMMAR B **1** aren't they **2** isn't it **3** don't they **4** is it **5** can they **6** are we

GRAMMAR C **1** isn't, don't **2** aren't, is **3** doesn't, can't **4** are, is

GRAMMAR D **1** ~~don't~~ do **2** ~~studies~~ doesn't **3** ~~doesn't~~ isn't **4** ~~aren't~~ are **5** ~~does~~ can **6** ~~don't~~ aren't

Lesson 2

LISTENING A **1** her routine as a dog trainer **2** her qualifications as a dog trainer **3** the things she teaches dogs to do

LISTENING B **1** b **2** c **3** a **4** a **5** b

VOCABULARY A **1** marine biologist **2** zoologist **3** veterinarian **4** zookeeper **5** breeder **6** horse trainer **7** wildlife photographer **8** dog handler

VOCABULARY B **1** wildlife photographer **2** veterinarian **3** horse trainer **4** zoologist **5** marine biologist **6** dog handler

GRAMMAR A **1** b **2** a **3** a

GRAMMAR B **1** a **2** — **3** the **4** — **5** an **6** the

GRAMMAR C **1** — **2** an **3** the **4** an **5** — **6** the **7** a **8** —/the

GRAMMAR D **1** A, a, an, the **2** A, —, The, — **3** A, —, the, — **4** A, the, the, a **5** A, an, —, an **6** —, —, —, the

Lesson 3

VOCABULARY A **1** Whales **2** turtle **3** Pumas **4** porcupine **5** polar bear **6** Tigers **7** Hippos **8** shark **9** crocodile **10** Dolphins

VOCABULARY B **1** crocodile **2** hippo **3** polar bear **4** porcupine **5** puma **6** tiger **7** turtle **8** dolphin **9** shark **10** whale

LISTENING A **1** square miles **2** natural habitats **3** not 100% natural **4** endangered animals **5** use the money

LISTENING B **1** thousands **2** rivers **3** fence **4** hippos **5** preservation

WRITING A **1** a **2** b **3** a

Unit 3

Lesson 1

READING A **1** a **2** a **3** b **4** b **5** **6**

READING B **1** ~~quick~~ slow **2** ~~often~~ rare **3** ~~happy~~ depressed **4** ~~chose~~ didn't choose **5** ~~positive~~ negative **6** ~~forget~~ remember

VOCABULARY A **1** c **2** c **3** b **4** a **5** b **6** a **7** c

VOCABULARY B **1** relevant **2** ignore **3** make an effort **4** pay attention to **5** concentrate on **6** rarely **7** evidence

GRAMMAR A **1** specific **2** future **3** present **4** before / after, before / after, doesn't

GRAMMAR B **1** will you attend, finish **2** buys, will regret **3** will not (won't), have **4** drive, will put **5** Will you get, are

GRAMMAR C **1** will be **2** until **3** finds **4** Before **5** after

GRAMMAR D **1** b **2** b **3** a **4** b **5** b

Lesson 2

LISTENING A **1** not worried **2** negative **3** impressed **4** confident **5** not be afraid

LISTENING B **1** a **2** a **3** b **4** a **5** c **6** c

VOCABULARY A **1** creative **2** powerful **3** solution **4** dangerous **5** employer **6** creation **7** powerless **8** thought **9** employee

GRAMMAR A **1** *has/have* **2** past **3** result **4** present perfect **5** *since* **6** *for*

GRAMMAR B **1** have been cleaning **2** have, for **3** been, since **4** working **5** have been, for **6** been trying, since

GRAMMAR C **1** ~~has~~ have **2** ~~since~~ for **3** ~~for~~ since **4** ~~was~~ been **5** ~~hadn't~~ hasn't **6** ~~since~~ for

GRAMMAR D **1** have you been doing **2** Have you been enjoying **3** haven't you uploaded **4** have been working **5** have been testing **6** haven't been using **7** has been using

Lesson 3

VOCABULARY A **1** come up with **2** make up **3** give up **4** take up **5** rely on **6** look up

VOCABULARY B **1** make up **2** take up **3** give up **4** rely on **5** look up **6** come up with

LISTENING A **1** students **2** have not **3** Convergent **4** Brainstorming **5** Deferring judgement

LISTENING B **1** False **2** False **3** True **4** True **5** True **6** False

WRITING A **1** c **2** h **3** d **4** b **5** g **6** e **7** f **8** a

Unit 4

Lesson 1

READING A **1** listener **2** eye contact **3** imagine in your mind **4** feel

READING B **1** b **2** b **3** a **4** b

VOCABULARY A **1** a **2** a **3** b **4** b

VOCABULARY B **1** persuade **2** common **3** connection **4** honest

GRAMMAR A **1** to express a purpose **2** after some verbs + direct object **3** after some verbs **4** after some adjectives

GRAMMAR B **1** to wear **2** to appear **3** to drink **4** to take **5** to learn **6** to give

GRAMMAR C **1** find **2** communicate **3** practice **4** smile **5** listen **6** let

Lesson 2

VOCABULARY A **1** volume **2** speed **3** distance **4** tone **5** space **6** touch **7** position

VOCABULARY B **1** distance **2** tone **3** speed **4** touch **5** position **6** volume **7** space

LISTENING A **1** a **2** b **3** b

LISTENING B **1** both hands **2** Africa **3** respect **4** not honest **5** appropriate **6** the Philippines

GRAMMAR A **1** can **2** noun **3** always **4** never

GRAMMAR B **1** hang the phone up **2** get off the bus **3** make an excuse up **4** come up with a plan **5** look it up **6** get along with them

GRAMMAR C **1** on it **2** it off **3** it out **4** it up **5** it down **6** into it

GRAMMAR D **1** I need to call my sister back. **2** My paper wasn't good, so I need to do it over. **3** Can you fill this form out, please? **4** If you get a bad grade, it's hard to get over it. **5** Our test is tomorrow, so we have to look Unit 3 over. **6** When I ran into Sonia, I stopped to chat.

Lesson 3

LISTENING A **1** b **2** c **3** c

LISTENING B Imagery of famous people with a bit of text which expressed an idea 3. Illustrations with text that focused on personal experiences 2. Illustrations with a great deal of text 1. Advertisements that flash and play videos 4.

VOCABULARY A **1** shake hands **2** wave **3** thumbs up **4** smile

WRITING A **1** Guess what? **2** How's the Blues Café sound? **3** Is 5:30 OK? **4** Can you come? **5** Text me back and let me know. **6** See you later!

WRITING B **1** take place **2** bring a guest **3** look forward

Unit 5

Lesson 1

VOCABULARY A **1** b **2** b **3** a **4** b **5** a **6** a

READING A **1** not everyone **2** not as bad as **3** contribute to **4** serious

READING B **1** a **2** b **3** b **4** a

GRAMMAR A **1** simple present verb, simple present verb **2** simple present verb, *will/won't*, base verb **3** simple past verb, *would/wouldn't*, base verb

GRAMMAR B **1** feels **2** change **3** would have **4** were **5** will need **6** calls

Lesson 2

VOCABULARY A **1** reduce **2** pay a fine **3** don't allow **4** provide **5** require **6** create laws

VOCABULARY B **1** provide **2** don't allow **3** pay a fine **4** reduce **5** create laws **6** require

LISTENING A **1** essential **2** hasn't always **3** they were doing **4** didn't have **5** Not everybody

LISTENING B **1** False **2** False **3** True **4** True **5** False **6** False

GRAMMAR A **1** simple past **2** simple present **3** present progressive **4** *would/could, would/could*

GRAMMAR B **1** will **2** would stop **3** were **4** is working **5** stops **6** could

GRAMMAR C **1** ~~will~~ would **2** ~~staying~~ stay **3** ~~will~~ would **4** ~~would not be~~ wasn't **5** ~~could~~ can **6** ~~got~~ get

GRAMMAR D **1** could go **2** can be **3** didn't have **4** can leave **5** is **6** would relax **7** is having

Lesson 3

LISTENING A **1** b **2** a **3** a

LISTENING B **1** c **2** c **3** b **4** b **5** b **6** a

VOCABULARY A **1** roof **2** rubber **3** net **4** steel **5** flip-flop **6** pot **7** coconut **8** tire

WRITING A **1** f **2** c **3** d **4** e **5** b **6** a

Unit 6

Lesson 1

READING A **1** True **2** True **3** False **4** True

READING B **1** the Chinese **2** rough materials **3** ancient Babylon **4** 1286 **5** 15th century **6** Benjamin Franklin

VOCABULARY A **1** ~~tiny~~ **2** ~~opening~~ **3** ~~usually~~ **4** ~~destruction~~ **5** ~~small~~ **6** ~~failure~~

VOCABULARY B **1** major **2** improvement **3** particularly **4** enormous **5** end **6** creation

GRAMMAR A **1** past perfect **2** simple past **3** *had*

GRAMMAR B **1** had already received **2** got **3** started **4** had gone **5** remembered **6** had hired

GRAMMAR C **1** friend found a cheaper one **2** not installed the software **3** received lots of likes **4** forgot about the event **5** posted a short video **6** not used a tablet

GRAMMAR D **1** ~~already learned~~ had already learned **2** ~~had set up~~ set up **3** ~~went~~ had gone **4** ~~had first appeared~~ first appeared **5** ~~didn't start~~ hadn't started **6** ~~started~~ had started

Lesson 2

LISTENING A **1** b **2** c **3** a

LISTENING B **1** uses passwords **2** robots **3** he might lose his job **4** drones **5** she has concerns about spying

VOCABULARY A **1** bored **2** amused **3** relaxing **4** amazing **5** disappointing **6** entertained

VOCABULARY B **1** amazed **2** boring **3** amusing **4** disappointed

GRAMMAR A **1** *who* **2** person **3** *where* **4** place **5** *when* **6** time **7** which **8** object **9** *that*

GRAMMAR B **1** where **2** who **3** that **4** which **5** where **6** when

GRAMMAR C **1** that **2** when **3** who **4** that **5** where **6** who

GRAMMAR D **1** b **2** a **3** c **4** c **5** b **6** a

Lesson 3

LISTENING A **1** an optical system **2** a source of a disease **3** a type of television **4** a type of jetpack

LISTENING B **1** 1958 **2** 1993 **3** 40 **4** 1833 **5** 1917 **6** 17 **7** 1954 **8** 1,450 **9** 13,500 **10** 30 **11** 125,000 **12** 30

VOCABULARY A **1** capable **2** thankful **3** successful **4** hopeful **5** incredible **6** hopeless

VOCABULARY B **1** hopeful **2** successful **3** capable **4** thankful **5** hopeless **6** incredible

WRITING A **1** gives an idea on what the topic will be about **2** sets a specific angle for the article **3** gives basic biographical facts about the person **4** restates the angle of the article

Unit 7

Lesson 1

READING A **1** b **2** c **3** a

VOCABULARY A **1** came across **2** burned up **3** turned out **4** looked into **5** went up **6** found out

GRAMMAR A **1** *have*, past participle, past **2** *not, should, have*

GRAMMAR B **1** ~~has~~ have **2** ~~send~~ sent **3** ~~should~~ shouldn't **4** ~~waste~~ wasted **5** ~~shouldn't~~ should **6** ~~had~~ have

GRAMMAR C **1** should have said **2** should have ignored **3** shouldn't have destroyed **4** should have done **5** should have acted **6** shouldn't have behaved

Lesson 2

VOCABULARY A **1** lose **2** waste **3** lose **4** spends **5** wasted **6** spend

VOCABULARY B **1** spend **2** lose **3** spend **4** waste **5** waste **6** lose

LISTENING A **1** negatively **2** essential **3** can

LISTENING B **1** Diana **2** Lucia **3** Lucia **4** Diana **5** Diana **6** Lucia

GRAMMAR A **1** didn't go **2** agreed **3** *wish*, *had*, past participle

GRAMMAR B **1** had flown **2** had made **3** had never met **4** had never gone **5** hadn't gone **6** hadn't thrown

GRAMMAR C **1** ~~complained~~ had complained **2** ~~did~~ done **3** ~~ever~~ never **4** ~~have~~ had **5** ~~took~~ had taken **6** ~~told~~ had told

GRAMMAR D **1** wish I had gone **2** wishes she hadn't lost **3** wish we hadn't / had never moved **4** wish I hadn't spent **5** wishes he hadn't sent **6** wish I hadn't chosen

Lesson 3

LISTENING A **1** nothing **2** have separated **3** not going to **4** criticize **5** an

LISTENING B **1** True **2** False **3** True **4** False **5** False **6** True

VOCABULARY A **1** miss **2** spend **3** lose **4** turn down **5** waste **6** get in **7** break up **8** stay

WRITING A **1** say **2** believe **3** feelings **4** opinion **5** feel **6** In

WRITING B **1** We are told that **2** Another argument is **3** I have mixed feelings about **4** I think that **5** I also believe

Unit 8

Lesson 1

VOCABULARY A **1** tidal wave **2** extinction **3** herbivore **4** asteroid **5** soot **6** crater **7** carnivore **8** debris

VOCABULARY B **1** herbivore **2** extinction **3** soot **4** crater **5** asteroid **6** debris **7** carnivore **8** tidal wave

READING A **1** b **2** b **3** b **4** a

READING B **1** False **2** False **3** True **4** True **5** True **6** True

GRAMMAR A **1** *if* **2** past perfect **3** past participle **4** hypothetical **5** past

GRAMMAR B **1** had hit, would have lost **2** had stayed, might have felt **3** had started, couldn't have burned **4** might have faced, had struck **5** would have covered, had erupted **6** wouldn't have discovered, had failed

Lesson 2

VOCABULARY A **1** shuttle **2** outer **3** capsule **4** zero **5** Station

VOCABULARY B **1** spacecraft **2** International Space Station **3** outer space **4** space capsule **5** space shuttle

LISTENING A **1** False **2** True **3** False **4** False

LISTENING B **1** second-closest **2** 34 and 250 **3** 6 to 10 **4** 438 **5** 20 to minus 125 **6** researching

GRAMMAR A **1** *be* **2** before **3** after **4** *yes/no* **5** *if* or *whether*

GRAMMAR B **1** the first person traveled **2** astronauts can live **3** if people will live **4** you move **5** if Mars has **6** there is

GRAMMAR C **1** Earth looks **2** zero gravity feels **3** Can people get **4** do astronauts return **5** the temperature becomes **6** it travels

GRAMMAR D **1** what living on Mars would be like **2** how you eat food in space **3** if/whether people in space get taller **4** how far you can go outside the spacecraft **5** what it would be like to stand on Jupiter **6** if/whether we will ever travel to Pluto

Lesson 3

LISTENING A **1** b **2** b **3** a

LISTENING B **1** True **2** False **3** True **4** True **5** True **6** False

VOCABULARY A **1** water filters **2** wireless headsets **3** memory foam **4** home insulation **5** cordless vacuums **6** foil blankets

VOCABULARY B **1** ~~blanket~~ vacuum **2** ~~insulation~~ filter **3** ~~foam~~ insulation **4** ~~vacuum~~ foam **5** ~~filter~~ headset **6** ~~foil~~ blanket

WRITING A **1** and **2** Furthermore **3** but **4** Nevertheless

Unit 9

Lesson 1

READING A **1** b **2** c **3** c

READING B **1** True **2** False **3** False **4** True **5** True **6** False

VOCABULARY A **1** government **2** effect **3** trend **4** human-interest story **5** industry

GRAMMAR A **1** adjective, noun **2** adjective, adverb **3** adjective, adverb **4** adjective, adverb, *enough*

GRAMMAR B **1** not good enough **2** such a **3** too **4** so **5** so much **6** not hungry enough **7** such **8** too

GRAMMAR C **1** such **2** enough **3** so **4** too **5** too **6** enough **7** enough **8** so

Lesson 2

VOCABULARY A **1** c **2** b **3** c **4** b **5** c **6**a

LISTENING A **1** d **2** e **3** a **4** f **5** c **6** b

LISTENING B **1** b **2** a **3** b **4** b **5** c **6** a

GRAMMAR A **1** *can't*, *be* **2** *might*, *be*, true **3** *must*, *be*, true

GRAMMAR B **1** can't **2** might **3** must **4** may **5** could

GRAMMAR C **1** ~~must~~ can't **2** ~~may~~ must **3** ~~must~~ could/may/might **4** ~~could~~ must **5** ~~can't~~ could/may/might

GRAMMAR D **1** could/may/might **2** can't **3** must **4** could/may/might **5** could/may/might **6** must **7** can't

Lesson 3

VOCABULARY A **1** photojournalist **2** translator **3** investigative journalist **4** news anchor **5** sports journalist **6** foreign correspondent **7** newspaper editor **8** reporter

VOCABULARY B **1** reporter **2** investigative journalist **3** newspaper editor **4** photojournalist **5** news anchor

LISTENING A **Brian** c **Jason** e **Leyla** a **Casey** d **Renee** b

LISTENING B **1** False **2** True **3** False **4** False **5** True

WRITING A **1** feel **2** it **3** find **4** As **5** In

Unit 10

Lesson 1

READING A **1** Opinion **2** Fact **3** Fact **4** Opinion **5** Opinion **6** Fact **7** Fact **8** Fact **9** Opinion

VOCABULARY A **1** identical twins **2** talent **3** theory **4** potential **5** memory

GRAMMAR A **1** simple past **2** past progressive **3** past perfect **4** past perfect **5** *will* becomes *would* **6** direct **7** past

GRAMMAR B **1** Frankie had potential in soccer **2** plays very well **3** she was practicing the guitar **4** You'll do well in math **5** he had lost the competition **6** They did very well

GRAMMAR C **1** she danced beautifully **2** the band was performing **3** he hadn't done so well **4** she hadn't performed **5** Maria would become **6** they had never sung

Lesson 2

LISTENING A **1** b **2** c **3** b **4** b

LISTENING B **1** a dance contest **2** second **3** improved **4** harm **5** is not happy **6** sci-fi series

VOCABULARY A **1** turned **2** turn **3** fill **4** come **5** kept **6** keep **7** turn **8** come **9** fill **10** show

VOCABULARY B **1** back **2** out **3** down **4** on **5** back

GRAMMAR A **1** a **2** a **3** b **4** b **5** b **6** a

GRAMMAR B **1** if she enjoyed **2** they had been **3** the lead performer was **4** had **5** was coming **6** if

GRAMMAR C **1** if she had heard about the talent contest **2** what she was practicing **3** if he would enter the contest **4** if he had taken lessons **5** where a good music school was **6** what day was the best for him

GRAMMAR D **1** ~~are my favorite comedians~~ my favorite comedians were **2** ~~was my dad~~ if/whether my dad was **3** ~~had I~~ if/whether I had **4** ~~has Rebecca~~ Rebecca had **5** ~~have they~~ if/whether they had **6** ~~am I not~~ I wasn't

Lesson 3

VOCABULARY A **1** Dream **2** be hungry **3** have your heart **4** who you know **5** set your sights **6** be in the right place

LISTENING A **1** False **2** True **3** False **4** False **5** True

LISTENING B **1** inspires you **2** set a work time limit **3** attend many events **4** expand your knowledge **5** do every kind of show you can

WRITING A **1** informal greeting **2** reason for writing **3** informal punctuation **4** informal closing **5** signature

WRITING B **1** b **2** a **3** a **4** b

Unit 11

Lesson 1

READING A **1** not what **2** similar to **3** the person you need **4** their strengths

VOCABULARY A **1** lay off **2** permanent **3** contract **4** in exchange for **5** hire **6** pension

GRAMMAR A **1** paying **2** forcing **3** *do* **4** persuading

GRAMMAR B **1** gets **2** to pay **3** look **4** written **5** makes **6** have

Lesson 2

VOCABULARY A **1** donation **2** contributor **3** donate **4** donor **5** contribution **6** contribute

VOCABULARY B **1** donation **2** contributors **3** donor **4** contribute **5** contribution **6** donate

LISTENING A 1 knowing where our money goes is important 2 feeling better about themselves

LISTENING B 1 False 2 True 3 False 4 True 5 False 6 True

GRAMMAR A 1 agree decide offer 2 deny keep suggest 3 prefer love hate

GRAMMAR B 1 to donate 2 to tell / telling 3 playing 4 to drive 5 being / to be

GRAMMAR C 1 ~~to dance~~ dancing 2 to eat ~~eating~~ 3 ~~going~~ to go 4 ~~to watch~~ watching 5 ~~to give~~ giving 6 ~~working~~ to work

GRAMMAR D 1 eating 2 working 3 to give / giving 4 volunteering 5 to go 6 wasting / to waste 7 to lend 8 working 9 to spend / spending 10 hiring

Lesson 3

VOCABULARY A 1 credit cards 2 debit card 3 cash machine 4 contactless payment 5 cash 6 change

LISTENING A 1 had money stolen from her 2 is 3 some 4 thinks 5 credit card

LISTENING B 1 a 2 c 3 c 4 b 5 a

WRITING A 1 you should only bring 2 in my opinion it's better 3 if I were you 4 my advice is to 5 I'd say that you should consider 6 I think it would be best if

Unit 12

Lesson 1

READING A 1 advertising strategy 2 oil companies 3 for problematic celebrities

READING B 1 c 2 a 3 d 4 b

VOCABULARY A 1 permission 2 criticize 3 remove 4 complaint 5 ban

VOCABULARY B 1 ask for permission from 2 banned 3 criticized 4 sent written complaints 5 remove

GRAMMAR A 1 simple present passive 2 simple past passive 3 present progressive passive 4 present perfect passive 5 past perfect passive 6 less important 7 don't know 8 transitive

GRAMMAR B 1 was criticized 2 is being shown 3 have been sold 4 had been heard 5 wasn't banned 6 have been made

Lesson 2

VOCABULARY A 1 manage a budget 2 designs a logo 3 come up with a slogan 4 promotes a product 5 launch a product 6 identify the target market

VOCABULARY B 1 come up with a slogan 2 launch the product 3 manage the budget 4 design the logo 5 promote the product 6 identify the target market

LISTENING A 1 b, c 2 a, c 3 b, c 4 b

GRAMMAR A 1 comparative 2 superlative 3 Irregular 4 before

GRAMMAR B 1 b 2 b 3 a 4 c 5 b

GRAMMAR C 1 ~~the most closely~~ more closely 2 ~~careful~~ more carefully 3 ~~fast~~ faster 4 ~~wiser~~ more wisely

GRAMMAR D 1 worse 2 the most easily 3 more beautifully 4 harder 5 more quickly 6 the most angrily

Lesson 3

VOCABULARY A 1 ~~because~~, ~~such as~~ 2 ~~however~~, ~~as a result~~ 3 ~~too~~, ~~although~~ 4 ~~for instance~~, ~~as well as~~

VOCABULARY B 1 as well as 2 such as 3 due to 4 whereas 5 for instance 6 as a result 7 although 8 In addition

LISTENING A 1 False 2 False 3 True 4 True 5 True 6 False

LISTENING B 1 a 2 a 3 c 4 c

WRITING A 1 True 2 False 3 True 4 True 5 False 6 True

Exam Training

Reading

MULTIPLE-CHOICE GAPPED TEXT 1 b 2 f 3 d 4 h 5 g

TRUE / FALSE / NOT GIVEN 1 False 2 True 3 False 4 False 5 Not Given 6 False 7 Not Given 8 True

Listening

SENTENCE COMPLETION 1 convince 2 reasoning 3 succeed 4 brand 5 react 6 trust 7 red 8 limit 9 hurry 10 changed

SHORT TEXTS, MULTIPLE-CHOICE QUESTIONS 1 a 2 b 3 a 4 b 5 c 6 c

MULTIPLE ANSWER 1 a and c 2 a, b, and c 3 a and c 4 b and c

Writing

WRITING A First

WRITING B 3, 6, 2, 4, 5, 1

Workbook Audio Script

Unit 1

Track 01

In this week's edition of Mindworks, we're discussing Savant Syndrome, which is when people with developmental disabilities such as autism also have incredible mental abilities in particular areas. There are many examples of savants but to begin with, we will look at the most famous example—the character in the 1988 movie *Rain Man*. Kim Peek was the man who inspired Dustin Hoffman's character in the movie. Peek was a savant who struggled with some everyday tasks but, in contrast, had other mental abilities far more developed than normal people. For example, Peek had great difficulty doing common tasks such as getting dressed, but he could read a book in only an hour. He could also accurately remember the details of 12,000 different books. When he met people in the street, by simply asking them their birthday, Peek was able to tell them what was in the newspapers on that date. So why does this happen? Well, there are different theories. One theory is that when there is brain damage in one area, there is greater connectivity in another area of the brain. Another idea comes from specialists who argue that savants do something called "hyper-systemizing." This means that they can process facts about the external world much better than other people can. This theory proposes that while most people think about relationships as well as the events in the outside world, savants, on the other hand, focus far less on relationships and this allows their minds to process external information very efficiently. For example in *Rain Man*, Dustin Hoffman's character is able to predict the next cards by remembering their order exactly. *Rain Man* won a number of awards, including the best actor, best picture, and best screenplay. In fact, the screenwriter, Barry Morrow, gave his award to Kim Peek as a gift. Sadly, Peek died at the age of 58 in 2009, but the movie which he inspired continued to make savant abilities famous. Peek redefined our traditional ideas of what it is to be a genius.

Another famous example of a savant is the British artist Stephen Wiltshire who can draw incredibly accurate pictures of cities, sometimes after having only observed the city for a very short time. Stephen started drawing buildings at the very young age of seven …

Track 02

Rolo: Hey Andi, did you hear that story about that brave guy from Ohio whose hand was trapped under a rock after a climbing accident in Utah?

Andi: Mm … no. What happened Rolo?

Rolo: Well, there's this guy called Aron Ralston, who was a really confident climber. He started climbing professionally in 2006. He was also very independent and he often went out climbing on his own. So, one day in 2003, he was climbing in a canyon when a rock suddenly fell on his left hand and nearly broke it! The rock then moved and trapped his right hand.

Andi: No way! What did he do? He must have absolutely panicked!

Rolo: Actually, he was relatively calm just after it happened. But he tried many creative ways to free his arm and it was impossible.

Andi: That's terrible! So, did he die?

Rolo: No, that's the amazing part. He survived for five days with almost no food or water, but he became convinced that he was going to die and even made a video of himself to say goodbye to his family.

Andi: So, what happened?

Rolo: Well, on the sixth day, he realized that the only way to get out would be to cut his arm off and he had to use a knife to do it, which took him about an hour. Then he managed to escape and he was rescued.

Andi: That's incredible! I bet he never wants to go climbing again!

Rolo: Actually, he's continued climbing since the accident. In fact, in 2005, Ralston succeeded in climbing all 59 mountains in Colorado.

Andi: It sounds like he's obsessed!

Rolo: Yeah, but he says he's changed these days. He says that he always used to look for adventure, but now he thinks about much more than climbing, especially since he and his wife had a baby in 2010.

Andi: Thank goodness for that.

Unit 2

Track 01

1

Donna: I love your dog, James. He's very intelligent, isn't he?

James: Yes, he is. We go to the park every day for a walk, and he knows when it's time to go. Dogs love to go for walks, don't they?

Donna: Absolutely!

2

Mark: It must be nice to have horses on your farm, Paula.

Paula: Yes, it is. They're beautiful animals, aren't they?

Mark: I agree. And your farm isn't exactly small, is it?

Paula: No. We have a very big field where they can run around.

3

Mary: Ah, look at your new puppy! She has such a cute face, doesn't she?

Nick: Yes, she's wonderful. And she's growing fast!

Mary: You can give her regular dog food now, can't you?

Nick: No, she still eats special food. She loves it!

4

Alex: Sonia, there aren't a lot of crocodiles near your house in Florida, are there?

Sonia: No, because I live in the middle of town. They live in areas just outside of town, though.

Alex: I see. I guess it's not safe to go to those areas, is it?

Sonia: That's right. It's dangerous, so you have to be very careful.

Track 02

Aiden: With us today is Sonia Flores. Sonia works at an animal shelter as a seeing-eye dog trainer. She's here to talk about what she does at her job, what experience she needed to become a dog trainer, and what she does with the dogs. Thanks for joining us, Sonia.

Sonia: My pleasure.

Track 03

Aiden: Can you describe for our listeners what a seeing-eye dog does?

Sonia: Of course. Basically, a seeing-eye dog helps people who can't see find their way in the world.

Aiden: How long have you trained seeing-eye dogs at the animal shelter?

Sonia: I've been working as a dog trainer for three years now. I started working at the shelter as a care worker, and after the shelter's seeing-eye dog trainer announced that she was retiring, I decided to study as a trainer.

Aiden: Can you describe your technique as a dog trainer?

Sonia: Yes, of course. Well, I start training the dogs when they are puppies. I love this part of their training, because they are so cute, but they are ready to learn as well. Once they are able to leave their mothers, I spend two or three months teaching them how to behave, how to sit, and how to take commands. When they get a bit older, I will start to take them out in public, so they can get used to these surroundings.

Aiden: That must be a very exciting experience for the puppies.

Sonia: Yes, and a very challenging experience for me. I have to teach them how to behave in a public setting, and also how to ignore other animals. But I don't really get into that until the puppy has become an adult dog, and that's after a few months.

Aiden: I see. So it takes a while before the real training begins.

Sonia: Exactly. When they are 12 to 14 months old, I begin to teach them how to recognize obstacles, you know, anything that might lead a person into danger. The most important obstacles are traffic intersections, but there are also things like low-hanging branches on trees.

Aiden: Oh wow, that's very smart. The dog could pass under it, but they understand that their owner can't.

Sonia: Exactly.

Aiden: If someone wanted to become a seeing-eye dog trainer, what qualifications would they need?

Sonia: Well, I have been to a four-year college, but I didn't train to work with animals. I started working at the shelter as a student, actually. I think the most important thing is to have actual work experience caring for and working around animals. This is how I was accepted into a training program. To become a seeing-eye dog trainer, I needed a license to train dogs, which I obtained at the shelter.

Aiden: So, if you're someone who has professional experience around animals, you could apply for this job.

Sonia: Exactly.

Aiden: Well, thanks so much for sharing your work with us. I'm sure you've inspired some of our listeners to become dog trainers.

Sonia: I hope so! Thanks very much for having me.

Track 04

Hi, I'm Jim Hernandez, and I've been a caretaker of animals for years. Some people believe that zoos are a terrible environment for animals. They are kept in cages, they are not living in their natural habitats, and it's a strange idea that humans should be allowed to view animals this way. Imagine if it were the other way around, right? While I think there are some benefits to zoos, in general I believe the better alternative is a wildlife park. A wildlife park is a very large area of land, sometimes thousands of square miles in area, for animals to live in safety and as naturally as possible. I work as a keeper at a wildlife park, and it's a very fulfilling job for me, especially since the wildlife park takes such good care of the animals.

Still, there are people who believe that even this type of environment is bad for animals. Animals should never be forced into a closed area. They should have the right to move freely in the forests, jungles, open plains, lakes, and rivers that are their natural habitats. I understand why they might feel this way. We try to create the most natural environment at the wildlife park as we can, but it's not going to be 100% natural. The animals will eventually reach a fence that they cannot cross, and there are also visitors to the park. So, the animals will encounter humans, something that probably wouldn't happen in nature, at least not very often.

This brings me to the greatest benefit of a wildlife park. You see, animals in nature do come across humans in their natural habitats. Many of those experiences are not positive for the animal, and it has led to many animal deaths. It is one of the reasons why some animals, such as lions, tigers and hippos, are endangered. Their natural environments are becoming more and more dangerous because of humans. So, it might be beneficial if humans created a safe environment for these animals.

Our wildlife park is designed to provide a safe habitat for large animals such as lions and hippos. We have many other animals at the park as well, such as birds, turtles, and even a few porcupines. The money we receive from visitors goes to the park's maintenance, but some of it also goes to the preservation of animals in the wild. We help organizations that monitor animals in their natural habitat and make sure they are not being hunted illegally. So, while it's not a perfect solution to helping animals in danger, I think it's one of the best.

Unit 3

Track 01

Welcome to the Futureproof podcast. Now, we've heard a lot about the possible dangers of artificial intelligence recently. Even the initials "A.I." make people think of evil robots or computers who are obsessed with taking over, and only humans can save the world. This is probably not surprising, as most Hollywood movies like *I, Robot* generally focus on our fears of being taken over by our own creations that have become more intelligent than their human creators. But think about how false that idea is … just one look at most of your everyday gadgets should show you that artificial intelligence is already part of everyday life, and we benefit from it all the time. Take your drive to work, for example. Using location data from a number of smartphones in the area, Google Maps analyzes the speed of traffic in your town. It can therefore tell you where there are traffic problems and recalculate your route in real time. Quite intelligent, right? And what about something a little closer to home, like your email account? A.I. works very hard to put spam emails in a special folder. Spam emails, by the way, are the kind of emails that try to sell you things you don't need. People who send spam emails update them frequently, so your email account actually learns to detect spam by specific words. But it also learns what spam is for *you*. Some people might want to get the same type of emails that you reject, so your email account's A.I. is able to learn who you don't want to get emails from. And have you ever wondered how on earth Facebook knows who is in a photo you've uploaded? Well, that's A.I., too. Facebook uses an artificial intelligence software called DeepFace to learn what people's faces look like. So, if you upload a photo of yourself with a group of friends, Facebook is able to instantly identify who is in the picture—and it can do this with 97.5% accuracy. That's nearly as accurate as a human. To put that in context, the FBI's software can only get to 85% accuracy. So, A.I. is everywhere already and helps us in many ways. And as the software engineer Grady Booch says, "I trust an artificial intelligence the same, if not more, than a human." So, let's relax and enjoy the fact that A.I. is making our lives easier and more efficient, not scarier. After all, you're not scared of your own cell phone, are you?

Track 02

Grace: Hey, Pablo. How's it going? Have you come up with any ideas for the end of term presentation for our psychology class next week? Remember that there's a prize for the best one.

Pablo: Oh, hi, Grace! I've been thinking about a few things but nothing that's really going to be that interesting! I keep looking at what we've been studying so far this year, but I'm not having any luck. I'm seriously thinking of giving up! I might take up philosophy instead. Psychology is too hard!

Grace: Maybe we can do our presentation about exactly this problem!

Pablo: What do you mean?

Grace: Well, I've been having the same problem as you. I've been trying to think of a presentation about something we've seen this year, but maybe we should be looking at some completely different options.

Pablo: I still don't get it.

Grace: Apparently, it's called divergent thinking. With normal problem solving, which is also called convergent thinking, you rely on logical steps to solve a problem. The solution you get to may or may not be the right one. But with divergent thinking, you look at a lot of different possible solutions.

Pablo: I don't understand the difference, really.

Grace: Right, well, think about this presentation. We've been trying to work out what to present on, based on what was in our psychology course this year—that's convergent thinking. We should be thinking about *other* psychology topics and plan a presentation about something totally different!

Pablo: Ah, I see! Our teacher will be impressed with that! OK, how do we start with this divergent thinking then?

Grace: We can start by imaging *all* the different topics that we could do a presentation about. That's brainstorming. And then we can do some question writing. That's when you write a lot of questions about a topic to get as many ideas as possible.

Pablo: So you don't reject any ideas, right?

Grace: Exactly, and that's called "deferring judgement." You don't make any quick decisions. In fact, you accept all ideas and look at them all equally.

Pablo: OK, great. I love it! Let's start then. I've actually been looking up some other topics that we haven't studied this year. Let's look at those!

Grace: Great! We might even win the prize!

Unit 4

Track 01

1

George: How do you make a connection with people at work?

Sally: I try *to find* things that we have in common.

2

Eve: Do you think it's difficult *to communicate* with people from other countries?

Sara: Well, if they don't speak your language, then it might be a challenge.

3

Juan: What do you say to your students about speeches?

Sam: I tell them *to practice* again and again until they feel comfortable with the speech.

4

Susie: How should I behave around my coworkers on my first day at work?

Dave: I imagine it's a good idea *to smile* so that people know you are friendly.

5

Irena: Should you raise your hand when someone is giving a speech?

Mark: I prefer *to listen* first, then ask questions later.

6

Marco: Oh, no. My teacher really didn't like my speech yesterday.

Laura: You should persuade him *to let* you do it again.

Track 02

Carla: With us today is international communication expert Lars Brown. Lars is here to talk about the different ways people communicate in different cultures when it comes to non-verbal communication, you know, facial expressions, body language, hand signals, and so forth. Lars, thanks for joining us.

Lars: Thank you for having me, Carla.

Carla: Well, I'm sure you have lots to tell us about this subject, but one thing that first came to my mind is handshakes. They are such a common form of non-verbal communication. How do they differ from place to place?

Lars: Well, here in the United States, people like to use a firm, quick handshake. They squeeze each other's hands very tightly. That's also the case in northern Europe. It seems to be a sign of confidence, but that is seen differently in other places such as the Far East. There, they view this as aggressive. They don't prefer handshakes at all, but rather, a bow.

Carla: What are handshakes like in other parts of the world?

Lars: Well, in Southern Europe, the handshake tends to be warmer and longer, and they often use both hands when shaking hands. In Turkey, it is considered rude to shake hands firmly. And in Africa, the handshake is very loose.

Carla: Interesting. What about eye contact?

Lars: Again, this something that is very different in Western nations versus the rest of the world. In Asia and having a long period of direct eye contact is considered aggressive. So, it is actually a sign of respect to avoid eye contact, or at least look away at some point. In Western cultures, though, if a person avoids eye contact, people may think that they are not honest. So, eye contact in Western nations is important.

Carla: And what about touching other people while you communicate? Is this a problem in many countries?

Lars: This is where Northern Europe, the US, and the Far East have something in common. Touching is not appropriate during communication. In Latin America, Southern Europe, and the Middle East, people sometimes touch each other when they speak, and it is not considered rude.

Carla: Lastly, I'd like to talk about hand gestures. Is there anything that's considered rude in one country but acceptable in another?

Lars: It is common for people to make the thumbs up gesture. This is fine in most parts of the world, but in Greece and the Middle East, it is considered rude. Another hand gesture where you use your index finger to call someone to you, where you "curl" your finger up, is very rude in many parts of Asia. In fact, in the Philippines, it's a crime and you can get arrested!

Carla: Well, that is very good to know! That's all the time we have today, but thanks very much for your informative talk.

Lars: You're welcome!

Track 03

I'm Leroy Thompson, linguistics researcher, and book author. Today I'd like to talk about the shift in communication that has been happening for many years now, in which there are more images because people pay less attention to words. There isn't a better place to study this phenomenon than in advertising.

Track 04

In the 1800s, when print media was the only form of advertising, you would see a lot more words featured in the advertisement than you do today. Naturally, there would be some illustrations, but often times you would see a great deal of text describing what was being sold and all of its benefits. And people actually read all of it! It was accepted that this was how you would be informed about a product.

In the early to mid-20th century, this trend continued, but a change occurred in the language that companies used in their advertisements. It became less about the product's benefits and more about what the product could do for you on a personal level. This "personalization" of advertising would continue for a long time.

In the late 20th century, you would finally begin to see what we largely see today—an image, and a few words—maybe just two words—that sold the product. For example, Apple computers began ads which simply had the Apple logo, with maybe a famous person like John Lennon and the words "Think different." It was so creative—and effective—that it still exists today.

Nowadays, we see a lot of different types of advertisements, but what's most notable are the advertisements that we see online, especially how we see them. Often times, they are posted alongside the news we read, and they feature eye-catching effects, for example, they flash their messages. Or, they include a video that sometimes plays on its own, so you can listen to the message while you read the news.

So, it seems that the focus on imagery and less on words is a trend that's likely here to stay. But is that such a bad thing? After all, they say that a picture is worth a thousand words, so perhaps it's more efficient to communicate with images rather than words.

Unit 5

Track 01

Every good cause requires a hero, someone who speaks about the idea and shows everyone why it's so important. Unless there is someone special speaking in favor of a cause, we pay less attention to it. Climate change is a good example of this. It has been in the news so much recently, because of a 16-year-old Swedish girl called Greta Thunberg, who used to be too shy to speak at all. Most recently she spoke to the European Parliament, reminding politicians that up to 200 species were becoming extinct every day because of climate change. This may sound impressive, but it all started when she was even younger. At 11 years old, Greta Thunberg was depressed and stopped going to school. She stopped speaking. Her parents decided they should provide her with the opportunity to talk, so they just waited and listened to her. When she finally started talking, she talked about climate change. She talked to her parents about the bad things that would happen to the environment if governments didn't create laws to reduce global warming. In fact, Greta managed to persuade her mother, a famous Swedish singer with an international career, to stop flying. She also persuaded her father to become a vegetarian. When she realized the power that she had to convince people, Greta decided to take action against climate change. She sat outside the Swedish parliament from 8:30 a.m. until 3:00 p.m. every day. And then someone joined her. And then someone else joined her. Eventually, she was asked to make a speech in front of thousands of people at a climate change event. Her parents did not want her to do this, because they were worried about her, but she did it. Soon after this, she got offers from all over the world to make speeches. So, we can expect to hear a lot more from Greta, although she is not saying something that everyone wants to hear. Because when people think about global warming, they still want to feel a sense of hope. They want to feel like they do not need to be too concerned. But with climate change, the reality is very different. In fact, as Greta said to all the business leaders at the World Economic Forum, "I don't want you to feel hopeful. I want you to panic. And then I want you to act." Climate change definitely has a new hero.

Track 02

Chris: Hello and welcome to Green Planet, where today we're talking to Dr. Linda Hamilton from our local environmental agency here in Chicago, who's going to tell us about some unusual environmental solutions. So Dr. Hamilton, we've heard of flip-flops made from paper and roofs made of earth, so what other solutions are there to help the environment?

Linda: Thanks for having me Chris and please call me Linda. So, solutions. Well, there's a whole range of fantastic ideas these days, and I have two of my favorites for you today. I hope they can inspire everyone! The first idea is the air well. Now, air wells were invented to help in areas which don't have enough water for people. The majority of air wells are made of stones, but they can be made of metal like steel or aluminum. During the night, water vapor condenses on the stones and becomes liquid water. That water then runs down the stones and is collected at the bottom the next morning. Some air wells can produce many liters of water every day.

Chris: How interesting! So, air wells don't need any kind of moving parts?

Linda: No, they don't, and that's what's so interesting about them. If you look up "air well" on the internet, you will just see a big stone building, a bit like a tower.

Chris: So, they're basic but very productive.

Linda: Exactly. The second is not exactly a single solution like the air well, but a concept called upcycling.

Chris: Isn't that supposed to be "recycling"?

Linda: No. Recycling is the way we find to use materials again for the same purpose. And there's also downcycling, when we use a high-quality product to make many lower quality products, like turning writing paper into toilet paper. But upcycling is different. It's the idea of taking a product that is no longer needed and turning it into something that is both useful and environmentally friendly, usually products we can't recycle easily. Tire walls are a good example of this.

Chris: Tire walls? You mean like using those black rubber car tires as plant pots?

Linda: Yes, but creating an entire wall. Imagine a wall that is made of tires filled with earth.

Chris: Why would anyone make a wall like that?

Linda: Tire walls are very strong, and they are good at keeping a home warm. The rubber tires contain a lot of earth, so they are very hard, almost as hard as concrete. During the day, the earth gets very hot in the sun and at night, when it's cool, they release heat into the home to keep it warm. That's a very good example of upcycling. It's easy to do and very useful.

Chris: I wish I could come up with an idea like that! Thanks so much for joining us today, Dr. Hamilton. Sorry, Linda!

Unit 6

Track 01

1

Bob: The price of these new e-readers is a bit high.

Sue: I know, but there are better prices. In fact, by the time I bought one, my friend had found a much cheaper model.

2

Jill: I just had a video call with my grandmother the other day. It's the first time I've used the service. I really like it!

Alex: That's really cool! I hadn't installed the software on my phone when my uncle tried to have a video call with me.

3

Gerri: How's your YouTube video going? Do people like it?

Jack: Yes, I think so. When I visited the site earlier today, it had already received lots of likes.

4

Barry: I'm glad I talked to you yesterday to tell you about the details of the event.

Liz: Thanks for that. I had totally forgotten about the event when you called to remind me.

5

Mario: How was science class yesterday?

Diana: It was amazing! Our teacher did this amazing experiment. By the time we left class, Yolanda had already posted a short video of it.

6

Linda: Technology has come a long way in education, don't you think?

Tom: I know. We all use tablets in school now. I hadn't even used one by the time I started grade school.

Track 02

Host: Good afternoon, folks. We've got a great show for you today. Our topic is tech fears, and the question is, "What scares you the most about technology today?" We've got a caller on the line … Caller, can you tell us your name and where you're calling from?

Sofia: Yes, my name is Sofia Sanchez, and I'm calling from Rolling Hills.

Host: Hi, Sofia. So tell us, what's your biggest tech fear?

Sofia: Well, I'm actually really proud of all the technology we have at our fingertips today, so I wouldn't say I have a really big fear. But one thing I worry about is information theft. You know, where someone breaks into your computer and steals all your data.

Host: Absolutely, it would be a person's worst nightmare. Can you tell us why you worry so much about this?

Sofia: Well, in my house, everybody uses a wireless device. My son uses a tablet, my husband and I use smartphones, and my daughter uses a laptop for all her schoolwork. What if somebody broke into the network and stole information, or even photos, from any of us?

Host: That would be a disaster. But I guess this is why we use strong passwords …

Track 03

Host: You do use passwords on all your devices, don't you, Sofia?

Sofia: Yes, and we change our passwords every so often. So really, that's why I'm not terribly worried, but that's my worst fear.

Host: Understood. Well, thanks for calling and keep those devices safe! We have our next caller … Caller, tell us your name and where you're calling from.

Sam: My name is Sam Flores, and I'm calling from Sherman Oaks.

Host: Hi, Sam. So, what's your worst tech fear?

Sam: Well, I work in an automobile factory. I love my job, but what if some day they build a robot that can do what I do? I won't have a job anymore, will I?

Host: Yes, that is a big worry. Tell me … are there any robots in your factory at the moment?

Sam: Yes, there is an area where robots put together some of the car parts. This is why I'm concerned. My job is to install electronics and test that they work. There isn't a robot that can do that at the moment, but I would hate to see someone make one.

Host: I agree. Well, we have to do our best to find ways to make ourselves useful. Surely there will always be something that humans can do that robots cannot. So keep working hard, Sam, and stay hopeful.

Sam: Thanks.

Host: We have time for one more caller … Caller, what's your name, and where are you calling from?

Trish: My name is Trish Spencer, and I'm calling from Round Rock.

Host: Hi, Trish. Tell me your worst tech fear.

Trish: We recently moved to a new neighborhood, and I've already seen three or four drones in the air. I don't know if they are our neighbors' devices, or where they're coming from, but I don't like them at all.

Host: And why is that?

Trish: Because someone may be using them to take photos, or record videos. I saw one fly straight over my back yard, right over my head! If I had a rock, I might have thrown it!

Host: Well, you know, drones are sort of the new thing in tech, and people are probably just using them as toys. You know, if you find out that someone is taking photos of you without your permission, you can call the police. I urge you to do that. Well, that's our show for today, and thanks for listening in. Up next … can people actually learn a thing or two from their house pet?

Track 04

It's National Hispanic Heritage Month in the USA, so for today's program, I'd like to honor a few Hispanic inventors who have given us some interesting and useful inventions over the years.

I'd like to start off with a woman who was both an inventor and an astronaut. Ellen Ochoa, born in Los Angeles, California, in 1958, is the first Hispanic woman astronaut, and her mission in April 1993 made her the first Latina to travel into space. She went on to do three more spaceflights, for a total number of 40 days spent in space. In addition to space travel, Ochoa invented a way to improve space exploration. She created a new kind of optical system, which is a system for seeing images and analyzing them. This greatly improved the job of astronauts.

Moving on to the field of medicine, I'd like to mention the work of Carlos Finlay. Finlay, born in Cuba in 1833, did research into mosquitos, those insects we all know and *don't* love for their

annoying, itchy bites. He discovered that they carry the deadly disease yellow fever. Before his discovery, people had no idea where it came from. As a result of his work, communities began killing off mosquitos in order to stop the spread of the disease. It worked.
Now for a little entertainment ... born in Guadalajara, Mexico in 1917, Guillermo Gonzalez Camarena was an inventor of a type of color television, which he invented when he was only 17 years old. While he was not the inventor of the color television, his type of television sold particularly well. It took him some years to get his television on the market, and he sold his first set in 1954 for about $1,450. I did some calculations, and $1,450 in today's money is worth about $13,500!
Last, we return to the skies with my next inventor, Juan Manuel Lozano Gallegos. Lozano didn't fly quite as high as Ochoa. We've all seen how a jetpack works: you put it on your back and you use it to rise up into the sky. While he was not the inventor of the jetpack, Lozano did invent a type of jetpack that actually works. Born in Mexico, Lozano was amazed by jetpacks as a kid and he spent 30 years developing it. He actually sells his jetpack today for around $125,000. While it does work, it doesn't take you very high, and he warns buyers that they will only be in the air for about 30 seconds before they have to land.

Unit 7

Track 01

Host: Hi there everyone, and welcome to another edition of The Mind in Society. Now today, I'm here with clinical psychologists Lucia Gimenez and Diana Partington, and we're going to be looking at a negative emotion, the feeling of regret. Lucia and Diana, I think we all agree that regret is a terrible thing, but that we all tend to spend a lot of time regretting things. Is that right, Diana?

Diana: Yes, indeed it is. Regret is something we all do because it's inevitable. You see, especially when an event occurs that we think of as big or important, our minds do something called counterfactual thinking. That's why regret is such a negative emotion.

Host: And what is counterfactual thinking, Lucia?

Lucia: Well, let me give you an example. Image you had just had some bad news, for example, being told that you had failed an exam. That situation might seem bad enough, but we then start imagining alternative realities where things happened differently.

Host: You mean like "what would life be like if I had passed the exam?"

Lucia: Yes, but not just that, unfortunately. Counterfactual thinking also means that we tend to think, "What if I had spent more time working?" or "I wish I hadn't wasted time playing video games." The problem with this is that you have already failed the exam. That's already happened, so there is nothing you can do about it.

Host: So why do we do that to ourselves, Diana?

Diana: There are a few theories about this. One of them is that we do it to avoid making similar mistakes again in the future. We take the pain from counterfactual thinking as a lesson for the rest of our lives.

Host: Ah, OK, so it's not all about humans just being negative creatures, then?

Diana: No, not at all. In fact, it's an essential way of learning and surviving. Also, we tend to do this in advance as well. So, we could think to ourselves, "If I don't pass that exam, then I won't get into college," and that makes us work harder to achieve our goals. The reality in this example is that we haven't failed the exam, but if we think about what it would be like, we want to take the necessary action to avoid it.

Host: I see. But what if you have already failed at something? How can that be positive? What if, for example, you didn't get an A, because you didn't study properly, Lucia?

Lucia: That's actually a good example of the positive effects of counterfactual thinking. You see, if someone gets a C, they may feel better than someone who gets a B. That's because the situation appears different to them. Someone with a B might think, "I wish I had got an A," but the person with a C is more likely to think, "At least I didn't fail!"

Host: Very interesting. Thank you both for joining us.

Track 02

Hey everyone, Cris Lopez from Chicago here with this week's podcast, "Cris Thinks." So over the last few days, I've been feeling kind of down about a couple of things in my life, and I have to admit that I really let it get to me a little too much. So, I don't want to miss the chance to share some of my ideas with you guys about how I've been feeling. So, I guess what started this off was that I broke up with my boyfriend, Troy. If you've been following my podcasts, you'll know he's a massive influence in my life, and he still is, but sadly we've decided to call it a day. We both decided that we were spending too much time fighting about stupid stuff and that wasn't helping either of us. I kind of wish we hadn't wasted all that time fighting, but I guess it was showing us that there were some problems that we needed to figure out. It's not like a permanent break up, I hope, but we're taking a break for now. So then, about a day after Troy and I broke up, one of the colleges I had applied to in the UK got in touch with me and offered me a place there to study English literature, and I turned it down immediately. I know you guys are probably thinking, "Chris, you should have taken that offer!" but I was really confused, and I wasn't thinking properly. I wish I had told them I'd think about it and get back to them later, instead of just turning it down right away, but it's too late now. But in any case, I've now decided I'm going to spend the summer working, because I really need to earn some money before applying to college again in the fall. Anyway, what all of this has taught me is that although life can be really bad sometimes, everything happens for a reason. Troy and I have promised each other that we won't lose touch and we'll see what happens. And I'm now thinking about studying English literature at a college a little closer to home. Well, that's all for now, guys!

Unit 8

Track 01

Host: Welcome to Life Beyond Earth, the show about the great outer space search for life. Today we're going to discuss what it would be like to live beyond our planet, specifically the planned manned missions to Mars. Space engineer Nina Garcia is here to give us the details. Nina, thanks for joining us.

Nina: Thanks for having me.

Host: Tell us why you're so excited about a manned mission to Mars. I mean, it's an incredible idea, but isn't it quite dangerous? And what do we hope to find there? Many scientists believe that Mars is too cold and harsh to support life.

Nina: You mention some good reasons why we shouldn't go there. But I'd like to share the reasons why we should. First of all, traveling to another planet is more or less a dream of mankind. We've traveled to the Moon, and if you think about it, that was a historic event. So imagine what it would be like for someone to step foot on Mars?

Host: But is that really enough reason to go? Just for the glory of it? I mean, I'm excited about a mission to Mars, too. I'm just wondering how we humans would benefit.

Nina: As you say, scientists have determined that it's very unlikely that there is life on Mars. But as far as studying other objects in our solar system goes, Mars is the closest after our moon, so it's the next logical place to go.

Host: OK, so we've gotten past the reasons for going there. Let's talk specifics. First of all, how far away is Mars? And how long would it take us to get there?

Nina: Well, Mars is the second-closest planet to Earth, after Venus. We don't want to visit Venus, of course, because it's incredibly hot. Mars is very cold, but it has some conditions that are similar to Earth. At any rate, Mars can be between 34 million and 250 million miles away, depending on where Earth and Mars are in their orbits. So we would need to plan our mission very carefully. As for how long it takes, it could take from six to ten months to get there, if we plan it right.

Host: Hmm. Well, that doesn't sound too bad. I wonder, though, if people can be in space that long. Can you tell me how long a person has been in space?

Nina: Yes, that is a good question and an important concern. Russian astronaut Valery Polyakov spent 438 days in space on the Mir space station. This took place in the 1990s. More recently, American astronaut Scott Kelly spent 340 days in space in 2015 and 2016, the longest for any American space traveler.

Host: In your best prediction, can astronauts really exist on Mars? I mean, for a long period of time. We see in movies that there are terrible dust storms and radiation. And the temperature is often freezing.

Nina: We are still looking into these things. The temperature on Mars ranges from 20 to minus 125 degrees Celsius. At its warmest, it is similar to Earth. Still, astronauts would have to wear a space suit if they were on the surface. There are plans to construct places for them to live and do research. So, the life of an astronaut on Mars would be building, doing research, and maintaining their environment. It sounds a bit lonely, but imagine how exciting it would be standing on the surface of Mars.

Track 02

Chair: Hi, folks. Recently, we have seen a trend in space funding—some governments are giving less money to their space programs. There is a debate as to whether space exploration is helpful or not. For our program today, we're joined by astrophysicist Julio Diaz, space engineer Viola Cruz, communications analyst Jeff Gomez, and laser technician Steve Walker. So, our topic today is this: Should we continue our efforts in space exploration? What does our panel have to say about this? Viola?

Viola: I believe that some people in government think that space exploration has not been worth it. It hasn't produced enough things to be worth the money we have spent on space travel. But let's look at it this way. Space exploration allows us to see what's out there—and what could possibly harm us in the future.

Chair: I see. Julio?

Julio: I totally agree with Viola's point. We need to know if there is a meteor or a giant asteroid heading toward Earth. This is important for human survival, isn't it? Scientists recently concluded that a large asteroid had a 10 percent chance of hitting Earth in eight years. That's a rather high chance, so we need to be looking out for these things.

Track 03

Chair: Jeff, your specialization is in communications. Do you think we will ever be able to contact alien life forms?

Jeff: There are a number of ideas about this. One is that there is life out there, but it's very basic. It's plant life, in other words, so we wouldn't be discovering intelligent life forms. So, I suppose that that is the best we have to discover, but that's fine. We would be discovering life, so that's important, right? Another theory is that there is nothing out there. I don't agree with this. We exist, so why wouldn't others? It must be possible that life exists, somewhere out there in the universe. A third theory is that there are life forms out there that are like us, but that have the same limitations that we have—distance, lack of technology, etc. They want to find us, but, like us, they can't because they're not advanced enough.

Chair: Interesting. Steve, you believe that space exploration can help us create better equipment on Earth. Can you explain?

Steve: In our efforts to explore space, we have made discoveries that help us on Earth: foil blankets, cordless devices, and memory foam are just a few examples. I specialize in lasers, which are used to cut through heavy materials like rocks and so forth. We use lasers in space to do this sort of thing. If we can improve lasers though space exploration, this technology can help us on Earth. Lasers help us in the medical field and with manufacturing. I am confident that advances in space exploration can improve laser technology and life on Earth, so I support space exploration.

Chair: Well, we have heard from four different people about the value of space exploration. What do you think? Post your comments on our website and answer the question: Is space exploration worth it?

Unit 9

Track 01

You might not know who Christopher Blair is, but you may know some of his victims, mainly because they are famous politicians: Barack Obama, Hillary Clinton, Donald Trump—the list is very long. But who is Blair, and what does he do? He writes news stories with very shocking headlines about famous people. This may sound like something that many journalists do, but in Blair's case, it's different. None of his stories are accurate at all. They are all invented. Blair is very good at this and has been called "the godfather of fake news" by the BBC. In the beginning, in early 2016, Blair created a website for fake news stories during the US election campaign. He said many things about the presidential candidates which were not true. In fact, they were all lies. But people thought they were funny, and his stories got over half a million shares in a very short space of time. How? Because Blair had also shared his stories on Facebook. This obviously brought more and more people to his website. So, he created another website. And then a third. And then a fourth. Blair soon figured out that this would make him a lot of money. And it did. Why? Because all this internet traffic then attracted advertisers to his websites. If he wrote a news story which over half a million people were looking at, companies wanted to put their advertisements on his websites. Blair was soon able to leave his job and make money just from writing fake news. Obviously, Blair also got many complaints about his stories. Many people started asking him to prove that his stories were true, so on his main website, he had to write the line: "Nothing on this page is real." But by then it was too late. Finally, in November 2016, Google and Facebook said they would stop making it possible for people to earn money from fake news and in December of that same year, many of Blair's websites closed down. So, was Blair's work just harmful lies, or was it a funny way of showing people the effect that the media can have on the way we think? That's up to you to decide. What we can be sure of is that you might not be able to trust any of Blair's stories, but you can trust him to make you laugh.

Track 02

Brian: Because I'm the studio's investigative journalist, I had a project to look into a local family company who were apparently polluting a river. I didn't really believe it, but I went anyway. Unfortunately, the security guard refused to open the doors for me, and so I spent about an hour trying to get in through a window! I then tried calling them and I spoke to 12 people, but no one knew anything about it. We finally found out that the company wasn't polluting the river anyway, so in my view the whole thing had been a waste of time. I'll make sure we investigate properly in the future.

Jason: I have to say that sometimes my job as a newspaper editor can be very difficult. I get stories all the time, and I have to ask the reporters to change them. As you can imagine, they hate rewriting their stories! But I've been here for about five years now, and I have a good idea of what makes a good story, so I have to explain to the reporters that I am not criticizing them, I am just trying to make our newspaper as good as it can be. They understand, so I feel like what I do improves the quality of the journalism every day.

Leyla: After I had done my training as a photojournalist, I had a really hard time, because I had to spend hours waiting around in the cold outside celebrities' houses. I couldn't stand that type of work. I used to think to myself, "Why am I doing this? This can't be as good as it gets!" But then one day, I was helping a new guy from Mexico in our office, and I was speaking to him in Spanish, and my boss offered me the chance to go to Colombia and start work as our magazine's foreign correspondent. Well, I accepted immediately!

Casey: So last week, we had the prime minister of Denmark in the studio, and I had to translate for her. I've been learning Danish for years, but it's not an easy language to learn and even more difficult to translate what someone is saying in real time, so I was very nervous. But as soon as she started talking about their economy, I was able to follow everything she was saying and translate everything only a few seconds after she had said it. I felt all my training as a translator worked perfectly, and I felt good about that. It was such a great experience. Everyone at the studio congratulated me afterwards.

Renee: I had a terrible night last night! As the anchor in the studio, it's my job to read the news, and I normally read my lines from a television monitor in front of me. But last night, just after we'd had the World Series report from the sports journalist, the TV broke, and the lines just froze. Of course, I couldn't say anything about the problem because I was on live TV, so when my producer finally understood what was happening, I'd been silent for four seconds! It doesn't sound like a long time, but it really is on live TV. It was so uncomfortable, especially because we have millions of people watching every night.

Unit 10

Track 01

1

Fran: How's my dancing practice going, coach?
Coach: You dance beautifully, Fran.

2

Olaf: Hi, Helen. I can hear the concert in the background. How is it?
Helen: The band's performing a great song!

3

Olga: Did you win the competition, Harry?
Harry: No, I didn't do so well.

4

Igor: I think we've seen this performance, Helen.
Helen: I haven't performed this routine before.

5

Anya: Maria is an amazing chess player.
Juan: She'll become a chess champion!

6

Lucy: I wonder if Tim's group is ready for tonight.
Frank: They have never sung in public.

Track 02

Host: Hi, folks. We're on the street today to ask for people's opinions about TV talent shows. There seem to be a lot on TV these days, so quite a few people are watching them. I hope we get a wide range of opinions. Let's see what this young woman thinks about them. Excuse me, ma'am. We're doing a survey, and I'd like to get your opinion.
Donna: Sure, I'll participate.
Host: Great! First, tell us your name, first name only.
Donna: Donna.
Host: Donna. Thank you. So, what do you think of TV talent shows?
Donna: Hmm, well, for the most part, I think they're OK. I don't really watch them that often, because I'm not a fan of television. I do like to see talented people on TV, though. I think a lot of people on these shows aren't very talented, and to be honest, I feel a bit bad for them. Occasionally, though, you see someone with a lot of talent who really impresses you. So, I think that makes them really fun to watch!

Track 03

Host: Let's ask this young man what he thinks about TV talent shows. Hi, would you like to participate in our survey?
Garry: OK.
Host: First, tell us your name.
Garry: Garry.
Host: Garry. Thank you. So, what's your opinion of TV talent shows?
Garry: Oh, I really love them. I watch them all the time. I think there are a lot of great talent shows out there with a lot of talented people.
Host: Is there a particular show that is your favorite?
Garry: Well, I like singing contests and variety shows, but I like the show Dance Off the best. My sister was on that show, actually, so my family and I watch it quite often. She danced with a professional dancer and she competed against seven other couples. She came in second place, so we were really pleased.
Host: Do you think some talent shows feature people who aren't very talented?
Garry: Of course, but that's OK. I think it's interesting to hear what the judges say, and yeah, some people don't take it very well, and they have a bad attitude, but I think the level of talent in shows today is higher than it used to be.
Host: OK, well, thanks for your time, Garry.
Garry: You're welcome.
Host: Excuse me, ma'am. Can I ask you a couple of questions?
Vero: About what?
Host: We're doing an opinion poll on how people feel about TV talent shows.
Vero: OK. Well, I personally don't like them!
Host: Well, great. You don't have to! But can you explain why? And please tell us your name.
Vero: Oh, sure. It's Veronica. But call me Vero. Well, I think TV talent shows do a number of things that I don't like. First of all, I think they use people to entertain others, and in a negative way.
Host: Really?
Vero: What I mean is, they will put people on stage who are clearly awful. Then we, as viewers, are supposed to laugh. I suppose not everyone laughs. I know I don't. But I think a lot of people do. That's terrible.
Host: OK, that's a good point.
Vero: Second, I think TV is something that we watch to get away from everyday life. A TV talent show is like a reality TV show, only perhaps worse. There is no plot to it and no characters, so I think it's kind of boring. I'd rather watch a sci-fi series. I mean, that's the type of TV show I'm into, not comedies or love stories.
Host: I see. Well, you've given us a very interesting opinion, and one that's quite different from what we've heard so far. Thanks for your time, Veronica.
Vero: You're welcome.

Track 04

Delia: Hi, Mateo. Thanks for meeting with me today. I'm having such a frustrating time, and I could really use your advice. You know how hard it is to break into the fashion industry.
Mateo: I'm happy to help, Delia. Yeah, I know how you must feel. Even though I've been a fashion designer for some years now, I've heard many difficult things from people in the business. An owner of a chain of retail stores told me, "You won't be successful in fashion. You should think about another career."
Delia: Oh, wow. I can't believe the owner told you that you wouldn't be successful and you should find another job.
Mateo: I know. Well, my first piece of advice would be to never give up on yourself. I told myself that a lot in the beginning.
Delia: Yes, well, I will definitely write that one down at the top of my list! What else can you tell me?
Mateo: Well, don't be afraid to dream big. A big part of fashion is having a great idea for your collection. Don't create fashion that you think will please other people. Create the kind of fashion that inspires you. If you love the countryside, put nature into your work. If you love technology, make your fashion look modern and futuristic.
Delia: OK, that's a start. Sometimes I have trouble finishing a piece of clothing. I can't stop working on it. I think, oh, let me try this, and let me remove that.
Mateo: Yes, sometimes it's hard to know when an item is complete. The best thing to do is to set your sights on a goal. Don't spend too much time on one piece. Set a time limit and say to yourself that you have to finish it in that time, then leave it and move on to the next piece of clothing. You can always go back to it later if you think it still need fixing.
Delia: OK. What about getting your work in magazines? Don't you need to be well-connected?
Mateo: That helps, but it's a matter of being in the right place at the right time. You should try to attend as many fashion shows as possible. You never know who you might meet at a show—a fashion editor for *Vogue*, for example. Don't just stay in your studio all day.
Delia: Yes, I understand. What do you think about this? They say it isn't what you know, it's who you know.
Mateo: Well, I think it's both. You should try to meet people in the industry. I think we've covered that. However, if you don't

know anything, you're not going to impress anyone, right? So, I suggest reading about fashion trends as often as possible. Don't just stick with what you already know about fashion. Broaden your horizons.

Delia: Yes, of course. I love fashion and want to know as much about it as possible. Do you suggest I try to get my collection into a big fashion show, or should I spend time doing smaller ones first? I don't want to waste my time with them if it's not a good idea.

Mateo: You must be hungry for success! Do all the shows that you come across, even if it's a show in a small shopping center that hardly anyone goes to. You will gain the experience it takes to put on a successful show. I wouldn't put all your energy into getting seen in a major event. It's very competitive, and besides, if your lack of experience causes a problem, a lot more people will see it.

Delia: I see. Get my mistakes out of the way before I hit the big time.

Mateo: Well, at least you're starting to believe you *can* hit the big time. I see my first bit of advice is beginning to have an effect on you!

Unit 11

Track 01

How did you feel the last time you made a donation to a charity? I am sure you felt good about it, because of course it feels good to know that you are making a difference. But are you really? According to some experts, simply giving money away to charity doesn't mean we are necessarily making a genuine difference. Economist Tim Harford says that "charity is selfish." We only do it to make ourselves feel good and not to really make the world a better place. The argument is that if we really wanted to make a positive difference, then we would find out exactly where our money was going. For example, if you donate a dollar to a charity in the street, you get the instant feeling that you did something good. But are you sure you did something good? Did you ask the collector how they would be spending your dollar? Or does it feel good enough just to be a donor? The problem is that simply giving is not enough, because you don't know how a charity is going to spend the contributions that they get. Maybe a charity will say they help homeless people and this of course sounds like a great reason to make a contribution, but it doesn't make sense unless you, and all the other contributors, really know how they are going to use your money. Robert Egger, who created an important charity project to help people who don't have enough to eat, thinks that it is often the most popular charities that get our cash. He thinks that we often give money to the charity who can sell themselves to us best. So, if all this is true, what should we do about it? It must be better to give than not to give, right? Well, yes, don't worry, it still is. But before you give money or anything else to a charity in the future, ask them some questions. Where's my dollar going and how are you going to use it to make a difference? That way we can make sure that we are not only feeling good, but doing good as well.

Track 02

Maria: I don't believe it! I've just tried to pay for our flights to São Paolo, and it says I've got no money in my account.

Maxi: Really? Look, if you used that app I told you about, that kind of thing wouldn't happen. It's the app I mentioned that helps you manage your money and see how much you're spending from your bank account, so that you don't overspend. It's even better than an accountant.

Maria: No, this is nothing to do with me at all. Look at the screen. It's impossible! It says I've made all these purchases with my debit card.

Maxi: Well, you do buy a lot of stuff by contactless payment. Think of all those times we've been to the store and bought little things. Some cost $5, some cost $15, but you buy so many. They soon add up.

Maria: But according to my bank, there were three identical purchases of $500 at the supermarket on the same day. That's really weird, especially because I didn't go to the supermarket on that day. I think someone's got my account details, you know.

Maxi: Maybe they have. Do you remember when that happened to me last year?

Maria: Yes, but that's because you left your card in the ATM! Nobody even needed to steal your personal identification number, or rob you. Of course your money was stolen.

Maxi: What do you think we should do?

Maria: I'll call the bank now and report those payments. They'll see that it's impossible, I'm sure.

Maxi: Yes, good idea. They're normally very helpful with this kind of thing. In the meantime, we could pay by cash, but it's a lot of money. And I don't have a debit card anymore. But we could pay by credit card. At least then we don't have to pay for it all at the same time. And I think we might get a discount on the vacation with the credit card anyway.

Maria: Yes, OK. How annoying, though.

Unit 12

Track 01

1

Juan: Hey Sally! Have you got 15 minutes before our next meeting?

Sally: Sure, I'm not busy right now

Juan: So, I've been trying to come up with a slogan for this product for a week now, and I can't decide which one would be better. Can I run them by you?

Sally: Of course, I'm in charge of managing the advertising budget, but I can give you my opinion as a consumer.

Juan: OK, well, the product is the new brand of dog food that the company has been working on. So, this is what I've come up with. The first one is, "Ruff's Dog Food ... so good, dogs ask for it by name."

Sally: Oh, I like that. That's great!

Juan: The second one is, "Ruff's Dog Food ... it may sound rough, but dogs think it's smooth."

Sally: Oh. Hmm. Well, it's OK. I like how you used the word "rough" in the slogan, since it sounds like the brand name. I think I'd go with the first one, though. It's smarter.

Juan: OK, thanks. I'll let the boss know!

2

Eve: Thanks, everyone, for coming to the meeting so quickly. We've got an issue with launching the product. It seems that there are some things missing from the launch. Can someone please explain what the problem is?

Gary: Yes, well, the posters are being printed right now. The job arrived at the printers late. It seems there was a problem with the ad message. Anyway, they are working on it more slowly than I expected.

Eve: Well, you've had weeks to get everything ready to launch the product, so honestly, I can't see how this is anyone else's fault.

Sue: If I may say, this isn't the first time we've had a problem with the printers. I've had problems with them as well. They take forever.

Eve: OK, so why aren't we doing something about that? We should be working with the fastest printer services out there. After we launch the product, we need to have another meeting about that.

3

Bob: Oh, look at this new brand of soda. I haven't seen this one before. It's cheaper than the one we usually buy.

Cath: Yes, but price isn't everything, is it? Cheap products sometimes aren't as good.

Bob: Well, we should give it a try. I mean, I love our usual brand, but you know, it's good to try new things. And it'll save us a bit of money.

Cath: Yes. I hope the kids will like it. It'll be a waste of money if they don't.

Bob: I can always come back and get we normally buy if they complain!

4

Girl: Mom, I just saw this great ad on TV for a new smartphone. It's the new version of my old one, and it's on sale for 50% off.

Mom: OK. Well, what's wrong with your old phone? It still works, doesn't it?

Girl: Um, well I suppose, but the new phone has more features. It has a better camera, and it has more storage. My old phone is nearly full.

Mom: OK. So, what does "50% off" mean exactly. What's the original price?

Girl: I think after you subtract the discount, it's 199 dollars.

Mom: What? So, the full price of the phone is 400 dollars! I got my new phone a year ago for free.

Girl: Yeah, but it takes terrible photos, and it's very small.

Mom: Yes, but it was free. I got it with my phone plan. Why don't you tell me what kinds of phones you can get with your plan, and we'll talk about getting you a new one then.

Girl: Mom!

Track 02

Host: With us today is Gerri Garcia, advertising executive for one of the most successful ad companies in the region. She's here to talk about false advertising and what we can do to avoid its tricks. Thanks for joining us, Gerri. Tell us what your biggest concern is about false advertising.

Gerri: Without a doubt it concerns ads for health products and services. We see so much false advertising in this field, and what's terrible about it is it concerns our health and well-being. False advertising in any field is bad, but sometimes it's not the worst thing in the world. For instance, if a restaurant advertises a meal that doesn't really look like the one in the photo, it's not going to be harmful to your health.

Host: Exactly. It's just not what you ordered.

Gerri: Right! However, if an over-the-counter pill promises to improve your health but it doesn't, it might cause someone to avoid going to the doctor, because they think the pill works.

Host: I do see a lot of food products making claims that seem true, but you don't really see any proof.

Gerri: Yes, well, that's probably because there isn't any! Companies can get in trouble for this. In the USA, consumers are protected by the FTC, the Federal Trade Commission, and they police this area. For instance, in 2010, the FTC accused POM Wonderful, the makers of pomegranate juice and pomegranate pills, of making false claims. Statements such as "Prevents or treats heart disease" had been put on the label, but they couldn't be proven.

Host: I think many weight loss claims are believed, even though there isn't any evidence.

Gerri: Exactly. It's not just adult food products that make false claims, it's also the companies that produce food for kids. Kellogg's, the cereal maker, put a claim on the box that said their cereal could help improve kids' immune systems. By eating their cereal, they could fight colds and the flu more easily. The FTC found out that the claim was false, and as a result, Kellogg's was forced to remove the claim.

Host: Goodness. These false claims must hurt companies, right?

Gerri: Yes, in fact they do. The famous yogurt maker, Activia Yogurt, who uses famous actress Jamie Lee Curtis in their ads, lost a lawsuit over false claims. A judge decided that their health claims were false and awarded consumers 45 million dollars. Furthermore, the judge said the company had to limit the health claims on their packaging.

Host: I've eaten that yogurt plenty of times! Well, I may have to choose more wisely in the future.

Gerri: I know people try to make good decisions about what they eat. I believe that's possible, although there are some companies to watch out for. We should read more about studies that health organizations have carried out and see what foods they recommend. Processed foods like cereals and fruit drinks often say "all natural," but a quick read of the label shows that it contains loads of sugar. So, look at those labels carefully!

Host: Thanks very much for your time. Real food for thought there.

Exam Training

Exam 1

Host: Hi everyone, and welcome to our series of podcasts on psychology in the world around us. This week, we're having a look at psychology in advertising. Advertisers have used psychology for many years. Since the nineteenth century, psychologists have studied the way humans respond to advertisements. Why? Because ultimately, advertisements are trying to sell people something. And to sell people something, you have to convince them that they need it. So this is where psychology is important. In 1896, psychologist Walter Dill Scott said that, with advertising, humans are not logical. He said that we follow our emotions, not our reasoning. In fact, he said that humans are "creatures of suggestion." This means that it is easy to predict how humans will react emotionally to something. And he was right. Recent research shows that 31% of advertisements with emotional content succeed, while only 16% of advertisements based on rational content do. Scott's work was developed by the American behavioral psychologist John B. Watson. In the 1920s, Watson was one of the most important people to use psychology in advertising. He noticed that humans respond to three basic emotions: fear, anger, and love. In fact, he used this with one of his first advertisements for a brand of toothpaste. He decided not to focus on the benefits of using the toothpaste for having healthy teeth. Why not? Well, because humans respond more to emotions than facts. He had an attractive woman in the advertisement with very white teeth. The suggestion was, that by using this toothpaste, you would become more attractive. This may sound very normal by today's standards. But it shows how long advertisers have been working out what makes us react, and what makes us buy. Fast forward to today, and psychology has become more advanced in the ways it affects us in advertising. Why? Well, one of the reasons is the massive number of advertisements that we see today. Back in the 1970s, people saw around 500 advertisements a day. These days, people see 5,000 a day, so advertisers need to make their advertisements more prominent. Many advertisers use something called "color theory" for this. For example, most advertisements for cleaning products have the color blue in them. That's because blue makes us trust what we are looking at: we feel like we can rely on blue products. Red, on the other hand, is associated with passion and hunger, and yellow is connected with happiness. That's the reason why one of the world's biggest fast food restaurants uses red and yellow as their main colors. Basically, they want to make you buy more food. But what about the emotions fear, anger, and love? Well, they are still used in advertisements every day, mainly online. The most frequently seen advertisements are not on TV or billboards, but on the internet—5.3 trillion every year. Many of these advertisements, especially those for clothes or vacations, use a very modern type of fear to sell their products: Fear Of Missing Out, or FOMO, for short. This is where the advertiser tells you that there is, for example, a limit to when you can buy a product. They do this through phrases like, "Offer available for 12 hours only!" This makes people feel that they must hurry. And if they don't, they'll miss something special. This emotion is stronger than our understanding of how good the product may or may not really be. So, even though advertisements and advertisers have changed, people have not. Walter Dill Scott is still right—we are much more emotional than rational.

Exam 2

Woman: So, how was that movie you saw last week? Did you and Sarah have a good time?

Man: Well we did, but something really frustrating happened. When we got to the movie theater, they said there was no way for Sarah to get her wheelchair in. So, they told us we couldn't watch the movie!

Woman: That's terrible! I'm sure Sarah was very angry!

Man: I was angry! I couldn't believe it! Anyway, I asked to speak to the manager, and he apologized. He also took us to the entrance at the side of the movie theater and it was easy to get Sarah's wheelchair in there.

Woman: How was Sarah after that?

Man: Well actually, Sarah didn't seem to care about it at all. And we both loved the movie, so we had a good time in the end.

Woman: Hey, did you see that documentary about A.I. in cell phones? Apparently, they react to how we use them, and they help us in lots of different ways.
Man: A.I. in cell phones? That sounds a bit scary! Anyway, I don't think my cell phone pays any attention to me.
Woman: Ah, but that's because you haven't been paying attention. It's nothing to be afraid of. Your cell phone just learns from your daily routine, so it's very useful.
Man: Not for me! I only use it to chat with friends.
Woman: Well, I think it's very useful. For example, I take the bus to my classes every day. After about a week, my new cell phone started telling me the bus timetable automatically.
Man: Really? Ah, so that's why I get those notifications! That's amazing!
Woman: I know!

Man: You know, I've heard a lot about climate change, but I don't know what we can really do about it.
Woman: I know what you mean. I think if most people knew where to start, they would do something to make a difference.
Man: Exactly, but people like you and I can't prevent companies from burning fossil fuels, can we?
Woman: Well, we can certainly do something on a domestic level. For example, we could always turn the lights off when we leave a room, or make sure the windows are always closed to save energy. Or we could even recycle all our paper instead of just throwing it away.
Man: It's really hard to recycle anything where we live, but we could definitely make sure we don't leave the lights on when we're out.
Woman: Ok, well, let's start with that.

Woman: What's the matter? You look exhausted! What time did you go to bed last night?
Man: Well, I should've gone to bed earlier, and I didn't study for the history exam tomorrow morning! In fact, I had planned to study over the weekend, but Tim had this party, so I went to that instead. I should've said no to Tim, but it was his birthday.
Woman: Oh no, not again! You should've told him you had an exam. He would've understood. Look, if I were you, I'd read those photocopies the teacher gave us. You can look at my notes, too, if you want.
Man: Thanks. I shouldn't spend so much time going to parties, should I?
Woman: It's not that you shouldn't go to parties, but you should plan your work properly!

Man: One of my friends shared a news story on his social media account last night. It sounded totally unbelievable, so I'm sure it can't be true. But all of our friends just started commenting on it anyway and saying how terrible it was!
Woman: So many people do that these days and it's really annoying. They post a shocking news story on social media and they don't even look at where it came from first.
Man: I know. If people did that, we probably wouldn't have so many problems with "fake news" all the time.
Woman: And it's not that hard to check whether a news story is true or not. You just need to make sure that the news is from a reliable website.
Man: Yeah, because a lot of stories are just invented to make people angry, which is kind of dangerous.

Woman: Hey, how's your sister these days?
Man: Not so good, actually. She started a technology company with one of her friends, but now they've got some financial problems.
Woman: Ah, did they have to spend a lot of money on computers?
Man: Well, they did, but that's not the problem. The thing is, they hired three employees, and my sister even had her apartment redecorated to make it more like an office. But they aren't getting as much new business as she thought they would.
Woman: So, I imagine your sister must feel like she's wasted her money.
Man: A bit. What's worse is that she and her friend are still paying the employee's salaries, even though they're not making much money.
Woman: I guess she must be spending more than she's getting then, right?
Man: It looks like it, yes.

Exam 3

Host: So we've recently been looking at how human beings communicate. Today we're going to be looking at a form of communication called haptic communication. The word "haptic" comes from the Greek word haptikos, meaning "able to touch." You see, haptic communication is about how we communicate by touching each other. Why is this so important? Well, imagine a situation where a mother has a baby but never touches him or her. What would happen? You might think that this wouldn't be a big problem if the baby is fed and looked after. But in fact, if a mother didn't touch her baby, the baby might become very stressed. This stress would mean that the baby might not develop normally. Children who grow up without being touched by their parents or caregivers can also suffer from depression and be aggressive. So why is this? For a start, contact between parents and babies is essential. It's also good for the parents and the child. For example, the child sleeps better and cries less, and the parents feel less stressed. In fact, the American psychologist Harry Harlow proved that children actually need to be touched, just like they need to be fed. Then later on, when people become adolescents and adults, touch continues to be important. Hugging and even play-fighting releases a chemical called oxytocin. This chemical makes us feels socially connected to people. This means that haptic communication is an essential way for communities to connect. In fact, in studies of haptic communication, there are "high-contact" cultures and "low-contact" cultures. What does this mean? Well in societies like Latin America, people generally touch and hug each other a lot. This reduces levels of a stress chemical called cortisol. In the US, people have less haptic communication and adolescents are more likely to be aggressive. As Dr. Tiffany Field tells us, "Touching each other keeps the peace." But what is haptic communication? Is it all about hugging? No, it's not. There are many, many forms of haptic communication, depending on the situation and the culture. When you say hello to someone in the US, you shake the person's hand. But in Latin America it is also normal to kiss someone on the cheek. People also use haptic communication to celebrate something. For example, friends or coworkers "high-five" each other to celebrate some kind of success. There's also the kind of haptic communication when people touch each other in a conversation to emphasize something they are saying. People also use this way of touching to show they are honest communicators. As I said, there are many types, and it is hard to define them all in one lecture. So, we can see that haptic communication is extremely important. But we have to understand how different people feel in different situations. At work, for example, if a manager puts his hand on an employee's shoulder, some people may think it's supportive, but others may think it's inappropriate. So, we have to be careful. But we can be sure that haptic communication is vital for all humans, from infants to adults. It's also essential for personal and social development at every level in society. So, at this stage, I'd like to ask if anyone has any questions.